Glauber Rocha (1939–1981) is Brazil's most important filmmaker and founder of the 1960s and '70s Cinema Novo movement. His films are landmarks of Brazilian and world film history. He was also a prolific writer and film critic, whose critical thought made a decisive contribution to the notion of Third Cinema.

Ismail Xavier is Professor of Film at the University of São Paulo. His book *Allegories of Underdevelopment: Aesthetics and Politics in Modern Brazilian Cinema* marks a milestone in Brazilian cinema studies.

'This book reveals to the world what Brazilian intellectuals already knew, that Glauber Rocha was not only a major filmmaker but also a major film theorist and an acute critic both of movements (the New Wave) and of individual directors, including mainstream American directors. His analyses are multi-faceted, bringing in industrial, production and aesthetic concerns.'
– Robert P. Stam, University Professor at New York University, USA

'At long last, Glauber Rocha in English. An essential collection of essays for all those interested in Brazilian *cinema novo* and world cinema.'
– Darlene J. Sadlier, Professor at Indiana University, Bloomington, USA and author of *Nelson Pereira dos Santos*

WORLD CINEMA SERIES

Series Editors:
Lúcia Nagib, Professor of Film at the University of Reading
Julian Ross, Research Fellow at Leiden University

Advisory Board: Laura Mulvey (UK), Robert Stam (USA), Ismail Xavier (Brazil), Dudley Andrew (USA)

The World Cinema Series aims to reveal and celebrate the richness and complexity of film art across the globe, exploring a wide variety of cinemas set within their own cultures and a they interconnect in a global context. The books in the series will represent innovative scholarship, in tune with the multicultural character of contemporary audiences. Drawing upon an international authorship, they will challenge outdated conceptions of world cinema, and provide new ways of understanding a field at the centre of film studies in an era of transnational networks.

Published and forthcoming works in the World Cinema Series:

Allegory in Iranian Cinema: The Aesthetics of Poetry and Resistance
Michelle Langford

Amharic Film Genres and Ethiopian Cinema
Michael W. Thomas

Animation in the Middle East: Practice and Aesthetics from Baghdad to Casablanca
Edited by Stefanie Van de Peer

Basque Cinema: A Cultural and Political History
Rob Stone and María Pilar Rodriguez

Brazil on Screen: Cinema Novo, New Cinema, Utopia
Lúcia Nagib

Brazilian Cinema and the Aesthetics of Ruins
Guilherme Carréra

Cinema in the Arab World: New Histories, New Approaches
Edited by Philippe Meers, Daniel Biltereyst and Ifdal Elsaket

Contemporary New Zealand Cinema
Edited by Ian Conrich and Stuart Murray

Cosmopolitan Cinema: Cross-cultural encounters in East Asian Film
Felicia Chan

Documentary Cinema of Chile: Confronting History, Memory, Trauma
Antonio Traverso

East Asian Cinemas: Exploring Transnational Connections on Film
Edited by Leon Hunt and Leung Wing-Fai

East Asian Film Noir: Transnational Encounters and Intercultural Dialogue
Edited by Chi-Yun Shin and Mark Gallagher

Eastern Approaches to Western Film: Asian Reception and Aesthetics in Cinema
Stephen Teo

Impure Cinema: Intermedial and Intercultural Approaches to Film
Edited by Lúcia Nagib and Ann Jerslev

Latin American Women Filmmakers: Production, Politics, Poetics
Edited by Deborah Martin and Deborah Shaw

Lebanese Cinema: Imagining the Civil War and Beyond
Lina Khatib

New Argentine Cinema
Jens Andermann

New Directions in German Cinema
Edited by Paul Cooke and Chris Homewood

New Turkish Cinema: Belonging, Identity and Memory
Asuman Suner

On Cinema
Glauber Rocha, Edited by Ismail Xavier

Pablo Trapero and the Politics of Violence
Douglas Mulliken

Palestinian Filmmaking in Israel: Narratives of Place and Identity
Yael Freidman

Performing Authorship: Self-inscription and Corporeality in the Cinema
Cecilia Sayad

Portugal's Global Cinema: Industry, History and Culture
Edited by Mariana Liz

Queer Masculinities in Latin American Cinema: Male Bodies and Narrative Representations
Gustavo Subero

Realism in Greek Cinema: From the Post-war Period to the Present
Vrasidas Karalis

Realism of the Senses in World Cinema: The Experience of Physical Reality
Tiago de Luca

Stars in World Cinema: Screen Icons and Star Systems Across Cultures
Edited by Andrea Bandhauer and Michelle Royer

The Cinema of Jia Zhangke: Realism and Memory in Chinese Film By Cecília Mello

The Cinema of Sri Lanka: South Asian Film in Texts and Contexts
Ian Conrich

The New Generation in Chinese Animation
Shaopeng Chen

The Spanish Fantastic: Contemporary Filmmaking in Horror, Fantasy and Sci-fi
Shelagh-Rowan Legg

Theorizing World Cinema
Edited by Lúcia Nagib, Chris Perriam and Rajinder Dudrah

Queries, ideas and submissions to :

Series Editor: Professor Lúcia Nagib - l.nagib@reading.ac.uk

Series Editor: Dr. Julian Ross - j.a.ross@hum.leidenuniv.nl

Publisher at Bloomsbury, Rebecca Barden – Rebecca.Barden@bloomsbury.com

On Cinema

Glauber Rocha

Edited by Ismail Xavier
General Coordination by Lúcia Nagib
Final text and notes by Cecília Mello
Translation by Stephanie Dennison and Charlotte Smith

BLOOMSBURY ACADEMIC
LONDON • NEW YORK • OXFORD • NEW DELHI • SYDNEY

BLOOMSBURY ACADEMIC
Bloomsbury Publishing Plc
50 Bedford Square, London, WC1B 3DP, UK
1385 Broadway, New York, NY 10018, USA
29 Earlsfort Terrace, Dublin 2, Ireland

BLOOMSBURY, BLOOMSBURY ACADEMIC and the Diana logo
are trademarks of Bloomsbury Publishing Plc

First published in Great Britain by I.B. Tauris 2019
Paperback edition published by Bloomsbury Academic 2022

Copyright © The Estate of Glauber Rocha 2019

The texts written by Glauber Rocha which comprise this anthology have
been previously published in the following volumes:
Revisão crítica do cinema brasilieiro © 2003 Cosac Naify, São Paulo, Brazil
Revolução do cinema novo © 2004 Cosac Naify, São Paulo, Brazil
O século do cinema © 2006 Cosac Naify, São Paulo, Brazil

This anthology is published with the permission of and by arrangement
with the Glauber Rocha estate.

The right of Glauber Rocha to be identified as the author of this work has been asserted
by the Glauber Rocha Estate in accordance with the Copyright, Designs and Patents Act 1988.

Introduction copyright © Ismail Xavier 2019
Preface copyright © Lúcia Nagib 2019

For legal purposes the Acknowledgements on pp. x-xiv constitute an
extension of this copyright page.

All rights reserved. No part of this publication may be reproduced or
transmitted in any form or by any means, electronic or mechanical,
including photocopying, recording, or any information storage or retrieval
system, without prior permission in writing from the publishers.

Bloomsbury Publishing Plc does not have any control over, or responsibility for,
any third-party websites referred to or in this book. All internet addresses given
in this book were correct at the time of going to press. The author and publisher
regret any inconvenience caused if addresses have changed or sites have
ceased to exist, but can accept no responsibility for any such changes.

A catalogue record for this book is available from the British Library.

A catalog record for this book is available from the Library of Congress.

ISBN: HB: 978-1-7807-6703-1
PB: 978-1-3502-5317-9
ePDF: 978-1-7867-3186-9
ePub: 978-1-7867-2186-0

Series: World Cinema

Typeset in Minion Pro by OKS Prepress Services, Chennai, India

To find out more about our authors and books visit
www.bloomsbury.com and sign up for our newsletters.

Contents

List of Figures	ix
Preface and Acknowledgements by Lúcia Nagib	x
Introduction by Ismail Xavier	1
Glauber Rocha's *On Cinema*	3
***Revisão Crítica do Cinema Brasileiro*/ Critical Review of Brazilian Cinema**	13
Introduction	13
Method	15
Humberto Mauro and the Historical Situation	19
***Revolução do Cinema Novo*/The Cinema Novo Revolution**	30
The Cinema Process (1961)	30
Barren Lives (*Vidas secas*) (1964)	37
An Aesthetics of Hunger (1965)	41
Revolution is an Aesthetics (1967)	46
The Cinematographic Revolution (1967)	48
Tricontinental (1967)	51
Positif (1967)	58
Cinema Novo and the Adventure of Creation (1968)	75
Tropicalism, Anthropology, Myth, Ideography (1969)	100
América Nuestra (1969)	104
Discussion of the Concept of Aesthetics and its Political Function	106
This Is How the Revolution in Cinema Is Made (1970)	114
An Aesthetics of Dreams (1971)	121

O Século do Cinema/The Century of Cinema — 126
  Chaplin — 126
  Welles — 129
  James Dean – Angel and Myth — 132
  David Lean — 133
  Juvenile Delinquency — 136
  John Huston – Physical Technique and Aesthetic Technique — 142
  Stanley Kubrick — 144
  Western – Introduction to the Genre and to the Hero — 150
  The Searchers — 152
  The New Western — 154
  The 12 Commandments of Our Lord Buñuel — 159
  The Morality of a New Christ — 172
  The Neorealism of Rossellini — 178
  Filmic Dramaturgy: Visconti — 187
  Cinema's Form and Sense — 192
  Visconti and the Nerves of Rocco — 193
  Viscontian Baroque — 199
  The Splendour of a God — 204
  Antonioni — 209
  Funeral Space — 211
  Glauber Fellini — 214
  Pasolini — 235
  New Cinema in the World — 241
  Alphaville — 252
  Do You Like Jean-Luc Godard? (if not, you're out) — 257
  Godardean — 265

Notes — 268
Index — 285

List of Figures

Figure 0.1 Facsimile hand-drawn cover for *O século do cinema* xi

Figure 0.2 Glauber Rocha in Jean-Luc Godard's *Wind from the East* xii

Figure 2.1 Glauber Rocha and Fritz Lang (Montreal, 1968) 112

Figure 3.1 Glauber Rocha and Luis Buñuel (Montreal, 1967) 160

Figure 3.2 Glauber Rocha and Roberto Rossellini (Venice, 1967) 180

Figure 3.3 Glauber Rocha and Jean Renoir (Cannes, 1969) 244

Preface and Acknowledgements

It is now eleven years since we first embarked, in 2007, on the project to bring for the first time to the English reader the key writings on cinema by Brazil's most iconic filmmaker and *cinema novo* leader, Glauber Rocha. The project coincided with the launch of the I.B.Tauris World Cinema Series, which includes among its aims to reveal to audiences around the world the diversity, creativity and originality of thought on cinema produced in languages other than English. A prolific and eloquent writer, Rocha left his thoughts and daily experiences minutely registered in thousands of press articles, letters, manifestoes, poems, novels and plays, many of them available in book form in the Portuguese language, collected in volumes prepared by Rocha himself or by dedicated scholars such as Ivana Bentes, who in 1997 edited *Cartas ao mundo* (Letters to the World),[1] a hefty and precious selection of his international correspondence.

The current collection of articles was facilitated by the fact that publisher CosacNaify, in São Paulo, had just launched, between 2003 and 2006, the most complete, entirely revised, superbly designed and richly illustrated editions of Rocha's three foundational books of film criticism he had himself organized: *Revisão crítica do cinema brasileiro* (Critical Review of Brazilian Cinema, first published in 1963); *Revolução do Cinema Novo* (The Cinema Novo Revolution, first published in 1981); and *O século do cinema* (The Century of Cinema, first published posthumously in 1983, two years after Rocha's untimely death at 42 years of age). Ismail Xavier, Rocha's greatest specialist and foremost Brazilian film scholar, having actively contributed to and introduced these new editions, graciously accepted to select and introduce writings extracted from them that would provide a concise but representative profile of Rocha as a film writer for the English reader. Because CosacNaify was in possession of all copyrights of the materials included in the three volumes, negotiations proceeded swiftly and cheaply, not least thanks to the goodwill and commitment on the part

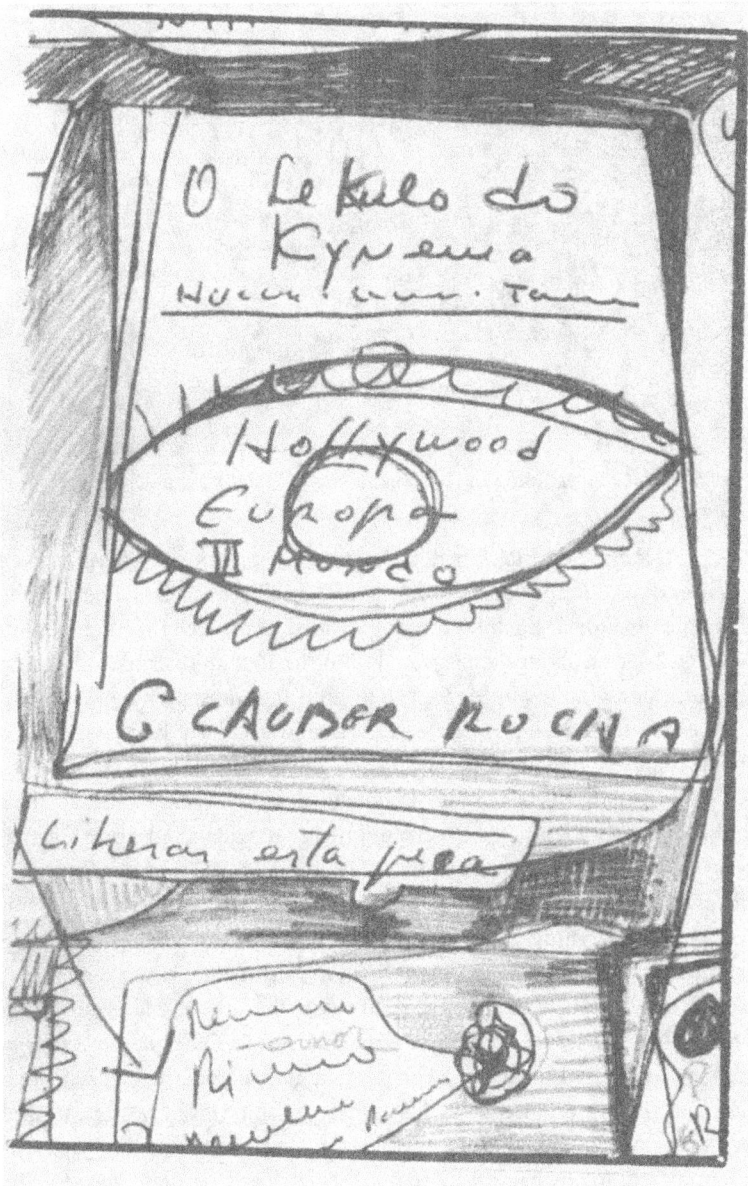

Figure 0.1 Facsimile hand-drawn cover for *O século do cinema*.

On Cinema

Figure 0.2 Glauber Rocha in Jean-Luc Godard's *Wind from the East*.

of CosacNaify's editorial director, Augusto Massi, and I.B.Tauris's visual culture editor, Philippa Brewster. Another key player was Leslie Bethell, the dynamic director of the then thriving Oxford Centre for Brazilian Studies who, on hearing about the project, did not hesitate to offer his support in the form of a grant from his Centre to fund the translation work.

Despite the backing of these cultural and scholarly heavy-weights, a major challenge remained, namely to do justice, in the English language, to Rocha's feverish, visionary and uniquely personal writing style. Rocha's ambition was not restricted to revolutionizing Brazilian and world cinema, but also language, to the extent that from the mid-1970s he started to use his own spelling of Portuguese, even revisiting and adapting to it some of his previous writings. Thus, for example, his groundbreaking 1965 manifesto, 'An Aesthetics of Hunger', or, in Portuguese, 'Estética da fome', was changed to 'Eztetyka da fome'; likewise, the title of one of his books utilised here, *O século do cinema*, was changed to *O Sekulo do Kynema*. Rather than based on a new, coherent linguistic code, Rocha's spelling testified, on the one hand, to his refusal to abide by any standardized practices and, on the other, to a strong visual element stemming from his talent as a draughtsman and visual artist, leading to a preference for the angular 'Y' and 'K' (nonexistent in the Portuguese spelling) and for the alphabet's last letter 'Z'. This, combined with his poetic verve – a ground of

Preface and Acknowledgements

aesthetic communion with Eisenstein's ideographic montage and Pasolini's 'cinema of poetry' – inspired him to create synthetic and often hilarious neologisms and puns in his writings which are, however, in most cases, untranslatable into other languages.

Again, on the translation front, we were lucky to meet with the willingness of one of Britain's top Brazilian film scholars, Stephanie Dennison, and a competent professional translator, Charlotte Smith, whose work cut through the major linguistic stumbling blocks; but time and money were exhausted before the many lingering queries were resolved. So more time was spent with funding applications with a view to enabling the work to continue. This time it was the Brazilian Embassy in London and the Brazilian Foreign Office in Brasília (the Itamaraty) who came to our rescue with complementary funding. With this crucial but rather modest help, we managed to lure into the team the brilliant Brazilian world-cinema scholar Cecília Mello, whose magisterial work on this book cannot be praised highly enough. Mello went through the entire text with a magnifying lens that exposed minor mistakes, information gaps and a great number of details that could prove mystifying for a non-Brazilian readership. She then undertook exhaustive research in order to clarify them all in more than a hundred endnotes, in addition to those provided by editor Ismail Xavier for the Brazilian editions; a few extra notes were added by the translators and by myself. Unfortunately, Rocha's creative spelling had to go, but the reader will hopefully recognize in the English prose his particular humour and inventiveness, alongside his uncompromising critical eye, in dealing with the work of others as well as his own.

But this is not yet the end of the story. Quite unexpectedly, CosacNaify closed its doors a few years ago, and the copyrights they held for the Glauber Rocha writings and illustrations returned to the filmmaker's estate, and had to be renegotiated from scratch. Another protracted round of correspondence and funding applications took place until the new acquisition of the copyrights was completed, thanks to a funding contribution made by the Centre for Film Aesthetics and Cultures (CFAC), School of Art and Communication Design, University of Reading, and goodwill on the part of the Glauber Rocha estate. Credit is also due to the Cinemateca Brasileira, in São Paulo, current holder of the Glauber Rocha collection, which granted us cost-free use of the cover image.

On Cinema

After this veritable saga, there are now, at long last, plenty of reasons to celebrate. In fact, this book is coming out as the world commemorates the fiftieth anniversary of May 1968 when politics ruled the day in cinema, and Rocha's work was being discovered and fêted in the United States and Europe for its revolutionary power. In particular in France, where he would go into exile in 1971 with the recrudescence of the Brazilian military dictatorship, Rocha's role as a trailblazer was hailed in unison by critics at the time and symbolically enshrined, in 1969, in a pivotal scene in Godard/Dziga Vertov group's film *Wind from the East* (*Le Vent d'est*). In it, Rocha appears standing on a crossroads with open arms, indicating the direction of political cinema to a heavily-pregnant passer-by and singing verses from Caetano Veloso's Tropicália song, 'Divino Maravilhoso' (Divine and Marvellous). As Godard had sensed, Rocha was himself an artistic and political event, and so is his film criticism, whether on the evolving *cinema novo* production, international idols such as Buñuel, Ford, Lang, Welles, Visconti, or direct interlocutors such as Pasolini and Godard. My sincere and heartfelt thanks go to all those who placed their trust in the risky and painstaking enterprise of translating to English this essential part of Glauber Rocha's unique, 'divine and marvellous' body of work.

Lúcia Nagib
General Coordinator of *On Cinema*, by Glauber Rocha

Introduction

Ismail Xavier

This collection brings together articles that reflect Glauber Rocha's thoughts at different stages of his life and career. Rocha's development as a filmmaker coincides with the rise and apogee of modern cinema, which found in the *Brazilian Cinema Novo* a privileged expression and in Rocha its uncontested leader. Before delving into his articles, a brief look at Rocha's biography is in order so as to offer a clearer insight into his development as a filmmaker.

Glauber Rocha (1939–1981) started to develop as an artist at the University of Bahia, in Salvador, where he was involved in theatrical performances and became acquainted with Bertolt Brecht's dramaturgy. His cinephilic initiation, enabled by the growth of cineclub activities in Salvador, dates from the same period. Still in his teens, and informed by the cineclub screenings and ensuing debates he regularly attended, Rocha started to contribute to magazines in 1956. He was soon established as a critic who combined cinephilic erudition in all kinds of cinema and engagement in the defence of a new cinema he called for in Brazil, inspired by Italian neorealism and the French *nouvelle vague*. He was soon travelling around the country, disseminating his militant ideas on cinema in Rio de Janeiro, Minas Gerais and São Paulo.

In 1959, he made an experimental short film called *Pátio*, the first evidence of his commitment to a cinema of invention, a position he would further develop in his first feature-length film, *Barravento* (*The Turning Wind*, 1961). This film leaves no doubt as to Rocha's intention to combine his aesthetic sensibility with the imperatives of political cinema, a feature that became distinctive of his cinematic output as a whole. Even before his

On Cinema

Cinema Novo masterpiece, *Deus e o diabo na terra do sol* (*Black God, White Devil*), came to light in 1964, he had already launched his campaign for Cinema Novo in the book *Revisão crítica do cinema brasileiro* (*A Critical Review of Brazilian Cinema*), which consolidated his position as leader of the new generation of filmmakers in the early 1960s. It was, however, with *Black God, White Devil* that his method of articulating aesthetics and politics came into full effect. The film was very well received by Brazilian critics, going on to be screened at the Cannes Film Festival in 1964 and to project Glauber Rocha's name internationally.

Terra em transe (*Entranced Earth*, 1967), another masterpiece, generated heated debates in Brazil, mobilizing artists from all branches (popular music, theatre, visual arts), as well as writers and political activists. The film's impact consolidated Rocha's cinema as the focus of attention for the Americas and Europe. It found particular resonance within the French cinematic context, bringing about the director's partnership with French producer Claude Antoine, who co-produced *O dragão da maldade contra o Santo Guerreiro* (*Antonio das Mortes*), the winner of the Best Director Award at the Cannes Festival in 1969.

Between 1969 and 1976, finding himself unable to return to Brazil given his opposition to the military regime, Rocha exercised his craft abroad. He wrote screenplays, some of which remained unfilmed, continued his militancy as a critic and shot films in different countries: *Der leone have sept cabeças* (*The Seven-Headed Lion*, 1970) in the Democratic Republic of the Congo; *Cabezas Cortadas* (*Cutting Heads*, 1971) in Spain; *Claro* (1975) in Italy. During a stint in Cuba in 1972, he edited the film *Câncer* (*Cancer*), shot in Brazil in 1968, and started to make *História do Brazil* (co-directed by Marcos Medeiros), which he completed in Italy in 1974. He found in this constant wandering a way of carrying out his function as a 'tricontinental filmmaker', an idea he had elaborated on in several of his interviews and articles.

Having returned to Brazil in 1976, he shot, in 1977, his documentaries *Di Cavalcanti* and *Jorjamado no cinema*. In 1980, Rocha completed his last film, *A idade da terra* (*The Age of the Earth*), which was screened in the same year at the Venice Film Festival, where he became embroiled in some disastrous polemics with Italian and French critics.

This last battle sealed the trajectory of a filmmaker whose talent combined the vigour of the polemist and the cogency of the critic and

Introduction

animated him until his death. His criticism was documented in two books he had prepared for publication before his departure for Venice in 1980: *Revolução do Cinema Novo* (*The Cinema Novo Revolution*) and *O século do cinema* (*The Century of Cinema*), both consisting of anthologies of his articles and interviews.

The last stop of his pilgrimage was Portugal, following his devastating experience at the Venice Film Festival. The excesses that had characterized his febrile and tireless confrontation with the world came to take their toll during his Portuguese sojourn, where he reeled from the accumulated tension of his convulsive career. In August 1981, at 42 years of age and in the last throes of a grave illness, he returned to Brazil to die in his home country.

Glauber Rocha's *On Cinema*

This volume brings together articles extracted from the three Glauber Rocha books mentioned above: *Revisão crítica do cinema brasileiro* (A Critical Review of Brazilian Cinema, 1963), *Revolução do Cinema Novo* (The Cinema Novo Revolution, 1980) and *O século do cinema* (The Century of Cinema, 1983), which express, each in their own time, Rocha's combative verve and unique style in distributing praise and blows. The latter book only saw the light of day after Rocha's death; its first, heavily copy-edited edition was based on a manuscript he left behind when he went, in 1980, to the Venice Festival where his last film, *The Age of the Earth*, was screened.

The first section of this volume starts with the Introduction he wrote for *A Critical Review of Brazilian Cinema*, his first book, in which the very young critic calls upon his generation to create a new cinema, even before his cinematic masterpieces had started to give shape to his revolutionary ideas. As the Introduction announces and briefly anticipates, *A Critical Review* sums up the militancy of a filmmaker who, at the age of 24, was already an influential personality in the defence of an authorial political cinema, a modern style that made ample use of the handheld camera and jump cuts, in tune with the scarcity of resources then available in Brazil. His agenda was in line with the *politique des auteurs* promoted by the *Cahiers du Cinéma*, albeit inflected by his radical attack on Brazilian cinema's 'industrial illusions', along the lines of his very personal mode of confronting the film industry's regulating powers and marketing imperatives. For Rocha, already at this early stage, aesthetic expression was necessarily a response to and a struggle against historical conjunctures that created all kinds of economic obstacles for film production in Brazil.

Guided by this principle, Rocha evaluates in the successive chapters the experience of the previous decades of Brazilian cinema and gives his opinion on its most important phases and filmmakers. In terms of historical importance, his preference lies with Humberto Mauro, whose silent films were shot in his hometown of Cataguazes. In a chapter about him, reproduced in this collection, Rocha warrants Mauro the status of a predecessor of the new generation and of a key filmmaker who, his lack of formal training notwithstanding, was capable of expressing a worldview, of being authentic while making films with minimal resources. In Rocha's view, Mauro's intuitive power should inspire youngsters to overcome their inferiority complex and embrace artistic creation under the principle of 'an idea in mind and a camera in hand'. This historical survey allows Rocha to proclaim what should serve as the matrix of Cinema Novo and what should be discarded. *A Critical Review of Brazilian Cinema* is not a history of cinema, but an act of militancy aimed at establishing a new project and, as is usually the case with the leaders of new movements, 'inventing a tradition' that will be in the leader's interest to cherish.[1]

The Cinema Novo Revolution is a collection of articles and interviews in which the voice of the experienced filmmaker, enjoying an international profile, prevails. The pieces contained in the book focus on two periods of Rocha's artistic trajectory: the 1960s and the period between 1978 and 1980. Together, they offer what Rocha seems to consider the legitimate legacy of Cinema Novo and of his experience as a 'tricontinental filmmaker', forged during his travels around the world.[2]

The first two pieces selected from this book are 'The Cinema Process' (1961) and the article '*Barren Lives* (*Vidas secas*)', written in 1964. They represent a first stage in the development of Rocha's ideas concerning auteur cinema and its particular predicaments in an underdeveloped country. The 1961 piece, more than a declaration of principles, is an expression of his anxieties towards the Hollywood film production that dominated the Brazilian market. Filmmakers have to face the permanent tension between the desire for undisturbed authorial expression and the inevitable economic and political constraints of their practice. The result is

Introduction

frustration and a sense of sacrifice, felt most acutely in the Brazilian context up to the late 1950s. The article on *Barren Lives* is a good example of Rocha's enthusiastic support of auteur Nelson Pereira dos Santos, who was able to overcome all economic and industrial obstacles and make one of the first Cinema Novo masterpieces.

'An Aesthetics of Hunger', written in 1965, is the first Rocha manifesto of major impact abroad, containing a synthesis of his criticism of the Europeans. It consists of a paper presented at the Instituto Columbianum in Genoa, on the occasion of a Latin American Cinema Retrospective, in which Rocha coined the formula 'an aesthetics of hunger'. It proclaims that revolutionary filmmakers in Latin America, instead of struggling to gain access to a film industry out of reach, should forge their own aesthetics out of the very lack of resources, taking hunger not simply as its subject, but also as its formal principle. Rocha was engaged not only in defending the social and political content of the Cinema Novo works but also in resorting to the semantic space of hunger which was comparable to the actual situation of filmmakers in need of a new creative method. By confronting the industrial codes of practice, a stylistic difference would emerge which would necessarily constitute an act of aggression – an aesthetics of violence.

In his speech in Genoa, Rocha comments on the inevitable misunderstanding, on the part of the developed countries, of the Third World experience, emphasizing what he sees as Latin America's structural condition of alterity with regard to Europe. His arguments lie on a geopolitical axis of confrontation and estrangement in which the oppressed only become visible (and occasionally a subject) through violence. Drawing on Frantz Fanon, he points to the social, economic, cultural and psychological barriers separating the universe of hunger from the developed world.[3]

'An Aesthetics of Dreams' (1971) can be seen as a sequel to 'An Aesthetics of Hunger'. Like the 1965 manifesto read in Genoa, it had a significant repercussion when it came out in response to the critical reception of his film *Antonio das Mortes* (*O dragão da maldade contra o Santo Guerreiro*, 1969) in the United States.[4] The paper gives Rocha the opportunity to adjust his principles to the new stylistic options adopted in this film and radicalized in his subsequent films made in exile, such as *Der leone have sept cabeças* (*The Seven-Headed Lion*, 1970) and *Cabezas Cortadas* (*Cutting Heads*, 1971).

On Cinema

In his writings during the 1960s, Rocha had emphasized how art's revolutionary vocation emerges within a geopolitical confrontation involving ethnic, class and transnational conflicts. In 1971, 'An Aesthetics of Dreams' makes clear that if art is a human practice pertaining to the symbolic field, it is not enough to defend its political dimension of confrontation and risk. It is equally necessary to understand that any poetic intervention in the social sphere requires a rupture with common sense, a disregard of all limits and conventions. For him, art should express human experience in its totality. Free from the strict control of rationality, art embraces the magical moment, tunes in with the dreams of the oppressed, gives voice to unconscious drives. Art, like revolution itself, expresses rebellions unleashed by unbearable situations, giving shape to the unpredictable in the historical world. Art is 'surreal, expressive, delirious', though not as in the surrealist automatic writing, but in its power to reach deep into the popular imaginary in a way that only art can do. This sign language acquired from popular culture is made of condensations which work in the manner of ideograms – and here Rocha's reference is Eisenstein. This is the filmmaker's raw material and it cannot be evaluated through the parameters of aesthetic realism – particularly if it is a criticism inspired by Georg Lukács who attacked Franz Kafka and other twentieth-century writers for their allegorical tendencies.[5] His reiterated aim is the epic-didactic cinema conceived as a ritual against the dominant reason, against cinema as a bourgeois institution, and in favour of an art in tune with popular mythology, an art that performs a material appropriation (of body, gesture and word) which is liberating in the face of the consensual social order.

Together with these two seminal papers, a group of articles published between 1967 and 1970 and an interview for the magazine *Positif* (1967) were selected from *The Cinema Novo Revolution*. They provide a multifaceted picture of the way in which Rocha's ideas concerning the new auteur cinema from Latin America were presented alongside and in relation to his explanatory and polemical accounts of the Cinema Novo aesthetics and political militancy.

'Revolution is an Aesthetics' (1967) expresses his principles for a revolutionary cinema in the form of an exposition and defence of the epic-didactic form as opposed to a realist cinema, combined with commentaries on the film cultures of Mexico, Argentina, Cuba and Brazil.

Introduction

'The Cinematographic Revolution' (1967) focuses on the social conditions and formal challenges faced by revolutionary cinema, commenting on the forms of organization that can provide a common denominator for politically engaged filmmakers. 'Tricontinental' (1967) is a provocative text, sometimes erratic and telegraphic, sometimes systematic in the development of Rocha's argument in defence of a tricontinental cinema: 'Tricontinental – auteur cinema, political cinema, *counter*-cinema, is a guerrilla cinema; in its origins it's brutal and imprecise, romantic and suicidal, but it will become epic/didactic'.

Why 'brutal and imprecise' in its origins? This question finds an indirect answer in his provocative comments on different experiences of Latin American cinema in its appropriation of national indigenous culture. It is a strategy he indeed supports but only when combined with that demand for the 'epic/didactic' which expresses his concern for the political effects provided by the incorporation of procedures taken from Bertolt Brecht's theatre. This demand for the dialogue with Brecht is yet another aspect of his concern for a productive interaction between Latin American cinema and different trends of the European modern cinema, a concern that he combines with his attack on filmmakers aligned with 'dogmatic socialism'. The following article brings the reader back to Brazil for a specific critical appraisal of Cinema Novo films, in 'Cinema Novo and the Adventure of Creation', a paper Rocha wrote after the filming of *Entranced Earth* (1967). This article conducts a broad review of Brazilian cinema history, with an emphasis on the major Cinema Novo films of the 1960s up to his own 1967 masterpiece, *Entranced Earth*, which launches a scathing criticism against the pedagogical premises of leftwing art and the strategies employed by Brazilian artists in general in their relationship with history. It is interesting to compare this historical appraisal with his interview with Michel Ciment published in *Positif* in 1967, where he clarifies many passages of *Entranced Earth* and its impact on Cinema Novo. The years 1967–1968 see the emergence of Tropicalismo, a new turn in Brazilian culture provoked by the veritable shockwave represented by *Entranced Earth*, ushering in a period of intense debate on the relationship between aesthetics and politics in which Rocha took centre stage. In 'Tropicalism, Anthropology, Myth, Ideography' (1969),[6] he refers to that 1967 cultural turn in order to take stock of auteur cinema's connection with traditions relating to both indigenous mythologies and the cultures of the European colonizers. Rocha's take includes an anthropological and linguistic interest, evident in his notion of 'ideography'.

In the two remaining pieces of this section, the reader will find examples of Rocha's informality in combining prosaic references to everyday life and conceptual remarks on cinema, culture and politics. The first contains his 1969 'untimely notes' for a never made film, the epic poem 'América Nuestra', written in a style which is at once affective and provocative. A mosaic of references describes his personal experiences in Brazil and abroad, including his relationship with filmmakers and writers (Eisenstein, Godard, Buñuel, Rossellini, Visconti, Brecht, Borges, Neruda, Guimarães Rosa, among others) whose works had inspired him and the major difficulties faced by Latin American artists in creating their masterpieces. The second, 'This Is How the Revolution in Cinema Is Made' (1970), reminisces about his encounters in Rome with Bernardo Bertolucci, Miklós Jancsó, Jean-Marie Straub and Pierre Clementi, rendering a friendly and erratic report on their personal experiences and thoughts concerning filmmaking and its predicaments, both in capitalist and socialist countries.

These two latter texts give us the basis for a better understanding of Rocha's articles and reviews selected from *The Century of Cinema*, the book collecting his criticism of American and European cinema, from his early days as a cinephile to the 1970s.

The Century of Cinema draws a retrospective of Rocha's encounters with his peers. On the one hand, it offers an enlightening summary of the evolution of Rocha's critical thought; on the other, it lays out the network of affinities and alliances he established in the international arena over the years. Once again, his aesthetic intuitions and political convictions gain expression in critical reviews where formal invention and ideological militancy are seen as a matter of style.

The articles and reviews from the 1950s and early 1960s show that Rocha the cinephile is a rigorous aesthete endowed with great intimacy with the film form and a passion for detail, be it in relation to American classical cinema or his favourite European films. At the same time, the way in which he expresses his judgement on film auteurs and their works is directly related to aspects of his own experience.

In our selection, the majority of the articles focus on filmmakers he admires. As we can see in those pieces, politics has always been a decisive

Introduction

and all-pervading element for him, stretching from major social events to minor daily issues, from the career of the statesman to the life of the artist, from the letter of the law to the dramaturgy of the zoom lens, for example, in a film by Luchino Visconti. Rocha sees politics in Orson Welles's search for the imponderable – Welles knew how to 'dramatize power'. He sees politics in Eisenstein's taste for graphics and the 'geometry of temporal processes'. He also sees politics in Godard's nervous poetry which saturates image, text and sound, capturing the spectator in a fascinating apparatus which Rocha defines as a 'poetic form of despair' (the reference here is *Pierrot le fou*, 1965). Like Godard, Antonioni, for Rocha, is another driving force of modern cinema. *The Eclipse* (*L'eclisse*, 1962) is the great 'funeral space' (as the title of another selected article goes), the document of a dead bourgeois world, a work which illuminates man, a monument to lucidity. Antonioni is a great master of the cinematic language, which is evident in the way he creates a 'dialectic of alienation' by means of mise-en-scène and images.

Politics tend to complicate rather than simplify things, as soon as the critic turns away from dogmatism, and this is precisely what Rocha does in his film reviews included here, be it in relation to Westerns (three selected reviews),[7] gangster films or those by his favourite filmmakers Welles, Eisenstein, Godard and Antonioni. Not by accident, these were the auteurs accused of formalism by some leftwing critics adept of Italian neo-realism and social pedagogy, who failed to understand Welles, 'the main interpreter of imperialist tragedy', or Rossellini, who created a 'new method to capture the real in its flow' and understood that reality cannot be reduced to logic because it is full of surprises.

For Rocha, form and style take pride of place, but only if they interact with life and history. The films he is interested in are pervaded by sex, politics, ambitions, encounters, passion and deceptions. Art does not allow for the separation of these elements, hence his praise of Eisenstein as a filmmaker who promotes a synthesis of sensibility and intellect, emotion and reason. Although there is no piece specifically devoted to an Eisenstein film in *The Century of Cinema*, he is a key reference in Rocha's articles on his favourite modern European filmmakers, such as Godard, Visconti, Buñuel and Resnais (see, for example, 'The Splendour of a God', 'New Cinema in the World' and 'Viscontian Baroque'). Eisenstein is Rocha's reference when he discusses Alain Resnais' use of the interior monologue.

On Cinema

For Rocha, Resnais has performed a revolution with which he has every reason to identify, given the nature of his own formal project regarding, for example, the complex sound–image relationship as seen in *Earth Entranced*. He compares Eisenstein's procedures with William Faulkner's use of '*simultaneous and progressive accumulation of conflicts*', as he says. The writer is a source of inspiration for him in his defence of modern cinema.

Distancing himself from realism, Rocha saw cinema as an art able to mobilize the great 'forms of culture', such as the myth, biblical narratives, the epic tale and tragedy. According to him, these genres are already cemented in the popular imagination and the collective unconscious. They are also rooted in national traditions, as is the case with opera in Italy, the ground on which Visconti's cinema thrived. Rocha is not worried about psychological realism and the trials of everyday life, but rather with ethical and political behaviours that establish a link between individual action and the movement of history, as the director of *Ossessione* (1943) and *Senso* (1954) did. For Rocha, Visconti is the most lucid of all the masters in his appropriation of melodrama.

Buñuel, in turn, is the filmmaker who has overcome the state of anguish which plagues twentieth-century artists. His cinematic strength derives from a single, primordial drive for freedom. The extraordinary force of his images comes from his particular ironical mode of unveiling an imaginary rooted in religious repression and of retrieving, on the symbolic level of experience, the 'creative' energy derived from the sublimation of desire.

Pasolini is the focus of a tense debate in Rocha's writings, as seen in the pieces about him included here. In them, Pasolini's films are the object of admiration and distance alternately, an ambivalence that reflects Rocha's own struggle with the commingling of politics, the body, sexuality and popular mythology, in particular Christian. Rocha finds in Pasolini's work the same popular Mediterranean imaginary brought into South America by the Iberian colonizers, which found fertile ground among the peasantry.

As for American cinema, aside from Welles, it is Charles Chaplin the filmmaker with whom Rocha identifies the most. In his words, Chaplin 'illuminates the twentieth century because through him the People are given Image'. He represents the underdog's ironic response to the

Introduction

inequities of the century. Chaplin produced an art of resistance that prefigured the kind of political and popular cinema that would flourish in postwar Italy. Generally speaking, Rocha was attracted to the historical and national significance of the Hollywood genres of his preference. He drew lessons from American cinema from the outset, establishing an intense dialogue with the Western as a genre where conflicts find a direct mode of expression. The sublimation of massacre into mise-en-scène transfigures history into myth and captures the fascination of the young critic when the legend proves more complex in the hands of someone like John Ford. In a pre-urban world, the characters' imaginary expands to the point of heroism becoming life itself, a life imbued with pathos and free from bureaucratic rationalization, bourgeois routine and the comforts of civilization. In the realm of modernity, Rocha's attention veers towards the radical authenticity of James Dean, a preference that many may find surprising. However, for him, Dean embodied a sense of tragedy and desperation in the face of material wealth, a kind of non-complacent egocentrism. Dean was the myth who conflated nihilistic youth and the violence engendered by the American Empire and its material power. He added a new and impactful iconography to the 'cultural malaise' of the 1950s: fast cars, black jackets and facial nervousness.

Resorting to Rocha's figurative language, we could say that the century of cinema is the century of violence. In it, one lives between the American tragedy and the betrayed revolution, between the dream of cinema and monetary reality. Banned to exile by society, the artist has no alternative other than subversion. Nobody staged the tragedy of Capital better than Welles–Kane, in the film that Eisenstein would have liked to have made in the United States; and no one represented the betrayed revolution better than Eisenstein, the Russian genius whose *Ivan, The Terrible II* is a poetic criticism of the ways in which Marxism had been reduced to techno-positivism in the Stalin era. For Rocha, many great auteurs should have incorporated the unconscious in the manner of Buñuel, who gave free rein to his transgressive imagination.

For Glauber Rocha, the century of cinema is a baroque drama which could have been conceived by a Shakespearean playwright. But it gave room to a heroic aesthetic whose best expression can be found in the Cinema Novo revolution. Rocha was part and parcel of it, not only as a filmmaker and critic, but also as the young author of a book which promotes a revision of Brazilian cinema and launches a new tradition, in Eric Hobsbawm's expression quoted above. Rocha's writings reframe art as an experimental laboratory of conflicts at all levels: formal, dramatic and thematic. His imperative has always been to stage experiences of great social resonance, combining collective destinies, the interests of power and the violence that forever postpones the utopian liberation of the oppressed.

Revisão Crítica do Cinema Brasileiro

Critical Review of Brazilian Cinema

Introduction[1]

Brazilian film culture is precarious and marginal: we have film clubs and two film archives, but we do not have a publication of either informational, critical or theoretical importance. When it comes to bibliography, apart from books by Alberto Cavalcanti (*Filme e realidade*)[2] and Alex Viany (*Introdução ao cinema brasileiro*),[3] there are only two or three translations of the most famous works (Georges Sadoul[4] and Umberto Barbaro),[5] as well as essays by Salvyano Cavalcanti de Paiva (that deal with American cinema),[6] *The Cinema Primer* by Carlos Ortiz,[7] and other film-related works.

The effort required to educate oneself in theory or practice is inhuman: critics usually begin work on student papers and steadily progress to the literary supplements of large newspapers or specialist pages in magazines. They earn very little, even if they get their own column. Their salary is not enough to pay for subscriptions to essential periodicals such as *Cahiers du Cinéma*, *Téléciné*, *Cinema Nuovo*, *Films and Filming* and *Sight and Sound*. Thus, critics, filmmakers and dilettantes are constantly behind the times when it comes to what's happening in the world of film. Ideas, when they reach us, are either old hat or obsolete.

Most critics are specialists in American cinema because it's easier to talk about these films without too much concern for cultural detail. If the critic is linked to foreign distributors, he suddenly becomes an expert in a given area: Japanese cinema, Russian cinema, French cinema; in most cases the critic has to survive by brokering publicity between his newspaper and a particular distributor. Every critic is an island; Brazilian film thought doesn't exist and it's for that very reason that the filmmakers, those sources that are isolated in intention and confusion, both genuine and dishonest, lack definition. Theoretically, the climate is one of 'everything goes'; after 1962, whatever was not considered *chanchada*[8] became *cinema novo*.

The novice director suffers more than the critic; the field in which he operates hasn't been professionalized, there's no training available in theory, and there aren't enough productions to sustain an uninterrupted and evolving practice. The novice is a suicide victim who is forced to abandon his commitments and suffer humiliation until, through pure chance, he is able to direct a film. In this process, the least pretentious among them, those who only want a career, and perhaps some money and success, will sooner or later find their feet: they'll dream up storylines with spurious narrative effects, and they'll show little interest in the ideological meaning of the films, or in the cultural significance of cinema. They'll make films despite cinema and without knowing the cinema. Meanwhile, the auteurs are easily defeated. While in Europe and the United States there are still opportunities to be had for directors blessed with intelligence, culture and sensitivity, in Brazil such qualities are synonymous with madness, irresponsibility and communism.

In our cinematographic environment a director is measured by the loudness of his voice; if he shouts in the studio or the dubbing suite he's a great director, respected by technicians, actors and producers. He's further measured by his so-called capacity to work, reflected in his willingness to carry the tripod to film some tale masquerading as a 'serious film'; he throws in naked women and pornography, he makes two films per year, and he acquires god-like status. On the other hand, there is the auteur director, who rejects the 'story', the 'studio', the 'star', the 'reflectors', 'box-office success'; the auteur who only needs an operator, a camera, some film stock and the basics for the lab; the auteur whose only demand is for freedom.

With the end of the *chanchada*, commercial cinema has appeared as the greatest and most complex enemy of cinema in Brazil. The auteur, in his creative obsession, will have to overcome incomprehension, bad faith, anti-professionalism, intellectual poverty within the field and a mean-spirited disrespect from the critics.

Revisão Crítica do Cinema Brasileiro

Method

François Truffaut rightly pointed out that '... *il n'y a pas davantage ni bons ni mauvais films. Il y a seulement des auteurs de films et leur politique, par la force même des choses, irréprochable.*'[9] Adapting the 'auteur method', first analysed by French critic André Bazin, the history of the cinema can no longer be divided into the silent and sound periods, according to which filmmakers are categorized as 'those who spoke through pure images' and 'those who speak through sonorous images'. The history of cinema should now be seen, from Lumière to Jean Rouch, as 'commercial cinema' and 'auteur cinema'. There are no limitations of sound and colour for auteurs such as Méliès, Eisenstein, Dreyer, Vigo, Flaherty, Rossellini, Bergman, Visconti, Antonioni, Resnais, Godard or Truffaut. Of course, with handcrafted composition, the quality of the editing, cinematography and sound is very important, but what makes these films eternal is the politics of their auteurs, the reality that, as much through the primitive lens of Tissé as the modern lens of Raoul Coutard, was captured on film as a vision of the world. In the timelessness of films such as *Breathless* (*À bout de souffle*, Jean-Luc Godard, 1960) or *Battleship Potemkin* (*Bronenosets Potyomkin*, Sergei M. Eisenstein, 1925), there are no temporal limitations: it would be like dividing the history of literature into before and after Gutenberg.

The 'auteur' in the cinema is a term coined by new criticism to situate the filmmaker as a poet, a painter, a fiction writer, that is, auteurs who have specific objectives. The 'director' or 'filmmaker', within the contradictions of commercial cinema, has lost his meaning. 'Director', 'filmmaker' or 'artisan' – as Paulo Emilio Salles Gomes[10] observed,[11] can, in rare cases, achieve an auteurist status through his craft, as long as he's not subjected to the mechanics of the studio, but instead is aiming to use his technical knowledge to fulfil an expressive ambition. It is then that he'll have crossed the line: he's an auteur. The advent of the 'auteur', as a noun meaning the creator of films, heralds a new kind of artist for our times.

In an attempt to situate Brazilian cinema as a cultural expression, I have adopted the 'auteur method' in order to analyse its history and contradictions. At any given moment in its universal history, cinema has attained greatness because of its auteurs. Thus, the conflict within a revolutionary communist like Eisenstein or within a surrealist poet like

Jean Vigo contains all the economic and political contradictions of the social process. If commercial cinema equals tradition, auteur cinema is revolution. The politics of the modern auteur is a revolutionary politics: nowadays it's not even necessary to describe *an auteur as revolutionary*, because the condition of an auteur is a totalizing one. Saying that an auteur is reactionary, in the cinema, is the same as describing him as a commercial film director; it's situating him as an artisan; a non-auteur.

Is it an alienated category? No, it's a new order that imposes itself in a fierce dialogue with the world through the specific myth of the century. It's the auteur who is most responsible for the truth: his aesthetic is an ethics, his mise-en-scène is political. How, then, can an auteur look at the world covered in make-up, misled by the use of gigantic reflectors, faked with cardboard scenery, disciplined by automatic movements that are systemized in dramatic conventions that inform a bourgeois and conservative morality? How can an auteur forge organization from the chaos in which the capitalist world lives, denying dialectics and systemizing its process with the same formative elements of deceitful and intoxicating clichés? The politics of the auteur is a free, non-conformist, rebellious, violent and insolent vision. It's essential to fire a shot at the sun: the gesture of Belmondo at the beginning of *Breathless* defines well the new phase of cinema. Godard, when capturing cinema, captures reality: cinema is living and breathing, it's an object, a perspective. Cinema is not an instrument, it's an ontology.

What launches the auteur headlong into this great conflict is the fact that his instrument for this ontology belongs to the objective world against which he aims his criticism. Cinema is a culture of the capitalist superstructure. The auteur is an enemy of this culture: he preaches its destruction, if he is an anarchist like Buñuel, or he destroys it if he is an anarchist like Godard. He contemplates it in its own destruction, if he is a desperate bourgeois like Antonioni, or he is consumed within it, in passionate protest, if he is a mystic like Rossellini; or he preaches a new order, if he is a communist like Visconti or Armand Gatti.

In Brazil, where a capitalist structure is consolidated against the contradictions of an agrarian and metropolitan sub-world, cinema has been a disastrous alliance between immature auteurs and amateur capitalists. Until now, with few exceptions, cinema has been produced by a petit-bourgeoisie anxious for provincial promotion, or by financial groups intent on patronage. In one or two cases in the last couple of years, we have seen a cinematographic conscience begin to appear within the producing class which, organically, is already converting amateurs into artisans. As a consequence, it's pushing the auteurs out to the margins of amateurism. Hence the creation of pockets of independent production as the only means of survival for auteurs.

Given the lack of professionalization in the past, the new generations in cinema were spurred on by an indispensable vocational motivation: in 1960 new film directors in Brazilian cinema were all 'auteurs'; in 1962 a new wave of impromptu directors appeared, from the theatre, television and the *chanchada*, who filled up the spaces created by the increase in production. What determined this growth was the mentality created by publicity (the public controversy) of the group of non-conformist auteurs who, in 1960, gathered at the office of Nelson Pereira dos Santos; the term *cinema novo*, born thus, was transformed into the promotional headline of the large production companies and the new financiers who were attracted to the film industry by the sudden novelty value of the business. The auteur, of course, was left with the crumbs; within his amateurism, with impossible resources, he was unable to make films that reached the public in a way that commercial films marketed as *cinema novo* could. The auteur lost ground and remained on the margins analysing the contradictions, exasperated and naturally weakened. Reorganized this year, together the auteurs have started over; now, with the death of the *chanchada*, they do battle with a much more powerful enemy, which has grown out of this death. The myths of Zé Trindade and Oscarito[12] have been replaced by the myths of the scandal of naked women and of the picturesque regionalism of *macumba*[13] and cowboy leather hats. The unsuspecting public was quickly overcome by films that imitate American cinema of the 1940s, especially Westerns (a cliché used spuriously in relation to *cangaço*)[14] and gangster films (here the same cliché is applied to metropolitan films). The public, unconsciously reacting against the poverty of the language of the copy, reacted primarily against these themes: both the *cangaço* and the *favela*, important thematic spaces in the Brazilian social process, are condemned before a cinematographic demonstration of greater stature. The Brazilian auteur is castrated in terms of such themes – ones that are popular, intrinsically expressed in their political aspects. He is castrated in relation to language, which is schematic, extrinsically prescribed as the grammar of American spectacle. The Brazilian auteur finds himself in what is practically a dead-end street. The industrial development of Brazilian cinema, which is half a century behind the times, can expect a cultural stagnation of thirty years. The mistakes affecting the industry, articulated by intellectuals divested of any modern concept of cinema, are helping to create a monster. The misguided intellectual stamps a false artistic seal on commercial cinema and imposes it as a truth that is praised by the critics who justify commercial cinema and give the public a false notion of culture.

The so-called artistic cinema produced within the industry is characterized precisely by neo-expressionist aestheticism and by the contemplative ideology of the bourgeoisie: humour, boredom and love are the grand themes of all the classes, while social problems are resolved by palliative reforms.

If class is identified by flesh and not by money, commercial cinema gains its ideal artistic form in melodrama: the pathological character, inherited from the standardized drama of American scriptwriters, is successfully opposed to the historical character: the historical character, like the auteur himself, is a conscious being, exposed, objective, strong and violent in practice. Thus, it needs to be exterminated.

André Bazin once said that the Western was American cinema par excellence: his words inspire us nowadays to consider the possibility that cinema is 'Brazilian culture par excellence'. With the destruction of the auteur, however, there will be no excellence at all about cinema in Brazil. It tends to fail, strangled as it is by the limits of the domestic market. The large foreign markets will not be conquered with sub-cultural production since, ironically, the world's greatest industries have already begun to be destroyed by auteur cinema, that is, the French *nouvelle vague*, the Italian auteurs, the American and English independents and even the new Soviet rebel generation, who shattered, in relentless battle, the myths planted by Hollywood. The auteur industry, a synthesis of this new dialectic of the history of the cinema, will be an important chapter in the future. In Brazil, stuck in pre-history, this dialectic has been precipitated. There's only one problem: while auteur cinema is political cinema and while commercial cinema reflects the evasive ideas of reformist capitalism, the problems of our industry, in the current historical period, are the same as all the others that the production and working classes experience in Brazil. Hence the delusion of organs such as the Executive Group of the Film Industry (GEICINE); hence the danger of improvised legislation in benefit of national producers who need a greater number of dates on the market. The only mission of Brazilian auteurs, assuming they form a class, is to fight the industry before it becomes consolidated. Thus, cinema has to be viewed with a universal perspective; to stifle the dialectics is to choose the shadow of inconsequential opportunism which will forever turn the history of Brazilian cinema into nothing more than an informative appendix in the universal history of cinema.

Once and for all we have to understand that a new culture proposes, given the difficulty of being an Antonioni, a Resnais or a Godard, the desire and the possibility of being a new cinema. It has grounds, more so than anywhere else on earth, the term: *cinema novo* in Brazil. Launched at the beginnings of a strange cultural phenomenon it will at least remain as a sign of a hypothesis.

This book adopts the auteur method. As a critic and practitioner, I have been linked over the last five years to the 'backstage' of Brazilian cinema. The book includes, on the one hand, personal opinion, and on the other impartial criticism. The result seems valid to me, as the first foundational stones of our cinema, after the introductory book by Alex Viany.[15] I may have omitted names and got my dates wrong.[16] However, recalling a minor observation made in a text by Caio Prado Júnior[17] (and recalling the economists of our cinema, Cavalheiro Lima and Jacques Deheinzelin!) I was not interested in listing numbers and figures, but rather in interpreting the facts where possible, 'if art and invention steer my pen'.[18]

Meanwhile, by way of humble homage, I dedicate this work to old Humberto Mauro – an auteur – and to the young Miguel Torres[19] – also an auteur – who died in a jeep accident in the state of Paraíba.

Humberto Mauro and the Historical Situation

The 1930s, before World War II, witnessed the third great cinema cycle, after the decline of German expressionism at the beginning of the 1920s and the Russian classical period, a phase that had revealed the genius of Eisenstein in *Strike* (*Stachka*, 1924), *Potemkin*, *October* (*Oktyabre*, 1928), *The General Line* (*Generalnaya Liniya*, Sergei M. Eisenstein and Grigori Aleksandrov, 1929); of Pudovkin in *Mother* (*Mat*, 1926) and *Storm over Asia* (*Potomok*

Chingis-Khana, 1928); of Dovzhenko in *Earth* (*Zemlya*, 1930), and Dziga Vertov's theories of the cine-eye. In the 1930s the great step forward in sound took place; persecuted by the Nazis, both Fritz Lang and Sternberg, creator of the myth of Marlene Dietrich, emigrated to the United States; then American cinema consolidated the gangster cycle; the sardine industry (in Stroheim's phrase) was built on the basis of names such as Rouben Mamoulian, Frank Borzage, Henry Hathaway, Sternberg himself, William Wyler, John Ford, King Vidor, Frank Capra, Fritz Lang (these last five being the major personalities), but above all in the great novelty of the musical, which industrialized the creative genius of Busby Berkeley, who found a solution to the impasse of Lubitsch's once-popular operettas.

In France it was the restlessness of the avant-garde – the golden age of René Clair, Renoir, Duvivier, Carné, Jacques Feyder, Marcel Pagnol – the tragic and remarkable episode of Jean Vigo – the restless talent of the Brazilian Alberto Cavalcanti. French cinema was born, whose industry went into dangerous competition with the American trusts; controversy stretched from naturalism to realism, from surrealism to anarchism. Experiments were made in drama, light comedy and literary adaptation: nothing was defined but while Hollywood destroyed talent, France flourished and welcomed new ideas.

In England, which was the destination of Cavalcanti, after a commercial stint in Paramount studios in Paris (which already existed!), the genius of John Grierson kickstarted, from within the famous General Post Office Film Unit, the 'British documentary' movement, which Cavalcanti chose to call neorealism.

The British realist documentary was without doubt more important at that time than the American industry or the restless French production. It was a movement that had clear definition and was not overtaken by time; it left lessons in style and in organization. But above all, and in a more meaningful way than the Soviet classical cinema, it invested film with a social and educational meaning. John Grierson was a Marxist and, despite being financed by the GPO, he never gave in to reactionary impositions. Improvements in film sound took place around this time and Alberto Cavalcanti was skilled in its use – he made up, alongside Grierson, Basil Wright and Robert Flaherty, the great quartet of the group.[20]

The 1930s were also the years that consecrated the name of the Dutch documentary maker Joris Ivens; but in the history of the *cinema novo* the

Revisão Crítica do Cinema Brasileiro

main significance of the 1930s lies in the fact that it was the era of Jean Vigo, Robert Flaherty and Humberto Mauro, in the far-flung Brazilian wilderness. Flaherty, like Vigo, symbolized the struggle against the lies of industrial cinema. He died a victim of the incomprehension of producers and exhibitors: his films, which according to Flaherty himself did not play or compromise with social themes, complete, more than in the case of Vigo, this profound sense of the truth and of a poetry that can be achieved only by a free cinema.

If Humberto Mauro, who started out in Cataguases, in the state of Minas Gerais, in 1925, with *Valadião, The Rogue* (*Valadião, o cratera*), had been in Europe and the United States in the 1930s, he would certainly still have made a film of the stature of *Rough Gangue* (*Ganga bruta*, 1933), but he would also have experienced the same difficulties as Vigo and Flaherty; he might have died sooner, from frustration. The fact that a Brazilian like Cavalcanti was one of the three or four most important figures of the period in all of Europe precludes any colonial references to Mauro. If *Limit* (*Limite*, 1930) by Mário Peixoto visibly corresponded to a symptom of the French avant-garde and revealed an artist impregnated with subjective aestheticism, *Rough Gangue* in 1933 not only corresponded to the poetic symptom of Vigo and Flaherty, but it was also associated with a reality that didn't limit it with an intentional language. Proceeding to an examination of *Rough Gangue* we can see that, while the dry style of the British documentaries would influence the French filmmakers, at that time fond of 'fusions', 'superimpositions', 'slow cameras', 'graphisms' and other practices that bordered on the ridiculous; and while in American cinema the German school was advocated (with the exception of the Frenchman Wyler, the Irishman Ford, and Capra, the Sicilian) as the beginnings of an industrial patent – Humberto Mauro, marginalized from the already established modernist movement, far from the film archives, linked to a primitive studio-laboratory, with no knowledge of criticism or specialist works – relying solely on disorganized information from Griffith, King Vidor, possibly John Ford and Stroheim; with a few expressionist films and a number of Russian, American and French ones – had before him the landscape of Minas Gerais; within him lay the vision of a filmmaker educated by sensitivity, intelligence and courage. Indeed, at a time of complex cinematographic creation, Mauro, in *Rough Gangue*, made an anthology that seems to combine the best impressionism of Renoir, the daring of Griffith, the force of Eisenstein, the humour of Chaplin, the composition in shadow and light of Murnau – but, above all, absolute simplicity, a sharp sense of man and landscape, a lyricism that, as José Guilherme Merquior eloquently put it:

> if it is emotion, but without the drifting of the sentiment and its disorderly dispersal; if it is imagination, but without the loose fantasy disconnected from reality; if it is consideration of the world, but without being subject to data, without pure description: if lyricism is also reason, or the emotional impulse of a reason that confronts the world and is ready to extract from it a meaning, then the object of lyricism is, not directly the reflexive conscience of an emotion, but first and foremost, the *pure* nascent meaning. What can be perceived in lyricism is the birth of meaning.[21]

This adaptation of a concept of lyricism by the literary critic perhaps illustrates the cinema of Humberto Mauro as well as it illustrates poetry itself. It's rare that, in *pure nascent meaning*, Brazilian lyricism is better expressed in the work of Jorge de Lima,[22] Carlos Drummond de Andrade[23] and João Cabral de Melo Neto[24] than it is in sequences from *Rough Gangue*. Photographed by Edgar Brasil, who also shot *Limit*, Mauro's film presents a quality that is equal to the best cinematographers of the time. When the history of cinematography is written, Edgar Brasil will be as important as Tissé was for Eisenstein; Kaufman for Dziga Vertov and Jean Vigo; Gregg Toland for Orson Welles and William Wyler; Figueroa for Mexican cinema, Otello Martelli for neorealism or Raoul Coutard for the *nouvelle vague*.

The explosion of Humberto Mauro onto the scene in 1933, bearing in mind that this was the heyday of the realist north-eastern [regionalist] novel – is so important that, if we were to look for a trace of intellectual identity in the formation of a character confusedly impregnated with realism and romanticism, we would see that Humberto Mauro is close to José Lins do Rego,[25] Jorge Amado, Candido Portinari, Di Cavalcanti,[26] and the first phase of both Jorge de Lima and of Heitor Villa-Lobos, whom he befriended and with whom he made *The Discovery of Brazil* (*O descobrimento do Brasil*, 1936).

The advance represented by the conscience of a realist such as Graciliano Ramos[27] meant that, only now, through Paulo Cesar Saraceni

Revisão Crítica do Cinema Brasileiro

(*Porto das Caixas/The Port of Caixas*, 1963) and Nelson Pereira dos Santos (*Vidas secas/Barren Lives*, 1963) critical realism has begun to define a Brazilian cinema style. But the initial link is found in Humberto Mauro. With its fragmented evolution, Brazilian cinema created its auteurs at unexpected moments and for this reason its artists remained in obscurity, at the margins of culture. In fact, that is the one great crime that Brazil committed against Mauro. From a professional point of view, Humberto Mauro was successful, having produced a filmography of 15 feature-length films, from 1925 with *Valadião, The Rogue*, followed by *In the Spring of One's Life* (*Na primavera da vida*, 1926), *Lost Treasure* (*Tesouro perdido*, 1927), *Dormant Embers* (*Brasa dormida*, 1928), *Blood of Minas Gerais* (*Sangue mineiro*, 1929), *Lips without Kisses* (*Lábios sem beijos*, 1930), *Woman* (*Mulher*, 1931),[28] *Rough Gangue, The Voice of Carnival* (*A voz do carnaval*, 1933), *Shantytown of My Loves* (*Favela dos meus amores*, 1935), *Woman-City* (*Cidade-mulher*, 1936), *The Discovery of Brazil*, with music by Villa-Lobos, *Clay* (*Argila*, 1940), *Secret of the Wings* (*Segredo das asas*, 1944) and *The Song of Sweet Longing* (*O canto da saudade*, 1950). Most of these films were made in Cataguases; with the advent of sound, Mauro moved to Rio de Janeiro at the invitation of Adhemar Gonzaga, where he directed the most important films of his career: *Rough Gangue* and *Shantytown of My Loves*. He also directed the unfinished *Conspiracy in Minas Gerais* (*Inconfidência mineira*), produced by Carmen Santos, which dragged on for years and years. As an actor, photographer, writer, editor, producer, director, stage director, electrician and machine-operator, he worked on all the technical roles. Today, as an employee of the National Institute for Educational Cinema (INCE), Mauro dedicates his time to documentaries and he has already made so many that even Alex Viany's insistent research fails to list them all.

To an extent Humberto Mauro was sacrificed, and his recognition was slow to emerge, because of the backwardness of film culture in Brazil. At that time Mauro was much more substantial than people realized. In Europe he might have made fewer films, because only in Brazil, in an amateur film industry, could he maintain his professional integrity and creative freedom. If intellectuals of the time had had a vision (the obsession back then was worshiping the hermetic *Limit*), and had there been a movement similar to that of 1962, lending cultural support to Humberto Mauro, demystifying the undeniable talent of Mário Peixoto, bringing

On Cinema

Cavalcanti back to Brazil and indicating directions to enthusiasts such as Adhemar Gonzaga and Carmen Santos, Brazilian cinema, at the moment when the American, British and French cinemas were being consolidated, would today be very strong. Mário Peixoto has been converted into a legend; Humberto Mauro has become isolated in bureaucratic professionalism. Cavalcanti would return to Brazil in 1949 to a climate of frank irresponsibility.

In an article published in 1961 in the Sunday supplement of *Jornal do Brasil* I wrote the following:

> Along with Ely Azeredo, Walter Lima Jr., Alex Viany, Sérgio Augusto and Paulo Cesar Saraceni – critics who attended the modest Cataguases festival, I concluded that Humberto Mauro and, of course, *Rough Gangue*, as the highlight of his work, should be the subject of a book, a project which in fact is already underway. We thus believe that the best policy would be to study Mauro and in this process rethink Brazilian cinema, not as a set of formulas linked to the industry, but in terms of film as an expression of humankind. Following in the path of Humberto Mauro's legacy is the greatest responsibility that any man in Brazilian cinema could take:
>
> (a) Mauro made in Cataguases, with the most limited resources, the best Brazilian films, and in Rio, also on a budget, he made one of the twenty best films of all time, *Rough Gangue*.
>
> (b) Mauro doesn't understand how one can spend 'thousands' on a film, because a film is not a structure made up of effects but a visual expression of problems.
>
> (c) In contrast, all Brazilian films after Mauro (the list would naturally include *The First Mass/A primeira missa*, 1961, by Lima Barreto or *Ravine/Ravina*, 1958, by Ruben Biáfora) have been made with increased resources and they are infinitely inferior.
>
> (d) The principle of production of *cinema novo* as a whole is the anti-industrial film: films that are born in a different language, because they are born amid an economic crisis, as a reaction against cinematographic capitalism.

Revisão Crítica do Cinema Brasileiro

So, the tradition of Humberto Mauro is not only aesthetic and cultural, but it is also the tradition of a producer, the likes of whom cannot be found in the millionaire delirium of today. Humberto Mauro – with the impact of his work – obliges us to rethink cinema in Brazil, at least those of us who are honest and who are not afraid to assume the necessary critical conscience. It's only then that the importance of Humberto Mauro will be fully recognized.[29]

In the same article I transcribed the view of Paulo Cesar Saraceni: 'A revision of the work of Humberto Mauro is now of extreme historical importance, because it is precisely this year that a new generation of filmmakers is being formed, not in relative terms, but on a level of universal ambition stimulated by the greatness of his work.'[30] At the beginning of the article I wrote, in reaction to the cinematographic moment:

> From *Rough Gangue* to *The First Mass* (from 1933 to 1961) Brazilian cinema has regressed violently. When we situate the latest film by Lima Barreto we don't include in this the opposition it suffered from an unjust political campaign – a backward and clumsy attitude from various factions. It's *critically* that we cannot endorse *The First Mass* in 1961, as it's earlier and more incomplete than *Rough Gangue* – a modern film from 1933, a silent film which represents a still valid watershed, an avant-garde work. By imagining a bridge going backwards from the young Humberto Mauro to the old Lima Barreto – it's possible to trace the involution of Brazilian cinematographic language.[31]

So we could apply, without a doubt, Saraceni's words: '*cinema novo* is a question of truth and not of age.'

Rough Gangue is a film that cannot be unpacked in terms of 'storyline' and 'direction', despite containing a story written by Octávio Gabus Mendes. It's classified as mise-en-scène cinema: the editing is not overbearing and it's the vision of the filmmaker before each dramatic phase that drives him towards this or that choice of camera, with the editing following an interior rhythm. Articulating the elements in a way that makes the traditional foundation (the fable) integral to the visual organism, evolving into a live filmic object, Mauro invests in a kind of expression that is contrary to the analysis of shallow critics who qualify him as primitive. If primitive in cinematic terms means directing the camera by intuition rather than restricting it with reason, then Jean Vigo, Robert Flaherty, Roberto Rossellini, Luis Buñuel, the Indian Satyajit Ray and many others among the great filmmakers would be primitives. Rather, filmmakers closer to the notion of primitive would be those who, while they ably manage the mechanics of filmmaking, they never manage, in the grammatical conjugation of shots, to transmit a single moment of truth. The camera is an object that lies. Talking about *cinéma-vérité*, Louis Malle said that every time a director limits a space of reality with a frame, he's lying about that reality, because he's dismantling it according to a given convention. The auteur, when he lies about the real, is *moved* by an interior impulse: but it's as a result of this determination to look that he captures the *truth of the chosen space*. The lyrical *pure nascent meaning* is in the shot itself and not in the sequence, in contrast to Eisenstein's theory of dialectical montage; the Russian filmmaker considered the shot to be abstract, so only the dialectics of this shot with the others could produce dramatic content. When Rossellini, at the end of *Il generale Della Rovere* (1959), denies the hero the close-up as he's about to be shot, his position in relation to heroism is revealed: after witnessing the inner revolution of a rogue who is converted into a martyr, Rossellini, in a crisis of doubt, withdraws from the great moment of sacrifice that would guarantee the hero a place in the history books. Any mechanical director, who sticks to the grammatical rules, would choose to have a close-up of the character dying, because that moment was merely a dramatic one. Who is the primitive? Rossellini or Henry Levin? On the subject of Eisenstein's *The General Line*, Paulo Emilio Salles Gomes observed:

> The rural theme and its process of renewal – the transformation of a *kolkhoz* from the private to the collective – the diverse demands of treatment of the agricultural world in contrast to the urban/industrial world, imposed a simplicity of lines which Tissé assimilated in the cinematography and a quality to the settings, which has nothing to do with the impact of intelligence of *October* and the revolutionary manifesto of *Potemkin* ... there are fresh touches in the spirit of *The General Line*, the most salient being its lyricism, which was not present in his previous films ... the figure of Marfa Lopkina insists on attitudes and reactions that are not symbolic, but instead come from a physical, moral and psychologically characterized creature ... It is evident that in the

Revisão Crítica do Cinema Brasileiro

> criticism of the *kulak* and its parasitic and bourgeois dreaming, in the satire of bureaucrats at the tractor factory and in the religious procession, Eisenstein the scathing critic maintained his integrity. But in his previous work there was no sequence like the lyrical, allegorical and sadistic wedding of *Fomka* the bull. Nor was there a sequence like that of the mixer, in which the exaltation of technical progress assumed the characteristics of an erotic liberation. The place of *The General Line* in the complex work of Eisenstein is as a more balanced attempt to firm up his aesthetic ideals, seeking as he was more objective results in terms of theme and less controversial and experimental ones in terms of form.[32]

It's worth noting that, in these poignant observations by Salles Gomes, Eisenstein was beginning to discover a truth that was greater than his theory. And it's precisely for this reason that *The General Line* contains more lyricism on the face of a peasant woman (only in close-up, without the need for a subsequent discourse with other shots) than in the famous scene of the bridge and the horse in *October*, a scene which seeks a poetics of violence.

Led by intuition, Mauro is dissonant and the root of his editing is lived experience. *Rough Gangue* isn't an uncomplicated film: it's a classic turned inside out. Being expressionist in the first five minutes (the wedding night and the murder of the wife by the husband), it's a realist documentary in the second part (the freedom of the murderer and his tram ride through the streets) and then a Western (the fracas in the bar, with the ensuing brawl in the best tradition of John Ford). It grows with the same force as classical Russian cinema (the sexual possession of the woman, with its erotic/Freudian connotations in the metaphorical editing involving machines/cranes in a factory); and, if in the argument between the groom and the criminal husband (the first anti-climax) the graphic evidences remind us once again of German expressionism, the entire ending is constructed in a climate of an adventure melodrama. But such dissonance doesn't make *Rough Gangue* an incoherent film: all these visions form a single filmic movement, corporified by a constant link of lyricism which forms the substance of Mauro's mise-en-scène. If the Freudian scene of the factory is the only moment to have been historically overtaken in the film, it's worth remembering that the work of Marx and Freud formed the basis of Eisenstein's theory. Mauro lacked knowledge of

Marx, and with regard to Freud I don't believe that the metaphors of the factory were a conscious experiment on his part.

The richness of *Rough Gangue* is not limited to this or that manifestation of talent: the editing, marked by a spirit of experience, today finds a connection with the syncopated rhythm of a Godard or the speculative rhythm of Resnais – to cite auteurs who, from the 1940s onwards, broke with the discursive editing patented in commercial practice. Evidently, being an inventive technician who confronted all the details of cinema, Mauro knew well the basics of narrative editing. His cuts, however, are free: there are no ecstatic moments in *Rough Gangue*; everything is moved by an interior rhythm; it explodes, withdraws, discusses, reflects and communicates a world in unexpected and increasingly suggestive mutations. And sealing his place as an auteur, what can be deduced from Mauro's camera position is an understanding of the objective values of the physical and social landscape. Aiming for understanding and avoiding ecstasy when faced with the exuberant Brazilian landscape – the kind of Brazilian romanticism that Lima Barreto would return to and in which the professionals of our misery immerse themselves – Mauro, although he was ideologically muddled, made a political statement divested of any demagoguery. He achieved a true picture of Brazil which is, through the alienation of customs, sociologically mystified by romanticism. In this picture he does not hide the violence of poverty. In a short documentary, already in the sound era, *Mills and Power Plants* (*Engenhos e usinas*, 1955) – a romantic film whose narration opens with the popular poem by Ascenso Ferreira 'of the mills of my homeland the names alone make me dream',[33] and soon afterwards led by the visual and lyrical movement of the folk song 'Engenho Novo', the naive poem organically establishes the economic and industrial evolution of the countryside, the power plants that destroy the slow watermills in the stagnant countryside; the advent of the machine, the lack of adaptation of primitive man to progress (through ignorance), the flight from industrial fever (causes of underdevelopment) – whose tragic path is nostalgia. Although certain criticisms appear to be made unintentionally, the truth with which Mauro penetrates the picture is enough to enable him to make a direct social comment. Thus, the beginning, with Mauro himself sitting with his back to us at the foot of a gigantic tree, looking at the vast, silent land, this which is the greatest moment in Brazilian cinema, contains an entire social cycle and the reflection of this landscape on primitive man. In fact, this could have been a documentary of three shots, if Mauro had wanted: after the force of the initial shot, having cut to a shot of the wheel of a mill and then one of a factory turbine – the whole history of the sugar industry in Brazil, which defined agriculture in the early colonial period, would be presented. Therein lies in this initial shot the root of the creative perspective of Brazilian film – a vision that would be re-established nearly thirty years later by Nelson Pereira dos Santos, Linduarte Noronha, Paulo Cesar Saraceni and Joaquim Pedro de Andrade.

When I point to the importance of a shot, I am not concerned with the preciousness of formal questions: what matters is not the quality of the lens or the lighting, or the rigours of composition, but rather the outpouring that comes from the true artist in his continuous dialogue with reality, a dialectical relation that leads him to transformational criticism and practice. It's a problem of truth and morality: it's being an auteur; it's making *cinema novo* as a challenge to mechanical cinema.

Humberto Mauro is the first figure of this cinema in Brazil. Omitting his name is like omitting the names of Gregório de Matos,[34] Gonçalves Dias,[35] Cláudio Manuel da Costa,[36] Jorge de Lima, Carlos Drummond de Andrade and João Cabral de Melo Neto from the history of Brazilian poetry, or José de Alencar,[37] Raul Pompéia,[38] Lima Barreto,[39] Machado de Assis, José Lins do Rego, Graciliano Ramos, Jorge Amado, Guimarães Rosa, Lúcio Cardoso[40] and Adonias Filho[41] from the history of Brazilian novel. Forgetting Humberto Mauro today – rather than returning constantly to his work as the only powerful expression of *cinema novo* in Brazil – is a suicidal attempt to start from scratch towards a future of sterile experiences, detached from the live sources of our people, sad and starving, in the midst of an exuberant landscape.

Revolução do Cinema Novo

The Cinema Novo Revolution

The Cinema Process (1961)

[1]

Is cinema doomed to disappear? Such a question could perhaps be puerile if considered from a traditional critical point of view. Since writing about films began, such a doubt has always existed: the fundamentally technical/economic conditions of cinema, its evolution and its increasingly complex consequences have made it not just an industry of thoughts but also a far-reaching political organization. The State always exercises on the product vigorous action, both in terms of the pre-defined *ideological* set of guidelines, and in terms of the effects that its mechanisms can have on Brazilian society: I refer here to censorship.

The *expression*, or *means of expression*, is also placed in the voluble plane of technology: *cinerama*, *technirama*, television and new processes of relaying the moving image concern producers in such a way that there is no time to care about thought or, rather, the form of thought that characterizes creators and poets seduced by the apparent aesthetic possibilities of the new art. I will return to such *possibilities* later. Everyone knows that films are the result of a production and production means capital investment like any other, with one particular characteristic: it requires sensitivity, good taste, intelligence, what is conventionally referred to as art, and other indispensable attributes to ensure that the merchandise is consumed by the *spirit* of the people. Merchandise is aimed at the spirit. Perhaps this is why – it's undoubtedly why! – poets are attracted to it. There is a greater possibility of expression than in humble and anguished forms of verse and picture. And, above all, there's the so-called profanity of the world which corrupts the poet, at the moment when he crosses the frontiers of cinema. In an article published in this very Sunday Supplement of the *Jornal do Brasil*, Ingmar Bergman speaks of the old humble artisan, of the gifted man who would work quietly and die happy in the knowledge that he was a worker like any other. Today, the artisan is an object of public fascination. He is an exception who attracts curiosity. If writers and painters are, in most cases, inscribed in this process of immortality that is organized by publishers and gallery owners, filmmakers, more than any other artist, are placed on the top of the pile. Producers invest millions in their work. It's necessary to turn the intellectual author of the film into a rare species. It's necessary to convert him into a sacred monster, as happened in bygone times with film stars.

Since neorealism, and before then French cinema, filmmakers have been taking the place of the starlet on publicity material. With the advent of the *nouvelle vague*, a whole traditional plane was subverted and newspapers found themselves invaded by photos and adventures of Roger Vadim, Louis Malle, Claude Chabrol, François Truffaut, Alan Resnais, Marcel Camus, Robert Hossein, Georges Franju, Jean-Luc Godard, Edouard Molinaro and a further dozen young film directors. Only Brigitte Bardot kept her promotional advantage. The social corruption of the creator of films became officially established; he was an artisan who, if beforehand he had been exaggerated in his own obscurity, was now exaggerated in his dependency on box-office returns.

Thus, we all know that the phenomenon of the *nouvelle vague* was merely a very clever production coup. What the French producers did also broke the routine production of the Americans: they gave the young filmmakers greater liberty and even fostered *intelligence* as a new ingredient in films. An intelligence, in this case a French intelligence, which was more capable than the scandalous version long ago industrialized by Elia Kazan and later by the transpositions of Sidney 'Paddy' Chayefsky, not to mention the new Westerns, with their injection of standard psychology into the genre with the greatest popular repercussion in the world.

Then the critics appeared as the greatest victims (consciously or otherwise) of the attack on culture and on all values considered dignified by the mighty human spirit. In the French case, we open a Bible like the *Cahiers du Cinéma* and we find high praise for names such as Alfred Hitchcock, Samuel Fuller, Richard Brooks, Nicholas Ray, Martin Ritt, Richard Quine and nearly all fashionable American directors who, with the exception of Hitchcock, don't possess the least creative sense (or are incapable of demonstrating it). They are merely contracted artisans, without ideas, but they do possess certain personal characteristics that help them establish new lucrative patterns. This minimum of permitted dignity means a lot within the industry. What modern American auteur is free of guilt, if even the great hope Stanley Kubrick has dived headlong into a super-production: *Spartacus* (1960)?

Although we can single out the case of auteurs such as Satyajit Ray (India), Federico Fellini, Michelangelo Antonioni, Visconti and Roberto Rossellini (Italy), Bergman (Sweden), René Clair and Alain Resnais (France) who fight to maintain complete creative independence, we cannot hide the fact that these names are today very worthy attractions at intelligent box-offices throughout the world.

[2]
It's not unusual for us to hear declarations by filmmakers who relate to the public their dreadful suffering. Producers are the enemy. The film in the eyes of the law is a piece of merchandise; the intellectual auteur has no rights over his work, which is mutilated according to distribution needs. And the filmmaker, without any alternative, is resigned to omitting even the slightest hint of creativity from his work. Orson Welles often gives such interviews. But is the author of *Citizen Kane* (1941) not fully aware of how much his name is worth in money?

The problem, recounted melodramatically by men who are already established in cinema, is more easily resolved than we think. Antonioni as an auteur was 'damned' until the explosion that was *The Adventure* (*L'avventura*, 1960). Then *The Night* (*La notte*, 1961) made at its first screening in Paris forty million francs. Today Antonioni is a bestseller. He did not make shameful commercial concessions. His art was simply discovered by the public. Mr Charles Malandra, supervisor of France Films in South America, told me that he had no faith in *Hiroshima mon amour* (Alain Resnais, 1959). The box-office returns were fantastic. Is it in order to lose money that French producers now spend it, allowing Alain Resnais

Revolução do Cinema Novo

and Alain Robbe-Grillet to have a romp in a specific castle in Austria? Grillet himself, one of the most outstanding names of the *nouveau roman*, is today, despite his literature still being linked to certain intellectual circles, a starlet in the making. His name, overtaking the success of his books, has been transformed into public legend, it has crossed frontiers. And just as the adventure of Marguerite Duras has resulted in millions of francs, there's nothing more appropriate than associating Resnais with another writer, and nothing more intelligent than associating the same writer with Roger Vadim, the Coca-Cola of filmmakers; sex and good taste at a bargain price.

Ideas come at a price. For this reason, it seems to me that critics either fool themselves or they try to survive. Without doubt, critics are more intelligent and cultured than filmmakers and at the same time they are artists who either have integrity or who are too shy to adhere to corruption. Would a sincere critic have the courage to deny cinema, if cinema was for him both intellectual motivation and his livelihood? In the Brazilian case, the only person linked to cinema who can live off the trade is the critic. Some receive decent wages from their columns as well as commission from publicity and promotion. They are honest, bar the usual exceptions, and they need to justify their existence.

[3]
In Brazil (and in other parts of the world – see Satyajit Ray's excellent commentary on this in the *Cahiers du Cinéma*), for any filmmaker who goes into film production the very experience of making a film can place him in an anguished labyrinth of doubt.

In the aforementioned article in this very Sunday Supplement of *Jornal do Brasil*, Bergman asks why he chose cinema. This question is the first form of anguish. We could reply that the problem (or trend) is organic. My own profoundly sincere reply (taking the cue from Bergman) is that cinema is chosen because it's a form of profanity against human integrity, and because it's the easiest way to save the artisan. This is a dangerous reply that I give without a trace of fear, and here I refer to both artisans and auteurs. In the case of the artisan (the metteur-en-scène) it's more profitable, less possible, and more promotional than theatre and television. I can even confirm that 90 per cent of theatre productions would disappear if directors were given their fair *chance*. In Brazil, then, not much attention is needed in order to ascertain that every man of the theatre possesses cinematographic ambitions. But since cinema doesn't exist here, the easiest form of survival is already guaranteed. Not that theatre is a lesser form of expression. But the conviction of a Bertolt Brecht would be indispensible in order to deny and reject as violently as the author did when he took Georg Wilhelm Pabst and producers to court over the film version of *The Threepenny Opera* (*Die Dreigroschenoper*, 1931).

In the case of the auteur who is essentially a poet or fiction writer, the greatest ambition in adhering to cinema is, in the first place, to create worlds that are more visible and marketable. Secondly, and this is a feature acquired as soon as he enters the world of cinema: a disposition towards self-flagellation. I refer to this second aspect merely to highlight yet another negative aspect of the filmmaker's condition. But what really interests us is to know the extent to which such physical and moral suffering ceases to be a possible masochism, and acquires instead the disguised form of demagoguery. Getting into cinema is a dangerous move. Every auteur (who is also a critic, a poet, a writer or a painter) who abandons his first interests and decides to make films brings with him unstoppable ambition. It would be necessary to preserve his humility to implicitly refuse fortune and glory. To make cinema is already to adhere to some disguised form of demagoguery. And this aspect becomes consolidated when the auteur sees, in the completed film, a mere shadow, or at best a sketch of his original idea. Vice already dominates him and it's difficult to turn back. The responsibility of the filmmaker is so great that turning back would mean destroying an entire group. It's for this reason, admits Ray, author of *Pather Panchali* (1955), that he couldn't give up once the desperation of dealing with 'the practical' overcame the poet.

But are material conditions really the principal cause of frustration?

Although making a film in Brazil and in other underdeveloped countries is a Via Crucis (according to Paulo Emilio Salles Gomes), it's also an arduous task to film in Hollywood or in France. Theirs are other problems. They exist on a large scale, and even in organized studios directors become caught up in basic, futile, serious, vulgar and even profound problems. The process is in fact inverted. In Brazil, a close-up is taken without much science. A close-up in Hollywood, which could destroy a great star, can take a whole day to resolve. It could cause neurosis. Therefore, such widely commented conditions don't strike me as just cause. Without a doubt, films are getting made. And they have been filmed under similar complications.

I hope we don't consider good films to be those that are commercially successful: the best of Hitchcock or the great literary works illustrated on screen, such as the case of Fellini and Bergman (whose own literature, given its hybrid character, is questionable) and, to a point, *Hiroshima mon amour*. When I say good I am not denying such films, but merely asking if they really are films. My question is not the old chestnut 'What is a film?'. Here, yet another critical revision would be called for.

The image, strictly speaking, should be a word and the filmmaker should write with the image. This theory, in various forms, has preoccupied hundreds of critics. But what image is this? The human face? Man? Nature? My reply is that this image has only existed in a handful of sequences made by a handful of filmmakers. Because cinema demands organization which in most cases is linear, the word interferes to assist the image, preventing the *being* of the cinema from becoming drained away into a complete artistic inconsequence, which would be the equivalent of the didactic documentary. Is not the avant-garde condemned by even the most formalist of critics? Cinema today is a betrayal of the sign. Like the Japanese ideogram and the Egyptian hieroglyphics, cinema is a language that is hidden and forgotten even by the great filmmakers mentioned above. It's not narrative editing, or even pianistic (atonal) montage that will make a film. A film will never be (*and it would be a cowardice of the spirit and imagination to admit it*) an illustrated fictional script paginated on the screen just as a report in a magazine is paginated. When a critic says that literary cinema is the real modern cinema, he is, in fact, seeking salvation. It's unacceptable for an intelligent man not to be aware of the incalculable intellectual task that is required to turn a film into an object, rather than just a conductor of dubious ideas.

When I accepted the profession of making films and duly performed my penance of ninety days on a deserted beach, without much money and with a heterogeneous crew, I only accepted the work which was against my original ideas on cinema because I was clear about the country, the basic problems of hunger and regional slavery, and I could decide between my ambitions and one of cinema's minor functions: being a vehicle of necessary ideas. Ideas that were not my frustrations and personal complexes, but which were universal, even when considered on the simplest level of values: showing the world that within the form of exoticism and the decorative beauty of Afro-Brazilian mysticism, there lives a race that is sickly, starving, illiterate, nostalgic and enslaved.

The example is not a case of exhibitionism but the frankness to confess that cinema as a vehicle of ideas can only be honestly accepted while it serves man in what he needs to live: bread. If he doesn't live by bread alone, in order to live off lyricism, metaphysics or pathos (as the critics like it), first it is necessary to have three square meals a day, even though, in order to do so, men must die in those parts of the world where blood flows that bit quicker.

Returning to another point touched upon earlier, I can practically confirm that the demagoguery of the filmmaker is born of this frustration. In the Brazilian case, where we still haven't got the conditions to make films as any human being goes about his work, or rather make films with the minimum of decent equipment and professionalism, such litanies will sound familiar. What's worse, the filmmaker here lives in a desert of incomprehension, which accentuates his drama. Being a filmmaker in Brazil means remaining in the waiting room of the great experience, and for this reason we cannot even reach the point of trying, being frustrated in the attempt and regarding that frustration as a concrete result. Our frustration is basic, superficial. It's more a result of a pre-existing economic and social ambition. It's no lie to declare that the Brazilian filmmaker is always heading in the direction of uselessness. His daily struggle with the sub-systems of production takes up all his time. He loses jobs and takes risks. He has no time left to read a particular book or to see a film. He becomes culturally weakened. In most cases, he veers towards a leftist position or else he's converted into an extremely reactionary anti-nationalist, going as far as to accuse the landscape of being responsible for his failures. Such filmmakers lack the courage to take a look in the mirror, and see that the asphalt of metropolitan centres is a pseudo-development and that, deep down, we are pretty much what the Europeans think we are: Indians in a suit and tie. And now I humbly ask: could we not, poor Brazilian filmmakers, expunge the sins of our ambition? Could we not return to that old condition of obscure artisan and seek out, with our miserable cameras and a few metres of film, that mysterious and fascinating writing of the real cinema that remains forgotten? I wouldn't even know what cinema this is, what truth this is. This proposal, which doesn't intend to be a manifesto, and which may well be a personal interrogation made public, could seem romantic and even idiotic. I do believe, however, that cinema will only be cinema when filmmakers are reduced to the condition of poets and, once purified, exercise their trade with seriousness and sacrifice. But, on the other hand, cinema has risen to become the greatest instrument for ideas in the universe. Would the desertion of filmmakers be fair if they themselves, despite being enslaved, speak at times so loudly?

We are undoubtedly in a vicious circle. Cinema is a profane art. Only the future, with the destruction or consolidation of this initial phase, can offer a response. Until then, between production and anguish, filmmakers will have to compromise or rebel.

Barren Lives (Vidas secas) (1964)

While the modernist generations from the 1920s and 1930s expressed themselves through literature – whose final polemical breath was the *concretist poetry* movement of the late 1950s – and while the theatre has always been an expression open to attack and crisis throughout this period, the *chief expression of the current national moment is the cinema*. Cinema novo didn't appear by chance or from a mystifying hypothesis: it was the result of a major crisis within Brazilian art. At the point when *concretism* decreed the death of our poetry, it was not a new generation of novelists that appeared, to shift the stones left by the authors of the 1930s – it was cinema auteurs, whose forebearers, from Humberto Mauro to Mário Peixoto, were powerless in their marginal situation. Nelson Pereira dos Santos, a possible throwback to 1945, 'happened' in 1962, forty years after the seminal Modern Art Festival in São Paulo;[1] and *Barren Lives*, in the cinema, provided a firmer revolutionary cultural basis in present times than the original work of Graciliano Ramos, the most important writer of the 1930s realist literature.

On the other hand, the crisis in literature coincided with the political crisis: the expression of the latter phenomenon was manifested through cinema projects while, years before – at the time of the Cuban Revolution (1959) that shook Latin America – Brazilian cinema was hardly connected to politics. Fatally, and with no other way out, for there could not have been a better context for the birth of a *new cinema* (*cinema novo*), Brazilian films were incorporated into politics and they tend, in this process, to influence the dialectical process of history.

Today, *cinema novo* doesn't project a solitary bourgeois revolution along the lines of the *nouvelle vague*, but a social revolution within the demands of the movement in which it exists.

Barren Lives, by way of synthesis, presents and signifies all these problems.

In Brazil, the cinema auteur is a rough sketch, a theory, and a crisis. If *Barren Lives* is a practice, whose greatest conquest for the history of cinema is the founding of another authorial language, this same film, by way of contradiction, reveals a crisis on the part of the cinematographic creator, overcome by the obsession of confirming his powers.

A revision of universal cinema leads us to conclude that the sub-process of production in Brazil has little to do with the realization of its auteurs.

Being a film auteur is the most dramatic and absurd condition – which suffers from external pressure but which is crushed by the inevitable conflict of the auteur. The way of looking at the world is so individual that, even in forced cases, it is impossible to discipline the vision to the regulations of traditional ways of viewing: those which are formulated to entertain and make profit. Orson Welles and Jean Vigo, Robert Flaherty and Max Ophüls, Eisenstein and Visconti, Rossellini and Buñuel – these are the heroes of the cinematographic saga at various points throughout the world.

At different moments: none of them succumbed, due to the resistance of their genius or to the greater force of the faith in ideas – but they all suffered and were mutilated by economic power or by censorship.

Before Nelson Pereira dos Santos became an auteur, he was a victim of this intention which defined itself over the years and was owing in particular to the commercial failure of his previous films; what made matters worse was that, despite domestic critical success, these creations – all of which were improvised – didn't satisfy the growing ambitions of the young director, who was precociously carrying the weight of Brazilian cinema.

The Via Crucis started to acquire new characteristics, carrying the stone from the beginning to the end of a film, and always returning to a successive film with the same pain. Nelson Pereira destroyed the notion of his *Brazilian* cinema: he ended up just with his cinema.

Revolução do Cinema Novo

And he began, calmly, to comprehend and define the project for *Barren Lives*.

Revolt was no dream, no mere detail; revolt was now a nucleus, and given that it was the thesis of the auteur, it would become the antithesis of the work.

In the cinema, the auteur is a 'monster' whose work confronts the intentions of a system aimed at commercial conquest and totalitarian politics. The problems of Eisenstein with Stalinism are not different from Orson Welles's experience with RKO or John Huston's with Metro: the auteur is a fierce and aggressive individualist, but his survival depends on integration in a collective practice. He has to concede so as not to die (like John Huston), or die so as not to concede (like Eisenstein), or run away and keep tackling so as not to die or concede (like Buñuel). Chaplin, Rossellini, Welles – the most aggressive – are barred at each step: Bergman, in Sweden, an exceptional case, is the only one who can manage a peaceful protest; like Antonioni or Resnais, Bergman is a peaceful and simultaneous balladeer of bourgeois decadence.

In Brazil – see, for example, Humberto Mauro – the auteur can perhaps go around undisguised and not be noticed. This was the case not just with Nelson Pereira dos Santos but with some other young directors of the *cinema novo*. What introduces greater drama, however, is not the fact of being an auteur, but the detail of being an auteur of films. One should not forget that Flaubert went to court for writing *Madame Bovary*, that *Ulysses* was banned, and that D.H. Lawrence is on the puritanical blacklist. But moralizing cannot prevent a writer from producing – even if it can prevent his work from circulating. In the cinema, the auteur cannot produce because his creation depends on technical means – he needs a machine to transform his ideas into an expression. This machine is denied to him; the auteur, in mystical renunciation, undresses and launches himself into the conquest of the means and of the film – he creates with hunger and with blood and only rarely is he not defeated – but what escapes, what survives this struggle is what remains eternal for cinema – like *L'Atalante* (Jean Vigo, 1934) or *Rome, Open City* (*Roma, città aperta*, Roberto Rossellini, 1945).

Is an 'auteur cinema' possible, or is the cinema, by its very composition, a minor art form which doesn't allow for auteurs? Are auteurs really possessed by cinema or by the authorial condition incorporated into cinema? Is it possible for an auteur to make his mark through the contradiction of a process? Would not the only way to deny such questions be, as Orson Welles says, a totally criminal manifestation of the auteur, criminal and suicidal to the point of subverting the order of the cinema and morality in the name of the myth?

Auteur cinema is free cinema! This freedom, fundamentally, is intellectual. For an auteur, as for Fabiano and Sinhá Vitória, the protagonist couple in *Barren Lives*, there are no moral dilemmas. The boss exploits because he's the boss. Government is government. For marginal beings there are no moral issues – there are the classic social and political issues. That's all: it's what stops your digestion but doesn't stop you from always leaving, even on foot, aimlessly, in a never-ending wilderness. Nelson [Pereira dos Santos] doesn't offer any ray of hope, Fabiano and Sinhá Vitória leave in the heat of the day; there's no morning, only the day.

More so than in the case of Graciliano Ramos, *Barren Lives* the film is the first autobiographical confession of Nelson Pereira dos Santos at a moment of success and on the verge of crisis. He sacrifices the dog Baleia to make the journey easier: Fabiano would in fact leave his wife and kids in the desert and carry on his journey alone towards hell before he would allow himself to be burnt alive by the sun. His struggle is against the colonel, against the soldier: the soldier and the colonel are more to blame than the sun. Fabiano is stubborn, an individualist, an auteur, while Nelson Pereira dos Santos and Graciliano Ramos want to conquer the sun and its transcendental beauty.

Discussions surrounding *socialist realism* find their response in this kind of modern cinema and at the same time they become unnecessary and even demagogic. Comprehending the essence of *realism*, auteurs such as Nelson Pereira, Francesco Rosi and those new faces around the world are beginning to create a new cinema in a phase in which the delirious expressionism of Bergman seems to determine that the greatest depth of a film in its search for knowledge would end in the domain of the literary gesture and conceptions. Tracing the line of a fictional and literary realism – where one can identify the best of American novels of the 1920s, the spirit of modern cinema seems to be, at least in the West, this analytical sharpness, the synthesis of man and his soul, filtered through the rigours of time. The freedom of the rhythm of a beating heart frees the filmmaker from the rules of editing in the attainment of a new interior time that from the inside out determines a style of mise-en-scène and defines itself.

In the Brazilian case, the auteur is impelled by a force greater than the force of the underdeveloped process: Nelson Pereira dos Santos takes a leap with *Barren Lives* and places himself on the same track where the great auteurs of today run – in the most part the Italians of the beginnings of neorealism and Jean-Luc Godard, who introduces dialectics into his (dis)montage.

An Aesthetics of Hunger (1965)

Thesis presented during discussions on cinema novo, *on the occasion of the retrospective which took place in January 1965 at the V Festival of Latin American Cinema in Genoa, sponsored by Columbianum. The theme proposed by Secretary Aldo Viganò was* 'Cinema novo and *world cinema'. A revision of this theme was deemed necessary: the paternalism of the Europeans in relation to the Third World was the main motive for the change in tone.*

Dispensing with the informative introduction which has become accepted practice in discussions on Latin America, I prefer to situate relations between Brazilian and civilized culture in terms that are less reductive than those which also characterize the analysis of the European observer. Thus, while Latin America laments its general misery, the foreigner develops a taste for such misery, not as a tragic symptom, but merely as a formal set of data within his field of interest. The Latin American doesn't communicate his true misery to the civilized man, and the civilized man doesn't fully comprehend the misery of the Latin American.

This, fundamentally, is the state of Brazilian Arts in relation to the world: up until now only lies passing as truths (*social problems conveyed through formal exoticism*) have been communicated in quantitative terms, provoking a series of misunderstandings which are not restricted to Art, but which above all contaminate the entire political terrain.

The processes of artistic creation in the underdeveloped world are only of interest to the European observer insofar as they satisfy his nostalgia for primitivism; and this primitivism is shown as hybrid, disguised beneath a belated inheritance from the civilized world, which is poorly understood because it's been imposed by colonialist conditioning.

Latin America remains a colony and the only difference between colonialism then and now is the more sophisticated form of colonizer and, as well as real colonizers, the subtle forms of those who also plan future incursions.

The international problem of Latin America is still a case of a change of colonizers. As a result, a possible liberation will for some time to come mean a new form of dependency.

This economic and political conditioning has led us to philosophical disability and to impotence, which, at times unconsciously and at times not, creates sterility in the former case and hysteria in the latter.

Sterility: those works found in great number in Latin American Arts, where the author castrates himself in formal exercises that still fail to achieve full possession of their forms. The frustrated dream of universalization: artists who never awoke from the adolescent aesthetic ideal. Thus, we see hundreds of paintings in galleries, dusty and forgotten; books of short stories and poems; theatrical plays, films (which, especially in São Paulo, have resulted in bankruptcy) ... The official world in charge of the Arts has created carnivalesque exhibitions in a number of festivals and biennials, manufactured conferences, easy formulas for success, drinks receptions in several parts of the world, as well as a number of officially sanctioned cultural heroes, academics in Letters and the Arts, juries of painting competitions, and cultural excursions abroad. University monstrosities: the famous literary reviews, the faculty selection process, the titles.

Hysteria: a more complex chapter. Social indignation provokes inflamed discourse. The first symptom is the anarchism that marks the work of young poets (and painters) up until now. The second is a political reduction of art that produces bad politics through an excess of sectarianism. The third and more effective is the search for a systematization of popular art. But the error in all this is that our possible equilibrium doesn't result from an organic body, but from a titanic and self-destructive effort in the sense of overcoming impotence, and as a result of this operation carried out with forceps we find our efforts frustrated, relegated to the inferior limits of the colonizer. If he understands us, then, it's not because of the lucidity of our dialogue but because of the humanitarianism that our information inspires in him. Once again paternalism is the method of comprehension for a language of tears or muted suffering.

Revolução do Cinema Novo

The hunger of Latin America, for this reason, is not only an alarming symptom: it's the nerve of its very society. Therein lies the tragic originality of *cinema novo* in relation to world cinema: our originality is our hunger and our greatest misery is that this hunger, while it's felt, is not understood. From Linduarte Noronha's documentary *Aruanda* (1960) to *Barren Lives*, *cinema novo* has narrated, described, put down in verse, discussed, analysed, and excited the themes of hunger: characters who eat dirt, characters who eat roots, characters who steal in order to eat, characters who kill in order to eat, characters who flee in order to eat, characters who are dirty, ugly, skinny, living in filthy, ugly, dingy homes; it was this gallery of starving characters that linked *cinema novo* to the 'miserabilism' that was so criticized by the government, by critics who work for antinationalist interests, by producers and by the public – the public could not bear such images of misery. The miserabilism of the *cinema novo* stands in contrast to the tendency of digestive cinema, advocated by the 'chief critic' of Guanabara, Carlos Lacerda:[2] films featuring wealthy people, in beautiful homes, driving luxury cars; happy, amusing, fast-paced, but ultimately meaningless films, made with purely industrial objectives in mind. These are films that work in opposition to hunger, as if, within greenhouses and their luxury apartments, filmmakers could hide the moral poverty of a fragile and ill-defined bourgeoisie, or even as if the very technical and scenographic materials could hide the hunger that is rooted in our uncivilization. It's as if, above all, within this apparatus of tropical landscapes, it were possible to disguise the mental poverty of filmmakers who make these kinds of films. What has given *cinema novo* its singular international importance is precisely its heightened commitment to portraying the truth. This same miserabilism which had been written about in 1930s literature has now been captured on film by the *cinema novo* of the 1960s. If in the past it was written about as a form of social critique, it's now discussed as a political problem. The very stages of miserabilism in Brazilian cinema are internally evolving. Thus, as Gustavo Dahl[3] has observed, it moves from the phenomenological (*The Port of Caixas*), via the social (*Barren Lives*), the political (*Black God, White Devil/Deus e o diabo na terra do sol*, Glauber Rocha, 1964), the poetic (*Ganga Zumba*, Carlos Diegues, 1963), the demagogic (*Five Times Favela/Cinco vezes favela*, Marcos Farias, Miguel Borges, Carlos Diegues, Joaquim Pedro de Andrade and Leon Hirszman, 1962), the experimental (*Sun on The Mud/*

Sol sobre a lama, Alex Viany, 1963), the documentary (*Garrincha: Hero of the Jungle/Garrincha, alegria do povo*, Joaquim Pedro de Andrade, 1963), to comedy (*The Beggars/Os mendigos*, Flávio Migliaccio, 1962), all experiments in one way or another, some frustrated, others successful, but all composing, in the last three years, a historical picture that, not by chance, would come to characterize the presidencies of Jânio Quadros and João Goulart:[4] a period of great crises of conscience and of rebellion, of agitation and revolution that culminated in the April 1964 coup. And it was after April that the thesis of digestive cinema gained impetus in Brazil, systematically threatening *cinema novo*.

We comprehend this hunger that most Europeans and Brazilians fail to understand. For the European, it's a strange tropical surrealism. For the Brazilian, it's a source of national shame. The Brazilian doesn't eat, but he's ashamed to say so. More importantly, he doesn't know where his hunger comes from. We know – we who made these ugly, sad films, these screaming, desperate films, in which reason hasn't always taken centre stage – we know that hunger will not be cured by government plans and that the cloak of Technicolor will aggravate rather than hide the physical evidence of this disease. Thus, only a culture of hunger, weakening its very structures, can overcome it in qualitative terms: and the most noble cultural manifestation of hunger is violence.

Beggary, a tradition established by redemptive colonialist piety, has been one of the causes of political mystification and of the jingoist cultural lie: official reports on hunger request money from colonialist countries with the purpose of building schools without training teachers, with the purpose of building homes without creating jobs, with the purpose of teaching trades without teaching the alphabet. Such requests are made by diplomats, by economists, by politicians; *cinema novo*, in the international arena, has never asked for anything. Instead, it has imposed the violence of its images and sounds on 22 international festivals.

For *cinema novo*, the precise behaviour of the starving is violence, and the violence of the starving is not primitive. Is *Barren Lives*' Fabiano a primitive? Is Firmino in *The Turning Wind* (*Barravento*, Glauber Rocha, 1962) a primitive? Is *Black God, White Devil*'s Corisco[5] a primitive? Is the woman in *The Port of Caixas* a primitive?

For *cinema novo*, an aesthetic of violence, rather than primitive, is revolutionary. Herein lies the first step enabling the colonizer to

Revolução do Cinema Novo

comprehend the existence of the colonized; only by recognizing violence as the only option of the colonized does the colonizer comprehend, in horror, the force of the culture that he exploits. As long as he doesn't take up arms, the colonized will remain a slave: that first policeman had to die in order for the French to be made aware of the Algerians.

From a moral point of view, such violence, however, is not subsumed in hatred. Nor can we say that it's linked to the old colonizing humanism. The love that encompasses this violence is as brutal as violence itself, because it's not a love of complacency or of contemplation, but one of action and transformation.

It's for this reason that *cinema novo* hasn't produced melodramas; the women of *cinema novo* have always been creatures in search of a possible way out for their love, given the impossibility of loving while feeling hungry. The prototype, the woman from *The Port of Caixas*, kills her husband; Dandara in *Ganga Zumba* leaves war behind for a romantic love; Sinhá Vitória in *Barren Lives* dreams of better times for her children; in *Black God, White Devil* Rosa turns to crime to save Manuel and love him in different circumstances; the young woman from *The Priest and the Girl* (*O padre e a moça*, Joaquim Pedro de Andrade, 1966) must defrock the priest in order to win her new man; the woman in *The Dare* (*O desafio*, Paulo Cesar Saraceni, 1965) breaks up with her lover because she prefers to remain faithful to her bourgeois world; the woman in *São Paulo S.A.* (Luís Sérgio Person, 1965) wants the security of a petit-bourgeois love and in order to achieve this she tries to reduce the life of her husband to a mediocre scheme.

Gone are the days when *cinema novo* needed to justify its existence: now, *cinema novo* has to advance in order to explain itself better, while our reality is more discernible in the light of thoughts that are not weakened or made delirious by hunger. *Cinema novo* cannot develop effectively while it remains on the margins of the economic and cultural processes of the Latin American continent. And besides, *cinema novo* is a phenomenon of colonized peoples and not a privileged entity in Brazil. Wherever there's a filmmaker prepared to film the truth and confront a hypocritical and police-enforced standard of censorship, there one will find the seeds of *cinema novo*. Wherever there's a filmmaker prepared to confront commercialization, exploitation, pornography, technicism, there one will find the seeds of *cinema novo*. Wherever there's a filmmaker, regardless of age or origin, ready to place his cinema and profession at the service of causes that are relevant to our times, there one will find the seeds of *cinema novo*. *This is the definition* and with this definition *cinema novo* marginalizes itself from the industry because *industrial cinema* is committed to lies and exploitation. The economic and industrial integration of *cinema novo* depends on the freedom of Latin America. *Cinema novo* is committed to this freedom in its own name and in that of its closest and most dispersed members, from the most stupid to the most talented, from the weakest to the strongest. It's a question of morality that will be reflected in the films, in the time it takes to film a man or a house, in the details observed, in the Philosophy: *it's not a film but an evolving collection of films which will eventually give to the public an awareness of its own existence.*

This is why we do not have greater contact with world cinema.

Cinema novo is a project that is realized in the politics of hunger, and it suffers, for this reason, from all the resulting weaknesses of its existence.

Revolution is an Aesthetics (1967)

The only way out for an intellectual from the underdeveloped world caught between being an 'aesthete of the absurd' and a 'romantic nationalist' is revolutionary culture.

How can the intellectual of the underdeveloped world overcome his alienation and contradictions and attain a revolutionary lucidity?

Via a critical examination of a reflexive production on two juxtaposed themes:

- Underdevelopment and its primitive culture.
- Development and the colonial influence of a culture on the underdeveloped world.

The values of the developed world's monarchic and bourgeois culture should be criticized in their own context, and then transformed into instruments of useful application to the comprehension of underdevelopment.

Colonial culture *informs* the colonized about his own condition.

Revolução do Cinema Novo

Complete self-knowledge should then produce an anti-colonial attitude, or rather, the rejection of colonial culture and of the *lack of awareness pervading national culture*, which are erroneously regarded as values by nationalist traditions.

From the violent dialectical process of information, analysis and rejection, there will emerge two *concrete forms* of a revolutionary culture:

> the didactic / epic
> the epic / didactic

The didactic and the epic should function simultaneously in the revolutionary process:

> The didactic: to teach how to read and write, to inform, to educate, to raise the consciousness of the ignorant masses and of the alienated middle classes.
> The epic: to provoke the revolutionary urge.

The *didactic* would be scientific.

The *epic* would be a poetic practice, which would have to be revolutionary from an aesthetic point of view so that its ethical objective can be projected in a revolutionary way.

It will demonstrate the underdeveloped reality dominated by the complex of melancholy impotence, by the unconscious admiration of colonial culture, the *very possibility* of overcoming, through revolutionary practice, creative sterility.

The *epic*, proceeding and being processed in a revolutionary way, establishes revolution as natural culture.

Art, therefore, becomes revolution.

At this moment, *culture* becomes the norm, at the moment when revolution is a new practice in the intellectualized world.

The *didactic* without the *epic* generates sterile information and degenerates into passive conscience in the masses and into a clear conscience in intellectuals.

It is inoffensive.

The *epic* without the *didactic* generates moralistic romanticism and degenerates into hysterical demagoguery.

It is totalitarian.

The new revolutionary culture, a revolution in itself at the moment in which *creation* equals *revolution*, in which creating is to act not only in the field of art but also in the political and military fields, is the result of a cultural-historical revolution that consolidates the links between *History* and *Culture*.

The infinite objective of revolutionary liberation is to afford to man an increasing capacity to produce his materials and use them according to a profound mental development.

An economic and political revolution which is detached from a cultural revolution becomes insufficient in the sense that it creates conflict in man between his economic freedom and his mental backwardness.

The revolution will raise underdeveloped society to the developed category and from there will appear a new necessity: the demystifying action of cultural nationalisms; the civilizing action against myths and conservative traditions; the substituting action of integral values of human collaboration, to which it is limited by the remains of the bourgeois defect of individuality.

The sense of human collaboration renews and reveals a new category of individual, but for that to happen it is necessary to revolutionize the old culture.

At this stage, the *didactic epic* needs the scientific psychoanalytical instrument in order to make of each man a creator who, informed of all his mental instruments, can provoke a revolution among the creative masses.

The Cinematographic Revolution (1967)

For *revolutionary cinema* there are no cultural or ideological frontiers. Since cinema is a method and an international expression, and since this method and this expression are dominated by the *American cinema associated with the large national producers – the struggle of genuinely independent filmmakers is an international one.*

Independent filmmakers need to organize themselves in the common struggle. Cultural power doesn't exist without economic and political power. The purpose of independent filmmakers must be to conquer the power of production and distribution in all countries.

All independent filmmakers need to be organized nationally into groups linked to production and distribution and they need to rely on the effective action of economic denunciation and aesthetic demystification of the *American cinema* and its respective by-products. The independent filmmakers should produce films that are capable of provoking in the public a shock that will change their moral and aesthetic education imposed by *American cinema*. This revolution is not the work of a film but of a whole international production that is permanently revolutionary. For this reason, the national organized groups should relate to one another on an international level, in order to facilitate co-production and distribution. This international organization should have roles that imply responsibility and sacrifice. For this, it is necessary that critics take to task not only filmmakers but also themselves, in order to transform the academic and mythological concepts of cinema, nearly all of which are founded upon the colonizing efficiency of *American cinema*.

The struggle should be aesthetic, economic and political.

In the capitalist world, the pernicious point of the cinematographic process is distribution. Distributors receive an inflated commission just for establishing a flow of contacts between producer and exhibitor. The distributor invests 90 per cent less than the producer. As a result, a film, in order to be produced, requires a prior agreement with a distributor. Failure to do so results in paralysis. Therefore, the distributor advances to the producer, for the rights of distribution, the producer's own money. In order to fight against this, filmmakers must transform themselves into producers and distributors. The producers then organize the flow of prestige of actors and filmmakers, through whom they make contact with distributors. Thus the real intellectual producers of films, filmmakers and actors in the first place and technicians in the second, are alienated from their work and accept, in the name of a *possible* opportunity for self-expression, the exploitation of producers and distributors. It is necessary to replace the concept of *capitalist producer* with the concept of *producer-creator*, that is, a professional trained in the organization of the production of a film in terms of participation, and equal to other technicians and specialist artists. Thus, the contact between the *product/film* and the exhibitor should be direct. The organization of distribution should be controlled and placed at the service of *new producers*. As a result of the development of production in different nations, the development of a *Filmmakers International*, capable of confronting *American cinema* in terms of quantity and quality, is made possible. In order for this to happen, independent filmmakers need to remain firm in their decision to make a *new cinema from the point of view of aesthetic/ethics*. Only then, through a *qualitative international action*, can cinema become *an instrument of revolution that is as efficient as the political instrument of colonization which is the* American cinema.

In relation to socialist countries, it is necessary to replace nineteenth-century notions of realist art with contemporary notions, and for socialist cinema to free itself as soon as possible from the aesthetic influences organized by the western capitalist world, which are in crisis and sustained only by the need for theoretical survival. At a time when capitalist *western culture* is questioning its own values, socialist cinema needs to concern itself with a new culture and to contribute, in an efficient manner, to the international struggle of the revolutionary cinema in the capitalist world.

Serious aesthetic vices belonging to American cinema *can be found in socialist cinema*. It's not enough *to replace capitalist morality with socialist morality and conserve the structure of* American cinema *in order to create a new cinema*. What needs to be transformed radically is the very structure of American cinema, grounded in anti-dialectical thought.

Independent cinema is facing a cultural revolution. This revolution must raise its consciousness through the use of the very techniques of production, whose particular and disorganized examples can be taken from neorealism and the *nouvelle vague*, movements that destroyed themselves because *they were not organized on an economic and political level*. American cinema should be beaten on its own turf. *Art and essay films, fronts* of the struggle of independent cinema, are already becoming contaminated by *American cinema*. It is necessary that the greatest possible volume of independent production, with distribution controlled by filmmaker-producers, invade the large theatres.

An aggressive battle on the part of independent cinema *will provoke a controversy without precedent in the history of cinema*.

From this moment, an independent cinema will pass from cultural fact to political fact and it will be well prepared to confront all types of aggression and sabotage by *American cinema*.

In order to organize national movements of independent filmmakers *the very concept of cinematographic auteur needs to be revolutionized*. The filmmaker cannot be considered an isolated artist like the poet or the painter. The filmmaker should be a technician, an economist, a publicist, a distributor, an exhibitor, a critic, a spectator and a polemicist. The

Revolução do Cinema Novo

filmmaker should be a man of action, physically and intellectually prepared for the fight. An independent film should be improvised with whatever means available, at a low cost and in a short period of time. But, fundamentally, the technology of production should allow cinema to develop, because only after a complete revolution could cinema overcome the aesthetic, political and economic domination of *American cinema*. Thus, the filmmaker should be, first and foremost, a creator, an intellectual, a politician, an artist and a scientist. Above all, the film should be made by the filmmaker, a creator who should have knowledge of both cinema and politics. Cinema should be both a method and a form of expression. And this expression should be both confrontational and didactic. That's how cinema should be integrated into the revolutionary process.

That is Epic/Didactic Cinema!

(a) The cinematic avant-gardes of each country should get together to organize a new production and distribution policy based on the specific set of contradictions of each country.
(b) These avant-gardes, once organized, should promote a Cinematographic International in order to create the means for inter-production/inter-distribution.
(c) The national and international organization needs a *front* of filmmakers, critics, professional producers, actors, technicians and people who are directly and indirectly interested in a cinematic revolution.
(d) It should be considered at all levels that cinema, given that it is the most powerful instrument of communication that exists (*whether it's shown in theatres or on television*), is an indispensable and fundamental weapon in the fight against imperialism.
(e) It should also be considered that only with an organized international action can the individual talents of filmmakers be integrated, and that any individual talent that is marginalized from the international revolutionary process is transformed into an instrument that is dialectically useful to imperialist thought.

Tricontinental (1967)

Tricontinental – any camera switched on to the evidence of the Third World is a revolutionary act.

Tricontinental – the revolutionary act is a product of an action that becomes a reflection on the process of the struggle.

Tricontinental – the political choice of a filmmaker is born at the moment in which the light pierces his film. This is because he chose the light: the camera on the Third World, occupied land. In the street or in the desert, in the forests or in the cities, the choice is imposed and, even if the original material is neutral, in the editing it constructs a discourse against that material: it could be imprecise, rambling, barbaric, irrational. But it's a biased *refusal*.

Tricontinental – is the film important? What's a tricontinental film? Here, a producer is like a general. The instructors are in Hollywood just as they are in the Pentagon. No tricontinental filmmaker is free. I don't mean *free* from imprisonment, or from censorship, or from financial obligations. I mean free from realizing that he's a *man of three continents*; but he's not imprisoned by this concept: rather, he finds freedom within it. The perspective of individual failure is diluted in History. In the words of Che Guevara:

> Notre sacrifice est conscient, c'est le prix de la liberté ... [Ours is a conscious sacrifice, it is the price of freedom ...]

Tricontinental – any other discourse is beautiful but inoffensive, rational but tired, cinematographic but useless, reflexive but impotent, and even lyricism, it hangs in the air, it's born of the word, it becomes architecture, only to turn all too soon into a passive or sterile conspiracy. Here, recalling Regis Debray, words become flesh.

Tricontinental – auteur cinema, political cinema, *counter*-cinema, is a guerrilla cinema; in its origins it's brutal and imprecise, romantic and suicidal, but it will become epic/didactic.

Mexican cinema suffers from a nationalist malaise. D. Luis Buñuel, an Ibero-American, considers *Que Viva Mexico!* to be an 'artistic' film. Eisenstein did not comprehend the spontaneity of Aztec architecture or the substantive monumentalism of the deserts and volcanoes. His attempt to *aestheticize* the new world is akin to the attempt to take the word of God (and the interests of the 'Conquistador') to the Indians. *Culture* also belonged to the Indians. These Mayan, Aztec and Inca *cultures* were discovered and civilized. In the land of magic, the Indian allowed himself

Revolução do Cinema Novo

to be seduced by the mobile volume of the horse: the *quadruped* was a war tank, a sacred beast, invincible. Today, centuries later, Ho Chi Min resists the technological innovations of the invader.

Mexican cinema adopted the frames of Eisenstein disguised as a Jesuit, then mixed the frames with the marvels of Hollywood's technique, and from all this he produced *nuestro México*. Industry protected by laws and unions, *nuestro México*, romantic nationalism and the illusion of History, *nuestra revolución sombreros, mujeres y sangre* [our revolution of *sombreros*, women and blood].

Sun on the natives. Murnau (Gauguin) and Flaherty saw bodies and seas, smiles and tragedies, in the same way that these Latin Ports are a violent and liberating paradise where, *to have and have not*,[6] Humphrey Bogart feels and suffers the exoticism of revolutions. Before the Latin filmmaker had the right to put to use his old camera, the art and commerce of the large companies had given us *their cinema* and the laws *of their commerce*.

The Mexicans have banned and still ban anti-Mexican films. But they veto only a small part of American production that treats Mexicans as poltroons. But what's worse is that in the majority of films coming out of Churubuzco Studios,[7] Mexicans are either poltroons or naive creations of nature. The Mexican industry, while defending itself against infamy, copies it, in the same way that socialist cinemas copy Russian cinema which copies the American formula. Mexican nationalism isolated Mexico from Latin America. It's not by accident that, apart from some young filmmakers who only now are beginning to betray *nuestro México*, D. Luis Buñuel is considered a marginal filmmaker. But in his comedies and melodramas, also filmed in Churubuzco, we find the first essays on Latin American civilization, after the Catholic, Zapatista and ... Eisensteinian apocalypse.

Pampas or asphalt, Argentina brought stone by stone from Europe. Argentina, the fatherland of Che, discussing in excellent French the aesthetics of the absurd, didn't suspect that 'the progress of Perón did not mean *desarollo* [development].' With empty pockets, aristocrats were prepared to sacrifice food for a Dior neck-tie. The pre-Antonioni bourgeoisie of Argentine films had its incommunicability limited by malnutrition. But they never used the word: if the literature of Borges/ Cortázar precedes many of the experiments of the *nouveau roman*, it wasn't for this reason that time was (or wasn't) articulated in pre-Resnais films. Argentine cinema alone discovered Style before History. One of Leopoldo Torre Nilsson's characters, disciplined in a universe diffused in Bergman, can achieve nothing beyond discipline. An ahistorical discipline because it is acritical. He doesn't expose himself to light: neither does he leave himself open to attack, but rather he conspires in the shadows about a world that doesn't exist culturally in its superstructure. Here, word doesn't become flesh: it's shadow and light (grey and black) in a country that doesn't integrate well in America.

What kind of bad conscience for his isolation caused Che, an Argentine citizen, to become the legendary Latin American man and, going even further, the tricontinental man?

A declining cinema, even before it developed, in the same land and era as Che, cannot be saved by technology or by an aesthetics manual. More than any other tricontinental cinema, Argentine cinema needs a Vietnam.

God save America, in Cuba everything is yet to be done. A cinema that, concentrating on didactic films, has to make the important revolutionary contribution of completely detoxifying itself from *socialist realism*.

> Simplifying the terms of such polemics, which involved artists and some employees, we defended an art more or less akin to socialist realism, while on the other hand (in the vast majority of artists) we defended an art which did not renounce the achievements of the avant-garde. The defeat of the first point of view was consecrated when Che, in 'Socialism and The Man in Cuba', *castigated socialist realism*, without however finding the second point of view satisfying: for him one should not settle for this position, but go farther. But to go farther one must depart from somewhere, and the avant-garde seems like a good starting point, if not a finishing point. (Jesús Díaz)[8]

Other Latin countries (such as Paraguay, Peru and Bolivia) never have or only rarely have been able to switch on a camera: apart from official occasions where we see the Generals and their medals.

Tricontinental, Latin, Brazil speaks Portuguese. For the practice of what is called *cinema novo* in Brazil, it's necessary to explain that the Portuguese, less radical and more cynical than the Spanish, have left us a less nationalist inheritance. Perhaps this is why we don't have the complex of the

Revolução do Cinema Novo

Mexicans, or the frustration of the Argentines. For this reason, the independent Brazilian filmmakers have lost their religious respect for cinema. They preferred not to seek permission to enter the sacred universe and, even though they were clumsy, they picked up their cameras. Perhaps as a result of intellectuals and critics writing so much to convince the public to intimidate certain filmmakers into thinking that 'Portuguese was an anti-cinematographic language', *cinema novo* considered it absurd not to turn the word (and music) into cinematic material: the home of a verbal, vocal, energetic, sterile and hysterical people, Brazil is the only Latin country that had no bloody revolutions (unlike Mexico), baroque fascism (unlike Argentina and elsewhere) or political revolutions (unlike Cuba). By way of sad compensation, it has a developing cinema, with a production that this year will reach sixty films, and that next year should surpass this mark, or even double it. More than one hundred young filmmakers have premiered in 16mm and 8mm at the last two 'amateur cinema' competitions, and the public, disillusioned with the latest football defeats, discuss each national film with passion. Rio de Janeiro, São Paulo, Salvador and other important cities have art-house cinemas, two film archives, more than four hundred film clubs (even in the most distant parts of the Amazon you can find a film club). Today, Godard, in Rio and São Paulo, is just as popular as De Gaulle, and we can find cinephiles capable of competing with the experts of the French Cinémathèque. In Brazil, especially in Rio, over the last five years, there has been a real cinematographic carnival.

Tupi is the name of an Indian nation. Intelligence and technical incapacity. *Cangaço* is a kind of anarchic, mystical guerrilla movement, and it means violent disorder. *Bossa* is a *special style of style*, to move but to stay put, to threaten to attack on the right and wound on the left, with plenty of rhythm and eroticism. This tradition, whose values are discussed by the films of the *cinema novo*, absurdly draws a caricature of tragedy in a melodramatic civilization. There's no historical depth in Brazil. There's a process of anti-historical dilution, carried out by military coups and counter-coups, directly and indirectly linked to imperialist interests and carrying with it the national bourgeoisie. The populist Left always ends up signing pacts with the regretful Right to begin again, once more, 'redemocratization'. Until April 1964, with the fall of João Goulart, the majority of Brazilian intellectuals believed in 'revolution by the word'.

On Cinema

The Latin American political vanguard is always initiated by intellectuals and here, frequently, poems precede rifles. Popular opera – music and revolution go hand in hand and the inheritance comes from Spain. Today, in the Brazil of unexpected reconciliations, the urban Left is known as 'festive'. They discuss Marx to the sound of samba. But that doesn't stop the students from going out onto the streets in violent demonstrations, and teachers from being arrested, universities from being closed, intellectuals from making periodic manifestations of protest, and union offices from being invaded. Political film is made when it's produced, which must be followed by publicity, distribution, exhibition. Politics as the art of opposition to systems of oppression.

In relation to a public that is less literate than the public of the developed world, a cinema that accumulates the inconveniences of tricontinental cinema doesn't create an easy communication. Communication, in populist vocabulary, means to stimulate revolutionary sentiments.

This cinema provokes, at various levels, a clash that is another style of communication. A *cinema novo* film is polemical before, during and after its projection, and the concrete fact of its existence is a new element in the paradise of inertia. Thus, while *Barren Lives* documents the peasants, *The Guns* (*Os fuzis*, Ruy Guerra, 1963) is an anti-militarist aggression which amplifies the discourse of *Barren Lives*, a discourse that is transformed into agitation in *Black God, White Devil*, a radical political demonstration which will be discussed under people's breath in *The Dare*. Even if *The Turning Wind* and *Ganga Zumba* talk about black people and with black people, and even if *The Deceased* (*A falecida*, Leon Hirszman, 1965) is the urban version of *Barren Lives*, it doesn't mean that the possibilities of *The Scoundrels* (*Os cafajestes*, Ruy Guerra, 1962) or *The Big City* (*A grande cidade*, Carlos Diegues, 1970) are invalidated. If, from *Plantation Boy* (*Menino de engenho*, Walter Lima Jr, 1970) to *Entranced Earth* (*Terra em transe*, Glauber Rocha, 1967), or from the latter to the next film by Dahl, *The Brave Warrior* (*O bravo guerreiro*, Gustavo Dahl, 1969), *cinema novo* becomes unbalanced by the difficult task of individual exercise, it soon re-establishes a cinematographic concert which, in a permanent state of controversy, carries political action.

The technique of past and present cinema of the developed world interests me in that I can 'instrumentalize' it just like *American cinema* was 'instrumentalized' by a handful of European filmmakers. What is

Revolução do Cinema Novo

this 'instrumentalization'? It is to apply, as a method, certain key cinematographic techniques, general touchstones that, in the evolution of technique, transcend the individual spirit of each auteur and implant themselves in the aesthetic vocabulary of cinema: if I film a *cangaceiro*[9] in the desert, what is implicit is a specific *découpage/montage* founded in the Western tradition, a *foundation* that is more closely linked with the Western than with Ford or Howard Hawks. On the contrary, imitation is born of a passive attitude of the filmmaker in relation to cinema, of a suicidal need to stick to established language, in the belief that, by sticking to imitation, the film will be saved. In an interview with *Cahiers du Cinéma*, Truffaut said, *'Mais presque tous les films imités de Godard sont insuportables parce qu'il y manque l'essentiel. On imitera sa désinvolture mais on oubliera, et pour cause, son désespoir. On imitera les jeux de mots mais pas la cruauté.'*[10]

Most of the films by young actors suffer, nowadays, from this 'Godard syndrome'. Only suffering coming directly from the real and a permanent dialectical criticism can overcome the level of mythological imitation of the cinematographic technique, 'instrumentalizing' the rules of the game in progressive expressions. Brazilian films such as *Barren Lives*, *The Deceased* or *The Guns* are examples of how *colonized* filmmakers can make use of the techniques of developed cinema and promote an international expression. The problem is not as radical for Americans and Europeans, but if today we watch films from socialist countries, we note that few are *revolutionary* films. The attitude of the majority of filmmakers in relation to their reality degenerates into a type of calligraphic, academic cinema which, clearly, denounces a contemplative or demagogical spirit. And the festivals, especially in short film programmes, reveal a true 'cinema incorporated', a meaningless wave of imitations which, innocently fabricated on an editing table, fall apart during projections. Cinema has international stature and national contingencies do not justify, at any level, an abrogation of expression. If in the case of tricontinental cinema aesthetics precede the technique, it's because aesthetics have more to do with ideology than with technique. The technical myths of zoom, direct cinema, handheld camera, colour etc. are merely instruments. The Word is ideological and there are no more geographical frontiers. When I speak of tricontinental cinema and when I consider Godard a tricontinental filmmaker it's because, by opening a guerrilla front in the heart of French cinema and attacking repeatedly and unexpectedly with films that are impiously aggressive, he becomes a political filmmaker, a strategy and tactic that are exemplary in any part of the world. This example, however, is useful in terms of behaviour.

I insist upon a *guerrilla cinema* as the only form of combating an aesthetic and economic dictatorship of western imperialist cinema or of demagogical socialist cinema. We must improvise from our own circumstances, and avoid the moralizing that is typical of a bourgeoisie which imposed on both the public at large and the elites its right to Art.

My ultimate intention with a didactic cinema could not anticipate but rather be confused with the didactic epic brought to bear by Che. A Western, on the other hand, with the words of a new poetics, which a complete revolution provokes, will destroy the idealistic frontiers of cinema. If, pre-continental, Buñuel *re-moves* in precise pans, in tricontinental cinema it's necessary to demobilize and explode. From the moment Che's *mis-en-mort* becomes a legend it's impossible to deny, Tricontinental, that poetry is a revolutionary praxis.

Positif (1967)

(Interview with Glauber Rocha by Michel Ciment)

[Ciment] *The Turning Wind* is not well known in France, but those who have seen it say that it's a film about fishermen in Bahia, in which you already described a certain mysticism in relation to dance, music, the sea ...

[Glauber] *The Turning Wind* is not a film of mine. I made it almost by chance. It was started by another director, Luiz Paulino dos Santos; after an accident during filming, I had to carry it on. I filmed it pretty quickly on a budget of 3,000 dollars and on 6,000 metres of film. Then, when I saw the material, I didn't like it and I put it to one side. Eight months later, Nelson Pereira dos Santos saw the rough cut and found it all interesting. So we began once again to construct the film.

[Ciment] Had you not previously made short films?

[Glauber] Yes, at the time when I wrote film reviews and was involved with film clubs. I also did theatre, but I only ever staged poems. I saw myself as avant-garde and made my short films in that spirit: they were *Patio* (*Pátio*, 1959) and *Cruz na Praça* (*The Cross in the Square*, 1958), which I never finished [the latter], because when I saw the edited material

I understood that those ideas no longer worked, and that my aesthetic conception had changed.

[Ciment] I heard you have another short.

[Glauber] It is not mine; it's a short feature that I produced called *Rampa* (*Ramp*), directed by Paulino dos Santos, the original creator of *The Turning Wind*. But in between *Black God, White Devil* and *Entranced Earth* I made two documentaries, one in colour about the Amazon (December 1965) and another with direct sound on the political elections in Maranhão,[11] which is also a region in the Amazon (February 1966). The film on the Amazon was my first essay in colour. I arrived in the Amazon with a preconceived idea and I discovered that the legendary and mythical Amazonia, the Amazonia of crocodiles, tigers, Indians etc., did not exist. The other film is a reportage on the election of governor José Sarney in the north-eastern state of Maranhão. It was important for me because it was filmed using direct sound and it was a lived experience for *Entranced Earth*, as I took part in the stages of an electoral campaign. You can see excerpts of this material in *Entranced Earth*: a black car that drives into the middle of the crowd at the moment when Vieira is elected, a demonstration full of young people ...

[Ciment] What do you mean by staging poems?

[Glauber] I had organized a theatre group with Brazilian friends, the poet Fernando da Rocha Peres and the stage director Calazans Netto, as well as Paulo Gil Soares, who had for a long time worked with me in journalism, theatre and cinema (he assisted on *Black God, White Devil* and *Entranced Earth*). At first we wanted to stage Greek tragedies, but we found it difficult and also rather inappropriate for the circumstances. So we staged poems. It was a time when Brazil was experiencing a poetic craze. We staged performances that dramatized poems and transformed them into dialogue. But the performances were suspended by the censors.

[Ciment] When was this?

[Glauber] It was in 1957, before I made *Patio*, but it was in the same spirit as this film, or rather, an avant-garde spirit; it was very anti-clerical and we were censored for religious and moral, rather than political, reasons.

[Ciment] So *Patio* was similar?

[Glauber] Yes, and *The Cross in the Square* too. After meeting Nelson Pereira dos Santos I faced up to the possibility of making a film in Brazil.

In between filming *Patio* and *The Cross in the Square*, I assisted Nelson Pereira in Rio de Janeiro. I arrived in Rio from Bahia when he was filming *Rio, Northern Zone* (*Rio, zona norte*, 1957). When I was working on the editing of *The Turning Wind* he influenced me and trained me in the technical side of things. If anyone has been an influence on my life in intellectual and cinematic terms, it's Nelson. Even if I don't have any affinity with his style, he played a decisive role in my life.

[Ciment] In fact, Nelson was important throughout the *cinema novo* movement.

[Glauber] Absolutely, but it's worth saying that this importance should not be seen as deliberate on the part of Nelson. It is, rather, a subterranean influence; he's the conscience of our group. It was Nelson who made the first independent film, in terms of production: *Rio 40 Degrees* (*Rio, 40 graus*, 1955), and in it we have the first political positioning in the face of Brazil's colonial situation. He became a leader, a kind of inspiration and, to this day, a mediator of those who are in disagreement. Every time there is a crisis in *cinema novo*, his role is both human and very efficient.

[Ciment] After your experience with *The Turning Wind*, on what basis did you begin *Black God, White Devil*?

[Glauber] I filmed *The Turning Wind* in a state of crisis – I was abandoning the ideas of my adolescence ... Unlike the French intellectuals, we have a very confused cultural formation. First we read the Dadaists, then Greek tragedy. We get to know the work of Faulkner and then we discover Rimbaud and Mallarmé. Our universities really don't work, and books arrive in great disorder. The cultural background of a young Brazilian is incoherent, assuming he doesn't get the chance to study in Europe. Back then I was a surrealist, a futurist, a Dadaist and a Marxist all at the same time. In Brazil, for example, all of Eisenstein's theories arrived in Spanish translation and then in Portuguese, and, since film clubs and film archives are well organized, the work of Eisenstein was well known there. We are Eisensteinians and we would not accept that a film could be made except using rapid montage, close-ups etc. ... *Rio 40 Degrees* was influenced by neorealism. We really liked Nelson's film because it was in fact the first Brazilian film, but our support came with a caveat, because it was not an Eisensteinian film. In the early days of *cinema novo*, I remember that my friendship with Leon Hirszman was due to the fact that he liked Eisenstein. He was an engineer, he had Eisenstein's theories on the tip of

Revolução do Cinema Novo

his tongue, he would experiment. His first film, *São Diogo Quarry* (*Pedreira de São Diogo*, 1962), a short film, applied the ideas of Eisenstein. And I recall that, when Paulo Cesar Saraceni joined the group, because he liked Italian cinema, Rossellini, Visconti, Fellini, we would say, 'That guy does not understand Eisenstein.'

Patio is a film made up of metamorphoses, symbols, dialectical montage. *The Turning Wind* was made in a different spirit, a more direct, more truthful one: I even recorded Black music live. It's a film that is closer to reality because back then we had already seen *Rome, Open City* and *Paisan* (*Paisà*, Roberto Rossellini, 1946), and the discovery of Rossellini through these two films was a kind of reaction against Eisenstein. In *The Turning Wind* such an influence can be felt, but there are residual influences of Eisenstein, and opening shots in the style of *Que Viva Mexico!*

[Ciment] So when you began filming *Black God, White Devil*, you had already made a film ...

[Glauber] No one has asked me about it before and it's the first time I have spoken about *The Turning Wind* in these terms. In *Black God, White Devil* I developed some things that are present in *The Turning Wind*. It's impossible to deny that the shadow of Eisenstein is present in the film, especially in the first part. I like Eisenstein very much, but I live in a reality that is not an epic in the style of *Alexander Nevsky* (*Aleksandr Nevskiy*, Sergei M. Eisenstein, 1938). Nor is it a historical drama in the style of *Ivan the Terrible* (*Ivan Grozniy*, Sergei M. Eisenstein, 1944).

[Ciment] But the opposition of styles corresponds to the choice of the holy man and the *cangaceiros*.

[Glauber] In the part on the *cangaceiros* I could have veered towards a Western style, as in the case of the famous film *The Bandit* (*O cangaceiro*, Lima Barreto, 1953). I think I achieved a personal style, which I would not know how to define. I felt better filming the second part. I felt freer to stage shots, tracking shots, to make cuts in the editing, and to direct the actors. The part of the holy man, which was filmed first, was arduous to me.

[Ciment] You said that *Black God, White Devil* was in the style of *cordel* literature.[12] In what way?

[Glauber] As in the poems of the Middle Ages or the Westerns, there is a strong tradition of popular verse and song that we inherited from the Portuguese and the Spanish. The *cantadores*, who sing their stories made up on the spot, nowadays in the north-east of Brazil are often blind men.

Because they are blind, they have a more powerful imagination and they invent legends. The whole episode involving Corisco in *Black God, White Devil* was taken from four or five popular stories, and the sequence of his death follows the decoupage of a song. When I spoke to several blind people and to the man who killed Corisco in real life, they basically told me the same story, but each one mixed in with the truth some made-up detail. Major Rufino, the man we see in *Memories of the Cangaço* (*Memória do cangaço*, 1965) by Paulo Gil Soares and who inspired me to create the character Antônio das Mortes, gave me three different versions of how he killed Corisco. And in Paulo Gil's film, he gives a fourth version. What we know for sure is that he wounded Corisco's wife in the foot and I show this in my film. The following Portuguese expression is very popular in the north-east; the blind, in popular theatre, in the circus, and at fairs, say: 'I'm going to tell you a story, both true and imagined; or rather, it is truthful imagination.' The idea for the film came to me spontaneously, with a certain amount of evidence. I learnt everything I know in such a climate. There's nothing intellectual in my position.

[Ciment] So the film appeared to you like a vision?

[Glauber] Yes, that's exactly it.

[Ciment] In *Barren Lives* and in your film there is the same geographical context and the same story about a peasant couple, but you didn't go down the realist route.

[Glauber] I don't intend to say whether I make cinema of poetry or prose, because they are categories that belong to literature, and not to cinema. Nelson took as his starting point a realist novel by Graciliano Ramos, a novel that is a document. My starting point was a poetic text. The origin of *Black God, White Devil* is metaphorical language, *cordel* literature. I preferred this genre. I like *Barren Lives* too, even though I don't have much affinity with it. Nelson likes objectivity and efficacy and that is why he chose Graciliano and was faithful to him. He was criticized for not having come up with his own subject, but he said that he chose Graciliano because he liked him and the difficulty was precisely in remaining faithful to his work.

[Ciment] Are the speeches by Sebastião and Corisco entirely your own creation?

[Glauber] Yes, but the style of speech is a popular one. We have three types of literary tradition: a European tradition – Stendhal, Flaubert etc.... Graciliano Ramos wrote in Portuguese like the French realists; then we have a baroque tradition which came from Spanish writers such as Cervantes and Quevedo and from the Portuguese; and finally we have popular literature which comes from the people. Someone born in São Paulo and who has been to university will have a more Anglo-French educational background; there are people in Brazil who have never read *Don Quixote* but who know Joyce inside out. All these traditions are present in Brazil. They are there in the north-east, as well as in São Paulo, which is another, Americanized type of Brazil.

[Ciment] The female characters in *Black God, White Devil* have a more important role than is generally accepted.

[Glauber] I have been told that on a number of occasions and I've never reached a truly objective conclusion on the subject. In *The Turning Wind*, *Black God, White Devil* and *Entranced Earth* the women are aware of what is going on, they are aware of 'History'. In *The Turning Wind* a female character gives her own life as an example, she sacrifices herself for the people, she leads a man to assume a political position and she dies. I find it difficult to work with female characters. I have written a number of scripts for films that have not been made, in which I had trouble creating female characters who are for me very conscious and who have moral and political influence.

[Ciment] But not Sílvia in *Entranced Earth*?

[Glauber] No, definitely not Sílvia, but she is a secondary figure; she is a kind of muse, an expression of adolescence, who becomes a fleeting image. Sílvia, in fact, says nothing in *Entranced Earth* because I was unable to place a single word in her mouth. Her words were cut from the film because everything she said sounded ridiculous. Sara, perhaps, says things a bit like a man. Perhaps there is the 'phenomenon of compensation' going on here because in the context of Brazil I don't often meet women with such a level of awareness.

[Ciment] How did you find and choose your cast? I'm told this can be problematic in Latin America. Buñuel, for example, had difficulties in Mexico.

[Glauber] It's different in Brazil. We have a great theatrical tradition. We perform Brecht. Many actors have been to the States and have trained at the Actors Studio. Othon Bastos (Corisco in *Black God, White Devil*) is the Brazilian actor who best performs Brecht in the theatre. I think he brought a particular dimension to his character and when I discussed his part with him he made many useful suggestions. He's a cultured man and he has an exceptional voice. He was responsible for the dubbing of Sebastião, played by an amateur, a member of the Black aristocracy of Bahia, who also has a part in *The Turning Wind*. Maurício do Valle, who plays Antônio das Mortes, is a television actor. He had starred in *Zorro*. I chose him because he was a familiar face and Antônio das Mortes is a popular hero. Geraldo D'El Rey, who plays Manuel, is a well-known actor in Brazil, a star. Othon Bastos, D'El Rey and Sônia dos Humildes (Dadá) are actors in a theatre group in Bahia, where they studied at a very good school. In *Entranced Earth* there are great theatre actors, but I chose them because of the subject matter. José Lewgoy, who plays Vieira, is the most popular film actor in Brazil: he always plays the leader of the criminals in gangster films, and he also appears in comedies. He is spontaneous and intelligent. Paulo Autran is practically our *official* theatre actor. He performs Greek tragedies, so in the film his role is theatrical, that of a mystifier. Jardel Filho, who plays the hero in the film, is also a well-known actor in Brazil. He has starred in more than forty films and he has worked in Spain and Argentina.

[Ciment] When you did theatre, did you already use music?

[Glauber] No. Just words and lighting.

[Ciment] Where did you get the idea from to place so much importance on musical commentary, such as that song that illustrates the closing message of *Black God, White Devil*?

[Glauber] Firstly, it's worth pointing out that music plays an important role not only in my films, but in other Brazilian films too. In fact, we are perhaps an underdeveloped people from a cultural point of view, but we are well developed in relation to music. For example, Ruy Guerra is a film director and a musician too, and he's a good musician. And everyone in Brazil plays an instrument; I don't but I have written some songs. We are all musicians. Hirszman has just made a musical. Music had such power in his films that he asked himself: Why don't I make a musical? And he made *Girl from Ipanema* (*Garota de Ipanema*, 1967), in which the characters are composers and singers in real life. In *cinema novo* there is a tendency to make films where music doesn't only provide a commentary, but it's just as important an element as the dialogue and photography. I was inspired by Villa-Lobos when I made *Black God, White Devil*. There's a scene in the

Revolução do Cinema Novo

film which I thought of filming because I had heard the music – the kissing scene between Corisco and Rosa. I was worried about filming this indispensable scene. I listened to the record at night, the 'Bachiana Brasileira n. 9'. I discussed it with the cinematographer and the assistants and we devised the scene. Then I did the editing based on the music, the rhythm.

[Ciment] Othon Bastos, the importance of the music, all this leads us to Brecht...

[Glauber] I should say that my favourite play, of those I have seen in Brazil, is *The Threepenny Opera*, a play that affected me greatly, me and everyone else in Brazil. I went to Berlin just to see the Berliner Ensemble. It's worth saying that Brecht is performed widely in Brazil.

[Ciment] Which Brecht is more important in Brazil? Because in early Brecht the use of music is very different from the later Brecht.

[Glauber] Before filming *Black God, White Devil* I had only seen *The Threepenny Opera*. The first of Brecht's plays to be performed in Brazil was *The Good Person of Szechwan*, but I did not see it. I saw *The Threepenny Opera* in the middle of filming *The Turning Wind*. One day I went to Salvador to watch the performance. And it really shook me; it was a belated but extremely important discovery.

[Ciment] What about directing the actors?

[Glauber] It was easier in *Black God, White Devil*. There was an extraordinary atmosphere, a wonderful crew. The cameraman Waldemar Lima liked the film and he was a good friend of mine. Then there was Walter Lima Jr and Paulo Gil who worked closely with me as assistant director and art director, respectively. The actors liked the subject, and since we didn't have any money it was a kind of romantic adventure. We shared a common spirit and a pure élan. There were the inevitable technical problems, but I remember that we would work hard together through the night, we would rehearse the actors etc.... In *Entranced Earth* it was a different story – professional actors, with fees and contracts, who had to work in the theatre in the evenings, who would film until four in the afternoon, and some even refused to speak to the assistants. Relations with the main actors were professional. It was frustrating because I thought that I would get more from the film if the actors understood their roles better. They wanted to work on the film because they thought that it was an important film – that's all. The one who played Diaz said that he did not agree with his character because he himself was left-wing and he did not want to interpret a man of the Right. The one who played Vieira tried hard to be sophisticated, and that's why he couldn't interpret a populist hero. The main protagonist was comfortable and enjoyed his role.

[Ciment] In *Black God, White Devil* the character Antônio das Mortes is at the service of the forces of repression, and at the same time he's an agent of history, a critical conscience in relation to the other characters. You didn't turn to this type of character in *Entranced Earth*. You jettisoned the character-as-witness construction.

[Glauber] Antônio das Mortes in *Black God, White Devil* is the only character that I really invented. The others are real characters from a specific historical context and they're recognizable. With Antônio I presented a description of a conscience that is ambiguous, that is in anguish. Antônio, the primitive, peasant adventurer can be seen in a more developed form in Paulo Martins, with all his contradictions in *Entranced Earth*. Paulo Martins, like Antônio, is a guy who swings from Right to Left, who has ambivalent concerns about political and social problems. We find in him a revolution that's falling back on contradictions, and this brings about his death. It is, in fact, a parable about communist parties in Latin America. For me, Paulo Martins represents, deep down, the typical communist from Latin America. He belongs to the Party without really belonging. He has a lover who belongs to the Party. He places himself at the service of the Party when pressurised to do so. But he also really likes the bourgeoisie that he represents. Deep down, he despises the people. He believes in the masses as a spontaneous phenomenon, but it so happens that the masses are complex. Revolution does not break out when he wants it to and so the position he assumes is Quixotic. At the end of the tragedy, he dies. Antônio is more primitive, he takes money from those in power, he must kill the poor, the holy man and the *cangaceiro* Corisco, and he knows that these people are not evil because they're merely victims of a particular social context that they have no knowledge of. Antônio is a barbarian, while Paulo is an intellectual. In *Entranced Earth* I wanted to return to certain elements of the structure of *Black God, White Devil*. We find in the cities the same hierarchy as in the countryside; it's the legacy of the *latifundium* plantation system, of a mentality left over from the Middle Ages, and inevitably mixed with influences from modern civilization.

Revolução do Cinema Novo

In *Entranced Earth* my greatest ambition was to denounce these structures and in parallel show a dramatic structure that was on the point of being destroyed. That's how *Entranced Earth* is linked to *Black God, White Devil*. It's all about the destruction of a discourse that had already begun in *Black God, White Devil*.

[Ciment] Did you also try to carry out this destruction from an aesthetic point of view?

[Glauber] *Black God, White Devil* is a narrative film, a discourse. *Entranced Earth* is more anti-dramatic; it's a film that destroys itself, with an editing full of repetitions. At the moment I would like to change, because I think that there is a political way out which really is current and valid, and which responds to all the theoretical insufficiencies of the traditional Communist Parties in Latin America. Characters like Paulo Martins or Antônio das Mortes no longer interest me. I think, for example, that Che Guevara is the genuine modern character. He is the real epic hero, neither an intellectual like Paulo, nor a primitive like Antônio.

[Ciment] But the implicit meaning of *Entranced Earth* is that the alliance between the intellectual and the bourgeoisie is doomed to fail.

[Glauber] I think the answer to doubts such as those of the character Paulo – which by the way characterize a whole generation, including myself – is the figure of Guevara. I am not just saying this because everyone has been talking about his death. I have thought long and hard about this and I feel inclined to make a film about a character like him, a bourgeois who disconnects himself from his culture and makes revolution. He articulates an answer through his own existence, and now with his legend he brings an answer to a series of problems in Latin America.

[Ciment] Antônio das Mortes is beyond Paulo Martins. He's a sort of rationalization of History.

[Glauber] Given the fact that Antônio das Mortes is a primitive, a man who did not experience the commitments and the bourgeois education of Paulo, he can become more quickly a revolutionary character; but Paulo can also become a revolutionary. I haven't abandoned Antônio's character; I want to return to it at a later stage. In Brazil, he became the most popular character in the film and *Black God, White Devil* owes him its semi-success; he communicated with the public. I want to make a sort of anti-Western, with fights between the landowners and the peasants etc., and I want to introduce Antônio in this situation.

[Ciment] In the end of *Black God, White Devil* it is said that 'the sea will turn into backlands',[13] and the beginning of *Entranced Earth* also has the sea, the ocean: was this a conscious choice?

[Glauber] Yes, it's very clear, not even a symbolic reference – I think that *Entranced Earth* is the natural development of *Black God*, the people have reached the sea. From the sea we reach the city and, finally, we end up in a desert where there is no hopeful music like there was in *Black God*, but the sound of machine guns which can be heard over the film's music. Music and machine guns, and soon after the sounds of war, that is, a song of hope. It's not a song in the *socialist realism* style, it's not the feeling of revolution, it's something harder and graver. I was happy to have included this in the film because a month later I read Che's essay in the *Tricontinental* which said: 'The place I should meet my death is of little importance. May it be welcome if our plea is heard ... and that other men rise up to the rattling of machine guns, to intone funeral songs and to launch new cries of war and "victory"'.[14]

[Ciment] What is the song from the beginning of *Entranced Earth*?

[Glauber] It's an African song, sung in Brazil in an African language and its sole purpose is to evoke a certain place, a certain atmosphere of tropical seas, or baroque palaces. This song is sung in various places, but especially in Bahia; *The Turning Wind* also begins with an African song. The sea is a myth for the poor peasant, and it was via the sea that the Portuguese reached Brazil.

[Ciment] You said that there is an António das Mortes side to Paulo Martins, but there is also a Manuel side to him, because Paulo also goes from one to the other, just as Manuel went from the Black God to the White Devil. One thinks also of Corisco. The character Corisco is obsessed with death and with a kind of metaphysical dream which is unusual in an outlaw, and Paulo, the poet, also thinks about death.

[Glauber] That's right, because he is as a poet a little of what Corisco is as an outlaw. He's also an adventurer who courts danger. In fact, Paulo Martins can only save himself through death; because if he chooses revolution or, rather, if he becomes a revolutionary, he's also choosing death and this choice offers him the possibility of victory. He should, therefore, prepare himself for death. It's a decision in preparation for which all ties should be severed. I'm not ready for that. It's a tragic eventuality that all men of the Third World must face. It can be treated as a

Revolução do Cinema Novo

neo-romantic position, if you like, but it's also a very didactic one. What matters to Guevara is that guerrilla warfare is not a romantic adventure, but a didactic epic. Rather like the characters in a Western, but with one caveat: the mission is very precise; it's about politicizing. In fact, I see in this the beginnings of a new culture, a new form of behaviour, a new style of man and action; in detail – the speech, clothing and behaviour of the guerrilla warriors is something new.

[Ciment] The monologue in *Entranced Earth* is very beautiful and it's interesting to know that you wanted to call your film *Maldoror*.

[Glauber] I have read a great deal of *The Songs of Maldoror*, unfortunately in Portuguese, because I could not get hold of the French edition in Brazil. What left a lasting impression on me in the book was the sense of permanent torture. It has the realism of vomit. The structure of the film and its derisory aspect were widely criticized. What I wanted was this appearance of vomit and I think that Paulo is a man who vomits even his own poems. The final sequences of the film are of continuous vomit. The discourse is evidently inferior to that of Lautréamont, but there is within it the same level of anguish.

[Ciment] Did you write this monologue first?

[Glauber] Yes, then some other poems and lastly the script. I shot the film and when I was editing it I inserted the monologue.

[Ciment] The death of Paulo has an aesthetic quality. In itself, it is of no significance, because it changes nothing.

[Glauber] Yes, because he gains awareness; at this precise moment, he dies because of an accident, but he declares that 'one shouldn't'. He says that it is necessary to accept violence, to confront destiny head-on. At another moment in the film he tells Sara that when one has a clear and complete awareness of everything, only violence will remain. He says this after the political rally; he reminds her that within the masses man can be found, and that man is difficult to manipulate, more difficult than the masses. He, of course, cannot accept violence, because he's impotent, he lacks the organization for this. At the moment of his death, he understands that violence is the path to revolution.

[Ciment] Almost at the beginning of the film there's a quote by Mário Faustino that is not subtitled.

[Glauber] Mário Faustino was the greatest Brazilian poet of my generation. He died in a plane crash aged 33. He wrote a book that became very popular with the younger generation called *O homem e sua hora* [*The Man and His Hour*]. And in the poem 'Balada (*Em memória de um poeta suicida*)' ['Ballad (In Memory of a Suicidal Poet)'] he wrote:

> He was unable to sign the noble pact
> Between the bloody cosmos and the pure soul
> [...]
> Gladiator, defunct but intact
> (So much violence, but with so much tenderness)[15]

That's what I put in my film, as a homage; he was a little like Paulo Martins.

[Ciment] In a very realistic scene, you use what ends up being the whole structure of *Black God, White Devil*: a character speaks on behalf of the people. Is this kind of symbolic play common in Brazil?

[Glauber] In order to film this scene I placed Vieira, the actor, in the middle of the people, and they thought that it really was a political rally, and that Vieira really was a candidate. And even in the indoor scenes, when Vieira greets people from the city, it was like a political rally. He arrived and started to make his speech, and at that moment the police wanted to interrupt filming because of the commotion – people wanted to vote for that man (it was during the elections for state deputies). I took the opportunity to film it all live, very quickly, one Sunday afternoon. It's the scene at the beginning of Vieira's electoral campaign, and everything in that scene was created spontaneously.

[Ciment] Is Eldorado the name of a city?

[Glauber] No, Eldorado is the Latin American myth of gold. When the Spanish reached America, they spoke of Eldorado. In the film, Eldorado is at the same time the name of a capital and of a state, while Alecrim is the name of a town, a region in the state of Eldorado. This could create some comprehension problems in Europe where, unlike in Latin America, there are no capital cities with the same name as the country. Alecrim, given that it is the name of a well-known province in Portugal, also brought problems for the Brazilian spectators.

[Ciment] This kind of confusion, such as Alecrim, for example, is serious because it hinders our understanding of something important which is the structure of the film, the fact that it is clear-cut. Don't you think that in the end you show the situation in a manner that is too direct, because you are so involved in it, and that this hinders our understanding?

Revolução do Cinema Novo

[Glauber] The final shot is long (one minute) and it's rather disturbing, but I think that after forty seconds, people begin to understand that the machine gun means something; I insisted on the duration of the shot. As for the dislike of the hero for carnival, perhaps it is very vague, in terms of the word itself, but Brazilian political life really is like carnival. Brazilian civilization is declining. We truly are rotten, sterile and lazy, we are highly unskilled artisans, and we have an irrational energy that always ends in nothing. I tried to make the film an expression of this carnival and of my violent disgust in the face of this situation.

[Ciment] Paradoxically, the part dedicated to the imaginary is perhaps greater in *Entranced Earth* than in *Black God, White Devil*.

[Glauber] When I made *Black God, White Devil* I really liked the landscape and the figure of Corisco too, and even if I adopted a critical standpoint, I felt linked to these characters. In contrast, as I detested all the things that were represented in *Entranced Earth*, I made it with a certain repulsion. I recall that I would say to the editor: I am disgusted because I don't think that there is a single *beautiful* shot in this film. All the shots are ugly, because it's about harmful people, in a rotten landscape, and it's falsely baroque. The script prevented me from reaching a point of visual fascination that is found in *Black God, White Devil*. At times, perhaps, I have tried to escape that environment, but there was a danger in attributing *value to alienated elements*.

The film made frequent use of handheld cameras, for increased flexibility. One can feel the skin of the characters; I was attempting a documentary tone. Everything that may seem imaginary is in fact real. For example, I consulted newspaper archives for photographs of politicians. When president Juscelino Kubitschek arrived, in 1956, in the site in which Brasília was going to be built, for example, the Indians took him a feather headdress etc. When I filmed the rally where the old senator begins to dance with the people, I invited a real-life samba school and I set Vieira among them. I had done the same thing in *Black God, White Devil*. In that film the peasants also thought that the man who played Sebastião was a real holy man. I hadn't planned the senator's dance scene, but at a certain moment the actor got carried away by the music and by the political speech: he started to dance and we filmed the sequence with a handheld camera. Pablo Neruda has spoken of concrete surrealism, since this surreal aspect is a fact in the reality of Latin America and the Third World.

We find this concrete surrealism in Miguel Ángel Asturias, Alejo Carpentier and Nicolás Guillén.

[Ciment] What about the song 'The square belongs to the people as the sky belongs to the condor'?[16]

[Glauber] It's a verse written by a nineteenth-century Brazilian Romantic poet, Castro Alves, who died aged 23 from tuberculosis. He is very popular. He fought in favour of the abolition of slavery. He was against the monarchy and was pro-Republic. He would hold rallies in which he would improvise poetry and he wrote a poem entitled 'O povo ao poder' ['The People in Power'], which contains the lines found in *Entranced Earth*.

[Ciment] What about Martín Fierro?

[Glauber] Torre Nilsson is making a film version of the Martín Fierro epic. It's a revolutionary epic poem of the gaucho people of Argentina; and since I was making a film in the spirit of Latin America, I thought it was a good idea to include a quotation from Martín Fierro. Vieira, the populist leader, reads this work and it's a progressive poem.

[Ciment] You like conflict: between passion and explosions of violence in *Black God, White Devil*, and between the image and a commentary that is not directly related to it in *Entranced Earth*. You place great importance on the editing.

[Glauber] A few days ago a Brazilian friend asked me when I was going to *tell a story in a film*. I always end up with a conflict and I try to open up a critical discussion on the story. *Political cinema* is a discussion about those facts. And I think that the editing is linked to this accumulation of various conflicts which are at the same time subjective and objective. What I really like about Faulkner is that with him there is always a *simultaneous and progressive accumulation of conflicts*. On the other hand, the social milieu, the blacks people, the people from the south, this could also be the northeast of Brazil, or some country in Latin America. There is in fact a Faulkner novel that I want to film – *The Wild Palms*.

[Ciment] They say, in our opinion with no good reason, that you are a disciple of Buñuel, when, in contrast, at least formally, we think of Welles in *Entranced Earth*.

[Glauber] Yes, in the same sense that you could make a Western or a *cangaceiro* film by borrowing from Hawks or Ford, but inverting content and form: this is aesthetic anthropophagy.

Revolução do Cinema Novo

[Ciment] In your film there is a very strong sense of violence, but you don't depict it. We see the revolver in the mouth of the peasant and that's all, or in the case of the suicide of Álvaro, which is merely suggested.

[Glauber] When violence is shown in a descriptive form, it pleases the public, because it stimulates their sado-masochistic instincts, but I wanted to show the idea of violence, and on occasions even a certain frustration brought on by violence. We ought to reflect on violence and not make a spectacle out of it.

[Ciment] There is in fact an interesting detail about *Entranced Earth*: everyone always exhibits their guns and weapons, stretching their arms.

[Glauber] Yes, like Brazilian politics, a politics in which no one ever fires a shot; it's an ironic comment on the situation.

[Ciment] Why is there a constant police blockade?

[Glauber] It's a government-controlled area, and there is a coup, so the presence of soldiers is normal. And anyway, since the film develops in flashback, we see at the end that when Paulo flees he passes a number of army trucks.

[Ciment] There is something which lends to Paulo's flight an imaginary quality, and in particular the fact that he is wounded by the police: when the policeman shoots him the action is fragmented into several shots, and this makes his movements look mechanical and unreal.

[Glauber] In a Western or in a police thriller you can include the whole movement; you make a film for the pleasure of filming that kind of thing; but in *Black God, White Devil* when Antônio das Mortes is presented for the first time in action, or rather, killing someone, I also fragmented that scene, because what is interesting is not the action in itself, but its symbolic value.

[Ciment] Paulo says to Sara: 'I'm hungry for the absolute' and she replies 'Hunger', physical hunger. Sara is a character who has a more direct and realistic experience of the political situation, but at the same time she stays with Vieira, the mystifier.

[Glauber] She is lucid, but she is forever the Communist; she is always faithful to the Party. When Sara goes with her two friends to see Paulo to get him to confirm his support for Vieira once and for all, he's conscious of the fact that a union with Vieira will not lead to anything positive, but at that moment his political conscience suffers existential interference: *since he loves Sara, he joins Vieira because of her*. In the end Paulo is defeated and she leaves him; she is a lucid and political character; she continues the struggle. This is the only 'coherent' feature in *Entranced Earth*.

[Ciment] The character of the Black man who appears in the political rallies is interesting: he's like the blind man in *Black God, White Devil*.

[Glauber] He's someone who will preserve the memory of events, and he's also a reference to *direct* cinema.

[Ciment] You used Villa-Lobos, Bach, Verdi and Brazilian composer Carlos Gomes in your latest film.

[Glauber] Villa-Lobos had a profound influence on me as I had mentioned before. Carlos Gomes is a composer of Brazilian opera of the nineteenth century; he was inspired by Verdi and he's still widely appreciated. In the Federal Official Radio programme called 'A voz do Brasil' ['The Voice of Brazil'], when the President is about to speak, Carlos Gomes is played.

I used his music for the sequences with Díaz, when he's walking around his garden and when the film is being deliberately parodic. I used Verdi's *Othello* because of the discussion of envy and friendship and because I wanted to suggest a homosexual and solitary side to Díaz.

[Ciment] In the text that *Positif* (no. 73) published with your essay 'An Aesthetics of Hunger', you said that the *cinema novo* now needed to carry out a revision of itself. At the end of 1967, what point is it at?

[Glauber] After the first *cinema novo* films, we set up a distribution company in Brazil which also aims to place the films in the international market. We have a certain economic freedom which allows us to produce our own films with complete independence. At the same time, I think that there has been a certain development of ideas and also of technique and expression. Nelson Pereira dos Santos's next film, for example, is much more ambitious than *Barren Lives*, just as Carlos Diegues's *The Heirs* [*Os herdeiros*, released in 1969] will be more political and more ambitious than his previous films. There is also Walter Lima Jr, who is making *Brazil Year 2000* [*Brasil ano 2000*, released in 1969] and Joaquim Pedro de Andrade with *Macunaíma* [released in 1969], Hirszman with *Girl from Ipanema*, Gustavo Dahl with *The Brave Warrior*, Paulo Gil Soares with *Satan's Feats in the Town of Back and Forth* [*Proezas de Satanás na vila do Leva-e-Traz*, released in 1967], Júlio Bressane with *Face to Face* [*Cara a cara*, released in 1967] and Paulo Cesar Saraceni with *Capitu* [released in 1968]. Many films are being made. 1968–1969 will be decisive years for *cinema novo*. If four or five films reach the standard of *Entranced Earth*, we will have a real revolution within the movement and *cinema novo* will find a way of surviving. Failing that, *cinema novo* will experience a crisis, which will only happen if there is a political crisis, with total censorship etc. We have reached the conclusion that without a certain economic freedom there will be no artistic or political freedom and that's why *cinema novo* doesn't have any clearly defined aesthetics.

[Ciment] It appears that *cinema novo* is at the moment moving from the country to the city. The first three important *cinema novo* films (*Barren Lives, Black God, White Devil* and *The Guns*) were about the north-east, and now the films are delving into the problems of the city, at a time when Guevara is teaching us that it is necessary to leave the city and begin in the countryside.

[Glauber] Theorists used to say that you should not make films about the countryside, because politics happen in the city. In Brazil it happens in the city, in the desert, everywhere. In Walter Lima Jr's film [*Brazil Year 2000*] politics do not happen in the city or the countryside, but in the year 2000; it's a kind of political *science fiction* film. Nelson Pereira is going to film politics among the Indians. It's a story about cannibalism with a very funny title in French: *Comme il était bon mon petit français* [*How Tasty was my Little Frenchman*, released in 1971]. He made use of the narration of a young French soldier who, during the French invasion of Brazil, was captured by Indians; he teaches them French and warfare. He is given a woman as a present, and then the anthropophagous Indians want to eat him because they respect him. Nelson wants to make a commentary on relations between colonizers and the colonized, and on cultural exchange. It's very interesting because even if anthropophagy no longer exists in Brazil as such, there is *a philosophical spirit which is anthropophagic.*

Cinema Novo and the Adventure of Creation (1968)

To Zuenir Ventura[17]

There exists no individual in today's technology-dominated world who has not been influenced by cinema. Even if they have never been to the cinema in their entire lives, each individual feels the influence of cinema. Not even the most nationalist of cultures is able to resist a certain form of behaviour, a certain notion of beauty, a certain moral code and, above all, the fantastical stimulus of cinema on the imagination. Our cinematic reflexes are formed both in the short and long term and the establishment of a cinematographic culture is an ingrained feature of contemporary life. It's impossible, however, to talk of cinema without talking of *American cinema*. The notion of *cinema* and *American cinema* are practically the same thing: the aforementioned influence of cinema is, then, the influence of *American cinema*, as the most aggressive and widespread form of American culture inflicted upon the world. This influence, moreover, has touched upon the American public itself in such a way that the public, thus conditioned, now in turn demands a cinema made in its own image. A monster which creates illusions and devours people's alienations, *American cinema* cannot help but spawn similar cinemas which will then feel the need to kill their paternal figure to ensure their own survival. Any conversation about cinema which takes place outside of Hollywood inevitably begins with Hollywood.

Much closer economically and culturally to the United States than to Europe, Brazilian cinema-goers have developed a vision of life by way of *American cinema*. When a Brazilian citizen thinks about making their own film, they think of an 'American-style' film. And it is for this reason that the Brazilian cinema-goer watching a Brazilian film demands, first off, an 'American-style Brazilian film'. Because it is a *national* film and not an *American* film, it disappoints. The conditioned cinema-goer imposes, *a priori*, an artistic dictatorship on the national film: he doesn't accept the image of Brazil as viewed by Brazilian filmmakers because it doesn't correspond to the technically developed and morally ideal world as shown by Hollywood films. It is therefore no surprise when a Brazilian film is a popular success: all successful Brazilian films are those which, even when addressing national issues, do so using art and techniques which imitate those of American films. Obvious examples are as follows: *The Bandit*, by Lima Barreto, creates an American Western-type plot in the heart of the *cangaço*. In order to do this, he twists the social roots which are the basis of the bandit phenomenon in the Brazilian *sertão*,[18] and makes use only of those symbols which serve the Western plot: big hats, aggressive landscapes, guns and horses (it's well known, for example, that these Brazilian bandits rarely travelled on horseback), music and folk dance. The plot, as we can all remember, divided men into good and bad. Galdino was bad and Teodoro was good. Galdino, however, as a boss, showed some moments of greatness and humanity. And Teodoro, even when caught in the web of evil, doesn't hesitate in his decision to follow the right path, as soon as he's touched by a mixture of love and pity for the young captured school teacher. When Teodoro escapes with the school teacher, the film adopts the classic, progressive storyline of many Western films. The action is divided between the good being pursued and their evil pursuers. At the end, the little teacher, who is pure through and through, escapes. Teodoro, who had been bad in the past, has no hope of staying good and dies, prey of a nationalistic fit, kissing the earth. The technique of this film is artificial, it follows the American model. Virile actors, typical of the genre; romantic cinematography using shots of sunsets and heavy clouds; rapid, descriptive rhythm. At no point does the camera stop to analyse: the camera shows an array of characters in movement, delving no deeper into the conflict. This *realism*, as can be seen, is *unreal*. It creates an illusion of the world of Brazilian banditry in the image of the illusionary world of the Texan outlaws. The public, which was brought up entirely on *cowboys*, makes not the least effort to understand the film which is offered to them in the form of a generous imitation of what the public's warped taste requires. At the same time, the film soothes the inferiority complex of the Brazilian cinema-goer, who happily exclaims:

> At long last we can compete with American cinema. *The Bandit* is our own *Stagecoach* (John Ford, 1939).

The spectator doesn't know that the true phrase is in fact:

> At long last we can *imitate* American cinema.

Satisfied with the ability to imitate, which he understands as to be 'competing', the spectator will naturally react against any other film which, in its desire to show that Brazil is not the United States, exposes another type of conflict in its narrative, and, as a consequence, uses a different type of language. As the spectator is ignorant of their own country, the image of his own world is shocking to him.

Assault on the Pay Train (*Assalto ao trem pagador*, Roberto Farias, 1962) also repeats, this time via the crime genre, certain principles of American gangster films. The characters, although motivated by poverty, don't reflect upon it. The director creates a structure according to which the characters move and travel towards an irreversible destiny. The public here, watching the chronicles of the Brazilian nation by way of the American film form, can identify with the misfortune (not the tragedy) of Tião Medonho, whom they believe to be a 'victim of society', just as he does. The social issue is portrayed as being the divide between rich and poor: the poor man, like the humanist of yesteryear, Robin Hood, takes from the rich to give to his own. The police, even if they use brutal methods, are acting in the defence of society. In the end, society creates its own victims, but it has to punish them. Failing to do so, society itself will be threatened.

These ideas are already in the minds of the general public, basically comprised of the middle classes. This is why *Assault on the Pay Train* received international acclaim: the public, conditioned by the ideology of Hollywood, is the same throughout the whole world.

In his next film *Tragic Jungle* (*Selva trágica*, 1963), Roberto Farias made a big effort to move away from *American* film forms. This time he considered the problem of slavery on the large tea plantations in central Brazil by not dividing society into good and bad people, and invested in a more profound analysis. By penetrating into a complex structure, the resulting film was a flop at the box-office. The critics reacted and classed *Tragic Jungle* as a step backwards in comparison with *Assault on the Pay Train*. The *disconnection* within this film, however, is more realistic than the predetermined formula of *Pay Train*. *Tragic Jungle* was not an American imitation; it was a Brazilian social criticism film, a strong and sad film, more Brazil than United States.

The public's rejection caused Roberto Farias to realize that his ability to *communicate* was not linked to his personal talent as a director, but to the way he could apply this talent to approach a subject. And, once again, the director used an urban background, a view of middle-class morality applicable to the bourgeoisie. The film *Every Maiden Has a Father Who Is Angry* (*Toda donzela tem um pai que é uma fera*, 1966) proves the theory that using an *American narrative* for the subject matter is a *recipe for success*.

The international acceptance, both by the critics and in artistic circles, of *Tragic Jungle*, divided Roberto Farias into two directors where the craft ends up by conquering the author. Thus, his latest film *Roberto Carlos in the Rhythm of Adventure* [*Roberto Carlos em ritmo de aventura*, released in

Revolução do Cinema Novo

1968] combines national subject matter with American formulas and is destined to be a box-office success.

Is giving the public what it *wants* a way to triumph or rather the economical exploitation of its cultural conditioning? Would *Tragic Jungle* not be the true path in the battle to *win over* the public?

The answers to these questions, if not burdened with ideology, are at least complex. Roberto Farias would answer that cinema is an industry and that Brazil needs a cinematic industry in order that, at a later date, an original national cinema, which concentrates on our problems, may exist.

But how is a national industry formed? Cinema is an industry which generates *culture*. If *American cinema* created a certain type of taste and if *Brazilian cinema*, in order to develop, needs to take the easiest path, which is to use American forms, Brazilian cinema industry will be nothing more than a highly potent contributor to the dominant culture. This *culture* could quite easily be French, Russian or Belgian; it's irrelevant. In an underdeveloped country, it's essential that the way that society behaves is born of the circumstances of its economic structure.

The first challenge of the Brazilian filmmaker is this: how can we win over the public without using *American* film forms, which are already diluted into other *European* sub-forms?

This impasse, which reflects the modern view of underdeveloped tropical civilizations, has a moral repercussion which is two-fold and diverse: on the filmmaker who 'produces the imitation' and on the public who 'rejects that which is original'.

For the public, however, the stakes are higher. As a consumer, the public is unaware of the process involved in making original cinema as opposed to imitation cinema. And as imitation cinema gets much closer to the *public's concept of perfection* than original cinema does, which, by virtue of being new is *imperfect*, the public, by accepting the imitation cinema, gives strength to the Roberto Farias who made *Roberto Carlos in the Rhythm of Adventure*, and indirectly kills the Roberto Farias who created the original film *Tragic Jungle*.

From this concept of imitation cinema and original cinema was born the term *cinema novo* in Brazil. However, upon the head of *cinema novo*, which has given us the opportunity to face the truth of what Brazil is, a new challenge is laid down: what original language should be used, given that the language of imitation has already been rejected? The implacable consumer is unaware that from the moment in which the concept was inverted he was also being called to participate in the cinematographic process. He doesn't know, and with good reason, that the *national* filmmakers have begun to view him with respect, that is to say, they have begun to consider his artistic taste and his morals, and for that reason they are trying to invent a new language.

The problem with the language is a problem of awareness, the latter replacing the conceited concept of romantic nationalism. This language is not created overnight, in the same way that the Brazilian awareness has not yet reached a level which allows us to conceptualize *our civilization*. Even though social, economic and political aspects have already been subject to a more precise conceptualization, the resultant information is still insufficient to formulate a 'Brazilian civilization'. Cinema, inserted in the cultural process, should be, in the final analysis, the language of a 'civilization'. But what civilization? An Entranced Earth, Brazil is both indigenous/proud, romantic/abolitionist, symbolist/naturalist, realist/Parnassian, republican/positivist, anarchic/anthropophagic, national/popular/reformist, concretist/underdeveloped, revolutionary/conformist, tropical/structuralist etc.... etc.... Information about the prolific oscillations within our superstructure culture (because we are talking about an art form produced by elites, which is very different from 'popular art produced by the people'), is not enough to understand who we are.

Who are we?

Which is our cinema?

The public does not wish to know anything about this; it goes to the cinema to be entertained but instead finds a national film on the screen which requires of it an abnormal effort in order to establish a dialogue with the filmmaker who, for his part, makes an abnormal effort in order to speak to the public ... in another language!

Discussions on the subject of this 'language' are both verbose and revealing. *Cinema novo* has rejected imitation cinema and chosen another language, and it has also rejected the easier path of this 'other language'. This other language, typical of the so-called nationalist art forms, is 'populism'. It's the reflection of a political attitude that is very much our own. Just like the populist *caudillo*, the artist sees himself as the father of the people: the order of the day is 'we're going to talk of simple things that the people understand'. I consider it disrespectful to the public, as

Revolução do Cinema Novo

underdeveloped as it may be, to 'do simple things that the people understand'. In the first instance, the people are not simple. Sick, starving and illiterate, the people are complex. The artist/paternal figure idealizes popular characters, fabulous fellows who, even in poverty, have their own philosophy and, poor things, all they need is a bit of 'political awareness' to invert the historical process overnight.

The elementary nature of this concept is more damaging than the art of imitation, because the art of imitation justifies the 'industry of artistic taste' by way of its clear objectives of making profit. Popular art justifies its elementariness by way of its 'good intent'. The popular artist always says, 'I am not an intellectual, I am with the people, my art is good because it communicates etc.' But what does it communicate? It communicates, in general, the alienation of the people itself. It communicates to the people its own illiteracy, its own vulgarity born of a misery which conditions them to view life with disdain.

The Brazilian people always criticize, in a conformist manner, their own misery. In popular music there are countless Samba chants which exclaim 'having no beans to make soup, I make it from stones', 'I will die in the gutter, but with much joy', 'the *favela* is the waiting room for the heavens', 'I prefer to die in the dryness of the *sertão* than to live in a land of tarmac', and so on and so forth. *Populism* feeds from these sources and then regurgitates them to the people, offering no interpretation of them. The people, getting a skin-deep comedy version of underdevelopment, think their own misfortune is brilliant and splits its sides laughing. Hence the success of the *chanchada* films, all based on the picturesque misery of the *caboclo* [mixed-race peasant] or of the middle classes.

Populism also still defends that theory which says that the key is to use forms of communication ... to 'un-alienate'. However, such 'forms of communication' are, as we have already seen, the alienating forms of the colonial culture. An *underdeveloped* country is not necessarily obliged to have an *underdeveloped* art form. That's a reactionary and naive way of looking at it. *Cinema novo*, involved in the general concerns of Brazilian culture, rejected populism and consequently lost its own power to manipulate the masses.

While the problem of communication is discussed at length, *cinema novo* is discussing the problem of creation. Are creation and cinema irreconcilable? The majority of observers would answer that cinema is a communicative art form and there it ends. For these observers, *creation* sits in opposition to *communication*. The ever-faithful followers of communication have not, however, considered the following: on how many levels is communication processed, or, above all, what is true communication? *Cinema novo* confesses that it doesn't know what true communication is but is free from the constraints of the communicative certainty of *populism*, an audacious certainty, as, deep down, populism only cultivates the 'cultural values' of underdevelopment. These 'values' are worth nothing; our culture, a product of lack of craftsmanship, laziness, illiteracy, political impotence, and lack of social mobility, is a 'year-zero culture'. Set fire to the libraries, then! From zero, just like Lumière, *cinema novo* starts afresh with each film, splurting forth a brutal alphabet which tragically translates as 'underdeveloped civilization'.

When filmmakers are willing to start from scratch, to start talking about a cinema with a different type of plot, a different type of interpretation, with a different type of image, with another rhythm, with another type of poetry, they are launching themselves into the dangerous and revolutionary adventure of *learning on the job*, of placing, then, the theory alongside the practice, behaving according to an appropriate phrase of Nelson Pereira dos Santos, quoting I don't know which Portuguese poet:

I don't know where I'm going but I know I'm not going there![19]

And the public, which already knows how to SEE another type of cinema, finds itself assailed in the cinema stalls, forced to SEE another type of cinema which is technically imperfect, dramatically dissonant, poetically in revolt, sociologically as imprecise as official Brazilian sociology, politically aggressive and insecure just like the Brazilian political avant-garde, violent and sad, much sadder than it is violent, just as Brazil's Carnival is much sadder than it is happy.

NOVO [NEW] in this context does not mean PERFECT as the concept of perfection has been inherited from the colonizing cultures who fixed a concept of PERFECT according to the interests of a political IDEAL. The artists who worked for the princes created HARMONIOUS art according to which the earth was flat and all who lived on the other side of the border were barbarians. By way of the language it uses, true Modern Art (that which is ethical, aesthetically revolutionary) stands opposed to

Revolução do Cinema Novo

the language of domination. If the guilt complex of the bourgeois artists leads them to rise up against their own world, in the name of the conscience which the common people need but do not have, the only way to achieve this is to stand opposed, by way of the aggressive *impurity* of their art, to all alienating moral and aesthetic hypocrisies.

The secret of the cinematographic business is distribution. When the film is ready, the producer should launch it, but in order for it to get to the person who is going to show it, it is necessary to go through an intermediary, the distributor. The distributor only contributes contacts and organization. The promotional expenses are divided into three, but 80 per cent of them are payable by the producer. The exhibitor takes 50 per cent of the gross profit, the producer takes 30 per cent (while paying for 80 per cent of the promotional costs) and ... the distributor takes between 20 and 25 per cent, while spending only a small amount. However ... the distributor invoices directly and thus manipulates the producer's capital.

In general, at the end of a film, the producer has no money and ... he goes to the distributor. The distributor generously gives him an advance. But this money will be discounted, directly, from the first returns. And the producer, handing over the first returns to the distributor, will pay the banks with the returns he receives later ... which are always lower than those first returns.

Brazilian cinema is living through this drama. When capitalists in São Paulo created the big production company Vera Cruz, in 1950, they thought of everything ... apart from distribution, which went to Columbia Pictures. Columbia tried to distribute the films but made no effort to promote and market them. As the organization was being kept afloat financially by the returns of its own films, there was no need for any greater investment to be made in Brazilian films, which would directly fight for their own public in the arena of *American* film. But in that time of megastructures, the cinema theoreticians from São Paulo (the same ones who today influence the policy of the National Institute of Cinema) believed that studio-based cinema, with its stars, make-up artists, reflectors, astronomical salaries, Italian directors, was the best in the world.

Eighteen films later, Vera Cruz went bankrupt and even the success of *The Bandit* was not enough to prevent the fall of the Country Bumpkin Empire. Was it the fault of the financiers? The fault lies with the improvised producers, the imported directors, the irresponsible actors, the idealists who mystified the bourgeoisie saying that the art form was a product of money and that, by way of this art form, which had no market, São Paulo would have a cinema equal to that of the United States, given that it was Columbia itself that would distribute the films.

Offering an aesthetically dubious and culturally hybrid product, Vera Cruz did not even think to organize a market for its products.

Distribution, I should say, is not able to perform the miracle of making a bad film pleasing to the public or making a good art film be understood by the public. Distribution can, however, by way of persistent and skilful programming and efficient financing, circulate a film around our immense national territory and get back all the capital invested in it, with a profit.

An organized distributor can also create a public for a certain type of product. The best example of this is the increase in the market for *art house cinema*, on an international scale. With television reigning supreme, the film market managed to breach a gap, serving a section of the public looking to cinema for a more ambitious spectacle.

But what on earth is *art house cinema*? The term, used pejoratively by those who hate cinema, was a bad alternative for those who, producing and loving cinema as an art form and not as something banal, decided to unite to defend themselves.

But did anyone ever say, at any time, 'art poetry'? Or 'art painting'? Or 'art music'? Cinema, the art form of the twentieth century, cannot be considered an art form because 'art' in the minds of the conservatives is 'theatre' and cinema is 'entertainment'. These are subtleties which create large ripples within the industry itself.

The most ambitious of exhibitors understood that the only way to attract the spectator already a prisoner of television entertainment was to call him out to see 'art' in his film theatre. And thus began the commercialization of cinema, which, in order to become commercial, adopted the *anti-commercial* name of . . . art. Within these circles was born the French *nouvelle vague*, the names of the great Italians Fellini and Antonioni, as well as the Swede Ingmar Bergman, the Spaniard Luis Buñuel and many others, both young and old. At the entrances of *art house cinemas*, it was suddenly the director's name that was displayed and no longer those of the actors. And, with the exception of three or four individuals, very few of those names displayed at the entrances were of American directors.

Revolução do Cinema Novo

Is the *art house cinema* business then the response to *American cinema*? Is *American cinema* itself not an art form? Boasting an exceptional technique of creating and communicating the ideas of American civilization and already identified as having contributed to its formation, *is American cinema indisputable?*

History is not built on absolute certainties and it is the reverence shown towards *American cinema* itself which has resulted in the various independent production and distribution fronts operating throughout the world, fighting to bring another version of the world to the public. When the director stopped using his power to serve the physique and talent of the actor in order to fascinate the public, and instead began *to use* the actor as a way of starting a discussion with the public, the change was radical. The *auteur* appeared on the scene and with him, *art house cinema*. We could, therefore, conclude that the struggle between *cinema novo* and the public is not a struggle on a regional scale but a universal one, and it has the dimensions of a cultural revolution.

In 1964, Luiz Carlos Barreto recognized the phenomenon and had difficulties in convincing the directors/producers of *cinema novo* that imposing an original language could only be achieved through direct market control; that a long time was necessary in order for the films to modify the moral and artistic concepts held by the public and this required a self-sufficient distribution structure, working with the same type of product in an organized fashion. Hence the creation of DIFILM, a distributor of Brazilian *cinema novo* films which today competes on the same footing as other Brazilian distributors of commercial imitation films.

The multiplication of revenue was rapid. And the public's receptiveness to the 'cinema films' has increased by 40 per cent between 1964 and today. Any *cinema novo* film has, by way of efficient distribution, an audience of between fifty and a hundred thousand viewers in Rio alone.

DIFILM has fifteen films in distribution at the current time and this year will launch a further ten. The profit, without making great efforts, is between 10 and 15 per cent on the gross revenue; it does not serve to pay for the leisure activities of its associates but instead is invested in the company's organization and in film production.

DIFILM, moreover, has begun the exportation of its films by way of designated agents in Paris and Buenos Aires, international centres of distribution.

On Cinema

The acceptance of the majority of *cinema novo* on the *art house cinema* circuits abroad, as well as translating into an additional market which creates many possibilities, has given *cinema novo* a certain level of prestige which allows it to deal with more varied pressures.

One fact is irrefutable: an artistic language is not consolidated in an abstract manner; without economic power, it has no cultural power. DIFILM penetrated into the system by way of its objective grasp of reality, which is to use *business* in order to sell a subjective product, which is ... *art*. The increase in the market is a reality, as well as the increasing desire of the public to be informed about and to discuss its future. This desire demonstrates the mobilization, albeit a slow one, of an authentic Brazilian culture, contributed to by the avant-garde in our universities, the editorial movement, popular music, new theatre works, literature, new press and ... *cinema novo*.

Cinema novo is becoming a part of our society as an instrument of reflection and is trying, by way of a quality production, to create a language both *as different and efficient as* the language of *American cinema*.

Mário de Andrade, a theoretician and creator of great importance in the Modern Art Movement in 1922,[20] the first step in a Brazilian cultural revolution, wrote a book of as fundamental importance as *Rebellion in the Backlands* (*Os sertões*, Euclides da Cunha, 1902) in terms of the understanding of Brazil: *Macunaíma, the Hero With No Character* (*Macunaíma, o herói sem nenhum caráter*, 1928). The hero is an extraordinary person for any author of a novel, theatre production or film to choose to replicate for his story. Even the typical *hero*, the one which embodies the general aspects of society's fabric, is transformed, so long as it is *synthesized*, into the exception.

American cinema, by skilfully taking key elements from both novels and theatre from the last century, created heroes which were useful to its violent and humanitarian vision of 'the world in progress'. Handsome, strong, honest, sentimental and unyielding men. Independent, maternal, loving, sincere and understanding women.

This *hero couple* underwent various changes according to the type of actors embodying it. Obviously, a couple comprising Humphrey Bogart and Lauren Bacall would be different from a couple embodied by Errol Flynn and Olivia de Havilland, but the message of these heroes, whether in the Wild West or in the city, never underwent any radical changes: any internal social conflicts had to be remedied for the good of the nation; a tooth for a tooth, an eye for an eye, there is always hope for those who are just.

The *American* producers always made films for a specific time, and a minority even managed to take a critical stance, albeit going no further than social condemnation. Even arguments which today remain both bold and topical such as those put forward in John Steinbeck's novel *The Grapes of Wrath* (1940) could suffer an outrageous watering down: John Ford, a great technician gifted with a sense of humour, transformed a political subject into a socio-sentimental subject. The hero, played by Henry Fonda, who must have influenced the young Che Guevara, is shown here as a revolutionary son, completely inoffensive. We feel sorry for the hero, poor thing, who deserts his mother to join the revolution. And, if we were more mawkish, we would feel sorry for the mother, poor thing, who is left without her son, who was forced, by the changing circumstances within the city, to join the revolution. At the end of the film, Henry Fonda walks towards the horizons of glory in exactly the same manner that he walks at the end of another of Ford's films, *Young Mr Lincoln* (1939), on that occasion taking up the role of the patriarch, moving towards the horizons of imperialism.

John Ford, a good man, shows an enormous amount of pity towards the poor country folk who, thrown off the large estates, cross the United States towards California, the land of promise. It's a modern exodus and Henry Fonda never once stops playing Moses; at least, that is, a Moses as depicted by Cecil B. de Mille.

In 1929, the United States suffered a serious economic crisis. Unemployment. Social unrest. John Ford looks upon all this with both love and humour, without questioning the contradictions at play, wanting only to see 'the man' in the midst of his misfortune. What was cruelty and aggression in Steinbeck becomes gentleness and understanding in John Ford. The film is considered 'realist'. The actors wear authentic dress, a large part of the setting resembles reality, but all this is photographed with the care of someone taking pains to capture the radiance of a model: it is *the aesthetics of miserabilism*. Suddenly everything is beautiful, ideal and so harmonious that the audience feels a sudden desire to live in that world of hunger and unemployment.

This example of *The Grapes of Wrath* is an important one in the understanding of the secret: what makes the film is not the story but its direction. One of the mistakes made by the critics and the public alike is to consider *the story as being the basis of the film*. In cinema, *the story is only one of the elements of direction.*

In order to understand a film it is necessary for the spectator to at once observe the scenery, the tone of the cinematography, the set design, the actors' interpretation, to listen properly to the dialogue and to the music, to read the signs properly, to observe the camera movements from left to right and vice-versa, to understand what it means when only the actor's face is in close-up or when the actor is shown in an establishing shot, in the middle of the scenery, alone or in company.

In classic *American cinema*, everything was prepared in such a way that the viewer was faced with no conflict. The director tried to go over *everything* with a fine-toothed comb, in the most minute detail, to inject his ideology into it and present it to the public *already* cut into bite-size pieces. The public goes to see a film and it doesn't have to invest any thought in order to understand what is happening. They leave the cinema feeling good about themselves because they have had no involvement with what they have just seen. They feel stimulated only insofar as wishing to obtain for themselves some of the moral and physical advantages of the hero/heroine: beauty, strength of mind, courage, integrity, victory. Because life doesn't offer them this, they take refuge in cinema.

It's normal to overhear the phrase:

> Listen, I suffer so much in my own life that when I go to the cinema
> it's to see joy and not suffering.

A critic of French cinema told me that he loved the colour films of Metro-Goldwyn-Mayer because his own reality was so unhappy that for him Metro-Goldwyn-Mayer became a new *paradise*.

A paradise of unhappy souls, frustrated souls, impotent souls, victims of a system which oppresses them and, at the same time, offers them relief in a darkened room, a place where the failed man can anaesthetize his life.

The Brazilian filmmaker is aware of what's happening in Brazil and in the world, within society and within cinema. It isn't possible to isolate art, and cinema even less so: the filmmaker is a man who mobilizes himself on a daily basis, from the corridors of the banks to the labyrinths of the film laboratories, from the sophisticated world of the actors to the brutal world of the exhibitors, from luxury apartments to the depths of the jungle, and it's for this reason that, if he has a modicum of sensitivity, he will be touched by a reality so complex that it constantly calls into question the world in which he lives.

Our *hero* should be this *multi-faceted Brazilian man* living through each crisis in each stage of his life. The instability of this active and reflexive character is not to be found in our cinema – in the past he came already from our fiction and theatre and was linked to the understanding that authors themselves may have about reality. And he is also not yet untangled from the uncertainties of the *concept of realism*. In a *revealed*, developed society, it's much easier to conceptualize and practise dramatic realism than, as we saw before, it is in a society where there exists great uncertainty in the information available.

Our filmmakers join the adventure of learning about Brazil, in their desire to record its image directly and discuss openly what is known (or what is thought to be known), by our peoples, *by us and the others included.*

The false man, we know full well, is Capitão Galdino in *The Bandit*.

Not because he uses one or two too many stars in his bandit's hat, but because Lima Barreto says no more about him than what the viewer already knows: that he's a bandit and for that he will be punished, both by his own remorse and by the police. On the other hand, Fabiano, in *Barren Lives*, is authentic.

Barren Lives, a film by Nelson Pereira dos Santos, made in 1963, inspired by the novel by Graciliano Ramos, achieved no popular success, despite generating a cultural polemic. The hero, Fabiano, is a migrant from the north-east of Brazil. Weak, timid, ugly, hungry – he's not a coward but his fear of an unknown and oppressive political force leads him to take an honourable stance of non-vengefulness as recompense for his humiliation.

Luiz Carlos Barreto used direct cinematography when filming *Barren Lives*, to capture the sun of north-east Brazil, its effects on the landscape and on men. Ravaged by the sun, the characters initially move around the vast, stretching semi-desert region. The opening scene sets out a new type of cinema. The characters move in from a distance and slowly approach the spectator, led by the dog Baleia. The only sound we hear is the strangled creak of an ox-led cart.

The spectator, who came into the darkened room to *see* a drama about the drought, finds himself assailed by an opening which throws itself on top of him and tries to force him not to see but to *participate* in the drama about the drought. The film develops under this pretext. The white and glaring frames continue monotonously, one after another, but each one of them exposes a reflection on what is being seen, and it's irritating: if Fabiano, the hero himself, does nothing to change the situation, if he only manages to escape when the drought becomes life-threatening, why should the spectator, in the city, worry about Fabiano, and, moreover, get irritated with that useless Fabiano on the screen? They know that this film is different, they vaguely know that it is not rubbish, they have read about it in the newspapers and know that it's something arty, but they cannot stand it and protest: it could at least be in colour, move more quickly and be less sad.

A populist film would show Fabiano dancing *xaxado*[21] at the fireside, making sub-literature on the subject of a piece of grass. Moreover, at the end of the film, Fabiano would kill the military policeman, whom he finds lost in the *sertão*. Sinhá Vitória, with her sullen temper, would die, and Fabiano, receiving his strip of land as part of the agricultural reform, would marry the beautiful peasant girl and would build his ranch at the edge of the dam built by the Government Agency for the Development of the Northeast of Brazil (SUDENE).

This example is in no way funny; in art there is one option available: that which exists. The other option is a list of hypotheses. As on this occasion, watching *Barren Lives*, the spectator is not given a film which follows his mental movements trained like a monkey's to react this or that way, he refuses to move in the way suggested by the film in order to understand that Fabiano is not in an ideal world and, in order for Fabiano to change, it is necessary for both him and others to change the world etc.

The anti-hero grates. No one feels for him, just like no one feels for us. Lost, be it in the *sertão* or in the city, we have to take our future in our own hands. *Barren Lives* is a democratic film. Nelson Pereira dos Santos dissects one of the aspects of *the barbarity of the sertão*. He speaks the truth but few people *see and listen*.

Ruy Guerra, filming *The Guns*, took a different stance. He shows a group of migrants from the north-east (a mass of Fabianos) but prefers to look at things from the point of view of the soldiers (such as the man who humiliates and beats Fabiano in *Barren Lives*). The soldiers were called to the backwater town to keep order: to shoot down the first destitute man

Revolução do Cinema Novo

who tries to break into the food store building. The soldiers are human beings, some have rural origins, others are from the middle classes, but they live in their own world. The destitute man is, to them, an inferior being who has not freed himself, and no one really knows why, perhaps through laziness, perhaps because he likes being hungry. He, the soldier, has already lived his *revolution*.

In the little town they meet Gaúcho, now a lorry driver, previously a soldier. Gaúcho is an adventurer, ready for anything, a sceptic. A man without values, he's more than capable, irritated by their passivity, of taking up a gun and coming to the defence of the destitute men. He's shot down by the soldiers. As Gaúcho *is not victorious in the way a Texan sheriff would be victorious*, the spectator turns against the film which, in the end, neither offers him a solution nor an uncomplicated story to watch.

The Guns, different from *Barren Lives*, looks at another problem of the Brazilian north-east, that is the relationship between power and poverty, and uses violent language to try to express all angles of the drama. For Ruy Guerra, the story is not of great importance; the viewer, like the director, has to spend a lot of time on a long scene where a native of the *sertão* digs up a root to eat it, and another in which the soldier, following an injury sustained on duty, shows he is able to load a gun with his eyes closed and therefore to kill by conditioned reflex, without knowing what he's firing at and for what reason.

Within the context of the lavish natural setting in which the drama takes place, the spectator demands a cowboy film which is progressive and immediate, with no conflict between man, landscape and social fabric, where the soldiers, arriving in the name of the law, open fire against the exploiters of the poor and at the *bad elements* living amongst the people.

And Gaúcho, joining the soldiers, would feel stirring at his chest the old call of justice.

The Guns is seen as an *obscure* film. The lure of the images tires the spectator because they are forced to see and think about what they see.

In *Black God, White Devil*, I started from popular legends to show another side of the drama of the Brazilian north-east. Manuel, a poor cowherd, kills his boss and leaves with his wife in search of mystical salvation at the feet of the holy man. Losing the holy man, he continues in his quest for truth and ends up working as a hit man for a bandit. When the bandit dies, Manuel loses faith in everything, goes mad, leaves his wife and runs towards a sea glimpsed in a liberating delirium.

Another film causing a cultural polemic, just as *Barren Lives* and *The Guns* did, *Black God, White Devil* shocked the public and did not receive the success that was hoped of it. A young film programmer told me that if, in the film, Manuel had joined with Antônio das Mortes to kill the bandits and the pious and, afterwards, as a reward, he had taken over a rich colonel's farm, the film would have been a success. But changing Manuel's path would be changing the true character of Manuel, as weak, hungry and confused as Fabiano. Fabiano, bewildered, sits on the floor. Manuel goes forth into the world, following the path of bloodthirsty mysticism, expending his energy in the name of an abstract moral code of physical and spiritual purification.

We therefore see that the hero's behaviour, chosen by the director and developed as the director constructs the film, is linked to the filming technique. When the director tells the cameraman to shoot the hero in close-up or from afar and when he directs the hero to walk left or right, it's because he knows that this way or that way are related objectively and subjectively to the hero.

The evolution from the rural heroes of 1964 to the urban heroes of 1967 takes place due to a new realization which, even if it's obvious, comes not a moment too soon: underdevelopment also exists in the cities, in the posh neighbourhoods, in the luxury boutiques, in Ipanema.

The character in *The Big City*, Maria (Anecy Rocha), who comes from the north-east to look for happiness amongst the concrete, finds another kind of poverty. And it's against this poverty that the middle-class character, Marcelo (Oduvaldo Viana Filho) of *The Dare* rebels, much more due to moral unease than due to his political ideology.

A clear, honest and direct documentary of the underdevelopment integral to who we are, self-critical and self-flagellating, *The Dare* had very few people speaking in its defence and once again it reopened the debate as to whether or not *cinema novo* had any real purpose.

The repercussions of the 'failure' have had the opposite effect because, from the privileged position of someone who still had the slightest possibility to reflect and the courage to denounce his own class, the filmmaker knows that his *pineapple*[22] scatters its seeds while it's smashed to pieces in public.

Revolução do Cinema Novo

A phenomenon took place with *Ganga Zumba* where, taking on the subject of the slaves' revolt in colonial times (focusing on the case of Palmares), Carlos Diegues gave priority to the Afro-Brazilian soul and left the idealistic Homeric epic to one side. The disappointment for anyone who already had the sensational adventure of Zumbi dos Palmares in mind was so great that no one saw the filmmaker's sense of understanding of the black people, with their sensitivity, their wish for freedom, different from that of the freedom of the whites, of how, as slaves, the blacks were already immersed in our country's formation.

Up until today, *Ganga Zumba* is the only film which has been made about black people where the filmmaker, a white man, doesn't take a paternalistic view of the blacks but rather identifies with them by way of their origins and creates a slow and sad anti-epic. For that reason, *Ganga Zumba* was received with enthusiasm by the African delegations in the 1965 Third World Congress in Genoa, and it's for that reason also that this film, scorned in Brazil, was a success in its recent showing in Paris: prophetic in terms of the cultural and political role of the black man in the Americas, *Ganga Zumba*, just like the aforementioned north-eastern films, continues to be a source of information and discussion.

The incursions of our filmmakers into other areas within our culture remained incomprehensible to the public in the case of *The Priest and the Girl* by Joaquim Pedro and *The Deceased* by Leon Hirszman and, to a lesser degree, in *Plantation Boy* by Walter Lima Jr and *The Hour and Turn of Augusto Matraga* (*A hora e vez de Augusto Matraga*, 1965) by Roberto Santos.

The information provided in the texts of José Lins do Rego and Guimarães Rosa, especially in the case of the first, provided filmmakers with the possibility of learning about universes which no longer exist. Walter Lima Jr filmed the decline of the sugar plantations without having any personal link with the subject. As the plantations really belong in the past, the public agreed with the final sequence, when the child bids farewell to the countryside. The message of *Plantation Boy*, however, stood at an advantage, independent of the wishes of the filmmaker, and that advantage was childhood. And, by chance, a childhood untouched by poverty, a childhood of the plantations and not of the slave quarters.

In *The Hour and Turn of Augusto Matraga*, a drama of moral revenge with no political viewpoint, the itinerary was easier. Roberto Santos didn't veer away from the myth-enclosed world of Guimarães Rosa, and instead constructed a human drama in an unyielding world: Matraga, however, dies in defence of a poor man, fighting against hired gunmen. The same young programmer who gave me his opinion on another version of *Black God, White Devil* said that if, at the end, Matraga had united with Joãozinho Bem-Bem and managed to destroy his rival, Major Consilva, the public would have been elated and the film would have been a success. Once again, we see that *the public refuses to follow the film but wants the film to follow its ideas.*

The Priest and the Girl and *The Deceased* are films which, like *Barren Lives*, penetrate into areas of underdevelopment and immediately place the hero in context.

Joaquim Pedro used a very witty poem by Carlos Drummond de Andrade as a basis for his mining tragedy, a low song of death in the faded mining areas where nothing exists bar the image of a rich and dispossessed past. And there, not even beauty flourishes. The film is sad, slow, bitter and mute. The ideal version, a sophisticated film made about our declining aristocracy, is not made because the filmmaker pits his talents against these rotten origins of our economy and culture in order to declare that they are worth nothing, gold is worthless, tradition is a lie: *it is the rejection of underdevelopment.*

In *The Deceased*, Leon Hirszman moved away from the fantastically moralist world of Nelson Rodrigues.[23] In this descent into the solitary hells of Rio's northern zone, where man, oppressed by the city's concealed underdevelopment, devises the most refined forms of self-destruction, Hirszman approaches Nelson Rodrigues from a critical point of view and, for the first time, *reveals the social auteur behind the sexual auteur.*

Unveiling Nelson Rodrigues sounded like a crime. Faced with the uncertainty in which we live, both the public and the elite need gods. Even the most fantasized myths must be upheld. Up until *The Deceased*, all directors, both in theatre and cinema, had seen Nelson Rodrigues as either pornographic or expressionist, depending on the commercial or artistic intentions of the production. Leon Hirszman was the only director who showed Nelson Rodrigues in the rough, Brazilian, the expression of a mystical conflict with an immutable and crushing reality.

In the film, the character Zulmira wants a luxury burial, and involves her husband in this obsession. The obvious sensationalism of the issue is wiped away by Hirszman who instead shows us the isolation of a character

Revolução do Cinema Novo

who is socially immobile. The premature rotting of a social environment beyond salvation is dissected, piece by piece, in gestures, in cracked walls, in lonely streets, in the trains and trams which crawl along, in the unemployment, in the chronic hunger.

An escape from misery to mysticism in an enclave of the Brazilian northeast within Rio's northern zone, *The Deceased* is a type of urban *Barren Lives*. The desire to die is not an abstract issue, it's a suicidal act against social immobility and for this reason Zulmira is an exceptional person, a heroine whose character is free of the morality which characterizes popular drama. And even after her death the frustration continues: she will have a non-descript burial and her husband, morally stricken, gives himself over to another mystical compensation, football, and not once is he rescued from his isolation by the masses.

An image of radical anti-sentimentality, *The Deceased* is a rare example of how a filmmaker can take a script and criticize it by the way he films it and directs the actors: here is a unique example within *cinema novo* of total integration between the camera (which corresponds to the point of view of the director facing each scene), the actors and the set design. The set design is not decoration but an object which, mute, is just as important as the actors: in the photography of José Medeiros (who used natural light), actors and set designs take on the appearance of an engraving.

A graphic, critical, anti-literature melodrama, *The Deceased* carries with it the weight of a cinematographic tradition which is highly specialized: through the material rawness of the set design and the actors it links itself to *Greed* (Erich von Stroheim, 1924); through the precision of the camera, the subtle exactness of the cuts and the perplexity betrayed by each face (above all in the hour of death), it links itself to Dreyer, the director of *The Passion of Joan of Arc* (*La Passion de Jeanne d'Arc*, 1928).

But it is, at the same time, a criticism of this type of fatalistic *realism*. Not even the slightest gesture in this film is out of place. Thus, the stripped-down urban reality becomes shocking. The public, assailed, shuts itself off.

Everything is clear in the film. But the truth is frightening. The critics, taken aback, react. *The Deceased* upsets Nelson Rodrigues, the actors and the authorities. It becomes a doomed film, and is only seen by an open-minded minority.

The mistake is bigger than it is at first thought: In 1965, Itamaraty [Brazil's Ministry of External Relations] refused to send the film to Venice.

At the last minute, the Director of the Festival, Professor Chiarini, suggested its inclusion. Shown *hors concours* it caused a big stir amongst the best European critics. It was swiftly invited to represent Brazil in the I Rio Film Festival. This was a political manoeuvre to please Nelson Rodrigues and to 'guarantee' the Festival with a Brazilian film already internationally approved. A jury of foreigners, wherein the Brazilians were a minority, gave the Festival's second prize to the film. Straightaway, the same film was selected for the *Cahiers du Cinéma* week in Paris. And then it started to travel the world.

Sold to various countries, *The Deceased* was lavishly praised up to the point where the critic of *France Nouvelle* and *Cinema 68*, Albert Cervoni, wrote that it was 'one of the rare films which are truly Brechtian'. Even so, it was shunned in Brazil. The producers, influenced by the irresponsible opinion of the critics and friends of the playwright, handed the film to a commercial distributor and it received little interest. Launched at the wrong time, with no publicity, the film was a failure, simply having the same fate as many other classic films like it in the history of cinema.

The intellectuals, defenders of Lukács' critical realism in Brazil, had no sensitivity to this rare example of *critical realism* which was realism Brazilian style and not German or Italian style. Just as the public, the critics also suffer from the complex of cultural colonization: they think like the Europeans and want to apply this way of thought to a reality like our own, where the public is sub-Americanized.

A non-fictionalized account of the people was provided by Hirszman himself, in a documentary made before *The Deceased*: *Absolute Majority* (*Maioria absoluta*, 1964). After the brutal filmic revolution of *Aruanda*, filmed in [the north-eastern state of] Paraíba, *Absolute Majority* was the first film which recorded the voices and thoughts of the starving masses of [the north-eastern state of] Pernambuco. People on the screen were very different from the people in foreign films and very close to the people who cultivate death in *Barren Lives* or *The Deceased*.

The repulsion of the people faced with their own image quickly becomes apparent in *Racial Integration* (*Integração racial*, 1964) and in *Public Opinion* (*Opinião pública*, 1967) by Arnaldo Jabor.

The *cinéma-vérité* movement gained weight within *cinema novo* and produced examples which serve to reveal the conflict between the public and film. One of the areas most explored by filmmakers, both in fiction and

Revolução do Cinema Novo

in documentaries, was mysticism. Here, *cinema novo* provided an *affective contribution* to the knowledge of Brazil, as it directly discussed something, through image and sound, which before was only statistics, and, to a large extent, bad literature, because in this literature mysticism is innocently incorporated as a cultural value.

The same happened with folklore: any work by past generations tends to aestheticize events, and in the example of Euclides da Cunha he is praised more for the book's [*Rebellion in the Backlands*] rumbling style than for the tragedy of what he documents. *The epic of the impotent – here's the ideal of dominant Brazilian culture, and within this wave is encapsulated a large part of the leftwing.*

Cinema novo, knowing that the hero has no character, went to the sources of the 'epic' and therein discovered the original corrosion, enveloped in myth, which begins in the times of Pero Vaz de Caminha's letter.[24]

In *Memories of the Cangaço*, Paulo Gil shows us the last days of embittered Lampião,[25] a far cry from Robin Hood-esque romanticism. Opting to document the entrance of north-eastern migrants from *Barren Lives* into São Paulo, Geraldo Sarno completed the circle in the story of those who leave the *sertão* with dreams of the sea: mysticism and unemployment, *viramundo* (the world turns full cycle); wandering spectres come and go, in a ghostly Portinari-esque epic, whose painting is used in the opening for the film *Viramundo* (Geraldo Sarno, 1965).[26]

The other side of *The Deceased* can be found in *Public Opinion*. Researching and making the film at the same time, Arnaldo Jabor broke into the world of Rio's middle classes, absorbed as they are by the pitiless humour of [TV showman] Chacrinha and others. He amassed a wealth of information. Distressed, the filmmaker refused to organize a rehearsal. *Public Opinion* strips the public of its *make-up*. Not showing the excrescences and absurdities of the middle classes as a 'a manifestation of God's will' (*mondo cane*-style, wherein all the misery means ... life is like that, there are lucky and unlucky people), *Public Opinion leans so heavily on the public, stimulates so much reflection on its current state that it pushes it away.*

The creators of the techniques which serve to dumb down the public are spread right across the world. Recognizing this structure is not difficult for an expert technician. The problem faced by Brazilian filmmakers is another one: we know like no one else the communication structure of *American cinema*, from its artistic techniques right down to its distribution mechanisms. And, more than the emotionless technician, living under the dependency on this structure, we feel it even more profoundly. We know about the system of actors, the keys of the stories, the attractions of each genre, about the advertising tricks, *every little thing*.

However, because we know it all, are we going to accept it, won over by its efficiency? The attitude of intellectual groups who decided to import theories, and moreover theories from the developed world, with no enforced brainwashing at customs, did a lot to contribute towards the worsening of the underdevelopment. The schematic nature of theory generated a sub-art of imitation. So worried are we about what the developed countries might think of us, we have forgotten to think about ourselves.

Cinema novo thinks about itself, and only evokes what is thought about it abroad as something else against which to compare native incomprehension.

The fact that *cinema novo* is well accepted outside of Brazil in no way justifies its lack of acceptance within Brazil. The fundamental problem is our public, due to interlinked economic and cultural reasons. Trying to get closer to the true elements of our culture, *cinema novo* collided against a precarious culture. It then tried to elaborate a culture out of this precariousness. In a succinct phrase, Gustavo Dahl said that *cinema novo was obligated to qualitatively overcome the cultural underdevelopment, a task which was attempted by some Brazilian artists, above all those of 1922.*[27]

Knowing the communication techniques and how to infiltrate them is of no use. What is important is to denounce these techniques and find alternatives. Brazilian cinema enjoys an exceptional advantage: built on a structure which is moving towards self-sufficiency, it will have (censorship battles aside) a freedom to manoeuvre which is infinitely greater than that of television, which is a slave to advertising and to its twisted public audience.

The danger for cinema is that, faced with a public addicted to foreign films and suffocated by television, communication becomes problematic. But it's not impossible to breach the overriding lack of interest. On one hand, the partial failure of *cinema novo* with the public can be traced back to the immaturity of the filmmakers who, jumping head first into the abyss without technique or experience, were knocked back by the impact and then made a counter effort to lessen it.

But a couple of things managed to pass through the glass wall and one of them was so important that it serves to counterbalance the monologue: cinema novo *became a political and cultural reality. It suffers, much like our legal and illegal political parties, from a forced isolation.* But, contrary to that which is said by the critic Jean-Claude Bernadet in his book *Brasil em tempo de cinema: ensaio sobre o cinema brasileiro de 1958 a 1966*,[28] cinema novo *does not live off the prestige of official culture and, moreover, has a great deal of disdain towards it*: this disdain can be seen on the screen, in the films, which earn prestige because they are *films* but not because of what they *say*. They are films, I mean, physical things, technical production, creative affirmation, which respond, victorious, to the challenge thrown down by this same official culture that 'Brazilians do not have the capacity to make cinema'.

From the first experiments in 1961 including *The Scoundrels*, *The Turning Wind* and *The Port of Caixas*, up to this year's productions which will be very polemic, like *The Brave Warrior* by Gustavo Dahl, *Capitu* by Paulo Cesar Saraceni, *Face to Face* by Júlio Bressane, *Satan's Feats in the Town of Back and Forth* by Paulo Gil Soares, *Bebel, Propaganda Girl* by Maurice Capovilla [*Bebel, a garota propaganda*, released in 1968], *Brazil Year 2000* by Walter Lima Jr, *Memories of Helen* by David Neves [*Memória de Helena*, released in 1969] *Macunaíma* by Joaquim Pedro de Andrade, *The Heirs* by Carlos Diegues, and around a dozen more shorts and feature-length films, *cinema novo* has moved away from the stage of pure discovery and intuition and has moved on to a stage of reflection and breaking away from its own roots. This is because the language that *cinema novo* is pursuing, a language which will depend upon socio-political and economic factors in order to communicate effectively with the public and have an influence on its liberation, does not claim to be an organized structure in the academic style, the style so dear to the theoreticians who need God's word to guide them, *but a proliferation of personal styles*, which bring into permanent doubt the concept of language, the super-stage of consciousness.

The quality of the work of art, as the poet Ferreira Gullar said to me the other day on the beach, will result from the artist's ability to elaborate his material within a stricter dialectic: it is he who will combine information, imagination, reason and courage, elements without which no piece of art can be made.

The avant-garde in the Third World, also according to Gullar, *is certainly not the same thing as the avant-garde in the developed world*.

Yet the problem doesn't exist, as some might think, between that which is *national* and that which is *universal*. The problem is to be able to create out of one's own insufficiencies and to turn these qualities into the mobile structure of a thought in progress. That will result in an international artistic style, thus an *avant-garde*. Therefore, the only factor which will be stimulated *in the development of cinematographic styles in the Third World will be the creation*, which starts from the tactics of production, takes shape in dialectical freedom and imposes itself in the strategy and tactics of distribution.

Tropicalism, Anthropology, Myth, Ideography (1969)

Let us consider 1922 as being the beginning of a cultural revolution in Brazil.[29] In that year, there existed a strong cultural movement which was reacting against the academic, official culture. The main spokesperson in this period was Oswald de Andrade. His cultural research, his work, which is truly amazing, he himself defined as anthropophagic, referring to the tradition of cannibal Indians; just as the latter ate white men, he claimed to have eaten all Brazilian culture and all that which is colonial. When he died, few of his texts had been published.

José Celso Martinez Corrêa, who is the director of Teatro Oficina, the most important avant-garde theatre group in Brazil, discovered the text *O rei da vela* [*The King of the Candle* by Oswald de Andrade, 1933], and produced it. It was truly revolutionary: anthropophagy (or Tropicalism as it is also known), thus presented to the Brazilian public for the first time, resulted in an opening up of all areas of culture.

Tropicalism, anthropophagy and its development, this is the most important feature of Brazilian culture today.

Brazil's history is small, reduced. We have a tradition of nationalism/ fascism which then transformed into nationalism/democracy, but when the country became aware of its underdevelopment, this utopian nationalism fell into crisis and faltered. First, albeit in a rather schematic

Revolução do Cinema Novo

manner because in Brazil our social sciences are primitive, we discovered our economic underdevelopment. Then came the discovery that our underdevelopment underpinned everything.

Brazilian cinema began against the backdrop of the realization of this totality, from the acknowledgement of it and the awareness that it must also be totally overcome, in the aesthetic, philosophical and economic sense: overcome underdevelopment using the resources of underdevelopment.

Tropicalism, the anthropophagic discovery, was a revelation; it stimulated awareness, an attitude towards colonial culture which is not a rejection of western culture as it was initially (and that was madness because we have no methodology). We accept this total *ricezione* [reception], the ingesting of the basic methods of a complete and complex culture, but also its transformation via *nostri succhi* [our juices] and via the use and elaboration of the correct policies. It's from that moment onwards that a search for a new aesthetic is embarked upon, and this is a recent event.

Right now, 'Tropicalism' is a name which means nothing, like *cinema novo*. What is significant is the artists' *apporto* [contribution] in this area.

Tropicalism is acceptance, promotion of underdevelopment. That is why there exists a cinema before and after Tropicalism. We are no longer afraid of facing up to Brazil's reality, our reality, in all senses and to all extents. Herein lies the reason why in *Antônio das Mortes* (*O dragão da maldade contra o santo guerreiro*, Glauber Rocha, 1969) there exists an anthropophagic relationship between the characters: the professor eats Antônio, Antônio eats the *cangaceiro*, Laura eats the police chief, the professor eats Cláudia, the assassins eat the people, the professor eats the *cangaceiro*.

This anthropophagic relationship is one of freedom.

I should have done that already, done it in *Black God, White Devil* but the relationships between the characters were stifled relationships, there were things left unspoken between them; they were more bourgeois because I was more bourgeois. In contrast, in *Antônio das Mortes* there was a complete frankness, and the same was the case for films of other directors: this freedom, new to us, created the possibility of a new relationship with the public.

Of late, we have not been making American films or populist films: I think the cinema we are making is less conceptual (and for that reason less schematic) and penetrates more deeply into a colonized public like our own. It's impossible to compete with the current imperialist system, but if a film is made which speaks directly to the collective unconscious, to the deepest and most authentic dispositions, then it may even succeed.

On the other hand, this idea of succeeding was not calculated from the offset, it came about through natural growth. And we will still make some unappealing films. But what matters is the public, and there are many kinds of public.

Ours is an aesthetic-political search which sits under the banner of the individualization of the collective unconscious, and for this there is an approval of the typical elements of popular culture applied in a critical manner.

A few days ago, I spoke to Godard about the place of political cinema. Godard holds that we in Brazil are in an ideal position to make revolutionary cinema, yet we are still making *revisionist* cinema, that is to say, giving importance to the drama, to the development of the spectacle.

His view on it is that there exists today a cinema for four thousand people, militants speaking to their peers. I understand Godard. He is a European filmmaker, French; it's logical that he would propose to destroy cinema. But we, here, cannot destroy that which doesn't exist. And looking at the sectarian problem from this angle is, moreover, wrong. We are at a stage of national liberation, which is also sweeping through cinema, and the way we relate to the masses is of fundamental importance. We must not destroy but build: cinemas, houses, streets, schools etc.

Eventually, Godard understood the rest as well, and I had the opportunity to appear, as an actor, in one of the scenes of his film, which is very promising.[30] A structural inversion of the Western genre would be very interesting and useful to us. The Western genre is very important, but not just for me. We are a people historically linked to sagas, to epics. We have a long history of philosophy and that's a bad thing. But it would be a lot worse if it were an imported philosophy with no link to our history. For that reason, anthropophagy is more important.

We are in a position to create the traditions of an industry in which the producer is the auteur. At present, the producer figure is, for us, that of a technician who studies the market to find economically focused methods and solutions, before arriving at the point of actual planning.

There exists a Brazilian cinema which didn't exist before, and within it there are many differences.

Revolução do Cinema Novo

We had to build the structures and discover the filmmakers. This has been done. Now a change of tactics is taking place, and a great deal of work is being undertaken (but planned, organized) to transmit the possibilities of cinema.

Talking about myths and language is fundamental. It is the centre of our problem. If we are working towards a total global revolution, language should be understood in the Marxist sense, as an expression of consciousness.

For us, the problem is of more immediate comprehension, because illiteracy leads to a complex type of understanding and what we want is to develop our cinema within the context of a permanent historical dialectic, as the situation evolves.

There were various different phases. The moment of social condemnation, influenced by neorealism, and by American social-conscience cinema. The moment of revolutionary euphoria, which already had limited, schematic and populist characteristics. The moment, finally, of reflection, of meditation, of profound searching.

In these three moments, there were great differences in language, even in its use by each individual director. I, for example, feel that right now I suffer less external influence. *Antônio das Mortes* contains less detritus. The influences are more subjective, more intimate.

The cinema of the future is ideographic. It's a difficult investigation into the signs (symbols). Investigation in a scientific manner is insufficient; rather, what is needed is a process of awareness and self-awareness, which delves into every level of existence and which is then integrated with reality.

Myth is the first ideograph and it's useful to us; we need it to get to know ourselves and to learn from it. Mythology, any mythology, is ideographic and the fundamental forms of cultural and artistic expression refer to it constantly. From there we will be able to develop other things, but this is a fundamental step. Tropicalism is surrealism for the Latin American peoples.

There is a French surrealism and another one which is not French. Between Breton and Salvador Dalí there is a great abyss. And surrealism is a Latin thing. Lautréamont was Uruguayan and the first surrealist was Cervantes. Neruda talks of *concrete surrealism*. It's the discourse about the relationship between hunger and mysticism. Our surrealism is not the surrealism of dreams but that of reality. Buñuel is a surrealist and his Mexican films are the first films of Tropicalism and anthropophagy.

The historical role of surrealism in the oppressed Hispano-American world was to be an instrument of thought in the path towards anarchic liberation, the only liberation possible. In the present time it's used dialectically, in a profoundly political sense, in the path towards enlightenment and unrest.

Ideographic cinema means the following: a developed and profound form of awareness and self-awareness, linked directly to the building of revolutionary conditions. The intelligence of French criticism, although snobbish and academic at times, has saved cinema from a more widespread mediocrity. What demoralized Italian cinema was pseudo-Marxist criticism. Bazin is much more intelligent than Guido Aristarco, even though Rossellini, Visconti, Fellini and Antonioni are Italian. Bazin's excellent criticism moulded only Godard – although Truffaut could be a great filmmaker if he underwent psychoanalysis. Two French filmmakers who I am watching with interest are Resnais and Jacques Rivette. However, as long as French cinema stays within the domain of reason it will remain limited. And the worst of it is that this reason is anti-dialectical. Godard is Swiss, from an underdeveloped country overwhelmed by its neighbour. And he's Protestant – a timid moralist who self-detonates to stop himself from dying of fear.

América Nuestra (1969)

Epic poem, theatrical performance, commentary, polemic and politics in Latin America.

Begun in Paris in June 1967, reworking the 1966 version, written in Rio. From the treatment of 1966 a few ideas for *Entranced Earth* would arise. The 1967 version, written in Paris, was narrative, novelistic and quite influenced by E.'s revolutionary memoirs[31] and by D.'s book.[32] E.'s death resulted in a pause to my work.

It still lacked structure; the ideological conflict was impacting negatively on its development. A.[33] insists that I go and film on the island, without even having read the script. Walter Achugar and Edgardo Pallero plan on doing the production in Chile and Argentina. Zelito Viana insists on filming in Brazil. As I had never pushed the idea with Claude Antoine, he has shown no enthusiasm for it.

Revolução do Cinema Novo

Worried about the state of popular cinema, I wrote and made *Antônio das Mortes*. In Paris, after Cannes, I have an idea to transfer over to Africa a play I wrote for José Celso Corrêa. The play gets lost. I also lose the versions I had of my screenplay *América Nuestra* but Rosinha[34] finds them in my small apartment in Botafogo [Rio de Janeiro].

I am planning on filming *The Seven-Headed Lion* [*Der leone have sept cabeças*, Glauber Rocha, released in 1969] and *The Death of Don Quixote* (*A morte de Dom Quixote*) in Spain. I am thinking of abandoning these projects to make *América Nuestra* but I think I will need to redo everything and find a perfect place for the production, which will cost around two hundred thousand dollars.

Rosinha is a fan of the film and she gave me this notebook today. I decided to note down the whole film here, and through my necessity to criticize I decided to write a free-flowing narrative on it. We're going to have dinner in a short while with Visconti and I think that he would be the perfect producer for *América Nuestra*, although I believe that Zelito Viana should have some part to play in the film and that Luiz Carlos Barreto would be the most apt photographer. For the cast, I should perhaps use Geraldo D'El Rey or Alfredo Alcón. I did also want to use Francisco Rabal ..., Sílvia Pinal ... and the great Pedro Armendáriz, if possible ...

The other day, travelling by plane to Munich, I told ... about the film, and I had the idea of a tracking shot of the President doing the tango. I then thought of ... but ... informed me that Brasília is not a good place to shoot that scene and then I remembered the Governor's Palace in the state of Maranhão. The political situation in Peru might allow for the film to be made there, in 1970 or 1971.

> The innocence of Lumière
> The set design of George Méliès
> The magnitude of David Wark Griffith
> The dialectic of Eisenstein
> The poetry of Renoir
> The force of Welles
> The inventiveness of Godard
> The irreverence of Buñuel (and the romanticism)
> The sentiment of Visconti, from Bernardo,[35] the love
> The intuition of Rossellini, from Gianni,[36] the rigour

and something from Straub, the mysticism of Elia Kazan + *American cinema*, Bresson, the wackiness of cinema and the passion of Glauber Rocha. Another thing: the epic biography of Leon Hirszman. Talking to Leon develops my cinematic reasoning. Nelson [Pereira dos Santos] makes me doubt. Walter [Lima Jr] gives me comfort. Cacá [Diegues] sharpens my culture. Gustavo [Dahl] educates my taste. Paulo Cesar [Saraceni] boosts my integrity. Zelito [Viana] stimulates me. [Luiz Carlos] Barreto. David [Neves] is my confident. Antônio [Pitanga] and [Eduardo] Escorel are my collaborators ... they should make films and I'm thinking of producing those first films for them. Talking to Gianni Amico is fantastic. Gianni and ... there are no others. Gianni is going to help me get down a plan for *The Seven-Headed Lion*. Triguerinho Neto and Gianni taught me as much about cinema as ... and ... about theatre and art in general. In terms of criticism, Walter da Silveira introduced me to it. Paulo Emilio Salles Gomes, Alex Viany, the president of the Brazilian Film Archive Almeida Salles, Rudá de Andrade, Louis Marcorelles, even they, they taught me a lot. Even Salvyano!!![37]

I'm talking of these things here because perhaps I want to free myself of all influences, good and bad, to prepare myself for filming.

I'm thinking about dedicating the film to F.[38] and in memory of E. ... It might be interpreted as demagoguery.

I'll eat quietly ... Neruda, Astúrias, Alejo, Villar etc. ... to later spew out like a volcano.

I'm thinking about sending a wire to [American producer] Dan Talbot: produce a post-Eisensteinian film for me.

I'm thinking about both the anonymous and the famous people who died to liberate Latin America. I fear that I will not be able to make this film, but I am, at least, going to write it.

I'll keep hold of the different versions as far as it's possible, which may allow for a more in-depth analysis of the film as a whole.

Discussion of the Concept of Aesthetics and its Political Function

[1]

Once, in 1966, I asked [critic and writer] Paulo Francis to read one of the versions of *América Nuestra*. I had spoken to him about the vulgarity of the Brazilian bourgeoisie in its attempts to equal the already defunct European

Revolução do Cinema Novo

aristocracy, which instead managed only to imitate the international bourgeoisie which was even more vulgar than that which is usually seen as vulgar: prostitutes and criminals. Well, prostitutes and criminals are not sinful. In a film like *Bahia of All Saints* (*Bahia de todos os santos*, Trigueirinho Neto, 1961), or in the documentary made by Gianni about Samba,[39] there are shots which reveal the cultural influence of ordinary people. This can also be seen in Jorge Amado's work or that of José Lins do Rego. Zé Keti[40] is more elegant than any of Proust's barons – even if there are Brazilian black women who straighten their hair.

Proust wiping his behind with a page of *Última Hora*.[41] Francis told me that the script was good and that it's true that the bourgeoisie are cockroaches. He also told me that the script had a 'textual problem'. This sort of observation is typical of Francis's intelligence: he despises everything in Brazil, even the Portuguese language, despite being one of the best creators of text we have at the present time. Journalists Jânio de Freitas and Paulo Francis are strange creatures. One day I'll speak about them at length and of other Brazilian intellectuals that I esteem and admire.

Aesthetic ignorance is very widespread within Latin America. This doesn't mean that some of the best writers of our time are not Latin American: [Jorge Luis] Borges, [Guimarães] Rosa, [Julio] Cortázar, Alejo [Carpentier], [Carlos] Drummond [de Andrade], [João] Cabral [de Melo Neto], Jorge Amado, [Gabriel García] Márquez etc....

Within the artistic process, the greatest impediment is fear. The authors of great creative works in Latin America have overcome fear in order not to succumb to the terrorism of the inferiority complex. Even I myself have broken out of this complex, kicking and screaming. The first person who showed me the ridiculousness of it all was Luiz Carlos Barreto. But the most complex-free Brazilian I know is Zelito Viana. I'm not afraid of creating; if both art and resources are present I press ahead. And it's important not to be a complete idiot as idiocy is the enemy of the artist.

América Nuestra should be a film which is Eisenstein multiplied by Eisenstein.

My friend the diplomat Arnaldo Carrilho once said to me, as we were standing in front of the ruins of Pompeii (it was a Sunday between January and March of 1965) that Simon Bolívar climbed Vesuvius and from there meditated on Latin America: he then set out on his political action. Whether the story is true or not, I want to start from the volcano.

On Cinema

How can I disconnect from Camões' epic poem *Os Lusíadas* (*The Lusiads*) or [Fernando Pessoa's] *Ode marítima* (*Maritime Ode*) when thinking about a film? Visconti told me today that my aesthetic ambition has no limits (I'm only afraid of not being cultured and rational enough to discipline my imagination). My imagination astounds me but I know that it's not enough. Yesterday, sitting on the lavatory, I was writing the shots for *The Seven-Headed Lion* and I realized I was writing shots like a composer writes a score.

I felt closer to cinema. I lost my fear of Godard.

He's the greatest filmmaker since Eisenstein died.

Montage is a dialectics whose structure is comparable to poetry. It's not atmosphere, but the editing of the words which creates a 'superstructure' of the atmosphere.

América Nuestra should have an epic montage. But I want to go back and revise Eisenstein himself: a modern epic, produced as a result of a culture which is highly critical but which is still unknown. I have no choice but to bow to this ancient past. However, it's so dangerous to make cinema in Latin America that I want to run the risk of striving to cover everything.

Eisenstein was so pure that he felt no shame in saying that he felt the true ecstasy of creation when he was filming *Battleship Potemkin*; and he added that whoever had filmed *Potemkin* would have felt the same way. That's why Eisenstein made great films. He was not afraid, and his greatest virtue was to dare to show beauty. Revolutionaries are generally reactionary in terms of art. Whichever political leader is able to liberate Brazil from its dictatorship will always tend to react against the aesthetic avant-garde. Che wrote that the aesthetic avant-garde should be integrated into the political avant-garde. Cuba is taking a big step in this direction. I read one of Brecht's quotes in Walter Benjamin's work: 'The latest bad things are better than the good things of old.'[42] Revolutionaries are afraid of new things in art. They are traditionalists, hooked on bourgeois culture. They are not true revolutionaries because a socialist revolution can only take place by integrating economics and culture and, according to this dialectic, 'new culture' should be socialism itself, wherein man can create and enjoy artwork as the pinnacle of his individual/collective development. However, reactionary behaviour towards aesthetics is worsened by the fact that the revolutionaries feel protected by their good revolutionary conscience when they react against the aesthetic avant-garde. And in the

Revolução do Cinema Novo

case of cinema, the situation is serious because cinema is not considered to be an art in the bourgeois sense of the word (like theatre is, for example) and because, on the other hand, as cinema awakens an interest greater than any other art form, so people feel frustrated by cinema and unleash a great wave of bitter and destructive criticism upon it. And everyone wants to tell the filmmaker what 'he *should* film', with the greatest amount of disrespect possible. The 'antifascists' are in fact as fascist as the fascist censors in power. In Brazil, *cinema novo* is fighting alone against fascism.

Even though this is the case, *cinema novo* has become an international cultural phenomenon – the first one to come out of the Third World, much more aggressive than that of Cuban cinema: even the Cubans recognize the revolutionary spirit of *cinema novo*. The Brazilian theatre circles are jealous of *cinema novo* and counter this jealous feeling with forced disdain. A famous actor from Brazil responded thus to a journalist:

> Cinema Novo is having a lot of success in Paris, isn't it?

This is typical of national stupidity. Brazilian theatre is rubbish. These actors have no humility. They seek bourgeois glory or to make it big in European cinema, while they're living amongst the best filmmakers in the world. Yesterday a producer offered me Marlon Brando, almost begging me. That Brazilian actor should not have any complexes. Or the snobby woman who says in the same interview:

> I think that Brazilian films are too intellectual. I prefer the silly MGM films.

The truth is, this snob represents the most irresponsible side of the Brazilian bourgeoisie. By saying that she prefers the silly films, she's playing fascism's game, the game of the commercial producers etc., and she's sabotaging *cinema novo*.

The funding available for *cinema novo*, however, coupled with a successful launch onto the international arena, are allowing us to fight back. *Cinema novo* created Brazilian cinema and came up against our inferiority complex in such a violent way that it's normal that the reactions are as they are.

It's *cinema novo* which is the forerunner to the Brazilian Cultural Revolution; it's 'Chapter 2', coming after *Semana de Arte Moderna*.[43]

On Cinema

Our loneliness is increasing because contact with other intellectuals is difficult: even those with the best intentions do not understand cinema.

[2]

I don't believe it's possible to discuss an aesthetics/politics problem nor to speak of more general or apparently superficial problems. *América Nuestra* should be a film born out of all these contradicting factors. For example, it should have an Eisensteinian spirit but be anti *Que Viva Mexico!* I don't like the visual feel of *Que Viva Mexico!*: in that film Eisenstein transferred Da Vinci, Michelangelo etc., all the Renaissance idealization, to Mexico. The visuals of *Que Viva Mexico!* should have been modern, like the tracking shots used by Renoir in *Madame Bovary* (1933) and other films, or even the way that Rossellini photographed *Journey to Italy* (*Viaggio in Italia*, 1954). There are no limits or classifications in art: the surrealism of Jean Cocteau's *Beauty and the Beast* (*La Belle et la bête*, 1946) with its expressionist vein is more attractive than *Orpheus* (*Orphée*, Jean Cocteau, 1950), the realism of which possesses an expressive desire which borders on the ridiculous.

The other day, I was playing with Jean-Marie Straub, saying that the Henri Langlois from the future would show *The Adventure* alongside *The Cabinet of Dr Caligari* (*Das Kabinet Des Doktor Caligari*, Robert Wiene, 1920).

Cinematographic expressionism doesn't have much in common with Baroque style nor with the contrast of light and darkness in set design.

Fritz Lang is not an expressionist, although many critics link him with the famous German cinematic school. In *Die Nibelungen: Siegfried* (*Die Nibelungen: Siegfrieds Tod*, Fritz Lang, 1924), for example, you can see that the theatrical set design is cancelled out by the position of the camera and by the narrative editing. The interior rhythm is realist and the whole looks like a real document. Expressionist theatre is already in evidence in Welles, even though he uses cinematographic resources more abundantly than is the case with any other filmmaker. Nevertheless, Welles always leaves us with a lingering impression of theatre, behind mind-blowing cinema. *M* (1931) by Fritz Lang is the *Paisan* of its era. It must have inspired Rossellini; it certainly inspired Godard. *M* is a masterpiece.

The first post-Eisenstein dialectical filmmaker is Godard. Another is Straub, but his classicist rationalism hampers somewhat the rhythm of his

Revolução do Cinema Novo

films. *Entranced Earth* is a dialectic film. *Antônio das Mortes* is dialectic: it's influenced by *La Chinoise* (Jean-Luc Godard, 1967) and by Straub. With no complexes, it leans towards Eisenstein. Making *Antônio das Mortes* gave me freedom as a filmmaker. Enough of criticizing cinema, we need to transform it. The dialectical direction taken by cinema could generate new forms and introduce space into the editing, which still abides by a rigid temporal rule.

Breathless is a Joycean film. *La Chinoise* is a dialectic film. *Made in USA* (Jean-Luc Godard, 1966) is a futuristic film, *British Sounds* (Jean-Luc Godard, 1970) is a dialectic film – the most dialectic of all because it's not based on journalistic sociology like *Two or Three Things I Know about Her* (*Deux ou trois choses que je sais d'elle*, Jean-Luc Godard, 1967).

The *école du regard* is finished. Expletive, atmospheric cinema is over. Outside of dialectic cinema there is only Buñuel. Buñuel's language, moreover, has its own dialectic, and that's the imponderability of knowledge. I believe that the poetic dimension is the greatest stimulus of Marxism. Scientificist materialism is the basis of Neo-fascism (Benjamin says that Brecht was underlining the fact that in Russia there was a 'dictatorship *over* the proletariat').[44] The great contribution of Mao is to topple this dictatorship and bring a true revolution of the proletariat into being. The term 'dictatorship of the proletariat' is fascist in itself. A worker's democracy – that's to say a democracy amongst those who produce things – is the fairest democracy, and by way of this democratic principle we can understand democracy as dialectic. The dialectic seems to me to be like a sonnet; in Petrarch, for example, there is as much logic as there is imponderable sensation and perception; they are basic functions of the poem. From Petrarch to Mallarmé, like from Chaplin to Godard, here, in this moment, the work of art becomes practical (praxis), and in cinema there is nothing more fascinating.

Dialectic montage should start with an analysis of the structures. In *Breathless*, Godard, in the manner of Joyce, pulverizes the structures but only begins to communicate them, interruptedly, in *My Life to Live* (*Vivre sa vie*, 1962), although in other films we have already at least seen the structures exposed. Narrative cinema creates an ideal structure which censors others – a minimum of information and superfluousness – the idiocy of so many artists who believe they are modern because they

Figure 2.1   Glauber Rocha and Fritz Lang (Montreal, 1968).

discover the obvious, that is, they discover the structure of imperialist communication and they think that adopting this structure will be inventive and modern.

Cinema which calls itself Brechtian falls into the same trap: the only Brechtian filmmaker is Brecht himself. Joseph Losey has influences (above all over the actors) and Godard is a neo-Brecht, but it's ridiculous to see cold, narrative, condemning, introverted films which try to justify their neutrality in the name of Brechtian 'distanciation'. *Nouvelle vague* is full of examples of this type. It could be said that the *nouvelle vague* created a bourgeois aesthetic *par excellence*. This became confused with the so-called *auteur* cinema which is itself confused with inefficiency. The only films of this school which were successful were so for sexual motives, and others, like *Hiroshima, mon amour* and *The War Is Over* (*La Guerre est finie*, 1966) by Resnais, or a couple by Truffaut, were so for some unequalled break-out qualities. The rupture of Resnais is pre-Joycean. This is characteristic of the extraordinary capacity of the French to criticize their present lack of creativity. Resnais dis-articulated time without articulating a dialectic. His cinema could be dialectic if it were not literary (I want to say bourgeois) and didn't contain the classic guilt complex, as well as containing moralistic, snobby and childish details like the love scenes in *The War is Over*, a good example of a despicable 'artistic' measure. One weak point of Resnais: his actors. He is, however, an excellent documentary maker and is revitalizing the use of tracking shots in cinema. *Night and Fog* (*Nuit et brouillard*, 1955) is a film with dialectic structure and *Toute la mémoire du monde* (1956) an (antididactic) poem of great beauty. Just like the first moments of Hiroshima. But oh how disappointing is his episode in *Far from Vietnam* (*Loin du Vietnam*, 1967). *Last Year in Marienbad* (*L'Année dernière à Marienbad*, 1961) is a first-rate, expressionist, literary essay, subdued by the neoliteralist Robbe-Grillet. It's a fascinating film, however, even though its apparent modernity conceals a profound academism. If Resnais were German, *Marienbad* would be a masterpiece. There are some brilliant tracking shots! Eisenstein would love *Marienbad*. It's the magical peak of a post-Hollywood cinema – and would it have existed before *Lola Montès* (1955) by Max Ophüls? The latter is an extremely modern film and one of the masterpieces of cinema. I saw it in a museum, with Nelson Pereira dos Santos and Zelito Viana, and Nelson loved it. I think that not even Godard would be as great had he not seen *Lola Montès*. An example of complex-ridden and infantile cinema is that of François Truffaut. *The 400 Blows* (*Les Quatre-cents coups*, 1959) is a sincere film. But *Jules and Jim* (*Jules et Jim*, 1961) quickly became dated, and after *The Soft Skin* (*La Peau douce*, 1964) I had no further interest in seeing Truffaut's films. He has now already entered into high-end commercial cinema. A good, anti-intellectual, sincere and poetic director is Jacques Demy. I very much enjoyed *The Umbrellas of Cherbourg* (*Les Parapluies de Cherbourg*, 1964), the only film of his I have seen. Demy is a gentleman and Agnès Varda is a delight: I liked *Happiness* (*Le Bonheur*, 1965). I lost interest in Chabrol. Malle is talented. Malle is trying to transform himself – he's a rich man, he has no interest in social standing like Truffaut. *The Fire Within* (*Le Feu follet*, 1963) is a bourgeois man's confession. But *Viva Maria!* (1965) is very funny. Chris Marker, who is a very strong character, made some excellent films. *The Jetty* (*La Jetée*, 1962) is an intelligent and appropriate film. The scripts are literary, but isn't *nouvelle vague* a literary school of thought? The great thing about the *nouvelle vague* is its love of and respect towards cinema. This is due in a great part to the *Cahiers du Cinéma*.

On Cinema

This Is How the Revolution in Cinema Is Made (1970)

We are in Gianni Barcelloni's house, where all the young proponents of world cinema passing through Rome are obliged to stop. Today, four of the greatest figures in contemporary filmmaking are here: Bernardo Bertolucci, Italian, filmmaker; Miklós Jancsó, Hungarian, filmmaker; Jean-Marie Straub, French, filmmaker; and Pierre Clementi, French, actor.

Bertolucci made his name with *Before the Revolution* (*Prima della rivoluzione*, 1964), which caused a scandal when screened during the Critics' Week at the 1964 Cannes Film Festival. The film broke with the neorealism of Italian cinema and, dealing as it did with politics, it ran roughshod over hypocrisy, cowardice and bourgeois sentiments masquerading as revolutionary spirit. It concluded that the only way out for a young bourgeois revolutionary is to break with his origins (or join the system once and for all). This film would, in the Paris of 1968, influence the so-called students of May. Bertolucci made *Partner* (1968), adapted from a novel by Dostoyevsky, a continuation of the earlier theme. A radical film in both idea and form, it was mauled by the critics and was a failure at the box-office. Bertolucci is currently finishing two films: *The Spider's Stratagem* (*La strategia del ragno*, 1970), an Italian television production based on a novel by Jorge Luis Borges, and *The Conformist* (*Il conformist*, 1970), a Paramount production based on a novel by Alberto Moravia.

Miklós Jancsó was first spotted around six years ago with *The Round-Up* (*Szegénylegények*, 1966), but it was *The Red and the White* (*Csillagosok, Katonák*, 1967) that secured him an international viewing public. This Hungarian, who is over forty, wielded weapons against the Nazi invaders. *Silence and Cry* (*Csend és Kiáltás*, 1967), *The Confrontation* aka *Sparkling Winds* (*Fényes Szelek*, 1969) and *Winter Wind* (*Téli Sirokkó*, 1969) are other beautiful and controversial films by Jancsó. If Bertolucci is a rebel still in search of a style, Jancsó's fame rests on his creation of an original style of filming and directing actors. While developing experiments by Antonioni regarding the use of space and objects in scenes, Jancsó has practically destroyed the story, the plot. Instead, he makes films out of the evolution of characters, landscape, architecture, colours and sounds. The rhythm of his films is closer to music than the theatre, but all this aesthetic finery is not abstract and it seeks to put forth a revolutionary thesis: bureaucracy

Revolução do Cinema Novo

strangles man, freedom is a very high price to pay for progress, the revolution needs noble and pure men and not corrupt moralists etc. Thus, when considered within contemporary cinema, Jancsó reflects much more than he protests. His films are either adored or loathed – there is no middle ground. At the moment, he's in Rome, preparing a Hungarian-Italian co-production of a historical film of five one-hour episodes.

Jean-Marie Straub is another case in present-day cinema. A Frenchman, he deserted the army during the Algerian War and was exiled in Munich. He is married to the French filmmaker Danièle Huillet. Straub exploded onto the scene in 1965 at the Festival of Pesaro, with an hour-long film called *Not Reconciled* (*Nicht versöhnt oder Es hilft nur Gewalt, wo Gewalt herscht*), a 'pamphlet-film' and a political reflection on the rebirth of Nazism in Germany. The subject matter was strong, but it was Straub's filmmaking style that upset the applecart with the critics. He destroys any notion of spectacle, all the famous 'notions of cinema' that a critic or spectator might have. He simply uses actors, with their backs to the camera or in profile, who remain stiff and motionless, and he films the sounds – that's the secret! For Straub, cinema is something physical, concrete. In his simple, desperate language, this translates as: immobile actors in dialogue of a sophisticated literary quality. In extremely long, static takes. Movement derives from the rhythm of speech. In Straub's cinema words become music. And music became words in his next film *The Chronicle of Anna Magdalena Bach* (*Chronik der Anna Magdalena Bach*, 1967), an aesthetic biography of the composer. There are several static scenes where, along with a few brief interferences from dialogue, we see nothing but orchestras performing concerts by Bach. For Straub, the only way of filming the life of a musician is to film his music, 'because his music is his words'.

After Bach, Straub completed *Othon* (1969), an obscure tragedy by Corneille filmed in Rome, in a German-Italian co-production. Filmed in colour, the actors recite the unabridged text of the play against the backdrop of ancient Rome. With its complete simplicity in terms of wardrobe and scenery, the film, according to its author, seeks to awaken in the public a love for the wonderful language of Corneille. In *Bach* we heard the music of Bach; in *Othon*, we hear the verses of Corneille. The neutrality of the image and the dynamism of the sound are the great contributions made by Straub to invert and open up new paths towards the future of cinema.

On Cinema

Pierre Clementi is the actor made famous by Buñuel in *Belle de jour* (1967), the one who plays the crazy scoundrel who ruins the life of the heroine. Clementi comes from a theatre group directed by Marc'O, a young director who decided to put an end to the traditional monotone formalism of French actors. An international celebrity after *Belle de jour*, he created an exceptional double character in *Partner*. His fame increased and Hollywood beckoned, with its large contracts. Clementi resisted bravely and had a severe psychological crisis. He was hospitalized, he split up with his agent, he turned his back on commercial success and joined the American group Living Theater. Clementi is one of the rare cases of an actor who doesn't want to be a star, who doesn't want his name in lights, who doesn't want to adopt his own image in the mirror. His break with the 'commercial system' has transformed him into a rare case. Clementi is for Europe today what Marlon Brando was for America yesterday.

These four men are in Barcelloni's house and it's the early hours of the morning in Rome. They speak and I listen (and speak too).

[Straub] I hope the film industry comes to an end, for good. The film industry is run by gangsters who buy the conscience of writers, photographers, directors, actors, ad-men and critics. They force onto the public products that are absolutely pornographic. I say pornographic not because they deal with sex, but as an aesthetic concept, as a philosophical reflection, as a moral conclusion. Industrial cinema preaches conformity, false beauty, false art, all the while giving the impression that it's 'making art'. Even intellectuals, people with good taste, get sucked into the disguised pornography of Hollywood. One recent example of successful pornography is *Midnight Cowboy* (John Schlesinger, 1969). Hollywood carefully constructed a montage of every little aesthetic and dramatic effect of European and American cinema and they sell it as if it were art. It's as if I were to sell an imitation of a Rubens claiming it to be the genuine article. The bourgeoisie buys fake works of art thinking that it's art. This, for me, is pornography. And I prefer recreational pornography, the sex films that are screened in the *bas-fond*...

[Glauber] But the film industry will not end so easily...

[Straub] Even if it ends or not, today or tomorrow, I will keep hoping that it ends. I am filming on the margins of industrial cinema, filming as people paint, write poetry or music, with no interest whatsoever in commercial consumption. If I have financial difficulties, that's my problem. What is serious is having to sell your art to industry, admitting that cinema is like the potato industry. All these conceptions result from the fear of artists to assume their condition as artists, from the great hypocrisy of thinking that success with the public that industry offers you is genuine artistic success. If all filmmakers were aware of this, and decided not to serve the industry any longer, then the film industry would be lost, because without the intellectuals they could not make luxury pornography. And then, films would be made by artists and not by gangsters.

[Glauber] Do you think that European television will counteract in some way this commercial tyranny?

[Straub] Television is also run mostly by stupid people. They are not technicians – they are men with political positions. If the government is Christian Democrat, then the staff is Christian Democrat. If it's centre-left, then the staff is centre-left. And so on and so forth. But as it happens, TV in Italy and Germany is less commercial than the cinema, because it's State-run. It doesn't depend on advertising and so it can produce films without any commercial concerns and it can give us political and aesthetic freedom. This is a good solution, particularly because a film shown on television is seen by many more people than if it were shown at the cinema. In this sense films produced by TV challenge, in a meaningful way, the pornographic cinema of the film industry.

[Glauber] Jancsó, since you are from a socialist country with a State-run film industry, do you agree with Straub?

[Jancsó] Our problem is different in certain respects, but you cannot deny that our cinema is run, in general, by mediocre clerks who don't understand art and who believe they have the right to define public taste. The difference is that art films are being made, or rather, art is not as scorned as it is in the West. But we also have problems with censorship.

[Straub] But are your films distributed in Budapest like Soviet and French commercial films are?

[Jancsó] Distribution is programmed. There are art-house cinemas and commercial cinemas...

[Straub] Then it's the same system as in the West! The principle of *art-house cinema* and *commercial cinema* is a fascist principle, because it presupposes that the public doesn't have good taste, that only a few privileged people can see a good film. Now, what happens is that the public doesn't have the right to see good films, in New York or Moscow, because the industry puts commercial films on at the large theatres and art films in small ones. This has been going on since cinema began. The public was brought up seeing one type of film; they have been seduced by a formula of beginning, middle and happy ending, for a certain style of interpretation and a plot full of commonplaces. So, when the public goes to see a film that examines the contradictions of reality, the public reacts. They react – quite rightly – because they don't know any other language. Commercial cinema has taught the public a language which only allows them to read lies! But there is the famous test that Henri Langlois set up at the French Cinémathèque: for months, he showed to a group of children only the great art films of the cinema: *Battleship Potemkin, Citizen Kane, Sunrise* (F.W. Murnau, 1927), the films of Charlie Chaplin, Buster Keaton, and others; months later he screened a James Bond film and the children did not get it. They thought it was rubbish!

[Jancsó] In our country we make a great effort to fight against bureaucracy, to fight against the triumph of a sole concept of spectacle, and that is how the two tendencies can co-exist. My films are screened in art-house cinemas, some are shown in large theatres – it depends on the success of the film.

[Straub] The principle is wrong because it's better not to make films than to deceive the public or divide them into the *stupid public* and the *sensitive public*. What we see is that in both capitalist and socialist countries, the prejudices are the same. Everyone patronizes the public and everyone lacks respect for the public. Who can say, in a theatre with one thousand seats, which spectators are stupid and which are sensitive? The public should have the right to choose the film that they want to see. Good films should therefore be screened in large theatres and not in art-house cinemas. Art-house cinema made sense years ago, but now it's a ghetto, a form of censorship, a fascist principle for promoting cinema.

[Jancsó] For us it's different, in the sense that the commercial value is not as important as in the West ... and the revolution should evolve until it removes all conservative prejudices...

(At this point in the conversation Clementi, who had been listening quietly and drinking his vodka, joins in.)

[Clementi] The thing is that today there are 8 mm cameras and anyone can buy one and start filming...

[Glauber] Anyone with money...

Revolução do Cinema Novo

[Clementi] Yes, but it's relatively inexpensive to buy a Super-8 camera and make your film, as if you were buying a typewriter, a pen, to write a letter, a poem, an essay, a novel. This is the great freedom that cinema can give you nowadays. There will always be Hollywood and its moronic system ... Hollywood offered me a contract. I would earn one million dollars per year, but I would have to interpret idiotic roles, I would have to say lines that offended my sense of morality, I would have to assume an attitude that goes against my sentiments, I would be merely an instrument of the communication of pornography that Straub spoke of.

A female star can appear naked in a film and I'll find it beautiful, but I ask myself: if a star is paid to appear naked, to attract the public with her naked body, isn't she selling her sexual attraction to the producer, who later resells it to the public, at a much higher price? If she appears naked in a non-commercial film, then it's clear – her nudity is an existential gesture. I am against such prostitution of actors. I was in the United States, I bought a Super-8 camera and I made a film of my journey. Now I only make films that interest me and I'm becoming increasingly interested in *collective theatre*, in *tribal theatre*, in total artistic freedom. I want to be an art activist, I want my gestures and acts to be physical and mental, I want my life to be a theatre, a dangerous, prohibited one. The commercial system will die on the day that all actors do like me, and rebel together.

[Bertolucci] I don't think that the industry will die. On the contrary, I think that it will become stronger and stronger because now co-productions have begun between Italy and the Soviet Union, I mean between Italian producers who invest the money of Americans in co-productions with the Soviets. And when Mosfilm joins forces with Hollywood it will mean that a pact has been signed to exterminate Art once and for all. I'm not for or against the system, I can work within or outside the system, because I have a pessimistic vision and I think that Art is a solitary activity. That is why I agree with Straub, with Godard, and I can also agree with Hitchcock.

[Glauber] Bertolucci, did you know that in Brazil there is a theory that *cinema novo* is rubbish and Brazil should follow the example of Italian cinema...

[Bertolucci] Three of the best films of the 1960s were *The Guns*, *Barren Lives* and *Black God, White Devil*. I find it strange that a country which produces three masterpieces in ten years has a bad cinema. And anyway, cinema in Italy today is rubbish, apart from Pasolini, who is a poet, and Rossellini, who is a teacher and now only makes didactic films for television. What Brazilian critics don't know, perhaps, is that we are also underdeveloped, that Italy is an underdeveloped country, and that Italian cinema no longer exists, either culturally or economically speaking, that our entire economy is in the hands of Americans and that the only Italian producer who doesn't have American money is called Barcelloni. In fact, there is no Italian or French cinema, it's all American made in Europe!

[Straub] And European cinema made in Hollywood ... Hollywood imports the techniques of Godard and Antonioni and produces 'luxury art' like *Midnight Cowboy* or *The Graduate* (Mike Nichols, 1967). Americans, intellectually speaking, are provincial.

[Bertolucci] As I was saying, before Straub interrupted me, these days Italian cinema is the worst example of cinema that one can cite.

[Clementi] The worst thing nowadays is that most filmmakers who speak of politics, who are challenging, make pornographic films for the system.

[Bertolucci] Filmmakers should be free like Rossellini and Buñuel.

[Glauber] No producer, from inside the system or beyond, has ever dared to meddle in any film by 'Don Luis' and nevertheless he made commercial films in Mexico. When you see these films today – what great films they are! They are the greatest anthropological essays on the Latin American man. You could write two hundred-odd essays on *Nazarín* (*Nazarín*, 1959) and *The Young and the Damned* (*Los olvidados*, 1950).

[Straub] Buñuel made the best political film I have ever seen: *Fever Rises in El Pao* aka *Republic of Sin* (*La Fièvre monte à El Pao*, aka *Los ambiciosos*, 1959).

[Clementi] Buñuel is a free man, a man that no one can criticize because he is as pure as if he were filming with a Super-8 camera.

(José Celso Martinez arrives and arranges with Pierre Clementi an excursion of the Living Theater to Brazil, which should take place this April.)

A week later, in Barcelona, I meet Pere Portabella, the most important independent filmmaker in Spain. And he lucidly concludes this conversation about the future of cinema: 'I am filming with ten thousand dollars, with five thousand dollars. Now we have TV cameras and soon we

Revolução do Cinema Novo

will have cassettes which will distribute magnetic films the way music is distributed. The system will make commercial films and we, auteurs, will make our films with magnetic film stock, and we will distribute these films as if they were books. You can buy a film on a cassette the size of a bar of soap, in a bookshop, and you take it home and watch it on TV, just as you would put a record on a record player. So art films are going to be more widely distributed by cassette than even by television. And the freedom of magnetic film will allow us to reinvent cinema, it will create a new aesthetics, a poetic, didactic, scientific cinema. Anyone will be able to make a film, to give his words, his language to cinema. Cinémathèques will become museums, like the Prado, the Louvre. We will go to these museums to see *Potemkin*, *Citizen Kane*, Chaplin, Buñuel. Within one hundred years no one will have heard of James Bond, and meanwhile there will be queues at the museums to see Chaplin, in the same way that today they queue to see Picasso at the museum in Barcelona. But the independence of cinema depends on the filmmaker, because the worst kind of censorship is self-censorship.'

An Aesthetics of Dreams (1971)

At the Seminar on the Third World in Genoa, Italy, in 1965, I presented 'An Aesthetics of Hunger', on the subject of the Brazilian *cinema novo*.

My address situated the artist of the Third World as up against colonizing powers: *only an aesthetics of violence could integrate a revolutionary significance into our struggles for liberation.*

I said that our poverty was understood but never felt by colonial observers.

1968 was the year that young people rebelled.

The 'French May' happened at a time when Brazilian students and intellectuals were demonstrating in Brazil against the military regime of 1964.

Entranced Earth, a practical demonstration of the aesthetics of hunger, was met with intolerance on the part of right-wing critics and by leftist sectarian groups.

Amid internal repression and international repercussion, I learnt the most important lesson: the artist should maintain his freedom in all circumstances.

Only then shall we be free from a highly original form of impoverishment: the official consecration that underdeveloped countries often bestow upon their greatest artists.

This congress at Columbia University is another opportunity for me to develop a few ideas on Art and revolution. The theme of poverty is linked to these.

The social sciences have supported statistics and they enable us to interpret poverty.

The conclusions of reports produced by capitalist systems see the poor man as an object to be fed. In socialist countries we witness the ongoing controversy between the prophets of total revolution and the bureaucrats who treat man as an object to be massified. *Most of the prophets of total revolution are artists.* They are people who have a more sensitive and less intellectual relationship with the poor masses.

Revolutionary art was the rallying cry in the Third World in the 1960s and it will continue to be so in the 1970s. However, I believe that the change to political and mental conditions demands a continual development in the concept of *revolutionary art*.

Ideological manifestos are more often than not simplistic. The worst enemy of *revolutionary art* is its mediocrity. In the face of the subtle evolution of reformist concepts of imperialist ideology, the artist should offer revolutionary responses that are capable of rejecting, under all circumstances, evasive proposals. And, what's more difficult, we need a precise definition of what is *revolutionary art that is useful for political activism, of what is revolutionary art at the opening of new debates, and of what is revolutionary art that is rejected by the Left and used as an instrument by the Right.*

As an example of the first case, being a man of the cinema, I cite the film by the Argentine Fernando Solanas, *The Hour of the Furnaces* (*La hora de los hornos*, 1970). It's a 'pamphlet' of information, agitation and polemics of the kind currently being used in various parts of the world by political activists.

In the second case, there are a number of films of the Brazilian *cinema novo*, including some of my own.

And finally, there's the work of Jorge Luis Borges.

This classification reveals the contradictions of an art that expresses the contemporary case itself. A work of *revolutionary art* should not only act in an immediately political way, but it should also promote philosophical speculation, thus creating an aesthetic of the eternal human movement towards its cosmic integration.

The discontinuous existence of this *revolutionary art* in the Third World is owed fundamentally to the repression of *rationalism*.

The current cultural systems, both right and left, are tied to a conservative mode of reasoning. The weakness of the Left in Brazil is the result of this colonizing vice. The Right thinks according to the logic of order and development. Technology is the mediocre ideal of a power that doesn't have any ideology other than the domination of man by the need to consume. The responses of the Left, and my example is drawn once again from Brazil, were patronizing in relation to the cultural theme of political conflict: the poor masses.

'The People' is the myth of the bourgeoisie.

The reason of the people becomes the reason of the bourgeoisie about the people.

The ideological variations of this patronizing reason can be identified in monotonous cycles of protest and repression. The reasoning of the Left turns out to be the heir of European bourgeois revolutionary reason. Colonization, at such a level, rules out an integral revolutionary ideology that would find its chief expression in art, because only art can get close to the depths of the human dream allowed by this comprehension.

The rupture with colonizing rationalisms is the only way out.

The vanguards of thought can no longer support the hollow victory of responding to *oppressive reason* with *revolutionary reason*. Revolution is the *anti-reason* which communicates the tensions and rebellion of the most *irrational* of all phenomena which is *poverty*.

No set of statistics can demonstrate the full dimension of poverty.

Poverty is the principal self-destructive burden of any man and it has psychiatric repercussions which transform the poor man into a two-headed creature. One head is fatalist and submits to reason which exploits him as a slave; the other, as a result of the fact that the poor man cannot explain the absurdity of his own poverty, is naturally mythical.

The dominant *reasoning* classifies mysticism as *irrational* and it represses it at gunpoint. According to such reasoning, everything that is *irrational* must be destroyed, whether it's religious mysticism, or political mysticism. Revolution, as the possession of a man who follows an idea, is the highest point of mysticism. Revolutions fail when such a possession is not complete, when the rebel doesn't free himself completely from repressive reason, when the signs of the struggle are not produced at a level of stimulating and revealing emotion. And when, *still triggered by bourgeois reason*, method and ideology become so confused that they paralyze the transactions of the struggle.

While *unreason* plans revolutions, *reason* plans repression.

Revolutions occur in the unpredictability of historical practice which is the encounter of the irrational forces of the poor masses. The political seizing of power doesn't necessarily imply revolutionary success.

One must touch, through communion, the weak spot of poverty which is its mysticism. This mysticism is the only language that transcends the rational scheme of oppression. Revolution is magical because it's the unpredictable within dominant reason. At best it's seen as a comprehensible possibility. But revolution has to be impossible for dominant reason to comprehend, so much so that it denies and devours itself when faced with the impossibility of understanding it.

A liberating irrationalism is the revolutionary's most powerful weapon. *And liberation, even in violent encounters provoked by the system, always means a denial of violence in the name of a community founded on a sense of limitless love among mankind.* This love has nothing to do with traditional humanism, the symbol of the dominant clear conscience.

The indigenous and black roots of Latin American people should be understood as the only developed force on this continent. Our middle classes and bourgeoisie are decadent caricatures of colonizing societies.

Popular culture will always be a relative manifestation when it's merely inspirational of an art that is created by artists who are still suffocated by bourgeois reason.

Popular culture is not technically folklore; it's the popular language of permanent historical rebellion.

The encounter between revolutionaries detached from bourgeois reason and the most significant structures of this popular culture will be the first configuration of a new revolutionary sign.

To dream is the only right that cannot be prohibited.

The 'Aesthetics of Hunger' was the measure of my rational understanding of poverty in 1965.

Nowadays I refuse to speak of any such aesthetics. Life itself cannot be subjected to philosophical concepts. *Revolutionary art* should be magic that is capable of seducing man to the point that he can no longer bear to live in this absurd reality.

Borges, overcoming this reality, wrote the most liberating unrealities of our time. *His aesthetics is that of dreams.* For me it's a spiritual enlightenment that contributed to dilate my Afro-Indian sensibility in the direction of the original myths of my race. This race, which is poor and apparently without a destiny, elaborates in mysticism its moment of freedom. The Afro-Indian gods will deny the colonizing mysticism of Catholicism, which is the witchcraft of repression and of the moral redemption of the rich.

I do not justify nor explain my dream because it has its origin in the increasing intimacy with the subject of my films, the natural meaning of my life.

Columbia University – New York
January 1971

O Século do Cinema

The Century of Cinema

Chaplin

[1]
The first incarnation of Charles Chaplin, a phase that began with him filming in Hollywood in 1914 and ended with *The Immigrant* and *The Adventurer* in 1917, is the revolutionary antithesis of Griffith.

Chaplin played an adventurous immigrant, outcast and worker, wearing repressed popular masks in order to unmask the capitalist carnival.

The second Chaplin is unveiled from 1925 onwards, through *The Gold Rush* (1928), *City Lights* (1931), *Modern Times* (1936), and concluded with *The Great Dictator* (1940), when, upon finding himself repressed in the United States, he began the process of idealistic regression, leading to the death of Charlie and the birth of the anarchic bourgeois character in *Monsieur Verdoux* (1947), *Limelight* (1952), *A King in New York* (1957), and *A Countess from Hong Kong* (1966).

Chaplin tells the story of a European proletarian immigrant who enacts through cinema the humanist revolution of the people.

The capitalist State was Cyrus/Chaplin's Babylon: Presidents, Ministers, Senators, Judges, Deputies, Priests, Ministers, the Army, the Police, Bureaucrats, Shopkeepers, Businessmen, Manufacturers, Proletarians and Alienated Outcasts were all attacked by Charlie, who confronted the weapons of physical violence with the violence of psycho-political comedy.

O Século do Cinema

Just like Cyrus, Chaplin diverted the course of the river and, through his methods of production, he introduced his message while the State lost itself in wars and partying.

The cinema of Chaplin, richer in its expressiveness than traditional art forms and the theatrical/Romanesque cinema of Griffith, was made from the point of view of the oppressed character up to the point of *A King in New York*.

The only film which Chaplin made from the point of view of the oppressor was *A Countess from Hong Kong*.

Charlie, assassinated in *The Great Dictator*, reacts weakly in *Monsieur Verdoux*, as Calvero, The Clown, the King without a crown, where he eventually disintegrates.

Charlie, the materialist, is transformed into Chaplin, the idealist, projected through the actors Sophia Loren and Marlon Brando, the imperialist couple.

The cinematographic power of Chaplin unleashed great psycho-political unrest between 1925 and 1940.

Did the humorous language used by Chaplin contribute to the awakening of the revolutionary conscience?

The question is not exhausted by the scientific word which attempts to imprison the poetical metaphor in a laboratory of probabilities: Chaplin illuminates the twentieth century because through him the People are given Image.

[2]

> Charlie, My and our Friend, Your Shoes and your Moustache Travel a
> Road of Dust and Hope (Carlos Drummond de Andrade).[1]

[3]

At 68 years of age, after the five years of silence which followed *Limelight*, Charles Chaplin returned, to ask for peace, with his new socio-political satire, *A King in New York*.

Being over 50 and having lived through two world wars and because he wanted a third to be avoided, Charlie, The Tramp, continued to suffer persecution from the reactionary press and to be hated by the paranoid holders of atomic energy.

The North Americans, and in particular the cinemascopic Hollywood, trembled and roared against his genius, while the cowards and 'intellectuals' tried to reject him with anaemic arguments.

Chaplin, both the Man and the artist, remained impassive, loving, above all, the values of Humanity.

It was the same resolute enemy of technology, who sought, through poetry, relief from the wounds inflicted on him by the machine.

His attitude as a filmmaker – turning his back, as much as possible, on sound, colour and the big screens – or his political attitude – showing in *Modern Times* the machine destroying the man – are proof of his fidelity to the pure image, to the expressive force of cinema under threat and proof also of his horror of soulless capitalism.

Chaplin was the keeper of eternal values and for this reason he turned his back on false originality, on artistic masturbation and on the pseudo-innovations of an Art which only through him became the full expression of life, and which continues to live thanks to rare geniuses like him.

Attempting to position him as merely a filmmaker doesn't do him justice; Chaplin is an artistic complex which transcends cinema.

[4]
Modern Times, 1936, silent film.

Here I will quote the historian and critic, Georges Sadoul:

> Charlie had chosen to portray, in *Modern Times*, a rather new profession: he was a worker in a factory. The film presented itself, in its opening scenes, as 'the story of industry, of individual industry, of humanity in search of happiness.' Then the workers go to their jobs like sheep to the slaughter. Later in the film, jobless, Charlie leaves the psychiatric hospital and wanders the streets. He picks up, without thinking, a red flag which had fallen on the ground. Behind him the people become inflamed with passion, and thus begins a demonstration. The police accuse him of being a troublemaker and arrest him. Prison reminds him of the factory, but he feels that he is being treated more humanely behind bars.[2]

The scene with the 'red' flag (perceived even though the film was made in black and white) was enough to see him accused of being a communist by the North American capitalists, armed with the religious codes of censorship and preservation of public morals. They reacted mainly against the artist who was fighting against the destruction of man by machines; against the HEARST press, WALL STREET and the Nazism of DR GOEBBELS. In Hitler's Germany, *Modern Times* was banned and Chaplin was accused of plagiarizing a film by René Clair, *À nous la liberté* (1931), produced by Tobis Studios in Paris, which were part of German business trusts. In this manner, American Democracy united with German Nazism to tackle Chaplin ...

The infamy of the accusation was shattered by statements by René Clair who claimed he 'felt honoured to have contributed to the work of someone who he considered a genius and his greatest source of inspiration'.

The relevance of *Modern Times* remains unaltered. The eternal protests against the humiliation that economic bodies have put man through have not died. Chaplin, whether embodied in Charlie, The Tramp, or Calvero, The Clown, or The King who goes to New York to ask for Peace, still remains in those who Carlos Drummond de Andrade describes as 'dirty with sadness and angry disgust at everything/who entered into the cinema like rats fleeing from life [...] and discovered you and thus were saved'.[3]

Welles

If Orson Welles challenged cinema as an instrument of creation, it was not due to his lack of belief in the cinematographic event itself.

His indignation stems from the impossibility of having at his disposal the methods with which he could reach a New Dimension, the interpretative region still unattainable from human existence on earth.

When we talk about the 'imponderable' which the camera can discover and which the editing can create (make 'ponderable', 'real'), many people see this as a utopia or a 'formalist' attitude as if this 'formalism' were somehow reactionary.

The search for the cinematographic 'imponderable' was never an isolated game of form on form, shot on shot, nor of light on light, even though such abstract conflicts may have an important role as the best example of non-figurative modern painting.

The possibility of a formalist cinema is rejected because its own and uncontainable power to create, through conflict, an unpredictable problem, leads even the intentional game of form for the abstract form's sake to create an Entity.

From there (*and in the cutting room we can clearly see that the theoretical principle takes place in reality*), we can break away from narrative-literary cinema and move towards cinema in which the camera and the editing CREATE a cinematic dimension to the subject matter and don't simply TELL a HiStory already existent in literature.

After Eisenstein, there never was a filmmaker as cinematographic as Orson Welles.

To those who see the importance of the involvement of cinema in social conflicts and on the human psyche, this observation becomes fundamental in order to crush the pejorative accusation of formalism.

If Eisenstein was the main interpreter of the Russian Revolution and of the radical transformations brought about by socialism, OW was the main interpreter of imperialist tragedy.

His favourite theme was power as manifested in men, in the manner of Eisenstein in *Alexander Nevsky* and in the Ivan films: *Ivan the Terrible, Part I* (1944), and *Ivan the Terrible, Part II* (1945).

OW took up the position of vigorous attack on man as corrupted by power and always toppled this *Dictator* with the force of someone who knocks down and destroys a worm.

This denouncement goes as far as his overthrow through cinematographic symbolism, even though the theme continues after the plot ends.

OW doesn't interpret a transformation in the manner of Eisenstein, because the revolution Eisenstein portrays didn't take place in the United States.

But OW 'provokes' in the film this overthrow, he opens up the possibility of revolution without dogmatism, strong in his belief in the complete and inhuman corruption of those in power.

Welles detests and destroys the newspaper magnate in *Citizen Kane*, just as he does the Police Captain in *Touch of Evil* (1958), and Othello, Macbeth, Arkadin and buffoons like Falstaff.[4]

He demystified genius and turned into the alter ego of the United States.

Could OW be as powerful if it weren't for 'his style'?

Hollywood ousted OW.

In Europe he filmed Kafka, a metaphor for the true story of the Amberson Kennedy family (*The Magnificent Ambersons*, 1942; *The Trial*, 1962).

When Orson Welles filmed *Citizen Kane*, the United States was allied with the Soviet Union in the war against Nazi-Fascism.[5] *Citizen Kane* is the successor to *The Great Dictator*.

It is the tonal and dramatic montage of the psychological movement of its characters who remain unaware of the materialist process of History, within an alienated nature and an alienating set design.

Kynema is a total language due to the imaginary unpredictability manifested more frequently in audiovisual than in literary language.

The narrative editing produced an illusory effect of History which caused the theorist André Bazin to perceive, in the depth of field, a psychological space which shuts out the social time of History.

André Bazin overvalued the tonal dramatic montage (internal montage of literoplastic origin) and idealized the external montage as both a divider and unifier of time of the neurotic mise-en-scène within the deep focus shot, a technique developed by Orson Welles in *Citizen Kane*.

Class struggles are absent from the process which leads Kane to inherit a fortune, marry the President's niece, present himself as candidate for State Governor and create something aesthetic from the figure of his failed opera-singer wife.

Welles makes a psychological rather than an economic criticism of Kane, a metaphor for imperialistic phallic power, but he explains economic power through frustrated political paranoia.

Rosebud is a Psychological Theme, instead of class struggle in the United States, which is a Hitorical Theme; it's a focus on the infrastructure, and it's Kane's motive, which coincides with the nuclear explosion of *Ivan II*.

In the cinematic flow of Kane, the class struggle is reflected in the mystic psychology of the auteur/character, who doesn't refer to it because he holds the slave in contempt.

The proletariat is the conscience of the narrator as interpreted by Joseph Cotten, Kane's alter ego, the old and poor Rosebud in the happy retirement home.

In Welles's depth of field, inter-imperialist contradictions are being processed.

A capitalist may kill another capitalist but he can never destroy the system, which must be defended against the absent ghost of the proletariat.

Kane, the imperialist, dies and Welles filmedits the psychological reconstitution of Kane's story, identifying in the indecipherable mythironanism[6] of Rosebud a cosmetaphoric process of characters.

The dialectic limit is established through the method of rhetorical investigation that leaves intact the myth of Rosebud.

The Kubexpressionist editing of *Citizen Kane* brings to light a circular concept of History full of sound and fury, told by an idiot, signifying nothing.

It is the Shakespearean climax, the Othello/Caliban of Welles.

German expressionism creates a phenomenological aesthetic whose function is to mask History with the language which, in Hollywood, substitutes economics, sociology, politics, psychoanalysis, linguistics, anthropology and philosophy for the psychoidealist of Freud, social space without social time.

It's Quinlan,[7] it's Arkadin, it's Macbeth, it's Othello, it's Falstaff, it's Don Quixote, it's the Devil, it's Kane, it's Roosevelt, it's Truman, it's Rockefeller, it's Julius Caesar, it's Hitler, it's Stalin, it's Welles!

James Dean – Angel and Myth

James Dean, a young angel poorly coloured on celluloid, an adolescent at high speed as well as a man obsessed with mechanical oblivion, released with his death the *enfants terribles* without flowers, suns and rhythms.

When myths assume such proportions it is necessary to break through the barriers of the flourished legends which still exist, in order to dissolve both form and formula in gestures of spasm and pain.

James Dean saturates the tradition of myth and invades the space of desires.

A rebellious angel and an unsatisfied demon tormented by an unconscious Oedipus complex (his young mother cradled him and then gently vanished from his childhood), Dean smashed the tarmac and rode right over the curves in the road in search for life's meaning through every driving moment of his life.

As his eyes were weak, his spirit reached a goal and a car of polished steel, a racing car to cradle a genius (substituting, with its unbalanced

rhythm, his mother's arms) crashed through the wind and liberated the boy from his anguish, making his escape with his black leather jackets and faded jeans, crowned with unkempt medusa locks of hair.
Dean Was Not An Ordinary Star.
He is the symbol of a generation with no morals to obey and which took shelter in the refuge of formulas.
He railed against the idea of judgement over feeling and for this reason he loved animals and machines.
He carried within him a *mal de vivre* and was never surprised by death.
He was well versed in tragedy and precipitated it with one hundred and seventy kilometres an hour of inexplicable things.

> James like Joyce, Byron like the crippled poet, Dean like me ...
> – JAMES BYRON DEAN.

David Lean

David Lean, author of works inspired by Charles Dickens such as *Great Expectations* (1946) and *Oliver Twist* (1948), and of an endearing film, *Brief Encounter* (1945), also produced, amongst other works, a trilogy of comedy, lyricism and epic poetry in *The Sound Barrier* (1952), *Hobson's Choice* (1954) and *Summertime* (1955).

The lyricism, hand in hand with the epic and with humour, transcends and envelops everything which is touched by Lean's hand. It's the predominant feature, the nervous system around which the diverse characters gravitate.

In *Hobson's Choice*, a British comedy set at the beginning of the twentieth century, we are met with a predominant note of cynical humour enveloped in geometrically structured formalism. Therein, man is left exposed by his other side; we see the ridiculous mixed together with seriousness; a piece where the puerile and the tragic emerge both strong and fleeting. It's an extraordinary piece of work due to the human warmth and faith invested even in those who are imbeciles. A moving story, for it's told with love: that of a humble cobbler, a good man, dedicated to his work but illiterate, who is projected forwards into the world of business steered by the arm of a woman who wants him to be strong so she can love him better. The film's ending is a gentle lesson in humility: the son-in-law ends up dominating his father-in-law's (his ex-boss's) business, whereas the latter, the drunken Hobson, searches for an alternative way forward, in the same way in which he tried to reach the moon that jumped and escaped from puddle to puddle, all the time mocking him, an old, funny and drunken fat man.

Lean creates through this humorous sequence not a portrait of the schematic British mind but rather a universal moment of cinematographic poetry. The heavy Hobson (Charles Laughton's majestic creation), sodden with wine, tries to capture the moon, which is sleepily reflected in a muddy puddle. When the old man leans over the puddle, the moon hops into another, through skilful use of the camera. The sequence is almost entirely composed of pans and tracking shots.

There is a harmony of movement between the camera, the moon, the puddle and the actor, who together perform an unprecedented choreographical sequence. The musical score also emphasizes, through its hopping movements, the moon's rhythm. The old man Hobson huffs and puffs in pursuit. The moon, even in the mud, remains unobtainable. Hobson gives up, exhausted, and the stars once again take up their resting position in the dirty water.

In *Summertime*, cinema turns a city for the first time into a character, both shining and alive. The lyricism within its architecture is captured in detail and composed piece by piece, leading eventually to the formation of the poetic finale: the solitude of the woman lost in the overpowering architecture. Venice is clothed in beauty and the woman is wrapped in solitude.

It's the lyricism which flourishes, not tearjerker storylines nor dramatic embraces and not light-hearted ditties sung under the breath, tricks used by so many mediocre directors.

Infinity, supersonic jets and man's moral fibre are the central themes of *The Sound Barrier*.

First infinity, the white clouds of human ideals.

Man with his eyes and his very being focused on space.

Man himself tries to overcome the never-ending scheme of desire and conquest aimed at both humanity's salvation and its downfall.

In Terence Rattigan, the axiological or ethical problem is non-existent given that the 'ideal' is the central nervous system.

The only contentious issue is the concretization in pure form of this ideal, of the profound ideal, unfettered and beyond any imposed design.

The audacity of the pilots is almost incidental, as is the supersonic jet. What's vivid and what's interesting is that which transcends the bare framework of the drama, the essence as dragged from the core, the triumph of intelligence over nature; the honesty of the ideal. And then what? The spontaneous ideal: the ideal for the ideal's sake with no need for ethical hierarchy.

While people argue and accuse him, John Ridgefield, strong man of the telescope and the sky (the very image of an Idealistic Macho Man), lives a secure and alien existence in the eyes of his daughter, and the life of a visionary in the eyes of his son-in-law. He is also a figure of fear for his son who dies in order to 'uphold' the tradition of manly suicides on the air, following in a long line of sacrifices.

John Ridgefield does not waiver. On two occasions – when he hears the recorded voice of his son-in-law on the verge of death and when he asks about 'his' guilt – he verges on the pathetic; a super-man, he thus overcomes the problem of morality. Sacrifice and love join together and complete one another.

The epic ends with victory and with the acceptance of the absolute ideal with no barriers, just like the sky itself, in the souls of those who understand grandeur.

Revealing, as an authentic British filmmaker, his documentary tradition, David Lean reaches his defining moment in cinema, creating the modern-day epic. We are, perhaps, in dangerous territory in defining *The Sound Barrier* as a bi-epic. And even more so if we call the epic of the ideal a metaphysical epic. However, if we were to search within the problem and the exaltation of the ideal, which first Rattigan and then Lean worked with and raised high with exceptional artistic and philosophical ability, for a field of action, then this field would be concentrated on entirely metaphysical ground.

And it's to find something 'beyond the material' that John Ridgefield lifts his telescope. He doesn't want to conquer and go beyond the sound barrier. He wants to reach, propelled forward by an ideal which ordinary men judge to be homicidal, the transcendental mystery of the cosmos.

In order to achieve this, the first step is to break the sound barrier, launch oneself at supersonic speed and then travel beyond the speed of light, for the definitive conquest of space, time and eternity.

This is where the epic surges forward. The heroic pilots, young and possessing the courage for self-sacrifice, even if they are still unsure 'why' they are taking this path, defy the sky and send shockwaves through History. When the jet at its peak 'dominates' the European continent, Lean cuts to shots of the forgotten monuments of Greece or of Rome.

The leaning columns and the busts of solitary marble remain impassive and chewed up by the centuries, in magnificent close-ups.

Does one have to interpret such a pivotal moment?

Nonetheless, over and above the epic, lyricism once again takes flight.

The solitary and swift jet in the infinite and yearned-after space at times reminds us of the solitary woman of Venice.

Everything about David Lean is grandiose.

Juvenile Delinquency

A rich subject, the theme of young people without hope and without a cause, would, due to its novelty, charge and need for release, provoke new experiences in cinematic language. This would be more a consequence of the creative process than due to the necessity of determining a new form. The preponderance of the theme itself as determining the form is debatable; not that the latter is executed in a rigid, mathematically induced manner; the fundamental elements are born of the theme in a more evolved fashion by way of an elaborate plot, a story to be told from a specific angle.

The formal resources emerge from this.

The filmmaker varies the rhythm and the image from that of literary material, thus extracting from the process a truly creative dimension; it's where the novelist and the scriptwriter end and the filmmaker begins: the graphical transposition of a literary image or situation marks the boundary between literature and cinema.

Such considerations are prompted by the new language appearing in Hollywood in films made on the subject of rebellious youth. We need to take into account some consideration of 'formal characteristics' and 'cinematographic language'. This becomes vital in order not to view criticism as a mystery and to see it instead as a form of explanation; we are partisans of didactic criticism.

In Hollywood, three genres – 'Crime', 'Western' and 'Musical' – characterize the history of American cinema. With the involution of these

O Século do Cinema

genres, for various reasons, a sense of quest was born, awakening the ambitions, albeit disorganized, of some young filmmakers. A film is qualified by its theme and form. The conceptualization of form in cinema involves the use of both mechanical elements and aesthetic concepts. To achieve a greater conceptual frame we need to look deeper into the importance of the external contributions received by cinema from other art forms.

Cinema, according to the first filmmakers, is the art of synthesis. Nevertheless, later on it was possible, with the input of Eisenstein (*Battleship Potemkin*, amongst others) and Carl Dreyer (*The Passion of Joan of Arc*), to discover, feel and see the rhythm in cinema as a language, from the crafted and exacting approach of the Soviet cinema to the laidback approach of Italian neorealism.

If cinema possesses its own individual expression, independent from that of other art forms – as could be demonstrated by a cinema based on abstract figures in time and space – it would be wrong to see the concept of cinema as a 'snapshot' of various artistic elements wrought around a literary plot. Due to commercial pressures – cinema is the art of complexity – it follows that purity within it is an impossibility.

Cinema cedes position to other arts even though it comes close to poetical creation itself: an art which is only recognized when it appears as figurative and visual lyricism within the film.

Cinema has a grammar.

The problem then is to achieve the poetical over and above the theoretical, which is the focus of the emerging science of Filmology.

The rhythm of the editing is The Film Specific, just as the symbol is The Poetical Specific.

The other arts are accessories which can be dispensed with at a later point, when the emotional content is fully realized in the image.

Cinema possesses two fundamental expressions: (a) rhythm of images; (b) dynamism of synthesized arts.

The first is the sequence of shots linked with the interpretation of the scene and the film's plot. The second is the internal rhythm, the ground on which subjective realism can emerge.

Onto the latter is imposed, in conjunction with the former, the style of the filmmaker.

External and internal rhythm together steer a film, together create 'cinematographic art', cine-aesthetics.

On Cinema

The Wild One (Laszlo Benedek, 1953), *Blackboard Jungle* (Richard Brooks, 1955) and *Rebel Without a Cause* (Nicholas Ray, 1955) are not imitations of each other.

What they shared were running themes which determined similar situations: the troubled young man, violence and a visual representation in the figures of Marlon Brando and James Dean, characteristics of a genre bursting forth in search of definition. Just like the cowboy in the Westerns remains true to form within the genre in his visual representation: the leather waistcoat, the scarf around the neck, the large-brimmed hat, guns in holsters etc., the rebellious youngster has trademark features which distinguish him from ordinary youngsters: unruly hair, sideburns, blue jeans, leather jacket etc.

Alongside the running theme, and more significantly in terms of cinematographic rhythm, there emerged a formal characteristic which followed certain variations throughout the three films.

We're talking of that which the Brazilian critic Cyro Siquiera called 'choreographic realism'.[8]

In the Western, founded by John Ford, a slow, marked rhythm dominated, which denoted nostalgia and the unchartered plains of the West. The caravans were always shown travelling across the prairies in sweeping shots accompanied by sombre music: thus the rider came and went in an undecided fashion, with no fixed route, taking the drama with him as he went.

The rhythm only quickened when the situation required it: brawls, gunfights etc. A languidness in activity was the predominating feature and, if we go back to a more recent film, *Shane* (1953) by George Stevens, we observe the still atmosphere of the countryside and of the sleepy towns in repeated fusions, punctuating the film *ad infinitum*.

In modern films on juvenile delinquency, the rhythm follows a variation which is the direct opposite of the *Western rhythm*. It's agitated in order to reflect the desperate temperament raging in the rebellious and violent youth. As much in the shooting of scenes as in the light, sound and movement of the actors, the anguish is manifest.

From the slow panoramic shots used in the Western, we move on to rapid, nervy cuts, swift tracking shots, and the actors follow a ballet rhythm; they dance more than walk or run. There is harmony between the camera and internal elements. A new rhythm styled on the dominance of rock and roll: a style of music with a key role to play in youthful irreverence.

Let's look at *The Wild One*, directed by Laszlo Benedek from a screenplay by John Paxton and produced by Stanley Kramer. The initial shot of the approaching motorbikes denotes organized violence: the motorbike is the symbol of unity and speed.

From this initial linear advance, the bikes branch off in all directions and act in accordance with the psychological situation of the characters. In the sequence of the chase of the girl, the bikers begin to circle and the enthralling terror moves closer, surrounding the girl, who spins round and round, 'dancing' to the roar of the motors.

In *The Wild One*, we see the appearance of the first symbols which will later come to serve as the formal basis of the juvenile delinquency genre in the United States, post-Korean War.

The Wild One takes up an important position in the history of film. It doesn't just encapsulate the initial trend for 'choreographic realism', a style of language, of rhythm: it brings a perspective to the theme, it explores it with new courage, it extracts from it the most complex manifestations of humanity and within it stand forward, acting as a vestment of tragedy, the symbols of the motorbike or of the black leather jacket with its back emblazoned with the inscriptions and classifications of the young people wearing it, in their rebellious advance against nature, gratuitously predisposed to disorder. Moreover, there is the symbolism which Laszlo Benedek created through sound, with the noise of the motorbikes and the slang used by the boys, staccatoed with shouts and bebop music, later replaced by Richard Brooks with rock and roll in the film *Blackboard Jungle*, a sound which echoed the state of mind of the young people, and which was substituted by Nicholas Ray in *Rebel Without a Cause* for one with a more tragic content.

Of these symbols, only the leather jacket would be retained in the two subsequent films: both Brooks and Ray did without motorbikes. The leather jacket, still present but more subtly employed in *Blackboard Jungle*, acquired something more than simply a formal presence in *Rebel Without a Cause*, in the same way as the presence of the revolver in Westerns. In the latter, the leather jacket attained a mystical status and emerged as a key symbol of tragedy.

On Cinema

Laszlo Benedek, director of *Death of a Salesman* (1951) by Arthur Miller and of the dreadful *Bengal Brigade* (1954), developed the cinematographic language of Hollywood. What we saw up until this point, even in films of other genres, was a conjecture on themes, and this denoted a lack of variations in the plot, of nuances that could become a new shoot of originality.

An increase of characters, situations, or even of a new 'style' of acting (see actors launched by Elia Kazan), served to conceal the point of saturation at which the main American directors found themselves. The tools employed were brought from literature and theatre. The rhythm and the narration remained static at the peak which had previously been reached. A preference for filmed theatre or, better put, for 'cinematographic' theatre, began to conceal the crossroad which had been reached. We then had, amongst others, *A Streetcar Named Desire* (1951) by Elia Kazan, *Come Back, Little Sheba* (1953), by Daniel Mann, *Detective Story* (1951) by William Wyler and *Death of a Salesman* by Laszlo Benedek.

Benedek exploded theatrical limitations and introduced a background in which narrative theatrical dialogue is replaced with images. He managed to sacrifice acting – a theatrical tool – in favour of expression through image. All we have to do is remember Vivian Leigh and Marlon Brando in *A Streetcar Named Desire* and Shirley Booth in *Come Back, Little Sheba*, to see the intentions of the directors in their support of the actors' interpretation. If we count up the great American classics since 1945 and those which came before, we can see that the appearance of this film had a much greater impact than its '*precursory quality as a film about rebellious youth*'; it reached the position of a cine-aesthetic point of reference.

It's not the vibrant rhythm, the propensity towards choreography of movement, which enriches *The Wild One*; it's the '*feverish realism*' which bursts through the moroseness, the repetition of compositions and internal struggles. Working with new human material, different from the gangster, different from the cowboy, different from the serene middle-class citizen, was the violent rebel without a cause. Benedek extracted his rhythm from this new reality and transferred it to cinema in a revolutionary conception of Italian neorealism.

And if in neorealism the basic initial intention was simply to transpose reality – and from there was born the formal untidiness which would come

O Século do Cinema

to determine the decanted 'anti-formalism' of Italian cinema – in the form of Laszlo Benedek – *a man and not a movement* – there existed an aesthetic interpretation of reality which made 'choreographic realism' a movement which was eagerly followed by Richard Brooks and Nicholas Ray, and which might be able, thanks to the new perspective it opened, to inspire even more daring achievements.

Blackboard Jungle, scripted and directed by Richard Brooks, would not maintain the same artistic level as *The Wild One*. Regardless of the erroneous content of *Blackboard Jungle*, we can still find, in the field of action, a pretentious language which didn't truly take advantage of the lessons shown by Benedek.

Nicholas Ray, conversely, carried out poetically the intentions of Laszlo Benedek.

In *Rebel without a Cause*, the characters do not tiptoe like ballet dancers but they do dance to a music which was neither bop nor rock, but instead a music which obeys psychologically functional variations. Further to this rhythmical fulfilment, we also see the achievement of the Poetical in the symbol of the leather jacket, which moves from being a simple prop to having its own role in the film.

The motorbike is replaced by the flick knife and the furious cars, even though the visual performance does not possess the same stance, the belligerent and imposing flair imprinted by Benedek. The car moves forward like a new triumph, a mechanical symbol and an instrument linked to delinquent youth. It's an intense rhythmic symbol like that of the modern furore of the leather jacket appearing and breaking the monotony of the suit jackets, dressing the rebellious youth as an unexpected angel. And the colour of the jacket, black or red, serves to further confirm the protest because it provides a shocking contrast to the suit jackets and grey shirts: the colour of choice of the discreet American man (as Nunnally Johnson tried to prove in *The Man in the Gray Flannel Suit*, 1956), the colour of the ordinary man with an office job.

Neither are the socks uniform; they are different, a sign of refinement, a necessary attitude to have, given that the object is the scandal. Colours and pure violence are necessary, authentic, poetic.

Three sequences in *Rebel without a Cause* hang suspended like choreographic spasms: the knife fight featuring Buzz and Jimmy, the stolen car race to death between the two, and the final scene of pursuit.

In the first, the camera and the two fighting men dance around each other. The panoramic shot is favoured over the cut, which is only used as an emotional indicator. The fight is danced in a round, the two men leaping in time, their arms flailing. The camera flits from narrator to interpreter.

In the second, the race to death, two furious cars are driven towards a precipice; the editing is edgy, a shock rather than a flow (the antinomy of Eisenstein and Pudovkin) which also works as an interpreter.

In the third and last sequence, the pursued and their pursuers perform fantastic leaps, trace unexpected circles and assume a studied position. The editing moves in a progressive chain of events, growing in a measured dose of cuts and movement interspersed with a violent pan from right to left, which uncovers a policeman firing a revolver. The police cars arrive in an organized fashion and park in a strategic location. The policemen jump out quickly, ducked down. There is no room for doubt: what we are seeing is a new method of scene creation, a mise-en-scène which sits opposed to the simplistic and overused cinematic arrangements of the past.

Johnny (Brando), star of *The Wild One*, differs from Jim (Dean) in *Rebel Without a Cause*. They are both heroes born of the same theme but headed in different directions.

Violent young men, enthralled with dangerous adventures, rebels without a cause, disorientated, lost in American post-war society, nihilistic adolescents, devils clothed in vivid colours.

John Huston – Physical Technique and Aesthetic Technique

Always discussed primarily for his uncompromising independent take on themes, more than for his artistic talent – an aspect of his work already seen as absolute – John Huston is vying for the position of best filmmaker in Hollywood, part of the vanguard of filmmakers which includes William Wyler, Robert Aldrich, Billy Wilder, John Ford, George Stevens and, very new to the scene, Stanley Kubrick, as well as around half a dozen more who not only prevent the regression of cinematographic language but actually fight for its advancement and discover within it the best of its possibilities. Mainly from that angle is John Huston of enormous value to American cinema. However, he's also extremely important to the evolution of this

O Século do Cinema

new language in the face of the limitless phenomenon of cinematographic thought, both in the practical realization of this language as well as that which he provides as raw material to filmology discussions in the area of pure cinematic thinking.

John Huston is a filmmaker who plays an active and vigorous role in the realm of culture – the political or philosophical or sociological or psychological, whichever it may be – but he is also a stylist: man and cinematographic form, all equal to the filmmaker who, while dominating certain forgotten corners of the mind, is also defining his work in the parallel sphere of the 'physical technique' and the 'aesthetic technique', two revered monsters of cinema which, if not integrated, will rip apart the talent of filmmakers.

Heaven Knows, Mr Allison (1957) surges forth in cinemascope, vanquishing, without doubt, the fear which up until now was terrorizing the most enterprising of filmmakers such as William Wyler or Fred Zinnemann, to name but the authors of *Detective Story* and *High Noon* (1952), two flat-screen, black-and-white classics.

With regard to Huston finally embracing cinemascope, as pointed out above, we make a distinction, at first sight strange, between 'physical technique and aesthetic technique'. From this angle, of more direct importance to cinema, let's discuss *Heaven Knows, Mr Allison*, given that morals and reproach of a social or religious nature are out of place in objective criticism, and should be left for commentary of a doctrinal character.

Cinema can be distinguished as an art born of developing physical principles and of the necessary investment in the object of animation, that is, the moving image. There are other minor problems, indispensible, albeit small, to the technical body of the film: lighting, cinematography, framing, depth, composition and set design are all applied according to certain basic principles. This resulted, with the flat screen, in the reduction of the field of vision, the 'physical technique', which without doubt dictated certain aspects of the 'aesthetic technique'. We are seeing a continuance in the close-up, which is as much part of the vocabulary of cinema as the other shots. Yet, with cinemascope, the widening of the screen results in a certain amount of fuzziness at the edges, the 'physical technique', and this doesn't allow for the dramatic intensity of the 'close-up' itself, which has already lost its unity.

Heaven Knows, Mr Allison is important in John Huston's career firstly for its use of cinemascope and secondly in its demonstration that the phenomenon of cinema cannot create any problem insurmountable to artistic expression.

In the transcendence of the artistic phenomenon of creation, when the most conscious craft receives a breath of unconscious inspiration, the technical obstacles of the mechanism are destroyed by the determination of the imagination.

John Huston thus takes on cinemascope and its mise-en-scène challenges and overcomes them simply and exclusively with the specific and objective intention of telling a story about two characters on an island. And he does that without ever growing tired or falling into the trap of creating forced situations.

Stanley Kubrick

Stanley Kubrick, a new filmmaker who has bowled over critics with just two films on global release, the first, *Killer's Kiss* (1955), and the second, *The Killing* (1956), has appeared as a new ray of hope for American cinema. He is what critic Maurício Gomes Leite called 'a seventy-minute filmmaker', that is to say, short films, common process, flat screen, black and white, budget production, B-List actors, modest set designs.

In *Killer's Kiss* the plot takes a back seat: what's important is the cinema on cinema dimension. It's a work of visual power, of rhythmic expression, the grandeur of which was often not fully understood. In this film, the following points can be observed which reveal the revolution in cinematic language:

(a) The boxing match. Critics believed that after *The Set-Up* (1949) by Robert Wise the theme of boxing as a base for editing and framing exercise had been exhausted. However, Kubrick creates new angles and goes further than Wise. While the director of *The Set-Up* relied on the visual and psychological objectivity of the fight, Kubrick creates the fight as follows: initial shots of boxing gloves. An abstract view of the audience which seems compact, dark and disfigured in an establishing shot; the animal sound of the voices is barely audible. The boxers face one another and therein begins a slow fight. Without a sound the hands move heavily across the ring, flailing, reaching a crescendo until an abstract shot of a crazed, demented image is created, which only highlights, as an element exterior to the fighters themselves, the lights which shine directly into their eyes. The editing thus creates a cinematographic rhythm which arises from a real rhythm (the movement of the sparring men).

(b) The second fight at the end of the film, between the boxing hero and the gangster in a shop-dummy factory. Returning once more to the theme of violence, Kubrick creates another editing, this time with a psychological slant. The first fight, as detailed above, was a one-on-one for financial gain: a boxer fights in return for a salary. The fight in the shop-dummy factory, however, is on the level of emotional violence. The cause is self-defence and revenge. The motive, therefore, is psychological. The editing, for that reason, is not made up of rhythmic shocks but of a slow and detailed narrative of the fear felt by each of the adversaries faced with his armed foe. The images move slowly, like shadows in the sea of shop dummies, grey men illuminated by Kubrick himself who, in this film, is also cinematographer as well as editor, director, producer and screenwriter. The reflections of the fight are objectified in the images of the shop dummies which seem to be actively participating. Cuts on faces in the most varied of human expressions create a state of perpetual agony which doesn't end until the death of one of the opponents, in this case, the gangster, as the structure of the story is true to that of the classic American crime genre.

Through this exercise in search of pure filmic expression, Kubrick launches the premise of a new cinema.

Kubrick is revolutionary because he breaks with the traditional line of direct, chronological narrative, going backwards in a predominantly dramatic time, running the risk of destroying the rhythm of suspense, desired and vital to the film's ending itself. In the assault sequence in *The Killing*, three parallel actions take place at once: (a) the fight in the bar intended to attract the attention of security guards in charge of the money; (b) the killing of the horse on the racetrack by a professional marksman, intended to distract the public's attention; (c) the entry of Johnny, the robber, into the office where the safes are, where he goes on to steal two and a half million dollars.

Delivering a direct blow to the emotions of the public, Kubrick takes two decisive courses of action; the fight in the bar is told from start to finish and concludes with the stealthy entrance of Johnny through the door through which the last security guard had left to go and deal with the troublemaker. From there Kubrick doesn't follow Johnny's story; the action is interrupted in its main plotline as if the image had been frozen, and then the action goes back in time to a few hours earlier, showing us the marksman preparing to shoot the horse, up to the fulfilment of the act ending with the killing of the criminal by a racetrack guard. From there, Kubrick cuts again to the last scene of the first sequence (of the fight), and starts to recount the tale of the robbery with Johnny already in the offices, covering his face and armed with a machine gun, throwing a bag full of money out of a window which we don't see from the outside. Later on, when the other thieves are talking about the robbery, one of them states: 'The bag was thrown to me.' The scene is cut and the dialogue interspersed with a shot of the window viewed from the outside, from where the bag falls, in a continuation of the interrupted scene.

It is at that moment, thanks to this show of disrespect for the cinematographic monster of time and continuity, that Kubrick, who had behaved so well, who was secure in his well-constructed editing, even so far as making it dignified, for having rested the film's narrative and climatic suspense within it, emerges as a filmmaker who has caused the critics to pause and fully consider the possibility that there was something new afoot in the Kingdom of Hollywood. This time it wasn't the exuberant talent of Robert Aldrich (more courage than creation); it was instead something warm, visually rich. Kubrick is a disciple of John Huston, influenced by the fever of Orson Welles.

But it's not only in this revolution in the narrative in which Kubrick's style reveals its inner workings: on a par with the external editing of the narrative is the interior rhythm of the film, the composition, the role of décor over and above that of the decoration. Here we see the inheritance from Orson Welles which he himself had, in turn, learnt from the visual richness found in the cinema of the past: the lesson of how light can be a key tool in the editing, not as in darkening a part of the image, but as in the light composing and decomposing the face of the actor in the internal editing.

A lampshade is present in the majority of the interior shots, focusing the light directly onto the faces of the actors. When a character moves away

O Século do Cinema

or moves back, according to the dramatic intensity of the scene, the light REVEALS or CONCEALS their face.

In the sequences at the racecourse (given that the film revolves around a robbery on the day of a big race), we still note the abstraction of the image which is achieved with panoramic shots of the horses running, underlined by the hard sounds of hooves and shouts; as the speed increases, the image resists up to the point of its total abstraction.

While he toys with the image and keeps an eye on the mounting psychological tension, while he shuffles the editing to the point of making the viewer suspect that the film's projection is inverted, Kubrick films the racecourse in sweeping aerial shots, converting it into a dark mass already abstract in human terms, and which doesn't get involved in the small drama of crime and dream taking place: that is why we are not treated to any close-ups of the spectators.

The horses are only of interest as a specific narrative tool: at the beginning they underpin the theme and at the end they are used as a tool to facilitate the robbery. What is instead vibrant and pulsating with life and which furnishes us with the angle which is of key human interest at the racecourse (the result of the bets) is namely the four-sided loudspeaker, through which announcements are made. The loudspeaker also offers a visual counterpoint to the sequence, one of the most complex and homogenous seen so far: it's a mass of relentless, never-ending narrative shots, where nothing is rushed: and it's from there that Kubrick reveals the craftsman within him, straying far from the easy solution and building an atmosphere using shots of the loudspeaker, always returning to the image from above, which also serves as a counterpoint in sound.

Kubrick is so calm, so profound; always searching for the humanity in each individual, and he does this without the demagoguery, the pseudo, tiresome psychologism so in fashion in modern cinema.

There is a dream in all men: that of richness, inherent ambition. How then does man meet his downfall? In two ways: the first due to error and criminal ambition, thief robbing thief like in *Rififi* (*Du rififi chez les hommes*, 1955) by Jules Dassin. In a shocking turn of events, the thieves who, after the robbery, wait for Johnny with the money are visited by another group of bandits brought into the fray by one of the thieves' lovers. A sudden gunfight sees everyone killed and this is followed by one of the most beautiful camera 'surveys' we have ever seen: it's the 'cinematographic experience of death'. The camera moves in a strange way, attached to a crane, descending on each dead face, and we feel the profound irony of what it was that killed these men: the dream of land. This is now the second misfortune to befall Johnny, once so full of hope, now able to find the irony in every detail of life. Here, Kubrick moves forward even in the philosophical dimension.

The end is both poetical and bitter: millions of dollars flutter through the air at an airport, propelled by the engine of a plane: the very same plane which would save Johnny and his wife.

'Why flee?', Johnny asks when he realizes his misfortune. He does not flee. He waits for the police, embracing his wife. And when the police, armed with guns, advance from an establishing shot to a close-up, the film ends in a crescendo.

The downfall and the same bitter taste as that of *The Treasure of Sierra Madre* (1948) and *The Asphalt Jungle* (1950) are both present as a lesson given from Huston to Kubrick: 'The gangster is like a flower planted in tarmac: it doesn't flourish because the ground is dry.'

A great war film is one which seeks peace: *All Quiet on the Western Front* (1930) by Lewis Milestone, an example of the classic war films of the past, *Attack!* (1956) by Robert Aldrich and *Men in War* (1956) by Anthony Mann, could all be considered as the most important in war cinema, successors to *Grand Illusion* (*La Grande illusion*, 1937) by Jean Renoir.

Any comparison between *Paths of Glory* (1957) with other films of the same theme, in terms of the level and type of outcry, cannot be borne out to any real degree, since Kubrick doesn't denounce the violence within a war but the inhumanity of the army institution. It's also made clear from the start that it's not only the French army which is being accused here: all armies are, because the situations in which the characters find themselves are situations in which any officer could find himself. The men in charge humiliate, persecute and destroy their subordinates in a blatant show of savagery under the cover of law. On this point, Stanley Kubrick is incisive, direct and clear. Colonel Dax, a figure of justice, represents the ideal army man or rather, a man who is just, exact and heroic, who recognizes the courage of his men and who considers injustice within the armed forces to be shameful, not only from the point of view of a military man but also from the point of view of a human being: 'There are times I am ashamed of being a member of the human race,' Dax (Kirk Douglas) proclaims, when the execution sentence against the three soldiers is pronounced.

Stanley Kubrick can take any theme and make it the starting point from which to denounce man and his circumstances. Kubrick denounces both good and bad, never taking a political stance. In *Paths of Glory*, we become aware that the young director is an irreverent rebel and that he cannot resist the temptation of telling certain truths using the voices of his characters. Colonel Dax speaks as if he were the voice of Stanley Kubrick himself: a voice of indignation.

Taken from this aspect, at least from the outside, *Paths of Glory* should be viewed as a war film. From other, more profound angles, we may well consider it to be a film whose theme is not limited to the military, social, historical or political. It has a universal subject matter: inhumanity, given no specific location in History, but rather all the evil which has been innate in man since the beginning of times, and which is revealed through a war or in the hearts of officers. It could, however, just as easily be an injustice committed in any class, just as we see in our everyday lives and which we could identify in past events.

The plot of *Paths of Glory* is as follows: a French general orders Colonel Dax's regiment to take a well-defended position from the Germans during World War I. It's an impossible task. The attack is well countered and the French are forced to retreat. In order for the event not to have a demoralizing effect on the army and in order not to attract any criticism from the press towards the army bigwigs, two generals engineer a crime: they shoot three soldiers, having charged them with cowardice. This would serve as an example and it would thus be proven that the regiment was defeated from within, due to the cowardice of its own soldiers, and not due to the French army's weakness when faced with the Germans. It is a courageous plot and we can see in its outline that Stanley Kubrick has adapted it from Humphrey Cobb's novel[9] and transformed it using the visual dynamics of cinema.

And this cinematic creation can be observed in *Paths of Glory* in the following sequences.

The sequence in which the three soldiers go out on a reconnaissance patrol. The sound is created by pulsating drum rhythms countered with the staccato of machine guns, two sounds which join together, one transmitting the real noise and the other the imagined, psychological noise.

The pulsating sounds are like the pulsations of fear. The daring alternation of the editing between fusions of grand establishing shots and grand close-ups. In the establishing shots, we see the battleground and its dark ruins. Between the dead and the destruction, diluted within the scenery, the three soldiers advance. In the close-ups we see the images of fear. The individualization of man when faced with death in the depth of the violent night. Even the pulsating sounds rise and fall. Then a dangerous spot, where one of the soldiers is heading, is revealed in an establishing shot composed of a violent alternation of light and darkness, filled with smoke, hellish. This shot is held, interspersed by the close-ups of the two soldiers waiting for the third. This slow and profound game within the editing of 'hell' (the establishing shot of the destroyed ground where one of the three soldiers is killed) and fear (close-up shots of the two soldiers staring at 'hell') leads to a point of saturation in cinematographic time, which coincides with the psychological point of saturation within the soldiers/characters. Fear then explodes. The cinematographic time is that which reduces real time to dynamic time or rather, in which the facts become important for their nervous or dramatic importance. However, more daring directors penetrate into the analysis of time and follow an event faithfully, showing it as it would naturally unfold. Once the duration of time is broken, it's important to take control of the editing in order that this daring does not result in something incomprehensible or monotonous. Kubrick, in this sequence, even though he doesn't completely follow real time, creates a psychological time and alternates it with his cinematographic time until the two (an image which becomes insistent and a fear which becomes inevitable) explode the film specific.

Western – Introduction to the Genre and to the Hero

The hat is wide-brimmed. The gun of never-ending bullets is drawn at the speed of lightning. The horse is black or white, steadfast even when faced with the greatest danger. The fists are both swift and strong. The star on the chest is the symbol of good.

The cowboy comes from a place unknown to man and boy; he appears at the end of the prairie under the blazing sun, moving through the dry curtain of dust. He hums a tune, sometimes sad, he talks to a woman, he talks of a land...

The horse brings the man to a close-up and a myth is born and grows. Shots are fired as inexplicably as HE appeared. The stagecoach being pursued is carrying a pretty girl, the travelling salesman, the bad man, a rich man from the city bringing sin to the West. The masked bandits – sometimes with black handkerchiefs on their faces, sometimes with plumes and wearing war paint – must be defeated. HE draws his guns, aims well, each shot meeting its target. The song is no longer on his lips; it comes straight from his heart and wins over time, dominates the prairie, it's a variation which moves to the rhythm of the bullets.

Evil cannot resist HIM. The bandits flee. They will return to fight another day. HE is gallant. He wins the heart of the young girl, provokes the hatred of the bad man and earns the affection of the travelling salesman.

In town HE is idolized by the children. Because one of them is killed HE places the star on his chest, bursts into the saloon through the swinging doors and shoots down the light. HE overturns the card game table, takes on thirty men, knocks down the braggart. The head of the group challenges him to a duel. HE is courageous. For the heart of the girl, for good, in order not to lose the admiration of the children and for many more things besides, in order to uphold the myth that cannot be shattered, because all men believe blindly in the infallibility of the hero, HE accepts the challenge to a duel even though he knows for certain that there are more guns slyly pointed at his back.

The breaking dawn sees a deserted street. The same strained music returns, fearing for our hero's life. HE MOVES FORWARD, his steps are sure, his eyes are fixed on a point far in the distance. The moment is worth an almost unperceivable gesture which results in the firing of various shots. The music hesitates, the hearts of the men and boys taking refuge in a darkened room miss a beat.

When the bad man keels over and falls, we see a smile of release.

HE is indifferent. He takes the star off his chest, gets back on his black or white horse, and, leaving the woman he loves, goes forth to the ends of the earth.

He will return the following week for new arrests and new releases.

The Searchers

The Western, the first and only crystallization of the social aesthetic in American cinema, has, in the figure of John Ford, the person responsible both for its evolution and later its maturity. The Western, as a regional genre of the United States, is a testimony and dramatization of the events of the great march forward of the settlers, travelling deeper and deeper into the great country. Later it told the tale of the social positioning of these pioneers, their social adaptation, of their fight against feudalism which so quickly took root, already a dominating force and which found itself faced with a growing consciousness in the smallholders who were beginning to join together to defend what was theirs. It was a genre which asserted itself primarily through its poetical import: the intensity of the myth embodied in the legendary hero of good, shining forth in the fight against evil, born of the spontaneous good spirit of rural folk.

Once the essential foundations of the Western had been laid down, the cowboy, given that the genre evolved at the same time as the cinema industry itself, lost his innate dignity and began to take on attributes from other areas which diluted him within the genre, making him no more pure than the common man, no longer like Tom Mix or Habel William S. Hart or others who came and went, always defeating their enemy, loving from afar and drinking milk, much to the astonishment of the barman.

But if the hero regressed, the genre gained new perspectives, wide social and human aesthetic horizons. The Western is that which American cinema possesses as an authentic force, something pulled out of the earth trodden by its ancestors who tumultuously entered the Civil War, an event which radically changed the country's economic landscape and brought about an enormous imbalance, characteristic of a postwar environment.

The Western is the blood which runs through the veins of the American man; it is American popular culture, its ethical and religious formation, that which is impenetrable.

Everything else, far from the settler's epic tale, is no more than a rickety coastline, with its dirtied version of humanity.

The Western contains a moment of cultural instability. The land is being tamed and within it the heroes and the bandits take the position of good or bad in the fight for the creation of a nation. From out of this subject matter, rich in so many aspects, American cinema extracted, right up to the current point of saturation within the genre, all that which was left of upstanding humanity after the massacre of the Indians and black slavery.

The discovery, the perception and the assured dominance of the theme, in terms of its details and subtleties, provided a handful of filmmakers with the opportunity to make cinema of specific and particular formal fulfilments in terms of the rhythm and the language, at the moment when the plot began to obey that familiar structure along the lines of the hero who comes from afar, lives, fights, overcomes difficulties and, at the end of the film, leaves for that same 'who knows?' from whence he came.

From amongst these filmmakers, John Ford appears as the main figure responsible for the evolution and maturity of the genre. He established the fundamental principles of the influence of nature on man, of a man immersed and struggling in a developing society, of the visual and symbolic illustrations of characters hidden behind the myth of the gun, the horse and the sheriff's star badge.

In the Irish genius, the social aspect overcame the poetic even though the latter existed more as an accidental rather than an essential consequence. After *The Searchers* was released (1956), we are forced to revise our viewpoints, both with regard to the position of the poet and the sociologist, as well as with respect to references of the decline of the filmmaker, not only in terms of the genre, but also in terms of cinema. In *The Searchers*, the characters react like pieces acting in defiance of their craft, in a manner which is much more than a technical exercise, as Ford was by this point already a mature man in full control of his life and who had learnt his art, not through formal observations, but through the essence of humanity, all of which was spontaneously portrayed in a cinematic language which carried the mark of a mature artist, of a fulfilled inventor.

The Searchers is enough proof of his intentions to show the frontier society of the United States made aware of its role of taming the land and constructing a future upon it, in the face of inhospitable conditions. It also shows the imbalances which this struggle provokes as well as the groups born from it as a social structure is built.

However, if in *The Searchers* the sociologist is present, it is the poet who flourishes most vigorously: he surpasses the former because, while the sociologist situates, demonstrates and explains, a poetic shadow begins to separate our hero from the rest, elevating him to his mythical position, revaluing him in the manner of Shane by his creator George Stevens (*Shane*), getting lost in the vastness. By the way, this flight of the hero – evoked as commonplace but which is not so – is always taken up again by the great filmmakers from a different angle. Even in *High Noon* by Fred Zinnemann, wherein the hero is more cerebral both in his conception and in his behaviour, when he leaves, in a manner contrary to the norm (his destination certain and with the woman he loves), there remains, however faltering, a sense of yearning behind him.

When we accuse Will Kane, the hero of *High Noon*, of faltering, we are not completely inferring that he is weak when compared with a good hero on horseback of the kind which began with the 'Tom Mixes' of this world, a character who died and was reborn in the figure of Shane and is now reshaped in Uncle Ethan, by John Ford.

Here, even though the cowboy is brought back and becomes solid once more, he is no longer as pure as he was. Today's cowboy is valued in terms of the pureness shown by his predecessor.

Shane, as well constructed as he may be, is not pure in that same primitive sense. He carries upon him the mark of deliberation. He is, as invisible as it may seem, intentionally stylized, even though he is more coherent and integrated in society. This is something we already explained and insist upon. At first there was the hero, then came artistic and economic progress within cinema; then the genre appeared, larger than the language, the rhythm, the specificity of cinema; the filmmaker needed to eliminate the hero for his own gain; then he needed a morality and looked again for a hero; he tried to resuscitate him and instead made him into a caricature of himself; the filmmaker fought on and Shane was born, a lyrical return but never again that freedom of movement across the prairies, that rapid movement across the countryside, a pure movement, so much so that it gave to cinema, by way of the genre and through the genre, its poetic climax.

John Ford is responsible both for the epic Western – *Stagecoach*, and for the historical Western, *Fort Apache* (1948).

The New Western

Gunfight at the O.K. Corral (1957) breaks through the barriers of the psychological-choreographic Western (begun with *High Noon*), and creates a new characterization of the genre. Retaining the fundamental themes of the form (the opening ballad, the internal rhythm of the characters and of dynamic elements) to the most minute level, John Sturges searches for and achieves a way out of the formal sense in which the form had fallen, due to the constraints that it had begun to acquire, resulting in the genre reaching saturation point.

Framed and created in an expositional narrative structure replete with paragraphs which existed in fact but not in theory, later made compulsory due to the sheer quantity and persistence of diluted versions of Fred Zinnemann's *High Noon*, the psychological Western (or the anti-Ford-epic par excellence), precisely because it avoids the non-rationalized movement of the director of *Stagecoach*, could be seen as a conjunction of basic primitive Fordian elements, as well as elements from romantic or crime thrillers, resulting in a more intellectual category of film: the psychological Western born out of the choreographic essay.

Classically, the compulsory structure (just like quartets or trios in sonnets) of the opening ballads, of the solitary rider, of a situation marked in time (wherein the tension was built right up to that very moment), of a gun duel in the dusty street, followed by the departure, was being decomposed into sub-structures of which the third category was *Shane* by George Stevens, wedded together with the existing synthesis already achieved by *High Noon*.

In this way, the growing complexity of the Western took the directors on journeys which led them to identical visual and rhythmic solutions. The variations became exhausted. The films became even more ludicrously stylized and repetitive, with criticism also becoming saturated, committed from the start to the cinematographic autonomy of the genre in relation to the other methods of the seventh art; it knew how to accept this formal refinement/exhaustion as a supporting tool of its own conceptualization as classic cinema. The more worn out it is, the more it adjusts itself to the emotive power achieved through this or that framing or audio explosion. By the way, the mechanics of shock (a montage of analogies and contrasts in the internal and external rhythms of the film) became, despite maintaining the fundamental steady compass used by Ford, a constant indicator of easy modes of expression, not satisfactory in themselves but by what the Western in essence brings to each detail: the myth that still endures, even when its intentionality resides in the ludic aspect displayed by the movements of equipping and firing, blooming from an agonizing cinema that inaugurates new forms of communication.

As a film containing all the details and supporting tools of all variations, we will take as an example *3:10 to Yuma* (1957), by Delmer Daves. It contains the situation marked in time (within the framework of the narrative), the portrayal of the solitary, good-hearted bandit (in the mythological sense), the railroad track, the classic burial and the narrative ballad. Thus, it brings together the influences of *Shane* and *High Noon* in what was an excellent example of the final testament of a genre which had reached, by way of folding to internal thematic temptation, a level of exhaustion, satisfying to the point of heralding its extinction.

Regardless of the exact chronology of *Gunfight at the O.K. Corral* in the general landscape of the Western in the last three years, with it a new type within the genre is created: that of psychological realism, which substitutes the psychological-choreographic.

John Sturges, having exhausted in *Bad Day at Black Rock* (1954) (a new historical dimension in the Western and almost a new dimension in the Western style) several items in the repertoire of the so-called shock montage, of the arid atmosphere, of the upwardly spiralling psychology and choreographic staging, would find himself theoretically prepared to resist the new and yet repetitive lures in order that, returning to the same theme, but now placed in a different time, he was able to propose an execution of a film which could go beyond those exhausted limits. In *Gunfight at the O.K. Corral*, he did away with the shock montage which could not fit the events of Leon Iris's plot concerning the strange friendship between the gunman, Holliday and the sheriff, Earp. Given that violence works simply as an outward, tangible expression used to vindicate the internal existence of complex humanity, the editing couldn't ever embody another role other than that of a soothing compass (and even more so when the subjective psychological constant was pacific rather than ferocious).

In *Bad Day at Black Rock*, the syntax of cinematographic violence achieved a rare objective in modern Hollywood cinema, that is, the analytical tension of the characters, their behaviour developing horizontally in the passage of time and vertically in terms of psychological behaviour, without once resorting to the abuse of the dramatic pieces, a tactic which could have been employed in order to guarantee the success of

O Século do Cinema

the film by way of superficial shock. John Sturges knew, creating a new Western in terms of historical time, social context and poetical nature, how to apply the tools of choreographic realism (a chapter in cinematographic expression in which the technique of craftsmanship – aesthetic – is directly conditioned by the physical technique) to the point where, from the point of view of cine-aesthetics, he exhausted these tools for himself, aware of their saturation. With little of interest in his career between *Bad Day at Black Rock* and *Gunfight at the O.K. Corral*, we can still point, in a less successful Western, *Escape from Fort Bravo* (1953), to an accentuation of a language within the film which demonstrated his rejection of the craft of physical technique in cinema, preferring instead, through the editing (aesthetic, as already explained) to search for the rhythmic sense, something which later flourished in *Gunfight at the O.K. Corral* – the arid atmosphere, the long, mournful days, the double salvation/perdition of man told through a style anchored on establishing and panning shots.

In *Gunfight at the O.K. Corral*, John Sturges begins with the tried and tested opening scenes: the opening ballad, the yellow landscape against a blue sky. After this, inside the saloon the editing is relaxed (both in the use of the camera shots and that of the whole scene itself), breaking with the traditional rationale so painstakingly applied: the bandit shouts in a violently abusive way, without being a complex muttering character in the manner of Kazan. *Gunfight at the O.K. Corral* evolves, once the first part of the film has been vanquished, which still suffers in some parts from the influence of *High Noon* (like, for example, the entrance of Wyatt Earp into town, advancing sombrely in a slow panning shot, as if propelled by the narrative of the ballad, a valuable accessory, even though it sits at odds with the film specific, as it is an authentic way of telling the stories of the old West). The mechanical rationalism jumps (or flows?) to something close to the conceptualization of an Eisensteinian montage (the multiple interior shock, subjective, similar to that of the explosions of an engine, bringing with it a poetical maturing etc ... see *Film Form*):[10] moving within the restraints of the rhythm, in the absence of sound, in the manner in which a ball of yarn unwinds in silence, and thus moving towards a powerful epilogue (the gunfight at the O.K. Corral).

Sturges, in Eisensteinian mode, whether consciously or not, objectifies every small dramatic explosion which has taken place so far (like the initial pursuit by Earp and Holliday of three bandits, the invasion of the town by oxen-drivers, the humiliation to which Ringo submits Holliday, the death of Earp's brother, the attempt by Holliday to kill his lover) by following a logical path which has previously been laid down in advance, which already anticipates the interruption by dissonant compasses to the fluidity of the structural rhythm. It's for this reason that *Gunfight at the O.K. Corral* advances Western film form forward a category – the abrupt/internal interruptions in its fluidity, like a motor that changes its outlet without halting its action. This is best demonstrated, more than in the film as a whole, in the final sequence of the gunfight itself. Time slips away in the utter silence of the scene. The gunshots, the first audible denunciation of violence, signal pure barbarity. As this barrier is overcome, with Holliday realizing the passionate nature of the shooting (he decides himself to kill Ringo, using a bullet to pay the debt of the humiliation he has been subjected to), and on the other hand with Earp going out in search of the young gunman who embraced crime as an antidote to solitude, the music irrupts as a central theme of the O.K. Corral.

It could be seen as an ordinary tool of interference, but, incorporated in the events which unfold within *Gunfight at the O.K. Corral*, this music gains an aesthetic dimension.

Gunfight at the O.K. Corral brings together certain cinematographic lessons about human nature (of the spiritual, as spoken about by Jean Epstein), mainly in the configuration of the tragedy which involves Doc Holliday and his lover, played by Jo Van Fleet.

In terms of cinema as an autonomous art and more specifically where a story is staged in a completely different way from the theatre, there is a dimension wherein the actor functions as an image/piece of the internal editing, which, using Maria Falconetti in *The Passion of Joan of Arc* by Carl Dreyer as an example, can be seen to a much lesser degree in Holliday, as embodied by Kirk Douglas.

The level achieved by James Dean as Jett Rink – a character of utter fragility in the script of *Giant* (1956), by George Stevens – is a similar example of this.

It is not the interpretation of the scene by the actor, but rather his visual presence which condenses and creates the tragedy and comedy in the overall view of the anti-discursive staging of the film. This goes beyond the concrete interpretation driven by the editing, the cinematographic specific as shown by Eisenstein in *Film Form*, and something which has been taken as a theoretical accessory by the concrete poets in Brazil: an element which neither announces nor explains the object but around which is created a visual rhythmic existence; and from here the object speaks for itself; this is the cinema of imagery, like the extreme close-up shots of Falconetti in Carl Dreyer's film.

And within the new Western, which is *Gunfight at the O.K. Corral*, can be found humanism, in the sense that the film transcends the psychological constraints of the genre. The solitary rider has lost his mythical status. The time has come for complex heroes: within whom lie anguish, solitude and the necessity of communicating using bullets or caresses.

The 12 Commandments of Our Lord Buñuel

[1]

> Witchcraft blocks the doors of the church.
> The priests are paralyzed. The faithful strangely held back.
> People explode into the squares. The cavalry charge.
> While the masses fight the fascist police forces, the bells ring out.
> A flock of sheep, tame and servile, walks in the direction of the temples.[11]

[2]

The last damned soul in a cinema which was lost in the hysteria of artistry, Luis Buñuel was born in Calanda in 1900 – part of the same generation of Spanish sons which included Lorca, Picasso, Ortega y Gasset, Miró, Alberti, Dalí – and it was with the latter that he began his cinematographic career, directing *Un Chien andalou* in 1929.

Educated by Jesuits in his adolescence, he then attended the University of Madrid and afterwards moved to Paris: *Un Chien andalou* was his passport for acceptance into the Surrealist group.

When *L'Âge d'or* was shown in 1930 the conservatives threw a gas bomb into the small cinema in the Quartier Latin, and tore down the paintings exhibited by Max Ernst, Man Ray, Miró, Tanguy and Dalí.

In 1961, *Viridiana* was awarded half a Palme d'Or[12] at the Cannes Film Festival. Franco's censors went berserk, began legal proceedings, fired civil servants and managed to turn the Catholic world against the film.

Figure 3.1 Glauber Rocha and Luis Buñuel (Montreal, 1967).

In France, Malraux said that he could not ban a foreign film which had won an award in Cannes; it was a ruse: even though he is Spanish, Buñuel is considered by the critics and the public alike to have a 'French spirit'.

Between *Land Without Bread* (*Las Hurdes*, 1933), a documentary on a poverty-stricken Spanish region, and *Viridiana*, when he returned to work in Spain – Buñuel's career was adventurous and fortuitous: he moved between France, the United States and Mexico; he made archive documentaries; provided dubbing for American studios; and transmitted anti-Nazi radio speeches.

Fifteen years after *Land Without Bread*, he met the Mexican Oscar Dancigers,[13] who offered him commercial films to work on. Buñuel accepted and began, in Mexico, a film production marked by three masterpieces: *The Young and the Damned*, which received a prize for Best Direction at Cannes; *Robinson Crusoe* (1952); and *This Strange Passion* (*Él*, 1953).

Even when making commercial films, Buñuel managed to insert a little of his personality: he directed an old project, *Wuthering Heights* (*Cumbres Borrascosas* aka *Abismos de pasión*, 1953), based on the novel by Emily Brontë (1847), and *The Criminal Life of Archibaldo de la Cruz* (*Ensayo de un crimen/La vida criminal de Archibaldo de la Cruz*, 1955), based on a novel by Rodolfo Usigli.[14] In the same year, 1955, he returned to France and filmed *That Is the Dawn* (*Cela s'appelle l'aurore*). He returned to Mexico to make *Death in the Garden* (*La Mort en ce jardin*, 1956), but by this time he already carried some weight in the industrial process and was able to enjoy the freedom he had been waiting for for twenty-eight years, since making *L'Âge d'or*.

Nazarin was explosive at the Cannes Festival (1959) and won the prestigious Prix du Jury. *Fever Rises in El Pao* aka *Republic of Sin* slated the small fascist republics of South America. *The Young One* (1960) won a special award *hors concours* at Cannes. 1961 was the year of *Viridiana* and 1962 the year of *The Exterminating Angel* (*El ángel exterminador*).

[3]
When responding to journalists, Buñuel is frank:

> Bourgeois morality is, for me, immoral, something which should be fought against. It's morality founded on our unjust social institutions including religion, the fatherland, family, culture, or rather, that which we call 'the pillars of society'. Yes, I did make commercial films, but I always followed my surrealist principles: the need to eat doesn't ever excuse the prostitution of art. Amongst the twenty films I have made, there are some awful ones but I have never betrayed my own moral code. I am against conventional morals, the traditional ghosts; all those dirty morals of society which seep into sentimentalism. In my opinion, *The Young and the Damned* is effectively a film about social struggle. Because I think that I am simply honest with myself, I feel I have to make a film about society. I know that that is my path. But I don't want to make thesis-films out of social circumstances. I see things which affect me and I want to translate them onto the screen but always with the kind of love which I feel for the instinctive and irrational which can appear in any situation. I am always reaching out for the unknown and strange things which fascinate me even though I can never figure out why. Yes, I am an atheist, thank God. We need to look for God in men, and that's an easy thing to do ...[15]

Aged sixty-one and financed by the young producer Gustavo Alatriste, Luis Buñuel works alone in Mexico, fighting old age and death, as virile as a man of forty, in order to complete the most important cinematic works of all time.

On Cinema

The shocking surrealist of 1928 declared himself too old to be courting scandal. Nevertheless, every film he made rocked the structures of the Church and of Fascism. He said that he would not return to Spain while it was still a fascist and Catholic country: his hatred of Franco is symbolic of his hatred against the totalitarian State. His hatred directed towards the Church is symbolic of his eternal fight against the mutilation of man by dogma.

In *Nazarin*, it is Christ, betrayed by the Church and persecuted by the State, who is shocked by human pity. *Viridiana* is the demon who arrives to destroy the principles of Christianity and to set man free, even if in a cynical manner, in view of the deformed morals the latter pursues in order to survive. *The Exterminating Angel* is the lack of pity for this very man who, once freed, is subject to the laws of the State and the Church.

Yesterday's surrealist has become today's anarchist: he supports the revolution by attacking the foundations of capitalist institutions.

Always on the left side of politics and fighting against the established order, Buñuel will always be a condemned man.

[4]
From Eisenstein to Visconti and Antonioni, cinema has been rationalist, it has obeyed a historical revolution; from the expressionism of Murnau to Orson Welles, leaving a legacy for Northern Europeans and Americans, cinema has lived through explosions which have never managed to release it from its theatrical and literary origins. From Buñuel and Jean Vigo to Rossellini, cinema has been developing along a marginal path, characterized by liberty, mysticism and anarchy.

It is cinema which is most linked to the primitives, born unrefined from within Griffith, spilled forth romantically through Chaplin and flagellated through Fellini. It is the same cinema that, depending on the mind and flesh of its auteurs, would create, on the margin of history, the damned figures of Buñuel and Rossellini and generate the tragic figure of Jean Vigo, dead aged thirty, leaving behind his incomplete and mutilated oeuvre.

Jean-Luc Godard is the youngest son of this 'liberated cinema' which influenced Truffaut and Resnais, which bit, in India, the young Ray, and which brought a lesson to New York well adapted to the beat spirit of Jonas Mekas and Allen Ginsberg, directors of the key work in the new American cinema: *Guns of the Trees* (1961).

O Século do Cinema

It is a cinema which falls out with the industry itself, starts fights with the producers, with the public, with the censors and with those critics wishing to champion films of good taste, morality, respect and tradition.

These are the origins of the new cinema, the free cinema, the auteur cinema; of the film which killed the 'monster-director', the 'sacred film-star' and the 'brilliant photographer'; it's a mise-en-scène which broke out of the frame, broke the grammatical rhythm, strangled emotion, fled from the spectacle: the film which stopped being the graphical narrative of puerile literary dramas to achieve powerful expression in the hands of men free from the industry constraints. Then was born the political film, the ideas film; cinéma-vérité, the investigative film, of Jean Rouch; the fictional-reportage cinema of François Reichenbach; the social documentary of Chris Marker, the Brazilian *cinema novo*.

[5]
Gabriel Figueroa, the famous Mexican lighting director, is one of Buñuel's favourite cinematographers. Mysteriously in these films, Figueroa emerges as a different force, without his trademark heavy clouds and romantic backlit shot.

Responding to the French press he said 'when everything is lit and the frame is composed Luis comes close and gives a nudge to the camera and then asks me to start shooting ...'.

Cinema is not a monster. The world is not contained within the limits of a certain frame created by this or the other lens.

Rossellini said: 'Cinema is a very small thing ... it is very easy to photograph a face; it is very difficult to photograph the world ...'.[16]

Scorning years and years of theory, the books by Eisenstein, Rudolf Arnheim, Bela Balázs, Umberto Barbaro, respecting the man but never the ideas of André Bazin, as well as the sweet humanist pyramid which is Cesare Zavattini, Buñuel defines his style: 'I never have problems with technique. I detest "angled" films. I detest unusual frames. When I am working with the cameraman and he proposes a beautiful composition, I start to smile and I abort everything set up so far to film with no effects ... I also detest the traditional mise-en-scène, the shot/reverse-shot ... I like long takes, sequence shots ... I look at a script for five weeks and I get bored ... if I film two hundred and fifty shots the final edit will contain the same amount ... No luxuries ...'.

[6]

Buñuel's editing doesn't attempt to enlighten the audience in a logical manner. It awakens, criticizes and destroys through its violence, through the anarchic shot, profane, erotic – always employing the images forbidden by bourgeois mores.

His style is an idea in motion – the realist freedom of this action is always tempered by an eye which pays close attention to detail: the shower which flows hot then cold, irregularly; never permitting the audience to stop thinking.

The dialogue swings between the colloquial and the poetic: man always speaks in the context of his position on a specific problem. The violence is absolute against the weak: the blind man who is kicked in *L'Âge d'or*, the tortured paralytic in *The Young and the Damned*, the bee which is crushed in *The Criminal Life of Archibaldo de la Cruz*. Violence against the taboos of sex and love, the image of the adored woman in a toilet in *L'Âge d'or* or the indecision in the hands of the nun Viridiana when faced with the full udders of a cow.

Buñuel takes a stance against man's inhibitions; shows escape through masturbation – the solitary Robinson wandering around the deserted island and the homosexuality which is established between him and Man Friday. The handles in the form of a penis on the skipping rope which the little girl plays with in *Viridiana*, the very same rope with which the perverted uncle hangs himself; the mystical hysteria of the prostitutes who long for the saintly, pure, beautiful and virile Father Nazarin; the eroticism in the Washing of the Feet sequence in *This Strange Passion*, when the Church explodes in the atmosphere of a brothel. The camera which runs over the semi-naked body of the young man in *The Young One*; the debauched bourgeois man who abandons an orgy; the fantasy with Christ's clothing in the pathetic ending of *L'Âge d'or*. The fusion of the taboo symbols of sex and the Church in the crown of thorns that the little girl burns when Viridiana appears with her hair loose and a sensual face; the diseased wife in *Nazarin* who, upon receiving her extreme unction, expels the Father from the room to get into bed with her impassioned husband. Or the Church, like the eternal prison of man at the end of *This Strange Passion* when the character who seeks peace in the convent goes blindly to mass. Or in the sudden political and propagandist intrusion of Father Nazarin's character, who

O Século do Cinema

strays from his path to deliver hard truths to a fat and pretentious army officer.

This editing, suggestive and at times highly critical, sometimes propagandist, rarely impenetrable – always attacks the state of order which the spectator accepts as normal: the power of the State, the fear of God taught through Catholic dogma, the crisis of conscience or the necessity of being merciful in order to be at peace with oneself and with our fellow man: the moments of escape, the sublimations, the silent cult of frustration, the passivity.

It is clear that in Buñuel the strong will always devour the weak: the fox chases and devours the chicken in *The Young One*; a cat always jumps on top of the mouse.

In *Viridiana*, this editing acquires, for the first time in the history of cinema, a transcendental feeling, over and above the optical effect even of that used in the classics of Soviet cinema: the beggars, under the charge of the virgin nun, abandon the fields at midday and kneel down to pray an Ave Maria.

Disturbing images of manual labour are interspersed at irregular intervals as we watch the men praying, thanking God for the happiness of each day: the succession of these images of stonemasons, carpenters and sawyers, side by side in the praise of God, creates a monstrous feeling of slavery.

If the editing is the idea in motion, shot through with Buñuel's acute vision (non-exacting and marked by poetical irreverence), Buñuel's mise-en-scène is no less strange: *The Criminal Life of Archibaldo de la Cruz* is the greatest offering of bad taste that cinema has ever created: vulgar studio set design, the actors dressed as actors. *This Strange Passion* is charged with all the elements of a tearjerker and searches the most legitimate of emotions of ordinary and stupefied man for the roots of his slavery – the actors open their eyes, make speeches, walk and bang themselves against the walls. Just like in *Robinson Crusoe*, where the hero, dressed in leather and protected by a simple parasol, wanders around the island in semi-circular movements, solitary and free, looking for a man to love and devour.

From *Un Chien andalou* to *The Exterminating Angel*, Buñuel used cinema as a way for his characters to face themselves through their own unconsciousness: the naked man and from the inside out. For precisely this reason, Buñuel remains a surrealist like Dalí (with whom he fell out, accusing him of serving the facile whims of the bourgeoisie), but also as logical as he can be: the mise-en-scène of the unpredictable, always working in the direction of the mystery, but still linked to the rhythm, to the visual and to Spanish literature. In the Mexico of *Narazin*, Spain is recreated in the distinctive features of the colonial architecture and in the text directly influenced by Lorca. The images of water, the moon and the sensuous angels are omnipresent from *Un Chien andalou* to *The Exterminating Angel*; despite rejecting more unusual paintings, Buñuel works with Goya and Miró, which is reflected in the recreation of the Last Supper in *Viridiana* and in the visions of Robinson on the island.

What the French were searching to find in Buñuel's work, in terms of a reflection of their own culture, would instead carry the distinctive features of the aforementioned influence of the surrealists. The fact of the matter is that Buñuel met André Breton after *Un Chien andalou* and never acted as a spokesman for the group.

In France, where the *nouvelle vague* is taking its lessons from Buñuel (despite having its own problems and its own courage: the skin-deep anarchism of Godard, the wretched petit-bourgeois attitude of Truffaut, the craftsmanship of Resnais – inspired by *L'Âge d'or* both in image and in sound), they refuse to accept that the genius of their cinema is actually Spanish.

That's why, in a moralist country, Buñuel's work is not censored: the only place in the world where his films are shown without cuts is Paris.

[7]

Father Nazarin is a pure, pious and penitent man. He takes in a prostitute who has committed a crime, in self-defence, and falls out with the Church. In order to avoid scandal, he leaves the cloth and goes out into the world as a pilgrim, giving out bread and food, caring for the sick and even staging miracles, against his will, to bring happiness to the poor.

The prostitute, Andara, sets alight the priest's humble home after Nazarin has left and sets off in search of her protector, followed by another friend. Accused of conspiracy, they are pursued.

Held prisoner, Nazarin is thrown in a ditch in the company of criminals; he is beaten and abused.

He is released. Ragged and starving he meets an old woman on the road who gives him a pineapple as an act of charity.

O Século do Cinema

With the fruit held aloft in his hands, stupefied and shocked, Nazarin continues on his path.

[8]

Nazarin, Viridiana and *The Exterminating Angel* are the trilogy which offers the most definitive path to unravelling the mystery of Buñuel. Liberty, cynicism, humour and irreverence are not touches which point to an anarchist position.

If in *The Young and the Damned*, like in *Land Without Bread* and *Fever Rises in El Pao* their author is making films of clear social and political standing, if Buñuel challenges the morals laid down by the Church and State and yet does not take a moral stance, if he does not himself accept any form of current world order, all this doesn't mean that he denies the possibility of the existence of a new order.

He doesn't make didactic films because he doesn't wish to defend morals.

He is not an individualist because he's concerned with the roots which enslave all men.

In the between-the-lines discovery of the extreme happiness to be found in love and sex, what Buñuel proposes is a new order born of complete freedom.

[9]

In *Nazarin* we have a hero who is enslaved by the Church, who doesn't resort to trickery even if this results in insulting the faith of a desperate mother who believes he has the power to cure her sick son.

The same hero who, wounded in flesh by the stupidity of man, condemns the final words of Christ on the cross, the pathetic 'Forgive them, Father, for they know not what they do' and, leaving the prison, goes half-mad when he receives alms.

Buñuel doesn't hate the masses but he does criticize those who, once whipped into a state of hysteria, will follow the orders of fascists.

What he's trying to achieve, through the tragedy of Father Nazarin, is to show the real tragedy of someone who destroys himself through servility: he is accusing the sources, he has no logic to his argument but he does ask for reason. He is trying to achieve an order of free men, who, thanks to this freedom, can see clearly. There is nothing in law which justifies the oppression of humanity. For this reason, Nazarin goes to an army officer who earlier had humiliated the poor traveller and tells him a few hard truths.

The wish to start a revolution through the free conscience of each man, between Left and Right, is specifically a third position of someone who does not accept the capitalist, catholic and bourgeois world, of someone who does not trust the new world which is being created in the name of History.

Buñuel, however, never strays in his belief in a society in which man can be freer. Even though some people are quick to call him a right-wing anarchist, Buñuel, after *Viridiana* (which was a huge success behind the Iron Curtain) and *Fever Rises in El Pao* (the most direct attack that the likes of General Franco's and Fulgencio Batista's dynasties could receive), was on good terms with the Communists.

The Exterminating Angel was awarded the *grand prix* in the Jesuit festival of Sestre Levante, in the heart of Italy, and confused both left and right.

[10]
'I am an atheist, thank God ... the Church betrayed Christ...' he declared in all seriousness.

His greatest hero is a priest who was mistreated by the Holy Order.

Many artists used Christ in order to create stories in today's world.

In the case of Buñuel, it's different: from *Un Chien Andalou* onwards, his work has been characterized by elements taken from Catholic mythology.

There are those who say 'frustrated Jesuit preacher ... maladjusted mystic ...'.

When he filmed *This Strange Passion* he wore a cassock to direct Arturo de Córdova. He studied, above all, the lives of the saints – he was educated by Jesuits, he is a son of Spain, a Catholic land.

Stripped of any surrealist visions, *Nazarin* is his attempt to show his encounter with the world – it would be Buñuel himself, unmasked, if it were possible to identify a church lesson in this tale.

The autobiographical pain '... look, the best men are cast aside, and it's your fault...'.

The suspicion is not ungrounded: never was a hero so loved in cinema.

O Século do Cinema

There is no gesture of pity for the massacred hero: overwhelmed by the shock of the unexpected, impossible act of kindness, Buñuel and Father Nazarin carry on, stupefied, the pineapple in their hands.

After *Nazarin*, he directed *The Young One*: 'the most terrible virgins are those which are 13 years old...'. This is a film about a fall, quite lazy, but maybe it was discretion towards a growing *Viridiana*: 'the most terrible virgins are nuns...'. However, *Fever Rises in El Pao* came along.

For Buñuel, Viridiana is the virus which takes hold in a goddess. The doubt which grips Robinson as he walks in semi-circles: from *Nazarin* to *Viridiana* is yet another circle developing. I have the pineapple in my hands; I am left stupefied on this journey along the self-same path. I return to the convent and I hear Hallelujah by Handel, I find the chaste Viridiana in peace in a cloister.[17]

From there the young girl goes to visit her uncle; he tries to have his way with her but dominates his instincts. He tries to make her stay in the house, by telling her a lie. The young girl leaves. Tortured, the uncle hangs himself. The young girl is gripped by a crisis of conscience. She abandons the convent, inherits her uncle's farm and welcomes beggars into the home, in an act of charity. The beggars bring disorder into the house; one of them tries to deflower her again. Viridiana becomes aware of her own body, she lets her hair down. She plays cards with the beautiful Jorge, who is none other than the actor Francisco Rabal, who embodied Father Nazarin.

The priest is a virgin. What the prostitute Andara feels for him is love, sexual desire.

When her aunt asks her whether the religious adoration she portrays runs into other emotions, Andara opens her arms and shouts hysterically, 'Slander! Slander!'

All Viridiana's erotic charge is focused into adoration for the small crucified Christ she carries with her. Arriving at her uncle's house she goes to her room and takes off her habit.

The camera discreetly shows us her beautiful legs. The woman surges forward when the saint undresses.

In the living room, her uncle plays Mozart's *Requiem*.

In the bedroom, Viridiana, in a white nightdress, prays to her Lord.

The following morning she goes to the cowshed and sees a man milking a cow; she attempts to copy him, her hands, clenched, pause before the full, phallic teats.

Buñuel later explains: 'When I was taught by Jesuits, the priests suppressed our sexual instincts and all our energy was focussed on religious fervour...at night, we would masturbate in silence before the images of the Virgin Mary...'.

Father Nazarin does not give in to the sins of the flesh: I am with the pineapple in my hands, chaste and pure.

Viridiana does not despair.

She becomes aware of sexuality, of the uselessness of sanctity, of a world which cannot be faced with the purity of Father Nazarin but can, conversely, be faced with the naturalness of someone who is beginning to identify who they are; first having sex in order to then have her own ideas.

'In my opinion,' Buñuel said, 'Viridiana is more of a virgin after having slept with Jorge...'.

In this film, another path appears by which to identify the author within the influence of the Church. At the Last Supper, Christ already knew that Judas was the traitor. Like an anarchic Judas, working under the guise of an actor, Buñuel presides over the second banquet of betrayal, instigates an orgy, awakens the basest of instincts in the most humble. This is the orgy we don't see in *L'Âge d'or*: '...to carry out the most depraved of orgies they were holed up in that impregnable castle for one hundred and twenty days. They were four criminals who had no other God than their own lubrication, no other law than their own depravity... without principles nor religion... the greatest, ineffable act of infamy... they brought to their castle, with the unique purpose of serving their dirtiest desires, eight beautiful young girls, eight splendid adolescents and, in order that their imaginations, already corrupted to an unimaginable degree, were continuously excited, they also brought in four depraved women who fed, incessantly, the criminal voluptuousness of the four monsters...'. These fragments of the intertitle which precedes the final sequence of *L'Âge d'or* demonstrate to us a kind of scripted orgy scene which is then carried out by the beggars in the pious house of Viridiana.

The Church once again shook in its foundations; however, there was not one detail of bad taste, of easy shock tactics employed.

The bourgeoisie did not applaud – through the liberation of flesh and criminal instincts portrayed within it, Buñuel revealed the tragic face of all classes.

O Século do Cinema

And so what? I am no longer with the pineapple in my hands; I play cards with sex, I'd rather listen to rock and roll.

[11]
The angel descended with its witchcraft. It shuts the doors: no one may enter nor leave the luxurious mansion where a group of aristocrats reside.
A few sheep go by, a bear.

> The people cannot climb the steps of the garden. The whole city is afoot.

Where now, a few days afterwards, is that upright manner?
The men walk semi-naked and bearded, the elegant dresses are now in tatters, they all fight over a water pipe which they dig out of the wall.
The couple shut themselves inside the wardrobe and commit suicide. Another man dies of hunger.
A simple view of the sky, a little card showing a picture of Christ surrounded by flowers, cotton wool used to represent snow in the nativity scene – the ingenuity in front of the camera, which moves round in tragic circles in that room until someone, touched by a miracle, finds the key.
They have to assume the same places as before, on the first night when they were sitting at the table. Play the same music.
Return to tranquillity.
It's a group effort. Witchcraft opens the doors.
In the church, mass is celebrated to give thanks for the miracle.
Witchcraft once again closes the doors, entraps the priests. The people explode into the squares, the sheep enter the church.
What does the final sequence of *The Exterminating Angel* mean? A declaration that the Church and fascism walk hand in hand?
That there is a way out for those who play cards with sex and listen to rock and roll? The proof that the best road to follow is that which leads to the squares and not to the temples?
Is anarchy in crisis?
Does liberated man need to curb liberty and violence for political ends?
The final shots of *The Exterminating Angel* are rapid and incisive; at the square, with a newsreel-type of shot, the vision is dramatic; the quick movement towards the churches by the sheep touches on the hilarious.

[12]
Luis Buñuel, aged 65, while declaring that he is too old to be courting scandal, has directed another film in Mexico, *Simon of the Desert* (*Simon del desierto*, 1965).[18]

Gustavo Alatriste, a young millionaire, has financed a man who detests Hollywood, who is in the sights of the Vatican and of Franco's police and who is committed to no one. Damned within the industry, Buñuel waited more than thirty years to achieve freedom of expression.

He has become the most important filmmaker of all time and one of the strangest artists of our time.

If this as yet unreleased and most recent film does not show us a clear choice between the square and the church, he will be returning to the same paths he trod upon before and could now find upon them Michelangelo Antonioni with *The Eclipse* (*L'eclisse*, 1962 – the destruction of figurative cinema, the reduction of man to an object) or the mystical Rossellini who denies cinema, art and thought, insisting on the axiological dominance of science.

The last damned man, Buñuel; we will not see another of his kind.

The other possible ending, according to his friend and producer Óscar Dancigers, is as follows: '...he leads a quiet life, a middle-class family man, modest and not given to excess...he likes to drink, eat and seek out his few but good friends...'.

The Morality of a New Christ

Witchcraft blocks the doors of the church. The priests are paralysed, the faithful strangely held back. People explode into the squares, the cavalry charges. While the masses fight the fascist police forces, the bells ring out. A flock of sheep, tame and servile, walks in the direction of the temples. This is the final sequence of *The Exterminating Angel*. What does it mean? Is it suggesting that the Church and fascism always walk hand in hand, above all in Latin countries? Or that there is a way out for those who play cards with sex (*Viridiana*), proving that the most natural road to follow is that which leads to the squares and not to the temples? Is the anarchy in the old Spaniard in doubt? Does man, liberated from his alienation (the sheep), need to curb liberty and violence for political purposes?

O Século do Cinema

These questions, asked in 1962, when Buñuel was sixty-two, brought us closer to solving the enigma which *Diary of a Chambermaid* (*Le Journal d'une femme de chambre*, 1964) has still not cleared up.

In it, the critics only noted a more political and less anarchic filmmaker. Mature, bitter, feral: the language breathes a certain sureness; the sweeping tracking shots plunge deep into the French countryside, introducing the spectator to the anguish-filled solitude born of social conventions. It reminds us of El Greco, not because of the image which is created within it but due to the virility of the rhythm.

If, as this domestic chronicle unfolds, occasionally there emerges from within his editing a familiar shot (an air rifle destroys a butterfly just like in other films a fox eats a chicken or a cat crushes a mouse), it is, in fact, the dialogue, taken from Octave Mirbeau's novel,[19] which works as the film's commentary.

Faced with this new discourse, Buñuel's followers are now able to comprehend how much a revolutionary creator can transform his style according to an idea. In *Diary of a Chambermaid*, there was a need for a profound reasoning as to the motives which led to the moral rotting of the old bourgeois France; a situation which then weakened the country when facing two world wars.

Less anarchic and more political. Marcel Martin added: 'We could lament the fact that he expresses himself, here, in a gentler and more rational way than in his great films; we cannot, however, say that he has acted with less force, less conscience and efficiency....'.[20]

But one day Saint Simón departs from the desert, travelling in a jet plane which crosses through times. His guide is the devil and the devil is the beautiful Silvia Pinal.

Saint Simón descends into hell and hell is a dance club where the long-haired young people writhe to the furious rhythms. The teenagers undress: the temptation of the flesh. The saint resists.

In *Simon of the Desert*, Luis Buñuel, aged sixty-five, goes back to the sources of *L'Âge d'or*; the anarchic surrealism returns to its rightful place and the enigma gains a new dimension. Buñuel's followers are left bemused.

The history of cinema places Buñuel in the position of Auteur and, to our great triumph, he will be one of the few filmmakers who, in the future, will be a point of reference.

On Cinema

A mindset, almost a system, which, not having been rationally created, leaves the critics with a fertile theme with which to work, and from whence can be extracted an ethic-aesthetic.

They are rare, even amongst the cinematographic auteurs we have today, those who can be considered, as well as poets, thinkers.

Many of them *think*, in the manner of Bergman and Fellini, incorporators of a neo-spiritualism which is mystical and heavy with narcissistic romanticism; many of them *think*, in the manner of Visconti or Rosi, representing, respectively, the first and second phases of *historical and critical* realism in modern cinema; many of them *think* via the morality of cinema itself, bringing to life on screen the emotional crises of the European bourgeois society which searches for life's meaning through cinematographic mystification, amongst them the legitimate representatives of the *nouvelle vague*, each with their own take on the theme but all working from the same starting point, including Godard, Truffaut and Resnais.

Others *think* in the manner of Griffith, Chaplin, Flaherty, Stroheim, Murnau, Fritz Lang, Welles, Rossellini – above all Eisenstein who, even if he did not reach a *synthesis* in his work, created the *methods* for a revolutionary cinematographic aesthetic.

Others, much younger, reflect: Kubrick, Losey, Andrzej Wajda.

There are, in cinema, those who *sculpt* (like Resnais), those who *paint* (like Eisenstein), those who *philosophize* (like Rossellini), those who make *cinema* (like Chaplin), those who make *novels* (like Visconti), those who make *poetry* (like Godard), those who make *theatre* (like Bergman), those who make a *circus* (like Fellini), those who make *music* (like Antonioni), those who make *essays* (like Andrzej Munk and Rosi) and those who, dialectically and violently, materialize the dream: that is Buñuel.

The crisis of cinema will be the crisis of thought of the 'modern man'. By *modern man* is understood man living in the *developed* world: the capitalist European, the North American, the Eastern European.

Cinema, the industry of the superstructure (the fundamental communication of this modern man), has taken up the place of the novel and of theatre, empty since the death of James Joyce and Bertolt Brecht.

The conscience of the modern world since the end of World War II can be found in cinema. It can be found in the very *non-existence* of German cinema and, above all, it can be found in the cinema of Italy, France and Poland.

Italy reaching its crisis point through the conscience of Antonioni. France escaping its crisis via the irony of Godard.

While Truffaut searches for a new emotion in Jules and Jim, Resnais searches the memory for values capable of constructing a new conscience.

The phenomenon, in a more general manner, characterizes the cinema of the capitalist world, except in the United States where, neurotic and excitable, the younger filmmakers have only one worry: nuclear war, the conquest of space, the advance of Communism.

On the other hand, in the developed Communist world, only Poland has been undergoing a political evolution for the last twenty years, reflected in the cinema of Jerzy Kawalerowicz, Wojciech Has, Wajda and above all by Munk in *Passenger* (*Pasazerka*, 1961-1964).

A mindset which, according to Munk himself, marked the abandonment of the *positive hero, a sociological constraint*, and instead took up the dialectics of socialist society in progress: the heroism of the past during Nazi occupation and today's solitude, when the new man has to readjust his position within a new society.

What happened in Poland influenced Czechoslovakia twenty years later. A new Czech cinema began to emerge from 1962 and, having overcome the problem of the past (the war and the revolutionary conscience), the Czech filmmakers subtly returned to their greatest literary tradition: Kafka.

In the USSR, the crisis remains: it has been twenty years since the great revolutionaries disappeared, above all Vsevolod Pudovkin and Eisenstein.

While Stalinism was oppressive, Khrushchev's rule only produced debatable works, given their demagogic nature: the trilogy portraying the thaw of the Soviet Union, directed by Grigori Chukhraj (*The Forty-first/ Sorok pervyy*, 1956; *Ballad of a Soldier/Ballada o soldate*, 1959 and *Clear Skies/Chistoe nebo*, 1961) talked of a new morality but was wrapped in old language.

Pier Paolo Pasolini, in 1964, filmed *The Gospel According to Saint Matthew* (*Il vangelo secondo Matteo*).

A modern version of the life of Christ, a historical analysis of the Jewish phenomenon and an attempt at a new, revolutionary morality, Pasolini's film was attacked by certain circles of French critics.

Pasolini responded to this criticism and shed light on the situation: 'What's so underhand about these French critics is that they refuse to admit to the existence of a sub-proletariat which is evolving in developing countries; they refuse to understand the values of these new forces. French culture has fallen into a rationalism that Sartre has already denounced as "aristocratic and decadent"....'.[21]

Pasolini made it clear that the crisis of conscience in modern cinema is a reflection of the crisis within capitalist society in Western Europe.

His Christ, who preaches intolerance over pity, who preaches violence over complacency, and who revolts against the Father when, on the cross, he sees he's left helpless, is the voice of the new morality: *the morality of the conscious man in the developing world.*

Pasolini's Christ is a stigma against alienation: *alienation* is pity, complacency, hypocrisy, sexual taboo, servility, all the behaviour which characterizes the *developing man, or rather, the colonized man.*

Pasolini's Christ is a revolutionary; the successor to Buñuel's anarchic Christ.

Guy Gauthier pointed out, in a study on Chris Marker and neorealism:

> In *Land without Bread*, the simple representation of the living conditions of an impoverished Spanish village will necessarily include, due to the indisputable reality of facts, some of the cruellest images imaginable. In particular, the dead donkeys laid on a piano are counterpoised with a donkey being eaten alive by bees. This route is significant, in the sense that it is summarizes the whole direction of surrealism: something which emerges from a laboratory of images which are continuously replaced with images of real events... In today's world, news broadcasts and science-based documentaries are the true surrealist cinema....[22]

The surrealism of Luis Buñuel is the preconscious of Latin man; it's revolutionary in the manner in which it sets free, by way of imagination, that which is prohibited by reason.

This *liberation* is not, however, an escape but a weapon, used to flog the symbols of the *underdeveloped capitalist society*, just as Pasolini's Christ does.

Buñuel's hero, from Robinson Crusoe to the criminal Archibaldo de la Cruz, from Father Nazarin to the nun Viridiana to Saint Simon, is, when

O Século do Cinema

reduced right to the core, an organically starving Latin fanatic: the behaviour of a starving person is so absurd that capturing his real image creates neosurrealism; his morality, like that of the sub-proletariat, is more metaphysical than political.

From *L'Âge d'or* onwards, Buñuel's Spanish unconscious peopled his cinema with starving characters: beggars in *L'Âge d'or*, the impoverished in *Land Without Bread*, beggars in *Nazarin*, beggars in *Viridiana*, child delinquents in *The Young and the Damned* and the sub-proletariat in *This Strange Passion*.

In the face of his crowd of starving peoples (just like the sub-proletariat which followed Christ, colonized by Imperial Rome), Buñuel prepared, in the history of modern cinematographic thought, the path for Pasolini's new Christ.

In the light of non-esoteric study, Buñuel could be considered as a *left-wing anarchist*: he demolishes current Western Christian values (mainly those of the Latin underworld): he does not propose a new order, but he does not accept the current order.

Buñuel presents, within the absurd scenario which is the reality of the Third World, a *possible consciousness*: faced with oppression, the police, the obscuring of facts and institutionalized hypocrisy, Buñuel represents liberated morality, the opening of the path to the continuous process of enlightening rebellion.

The surrealism in his work is the language par excellence of the oppressed man.

Here we can find, without deciphering the enigma which is Buñuel, that which seems to me to be essential in his work; here is, from an intellectual and Latin point of view, that which can be extracted of historical value to inspire a politics of liberation in which, just like in all past eras, art will play an important role in the process of enlightenment of the population.

In his most recent interview with the press, in March of 1965, Georg Lukács declared that it would be necessary to revise the current political programme with regard to the developing world.

The alienation within the bourgeois world, which some European theorists – including himself – have raised in discussion, is of no *absolute* value when applied to the man living in the developing world.

According to Pasolini, it is the forces of the *irrational* which *generate* Christ in this man.

Here the Virgin Mary is the irrational, she is the very height of real; she is the image of a suffering people, the alienation of which sooner or later results in, by way of a forced birth, extracted by forceps, Christ the Redeemer.

The space race and the atomic crisis gradually turn cinema into a scientific instrument.

The crisis of the old Western Europe turns cinema into a mirror of its alienation.

The awakening of the Third World turns cinema into its mouthpiece: the brutal consequences of hunger will mark the images of this particular cinema, whether or not this suits the wishes of the heralds of a digestible and beautiful world: a world in which men are strong, beautiful and invincible, where borders are made of roses and ready-made phrases try to hide the cancer which grows on the lips of Miss Universe or the criminality which is brewing in the mind of the dictator.

The Neorealism of Rossellini

[1]
World War II produced two apocalyptic films (*Ivan, The Terrible* by Eisenstein, USSR and *Citizen Kane* by Orson Welles, United States), and a renaissance film, *Rome, Open City* by Roberto Rossellini, Italy.

Between the realism of the Lumière Brothers and the fantasy of George Méliès (creators of the Technique and the Aesthetics of film), cinema revolutionized the first half of the twentieth century, making History tangible through its quest to transform dreams into reality.

All the Arts have been integrated into the Seventh Synthesized Audiovisual art form. In *Ivan, The Terrible*, Eisenstein showed how Stalin was the reincarnation of the Tsar Ivan IV and restored balance to the historical dialectics. The film reaches the furthest limits; neo-medieval in style, it explodes into the Christian and Zoroastric domes of Savage Russian Eurasia. In *Citizen Kane*, Orson Welles portrays the Yankee Tsar rectified through the search for a Freudian-Jungian 'Rosebud'.... In him progressive civilization dies a solitary death in a decadent Art Nouveau palace posing as the sophisticated architecture of Kubla Khan.

German expressionism, which preceded and then glorified Nazism, revolutionized theatrical set design and found in cinema a fantastical canvas with which to work and shine through.

O Século do Cinema

Fritz Lang, inspired by David Wark Griffith, constructed the cinematic architecture of *Metropolis* (1927). World War II bombed and destroyed the castles of ancient civilization.

Mussolini was inspired by nationalism to unite Italy, a country made up of archaic city-states governed by tribes morally independent of the state system within which the highest moral code is that of the Vatican, even for the Communist Party.

Fascism is an abhorrent abortion in history's timeline. Mussolini's ideology was the 'renaissance of decadence' in search for a mythical Rome reduced to a tourist centre. The Italian dictator searched amongst the roots of pagan-Christian Imperial Rome for the script for his tragicomic spectacle. At that time, Italian cinema was producing either films of grandiose proportions or psychological comedies, hiding from reality using crowds of extras or the White Telephones of the *futurist* fascist style.

Paganism is the true underbelly of the Italian people despite their Catholic guise. Catholic morality is society's mirror which punishes or absolves its pagan immorality. Communist morality as founded by Antonio Gramsci is another mirror which dialectically reflects the historic compromise between the Christian Democratic Party and the Italian Communist Party. Pagans, in search of a Dionysian carnival, the Italians create and destroy alliances depending on the omens and the general flow of the times.

The success of the pact between the USSR and the United States in their stance against Germany, Italy and Japan divided Europe into capitalist and socialist blocks demarcated by the Berlin Wall.

Italy, like many European countries, was in ruins. The resistance movement, fighting against Nazism and Fascism, was headed by the Communist Party which was, in turn, fighting to obtain a significant part of the power within the country. A poor country, Italy was being reborn through its visionary and poverty-stricken people. Italy, a synthesis of East and West, released from its position as a Third World country in a renaissance explosion, the new reality: cinematographic neorealism.

Roberto Rossellini is the *new* intellectual and aesthetic reality of postwar Italy. He communicates through cinema, a technique abused to the point of saturation by the world which died in the war. He worked without a camera, without any film reel, without a lab, without the use of cinematic technique, without actors, without any means of production...without anything...just

Figure 3.2 Glauber Rocha and Roberto Rossellini (Venice, 1967).

ideas... Rossellini would say that 'ideas generate images', 'the desire within our ideas creates solid things....'

Marginalized and impoverished, Rossellini reinvents cinema. *A scientist and an artist* at the service of the philosopher. Cinema was, up until that point, something pieced together in studios. All great Soviet cinema (with the exception of the films of Dziga Vertov) was made in this way. Documentary makers like Robert Flaherty were suffocated by the industry of spectacle. French existentialism sublimated reality into acceptable bourgeois shapes (see the theatre of Jean-Paul Sartre or Albert Camus). Spain and Portugal were still under the reign of fascist dictatorships and English cinema had remade its links with Hollywood, its natural ally.

O Século do Cinema

Rossellini did not come from a university background. He entered the world of cinema as a cameraman and later transformed himself into an inventor of new optical techniques. Learning through people and books, Rossellini taught himself to be a *master*, developing a Socratic role which would transform him into the authentic Pope of the Cinematographic World: discussing, questioning, teaching, lying, misleading, informing, investigating, imagining, criticizing, enjoying – Rossellini reduces, in the manner of Leonardo Da Vinci, cinema to a question of method.

Director of a tale of 'fiction', *The Man of the Cross* (*L'uomo dalla croce*, 1943), and co-director of another, *The White Ship* (*La nave bianca*, 1941),[23] both produced as Fascist propaganda, Rossellini, above all in *The Man of the Cross* (the film's subject is the Red Cross...), strips naked the cinematographic set design of the Italian studios, introducing the horror of reality to the horror of fantasy.

He subverts the aesthetics of illusion for the aesthetics of matter.

Rossellini is the first filmmaker to discover the camera as an 'instrument of investigation and reflection'. His style of framing, illumination and his editing times created, from the advent of *Rome, Open City*, a new method of making cinema.

Dziga Vertov, Robert Flaherty and Jean Renoir preceded Rossellini in the technique of filming 'reality as it happens', but the Italian filmmaker would synthesize, from a philosophical point of view, lessons learnt both from the socialist reporter and from the idealistic romantic.

Luchino Visconti would open yet another route, so plentiful, fertile and in such contrast to that of Rossellini, but Visconti's land is a revolutionary utopia: where Visconti believes, Rossellini doubts. From that point, neorealism spills forth in multiple directions via Cezare Zavattini, Vittorio De Sica, Federico Fellini, Michelangelo Antonioni, Francesco Rosi, Pier Paolo Pasolini, Marco Ferreri, Bernardo Bertolucci, Marco Bellocchio, Gianni Amico, Gianni Barcelloni and Carmelo Bene.

Rossellini is a mystic before he is a neorealist. If in *Il generale Della Rovere* there exists a demand for heroism, in *Europa '51* (1952) passion is born of heroic necessity, wherein the Impossible Saint substitutes the hero: Ingrid Bergman goes mad and sanctity skirts around the altered frontiers of social norms. In *Europa '51*, Rossellini was wracked by political doubt, faced with the terrible dilemma of a continent freed from Hitler and caught between communism and capitalism. The exit leads to a mental institution. In *Germany, Year Zero* (*Germania, anno zero*, 1947), just like in *Rome, Open City* and *Paisan*, we hear the voice which cries out again and again against the destruction of man by man, shouting not just at historical fact and war but wading deep into other domains: *A Metaphysical Why*. The suicide of a child in the bombed ruins demands deeper investigation.

Stromboli (*Stromboli, terra di Dio*, 1950) began the first phase of the trilogy which we could call 'Bergmanian' – the period of the artist in love with Ingrid Bergman. However, if the questions posed in *Europa '51* are born of social and political issues and the madness of Ingrid portrayed within the film is simply a consequence of these phenomena (just like the suicide of the boy in *Germany, Year Zero*), in *Stromboli* and *Journey to Italy* the problematic is *Completely Existential*.

Rossellini believes in love and searches, by way of these two films, even faced with the progressive sickness of his own marriage, for the idealistic integration of time and space. The natural tragedy of a volcano erupting after the war, this is *Stromboli*, with Ingrid Bergman climbing (escaping) in the direction of the molten lava in the apparent ecstasy of the *Eternal Fire*.

The journey undertaken by George Sanders and Ingrid Bergman through Italy is one in search of the past, back to the origins of man: in the museum it is History which is immortalized in the statues which impress upon the character witnessing them a sudden awareness of human passion. Through the archaeological excavations, the unearthing of the bodies from the underground tombs propels man into History's womb and turns passion into a symptom which lies beyond human relations. The meeting which takes place in front of the church cannot be considered as an escape towards Christ, in search of Peace. The church is *only* a symbol of this Peace.

Man who yesterday called on God would later call for heroism, just like in other mythologies. The same strength of the great quests of old can also be found later in *Il generale Della Rovere*; the director gazing on from a distance and yet still suffering due to the times to which he is exposed.

Looking out into the universe like a cowering dog, Rossellini frees himself by firing out questions. Because perhaps he already sees straight through to the core of objects, the details of things, the misery and the goodness in human faces – due to these truths which he despises – Rossellini chooses not to approach the vision. He doesn't bring the camera in closer, he despises the close-up; he renounces the detail in favour of the general. He is an inverted pantheist, always focusing on the ruins of war, the fog of the hellholes of Italy, the smoke from the volcanoes or the archaeological dust.

It is a duel with the universe. His style is born of the flesh; the distance he assumes is the distance of the camera. He is the filmmaker of the medium shot and the establishing shot. He isn't rational and for that reason the editing is anarchic, the movements of the camera obey reality and not technique. Whereas Visconti *argues dialectically about the theme*, Rossellini *asks questions of the theme*. He always asks questions. His camera sometimes veers wildly, like a man lost. From this delirium emerges an *Original Visual World*. They are newspaper prints, tragic news events from our times. Adopting the photographical stance of a reporter, Rossellini uses the symbols of our century.

The graphical representation of today's Europe is shown through Rossellini's frames: concentration camps, mad saints, heroes executed by a firing squad, children committing suicide in bombed-out roads.

Rossellini doesn't add to what doesn't exist in order to create the heights of fictional existence.

He avoids rationalism because for Rossellini tragedies go beyond any material comprehension of history: reality has no logic, that's why there is a constant shift of values within it, from *The Flowers of St Francis* (*Francesco giullare di Dio*, 1950) to *Il generale Della Rovere*.

Bound only by academic concept, by an alienated existence, it is possible (albeit useless) to treat art as a privileged and exceptional phenomenon. And scientifically conceptualized art is nothing more than absurd nostalgia on the part of aesthetes who are misplaced in today's world. The anti-academic stance on art is the liberation of Rossellini: his *aesthetics* is his *ethics*. His objective is the Truth, just like the beauty in *Il generale Della Rovere* is its final shot, distant and swirling in mist, when the redeemed rogue is shot down, along with all the other heroes of the Italian resistance.

The take is conventionally ugly and the rhetorical spectator must have begged for close-ups of the dead man, and, in terms of a 'firing squad sequence', would have preferred the one by Stanley Kubrick in

Paths of Glory. There are, however, no set conventions on how it should be done: Kubrick's sequence is a denouncement which is designed to shock and revolt; that is why it is shot in such analytical detail (the tracking shots, the close-ups). Rossellini's execution scene is the bitter discovery of the failure of death. In the same way as the men in those tragic positions are simply heroes in a collective death, the *Establishing Shot* photography sweeps over the heroism.

Rossellini's is a journey *over and above the real, without transgressing the real*. It is therefore possible to define Rossellini's style as a mise-en-scène of Mysticism, given that his realism is a 'Why?', a lucid and free poetical interrogation.

In *Il generale Della Rovere*, the path which converts our rogue into a hero is not one of systemic political awareness but an awareness on multiple levels, forged from violence, love, death, respect for man and mainly for solidarity. The solitary prisoner placed in a bare cell where the only thing to be found is the writing on the walls by condemned men, standing out like ghosts of the past, finally understands the value of a *human being*.

Rossellini's politics is *mystical* and implies the negation of a being as compromised by exterior constraints. When the rogue understands the importance of heroism – something which surges from collective necessity – he himself becomes a hero, but because *being a hero* is to search for another, non-Christian form of salvation.

If the character of the engineer was attempting to achieve economic salvation in Italy during the war, now, faced with an immense fortune (one million Lira and a safe-conduct to Switzerland) and in the solitude of his cell-block, he prefers to save his conscience by taking on the heroic personality of General Della Rovere, a Myth, a new existence, even if it is achieved as a result of death.

The German commander cannot comprehend the new hero. Rossellini perhaps didn't understand him either, and that's why we are not graced with the close-up of the dead hero on the screen. Like Brecht, Rossellini allows the spectator to be a critic.

Achieving a new existence outside of life (for those who do not believe in the biblical God as converted into a Catholic or Protestant God), is the origin of a mysticism which, in Rossellini's case, could be called a *social mysticism*.

O Século do Cinema

[2]

The death of Rossellini in 1977 left cinema an orphan. No other filmmaker influenced the last three generations of cinematographic auteurs as much as he did. Via the Italian lineage, the blood inheritors were Michelangelo Antonioni, Francesco Rosi, Pier Paolo Pasolini, Bernando Bertolucci and Gianni Amico and they gave him their public vote of recognition. In *Before the Revolution*, a film which marked the revolutionary entrance of the young Bertolucci into world cinema, the filmmaker and co-writer Gianni Amico appears in a bar shouting: '...*Senza Rossellini non se puó vivere*' [Without Rossellini it is impossible to live any longer] – which embodied the feelings of all the young filmmakers of the world about the master. Jean-Luc Godard is the 'Son and the Holy Spirit of the Father' while Pasolini became the Secular Apostle and Michelangelo Antonioni constructed the perceptive perspective of the new visual space discovered in Rossellini's *Journey to Italy*. Jean Rouch, an ethnologist who is developing the technique of *cinéma-vérité*, recognizes the origins of Rossellini in his proposal for 'the discovery of cinema through reality'. The Hollywood filmmakers who were victims of the McCarthy trials (for affiliation with communism) were influenced by the 'social neorealism' of Rossellini, which had seduced Ingrid Bergman.

He was the cinematic anti-professional. His filmography is vast and is still incomplete. Adventurer, intellectual, Don Juan, scientist, historian, philosopher – Rossellini built a popular personality in Italy. He remodelled himself as a Professor of Civilization. In 1958, he denounced the domination of European cinema by Hollywood cinema. The deglamourization of Ingrid Bergman violated the rules of international censure. His Hollywood-produced films were box-office failures, incomprehensible to the critics and sabotaged by the distributors. The radical tones of his language were blocked by the mass communications network which was, ironically, developed in part by the medium of television using Rossellini's lessons of *Cine-journalism* and later those of Godard.

Twenty or so feature-length films produced by the multi-national industry represented the aesthetic surplus of a fight between the dream of cinema and the reality of the economy. *Rome, Open City* was born of an annihilated Italy: the economic conditions created Rossellini's 'neorealism' within the industry structures. Television would tolerate his extravagances in the form of Didactic Epic works.

His movement from cinema to television was his abandonment of Ingrid Bergman (fiction) for Sonali das Gupta (reality).

In 1959, Rossellini filmed *India as Seen by Rossellini* (*L'India vista da Rossellini*) for television and began an affair with Sonali das Gupta, the ex-wife of a minister, an event which caused political and religious scandal.

Rossellini would continue working in both commercial industry (cinema) and state industry (television) by way of RAI (the Italian television and radio network).

Rossellini enjoyed the most fantastical adventure for a filmmaker: he re-filmed (critically and poetically) the *History of Humanity*. Christ, Socrates, Descartes, Saint Augustine, Cosimo de' Medici, Garibaldi, Pascal, Louis XIV, man's fight for survival, humanity as a product of the industrial age, the biophysical genesis....[24] His next film would be about Marx's life.

In 1974, he completed his political memoirs of fascist Italy, filming *Year One* (*Anno Uno*) in which he depicts the formation of the Christian Democratic Party.

His last film was *The Messiah* (*Il Messia*, 1975), filmed in Tunisia.

Adriano Aprà, Italian critic and filmmaker who became one of Rossellini's most loyal disciples, said to me in Rome that '*Doppo Le Messie, Roberto muore... Adesso ha trovato Dio...il film è bellissimo...*' [After *The Messiah* Roberto died... At that moment he found God...the film is beautiful].

Rossellini also separated from das Gupta and married another woman, causing a furore which saw his entire army of ex-wives and children up in arms (Anna Magnani was already dead). He distributed money and knowledge to those who asked for it.

The Brazilian public is not very familiar with Rossellini's cinema, and his films for television are the most important creations of contemporary cinema, which laid the solid guidelines to be followed by television in the future.

The difficulty about Rossellini is that the materialization of reality subjugated his talent. As humble as a true Christian, he thought himself no more important than his characters. And these characters are consequently as dry as reality is. Rossellini made attractive films based on a hideous reality. Agnostic but always a Christian, Rossellini wanted to save us through the Didacticism of Art. He helped develop, to an as yet uncalculated extent, the theories of Giotto di Bondone and Bertolt Brecht.

His final film would be that of Karl Marx's life.

Through Rossellini, cinema broke away from the age of letters and from theatre and entered into its audiovisual specific. Godard elevated the method to paroxysm, which led to the crisis of contemporary cinema.

'Not the death of cinema but the death of civilization...' Rossellini said at the last Cannes Festival, where he presided over the jury which gave an award to my own film *Di Cavalcanti* (1976), of whom Rossellini was a friend – and it was 'Di', as he is in the film, who introduced me, in Bahia, to the *Maestro di Roma*.[25]

Filmic Dramaturgy: Visconti

[1]

It is important to acknowledge the problem of filmic dramaturgy, an element born of the binary external–internal editing, or more precisely of the conflict between the framing and composition. In the former, we find editing as a creative expression, and in the latter as a narrative system.

Eisenstein's theory of the dialectic montage, where meaning is born from the conflict created between two shots, doesn't imply a dogma: it was simply up until today the method which came closest to absolute film. This doesn't invalidate, however, the linear message preached by Pudovkin, close (with some slight variations) to the embodiment of the idea which marks the style of Luchino Visconti.

Let's then take Visconti as our focus, given that *Senso* (1954) is the most blatant example of filmic dramaturgy. All the linear structure in its exterior editing is developed within the slow cadence of saturation, an expository rhythm which allows, by way of the length of time conferred on the visual, the birth of a new Universe. We can deduce here, therefore, that Visconti's conflict happens from linearity to linearity, from the framing to the composition, and not from frame to frame. What LV adds to the growing filmic language is that which is most solid in this postwar counter-cinema period. If Visconti doesn't grab our attention using the shock element so specific to Bergman, Kazan and Welles, he consolidates, through calmness and subtlety, the definitive limits which separate the drama which *exists within* in the visual dynamic and which differs from the intended literary drama. Let's examine *Senso*, the most polemic, the most brimful of dialogue and of narrative monologues.

[2]
There will certainly be a shot of theatrical drama, a shot of literary drama, of drama which *exists within* the visual dynamic. At first it's impossible to determine the *filmic drama* because filmic would seem to imply the abolition of drama. In the case of Visconti, let's establish a terminological concession: being as he is a filmmaker of counter-cinema (according to the classification of this type of cinema in my past work on 'Dassin, Inverted Cine-Christ')[26] he manages to come close to absolute film, even though to reach this position he tramples on the general lines of the tired traditional narrative. His use of time, also his system of mise-en-scène, his *vision* which gets confused with the pictorial, his capacity for extreme psychology are the cells of his cinema which, without doubt, blazes a path forwards in a time of cinematic exhaustion.

Let's look in detail, however, at each one of these cells and how this cinema manages to liquidate the cinema of entertainment, reach a new universe and what the dimensions of this universe are, mainly focusing on *Senso*.

[3]
We have already said that Visconti liberates camera time to the very limits it can be taken. Even if the camera is not static it pans slowly across the landscape, and as a rule pulsates in another cadence, a determining factor in successive abstract conflicts which evolve to give the film a complete body.

In the battle sequence in *Senso*, for example, when the soldiers move across the flaming landscape, the camera pans horizontally in the opposite direction from the internal movement as well as the internal rhythm. A fine tree acts as a central balancing point to the framing and, as the abstract conflict of the camera against the rhythm and sense is confirmed, the tree detaches itself from the rest of the field of vision, as a separate entity from all which is displayed on screen: the fine tree acting as a pendulum in the centre of the frame. Vague aesthetics? No, because it's Visconti's focus on the pictorial which allows the suffocation of the word in favour of the image. Filming the panoramic shot in a horizontal sense counter to the direction of the march of the soldiers equals the fundamental subversion of the grammatical narrative, telling the tale from the end to the beginning and creating another viewpoint: a counter rhythm, further empowering this vision, giving further weight to Visconti's *vision*, which negates the rhythmic function. The tree sits in the centre of the shot; it plays a solid supportive role in the realisation of the film's architecture. There is no sense of great admiration for Visconti because his creative subtlety is one of the most complicated that exists. His importance doesn't lie in bringing the obvious to our attention, in fact what is most admired about him is his weakest point: his pictorial viewpoint. What he brings to cinema, his contribution, are the small and definitive coups, like those discussed above. Let's move on to the next point: the dynamics of the scenes.

[4]

If one takes a script where the takes are indicated in the margin, in the centre of the page is the description of the scene, on the other margin is laid out the dialogue and sound, it is easy to *make a film*, as is said within the cinema milieu. But making a film is not enough to make a filmmaker. To begin with, anyone who receives a detailed technical script from another person and is able to execute it line by line is more or less a good *master builder*, and this simply depends on that person's prior capacity to carry out the project or not. This is a valid analogy if we make a comparison between a person making a film and one constructing a building. However, this analogy cannot be applied in the comparison to a *filmmaker*. A filmmaker plans and executes his work: he builds the film from the script to the final editing. When making the film, there will be a shot which is not vital to the triumph of the film as long as it turns out more or less well. However, if this is a bad shot, it can damage the final editing and if it's excellent the film is transformed from cinema to theatre. It's the shot, as was said before, wherein it's possible – if we examine a fourth hypothesis (and Visconti is responsible for this) – to have the filmic drama *existing* in the visual dynamic, replacing the spoken word and destroying the pictorial illustration: it's more dependent on its mise-en-scène than on its composition. Fifty per cent of the latter is made up of the framing. When used by Visconti, the composition belongs to his visual system which is the third element in his film, born of the two inseparable roots of his cinema, taken from a static angle: the framing and composition themselves. His internal mise-en-scène (given that before we were speaking about external mise-en-scène) energizes the composition to such an extent that the actors end up breaking free of any plausible theatrical space. Even if initially the action develops within the limits of the theatre, these barriers are then broken and the action shot becomes the reality. In this reality there is a new shock: allowing the drama in essence to be realistic in such a way that it then begins to be a highly sophisticated version of reality. And from this state the drama evolves to its unique position: the filmic. Given the subtleties, it's really difficult to establish what the difference is between a Visconti drama and any counter-cinema drama par excellence, that of Christ recrucified by Dassin, for example...[27] We could say firstly that the *vision* within a Dassin film is radically one-sided; it does not agitate his theme but develops it within the atmosphere in which it belongs. The orchestral build-up within his film, a true example of the skill of a craftsman, which begins to grow from a determined point, is forgotten in favour of a false search: a search for the expressive force within the register of the ferocious landscape. The result is a document without its poetic specific, whether this be highly sophisticated like in Visconti's work or highly refined like in De Sica's work, another example of filmic drama: two creative opposites who are brought together in their objectives.

In terms of Visconti, looking at him as a neorealist, the starting point is the duality realism/fable. At base there is the real, available for observation; secondly the act of turning it into a fable which confers upon the real its atmosphere and its absurdity, which is in itself justification enough for his decision to approach it. It is for this reason that the actors in *Senso* behave more like objects embodying states rather than actual human beings representing states. If Alida Valli portrays varying shades of charm or repulsive behaviour, this is down to something more than the actress herself. She is a malleable sculpture, existing within that space and under the atmosphere of that space: an atmosphere of high tension, born of an operatic climax and which develops (as opposed to grows) within the same density, up to the climax of an execution by firing squad. Using as his starting point an outdated dramatization of the real – the opera – Visconti sustains his own fictional world, giving credence to melodrama as much in its conceptualization as in its expository treatment: moving from climax to climax he explodes the familiar explanatory language, the plot etc., adding, for the first time in such a defined manner, another type of script.

We spoke of the fact that his visual system gets confused with the pictorial. Let's take a look at that now.

O Século do Cinema

[5]

In cinema, the photographic visual and the pictorial visual destroy the filmic visual. Where the latter doesn't exist miserably disseminated in one of the former two, it rarely exists at all, as is the case in *Umberto D* (1952), *Bicycle Thieves* (*Ladri di Biciclette*, 1948) and, as paradoxically as it would seem, in *Senso*.

Breaking through the film's coloured surface, the visual in *Senso* is filmic. Let's look more in depth: the visual rests on the photographed object or actually within it. In the latter case it is truly filmic; in the former it is falsely so. In *Senso*, conversely, the visual, even though it may directly be the object, something which jumps into view, is soon 'transformed' by the camera and by the composition and thus begins to be of functional value to the filmic visual. How does it do this? Well, as an example, let's take the battle sequence of which we spoke earlier: the fine tree in the centre of the frame moves from being a decorative shrub to being the point of functional balance of a sequence with inverted movements and rhythm. The subtle changes in the shades of Livia's hair cease to be a photographed object and become a functional visual device within a complex emotional development; the same happens with Livia's gowns, with Valli's face, as well as in the subtle play of tones as mentioned above, all of which serve as a balancing point, anticipating the drama, in the manner of a chromatic chorus in an operatic tragedy.

The critics who accuse Visconti's work of being purely pictorial image are making a basic error: the failure to accurately observe the distinctive points of LV's style. The chromatic action gives the object pictorial value which in turn destroys its decorative existence and turns it into a visual agent. For this reason, the spoken word loses ground and works only in the sense of a dispensable accident, as a frame. And when a filmmaker uses the spoken word as mere decoration it's already drained of its literary specific and it's turned into filmic word, a supporting column and not a furtive means of expression.

[6]

Visconti's capacity for extreme psychology can be observed in his famous long take and its duration. His definitive refusal to employ the shock mechanism takes him on a trajectory of fairness and objectivity. A classic filmmaker who doesn't open up – in the baroque manner of Welles – but who contains himself to the max, in search of a sophisticated simplification, Visconti, in this way, positions himself as the most complex creator in today's cinema.

In various ways, as we've seen, playing with multiple and complex elements, not investing in more daring domains such as the problematic of time in the expository technique, but instead searching for real time within his theme of solitude – which runs through *Obsession* (*Ossessione*, 1953), *Senso* and *White Nights* (*Le notti bianche*, 1957) – Visconti manages to create a private universe, joining together in one body the aristocrat, the communist and the homosexual, and therein creating a cinema of existential density and, moreover, one of speculation and awareness of such phenomena. Placing himself in the centre of a universal polemic, he achieves (through his own force, but having had no real intention of doing so), the embodiment of his existence as a concrete expression of indisputable form. This balance places him in isolation as a consummate artist.

Cinema's Form and Sense

Where does film begin and literature end? Where do the vague philosophy devoid of method, recited theatre, and facile poetry all fall away, and film – that mysterious entity evoked by critics – filmologists and theorists, begin?

What Philosophy is that which is said to exist in Fellini and Bergman? How is it that Philosophy, having existed for centuries, appears so easily, speculating and imposing Ethics through a mechanism which is so specific to the twentieth century?

Absolute film, film which is no longer investigating expression, which is no longer experimenting, which is no longer proposing a problem but is resolving it at source and which emerges as a complete Universe.

Luchino Visconti concentrates on that other 'reality' born of the silver screen, the transference of his spirit to the Image. And from beginning to end there exists the image which I Am. Which you Are. Which is the world, its landscapes and circumstances.

Visconti surpassed the Cut. Surpassed Cinema.

What is interesting about the Artist is his Work and not Him, the Artist, the Man Ablaze.

The essence is the Image and the matter is the frame which frames it.

It's equipped with minimal details of light and decoration.

The hairstyle, the nails, the lips, the teeth of the Actor.

The image of a Human Being.

The landscape is the other Image which envelops Man.

Universe: the Work which creates the Artist.

The visible cut which slits a wrist like a razor, the Panoramic shot like the wild animal which chews at our nerves, the Shock Mechanism which marks the musical cadence of modern Cinema, all of this doesn't exist in Visconti.

His skill of integration is so great that through him Film is Film, like Fruit is Fruit with an outer layer and skin, like man as a whole, of whom the bones and blood cannot be seen.

It's a style which is defined in a Shot: Maria Schell falls into the arms of Jean Marais at the top of the stairs, the arm collapses, the music punctuates: the operatic dramaturgy, the recuperation of the melodramatic spirit of Visconti's race (Italy). National Filmmaker, all Culture put into one Film.

And the Word which is born on the lips of the Actors, and the Actors themselves, and the Narration, and the Music, and the Theatrical Stage Design? And the Drama? And the Dramatic Tradition? And the Chronology? And the demarcated, designed, limited mise-en-scène? And the Medium Shots? And the completely narrative Editing? And the Static Cameras? Are these all the elements of anti-cinema? But don't they all exist in *White Nights* (*Le notte bianchi*, 1957)?

A refined artist: VISCONTI IS THE PROUST OF CINEMA IN THE FORMAL SENSE OF THE GESTURE WHICH IS FOLLOWED UNTIL THE NAIL SCRATCHES THE DUST.

Visconti does not despise the Word nor Theatre.

The Drama is within the stage constructed by Visconti to arm the foundations of his Universe.

It's not a question of that old and foolish tale of showing a spoken-word film with no sound in order to then find that the sense is lost.

Visconti uses the Word as Man's Greatest Sound and the Stage as the Ideal Space for the *Dramatic Being*.

Visconti and the Nerves of Rocco

[1] THE AUTEUR

Rocco Parondi is the son of Visconti in the biblical saga of Joseph and his brothers (the Bible and Thomas Mann)[28] and in the fraternal tragedy with Dostoyevsky roots (Karamazov),[29] born of the greatest filmmaker alive in the Western world.

Pinpointing Rocco's paternity is one of the most important points to be made in order to understand Luchino Visconti's sense and mise-en-scène: it is not a visual narrative of 'emotional drama' but a dramatic style (melodrama), the origins of which are steeped in circus performance, in Greek tragedy, in opera, in classic tragedy as well as in the serial novel and in the novels of Dostoyevsky and Stendhal. If we also search the basic structure of *Obsession* and *The Earth Trembles* (*La terra trema*, 1948), we will find in the first the realist novel of James M. Cain (*The Postman Always Rings Twice*) and in the second the verism of Giovanni Verga.[30] This is without citing the influence of Camilio Boito,[31] Marcel Proust and the Western dramatic tradition.

The continuation of his filmic work throughout a period of nearly twenty years (six films) is exactly why many classify his position as historicist. Art for Visconti is not lyrical impressionism nor is it Romantic struggle and even less is it improvisation. Art is intimately linked to Politics. Being both an elitist intellectual, a somewhat traditionalist aesthete and for this reason oldfangled, Visconti, the artist, is an essayist in dramatic terms, a creator of beauty from the understanding of dialectic and historical materialism.

Visconti never paid homage to Social Realism in the Soviet Communist sense, even though *The Earth Trembles* was a communist-style manifesto about the lives of Sicilian fishers, so powerful that the censures banned it.

Exiled from modern society, artists who take the decision not to look to the Epics and Tragedies for the pillars of their mise-en-scène, and who refrain from thinking the dramatic text in Marxist terms, find it difficult to survive in the twentieth century. At least three of the biggest names of our time (in cinema and theatre) have taken this stance and succeeded. Two of them have now passed away (Brecht and Eisenstein) and one is still alive: Luchino Visconti.

Another example of this is an artist who was a classic exception to the rule and we cannot completely deny the possibility that a future 'culturalization' of Jean Vigo would not have taken place if death had not taken him first. Vigo was a poet in the times of surrealism and the influence his father, the anarchist Miguel Almereyda,[32] marked upon his young temperament the irresistible desire for creative liberty, the principle weapon of which was intuition. Marked by the social problems of his time, Jean Vigo attacked the structures of the establishment by investing in the intellectual anarchy of surrealism; intellectual anarchy which belonged to

O Século do Cinema

cinema and naturally having a social objective: *Zero for Conduct* (*Zéro de conduite*, 1933) is a manifesto.

When making comparisons between Luchino Visconti and Brecht and Eisenstein, it is important to distinguish that the German theatre director came from a petit-bourgeois background and his rebellion had to have sprung from a difficult, proletarianized adolescence, in one of the most critical phases of pre-Hitler Germany. Brecht, the revolutionary, was the angry man.

Eisenstein came from a socially mobile bourgeois background and was exposed to Western culture in a Russia under the rule of the Tsars. Becoming involved in the Russian Revolution aged around twenty, the young Japanese-language tutor took on the doctrines of Marxism at the time of the historical explosion of the ideas which would change man's destiny forever in the twentieth century. He was not a rebellious man but rather a revolutionary in progress. For that reason, he consciously abolished the fictional man from his work: in *Strike, Battleship Potemkin, October* and *The General Line*, the films' main characters are the masses. In *Ivan, The Terrible*, the film's main character is the historical figure himself, as would also be the case in *Que Viva Mexico!* Only later on, when he came into direct conflict with the violent limitations imposed by Stalinism, did Eisenstein, with his eyes wide open to culture, look to the works of Theodore Dreiser and James Joyce for inspiration for fictional films, which he never made. Even if Dreiser was the most important voice of social revolt in the United States at the time of *An American Tragedy* (1925), Joyce was not a Marxist. The author of *Ulysses* (published in 1922) had, in his own interpretation of History, the subjective veins of History itself. Joyce was a novelist, a solitary artist who, being as much a genius as Karl Marx himself, trampled capitalist literary language, exploding this Dominating Ideology at its linguistic essence.

Visconti is not a socialist man in the throes of rebellion and we cannot call him a revolutionary in progress. Coming as he did from aristocracy (there are numerous references to the Visconti family in Italy's political and cultural history), Visconti had no grounds to rebel against oppression, poverty or the moral limitations of the working classes. The position he chose to take against the world in which he lived was one of a critical attitude, the consciously intellectual stance of someone who, when studying the evolution of art throughout the centuries, found that art and politics were inextricably linked, no longer in terms of the two exchanging niceties or orchestrating massacres, but in the interpretation of History and attaining the objective of Revolution. Man's discovery of politics, which, in Visconti's case is an exception to the rule (because his was the case of a man who had exceptional moral courage), is, in *Rocco and His Brothers* (*Rocco e i suoi fratelli*, 1969), the result of the numerous paths in capitalist society which lead a man to rebel.

Taking up the position of philosopher on the world, Luchino Visconti doesn't just provide us with the best lessons in politics (as noble and elegant as one of the many shows of defiance of his family) but he also rushes to war, with his heart wounded by [his own] impossible humanism.

[2] SENSE

Rocco is this idealist version of Visconti reduced to despair, from which there are two possible outlets: alienation or political action. The self-justified version of Visconti is Ciro, the worker; the honest man within his social class who wishes for a perfect society in order that, within it, someone like Rocco could live. In the final sequence, when Ciro is talking to Luca and gives the little boy hope of 'a fairer world', Visconti condemns Rocco and assumes, by following other paths, the current Sartreist position: a man engaged, no longer held within the limitations of intellectual compromise, but instead a man reduced, the revolutionary man, the sectarian man. Ciro gives up his own brother, Simone, to the police because he realizes, in his most lucid moment, that condemning Simone means the destruction of Rocco. So long as Rocco (a Christian and Biblical being) continues to understand Evil to the point of loving him, Simone would remain in the bosom of the family, dragging everyone within it to an inevitably tragic end.

Today, Sartre's reductive sense of engagement is a kind of terrorism. So is Ciro's choice. Visconti loves Rocco but Ciro represents the truth within today's monstrous capitalist society. It is necessary to destroy both Good and Evil in order that a new world can consciously be reached, without having to struggle through all humanity's miseries. When Ciro rushes out to hand Simone over to the police, Rocco takes Luca in his arms and says: 'All is lost.' These are Christ's words on the cross. Rocco knows that there is no longer a place for Him. Luca perhaps doesn't understand him but he will later understand Ciro and, at the end of the film, walking along the road, surrounded by the earth's ballad which speaks of a utopian rural lifestyle – the ideal of the pastoral poets, the growing shadow of Virgil – Luca understands that the land of Lucania is also an impossibility because, if men remain pure, just as Simone was before, hunger will always be close by. Luca hopes, therefore, for 'a fairer world' and, if he grows to be like Ciro (his future is uncertain, and herein lies the contradiction of despair in Visconti's awareness of the world), he will fight for change. Visconti's dialectic is implacable: in Luca's final movements, the tragedy is complete.

Sartre's last movement is political action. His reduction to this state took place without knowing what a real man is. He is also a petit-bourgeois; he does not possess the necessary greatness in order to revolt without despair against the super-structure which surrounds him. Mathieu (the character in the novel *Les Chemins de la liberté*)[33] is an intellectual and for that reason he is not everyman. He is Sartre himself transposed. Just like Camus in *Caligula*[34] is ultimately the disdain for the common man. Visconti, possessing the still-Romantic realism of Dostoyevsky and Stendhal, shows his continued concern for the social man, for the peasant and for the factory worker. He doesn't saturate his dialectic with his despair but instead liquidates this despair dialectically.

It's not difficult to recognize the conscious Marxist within him when the curtain is lifted on the aesthete. It's easy, even, to understand the existence of an aristocrat of this kind in the Communist Party, without him having suffered, even today, a large amount of criticism – criticism of which revolutionaries such as Brecht, Eisenstein, Camus and Sartre were victims.

The character most easily identified with the present position of Sartre is Ciro, a character who Sartre never had in his hands. Visconti as a metteur-en-scène of his thoughts, arranges five theses within his film and moves the last one (Luca) in the direction of a future dialogue. After his sectarian political conversion, Visconti directs his ideas with the same precision with which he directs his actors. He throws Luca into the discourse between Marxism and humanism, and on top of this thesis he builds the myth of Rocco.

It's history undergoing revolution.

[3] CIRO FACE TO FACE WITH VISCONTI
What follows is part of an interview with Luchino Visconti by Guido Aristarco in *Tiempo de Cine*, Buenos Aires, December 1960.

> I will tell you now that the character of Ciro was a character that always featured in the script. I remember that for that reason I wasn't always in agreement with my collaborators who said to me 'No, it isn't necessary to give Ciro this characteristic, to give him this value...' 'No,' I responded, 'it is necessary to give him this value.' I remember there were huge arguments because I wanted Ciro to perhaps be a bit hard, perhaps a little cruel in relation to the luck of the fallen brother (Simone). I insisted: 'He is like that, it's normal that he is like that because Ciro defends certain values. Ciro acquires this conscience little by little when living in Milan, and when he becomes a skilled worker in a factory like Alfa Romeo he sees certain things in a different way from his brothers. That's why he can't help being a little hard.' 'But then he's going to change into a character who is too cruel and bad,' they replied. And I said, 'No, he's not cruel, he is just a little, how do you say it, intransient, and, well, to me that means being fair, and at the end of the story he suffers a real emotional crisis which, even then, doesn't make him turn from his path.' Ciro said: 'This is the right path.' Ciro is the only one who, at base, learns something.[35]

And Visconti continues: 'Ciro for me is the one truly positive character in the film, in the best sense of the word, and it is he who ends the film. That is: he ends the film in a positive way. Any other way and the story would be too negative...!!!'[36]

Visconti, however, doesn't prop up his character under the guise of an indispensible working man. Society corrupts, just like it corrupts the pure rural man of the likes of Rocco and Simone. Visconti said bitterly of Ciro, 'Ciro will probably end up a bourgeois man...perhaps an important one at that. I don't know. I still feel that way.'[37]

In giving Ciro's defence in this way, and also disguising in a public interview his revolt against the fable/Rocco, Visconti (who in the film edits Ciro like a thesis) has the uncomfortable feeling that Ciro's character would end up a bourgeois man in real life...it is a bitter disbelief in man, but ultimately a clearer vision of things.

These are the nerves of *Rocco*. Simone, Luca, Vincenzo, Nadia and Rocco himself are figures of tragedy: simple and traditional figures in the dialectic pyramid. The whole mise-en-scène is evolved towards Ciro. Without the film's epilogue, the rest would be no more than an outmoded waltz, and this is something that Visconti himself admits. However, always at the side of the thinker is the artist.

Viscontian Baroque

When discussing cinema in the light of the new lease of life given to cinematographic language with the coming of Alain Resnais, Jean-Luc Godard, Michelangelo Antonioni and other young men of the cinematic world, a film like *Rocco and His Brothers* throws into the fray a fundamental problem: the freedom of a conventional form or, rather, Visconti's denial of the new explosion of youth and at the same time the modern and familiar force of his discourse.

Visconti adds, by way of *Rocco and His Brothers*, a new chapter to the polemic between cinema and fiction, bestowing a novelist dimension onto the world of cinema. *Rocco and His Brothers*, as much as it is considered to be simply a 'masterpiece of traditional cinema', is actually as modern in its style as *Hiroshima mon amour*, a film which, although it appears to be something 'new', it is no more – if it were to be characterized structurally – than a film which is 'new in cinema' but not something 'new for cinema' or, rather, Resnais' narrative processes are 'nouveau roman' – to which are added chapters using Faulkner's atemporal technique, as well as still being sustained by the Eisensteinian theory of cinematographic monologue, as expounded upon in *Film Form*,[38] when the Russian master was studying the adaptation of *Ulysses* by James Joyce.

Cinema is an art form which is still precarious as a form of expression beyond the technical – it's an art form which has yet to free itself from the conventional limits of photography and the mechanical editing with their infallible results in terms of perception. The novel, as traditional as it may be, never suffered the anguished chronology of cinema. When Resnais broke with conventional cinematographic time, he was only doing what the novel had been doing since the arrival of Proust: highlighting memory and oblivion, *Hiroshima mon amour* tackles the problematic of Proust, which transcends the cycle of lost time.

Cinema, in its position as an art of the public, brought to the masses and even to a naturally alienated critical response the collision which was dubbed 'new', and there is no need for us to negate the enthusiastic logic of intellectuals who are extraneous to cinema when faced with Resnais' work.

On Cinema

The revolutionary discourse can in fact be found within the novels of the great authors – Dostoyevsky, Dickens, Stendhal, Proust, Joyce and Faulkner (to name just half a dozen representatives of this category) and in cinema it only began to exist from *Hiroshima mon amour* onwards, something which was both a consequence of the fictional influence and of the despair following the annihilation of this narrative form itself, not only due to the ends to which it was taken but also due to the evidence of the communicative force of cinema, both on a 'social' level and on levels of 'perception'.

However, if *Hiroshima mon amour* is also of value as it brings a new narrative process to cinema – a method of human awareness – *Rocco and His Brothers* is of value because it unleashes this awareness into the apparently traditional language – destroying at the same time the well-behaved line of the old cinematographic chronology while imposing the tortuous line of the novel onto the realisation of cinematic works.

Rocco and His Brothers doesn't tell a story within a specific timeframe. It is, instead, a narrative cycle of facts which complement each other in the evolution of the conflict. Being a realist, Visconti doesn't interrupt real time but dramatic time, not subjecting the form to an experience but handling it in the manner in which a well-structured element is handled in order to properly know it in all honesty: developing this form through the theme, achieving beauty via the consolidated roots of a conflict which becomes more and more intense. In short, a game played with the character who then loses his characteristic of 'character' and becomes instead an objective world, wherein tragedy seeps into every pore.

In this manner, in *Rocco and His Brothers*, Visconti no longer keeps to the operatic form we see in *Senso* and *White Nights*: he moves on from opera not to a modern novel of 'formal experience' but to a modern novel of 'grandiose experience'. If before, in *Senso*, the mark of Stendhal's spirit was present, now, in *Rocco and His Brothers*, not only the fraternal violent drama of the Karamazov is intertwined in the whole works but we also find the mythical tradition of the same dramaturgy as that of the biblical saga of Cain and Abel – Joseph and His Brothers. When Visconti is portraying brothers he is portraying the fraternal tragedy on a grandiose scale, and it is for this reason that he doesn't fixate on the individualistic provincialism. It's even for this reason that he doesn't fixate on tragedy in film form, in the way a film is conventionally considered. His conventions are those of

O Século do Cinema

human sentiment channelled through the expressive forms of emotion: theatre, novels, opera and cinema.

Evolving from a 'cinematographic' narrative – when he moves from neorealist documentary style (Vincenzo's wedding) to (an already classified) Latino expressionism (the hysterical weeping of Rocco and Simone in the bed, with the pathetic intervention by the mother), Visconti bestows upon Latin cinema its specific condition, isolating the aesthetic of a race and a culture. The passionate explosion is transformed into an object not because of the establishing sound shots but because, while rejecting the academic logic of emotion in its exact form, he both comments on and criticizes these forms through the masterfulness of his art: it's a Latin sensualist view of the arts and emotions, all of which translates into a complete revision of the artistic history of our basic culture, which is criticized, not on a moralistic level, but from the point of view of his awareness of the necessity of revolution.

Visconti's cinematographic work finds in *Rocco and His Brothers* a well-accomplished portrait of Latin culture.

What is drawn out as essentially baroque in *Rocco and His Brothers* is that which is the determining factor in the cultural-historical evolution of neorealism: from *Obsession* to *Rocco and His Brothers* the visual seduction has evolved, but it is within the baroque that the characteristics of the *verist Latin portrait* can be found.

It is the *Viscontian baroque*.

Rocco and His Brothers is one of those events which transcend a crisis: Visconti, being a great filmmaker, uses the mise-en-scène as something other than a fundamental focus which satisfies small human necessities. And by not being moralistic, his argument breaks free of the 'Latin' limits, breaks away from criticism of provincial mores, analyses humanity by way of its causes and consequences in the psycho-social conflict and in this setting, free of preconceptions, Visconti throws onto the table two elements which shock the bourgeoisie: sex and money. Money and sex! And its politics, treated in a pitiless and cruel way, without concession.

In *Rocco and His Brothers*, Visconti, like in all his work, descends into the condemnation of society and continues to despise the morality of society which exists *only* for the purpose of humanity's individual and collective despair. He believes in higher values, and they are those which shock the bourgeoisie as they are popular values: love of the land, affinity with the earth's roots and the awareness of its purity.

Rocco is bucolic – the goodness inherent in Rocco is the lyricism in the shepherd and his sheep. Rocco is good in the same way as Joseph is good – and his brothers do not understand him. It is for this reason that Simone beats him, in the same way that Joseph's brothers sell him to faraway Egypt. It is from this point that we see the culmination of real events which drive Rocco towards evil, to sin, the point to which Rocco evolves and where he ends up.

Luca sees the posters of Rocco, corrupted, announcing his success and when he walks on, it is Rocco's purity which sings and lays bare the hope of a possible rural paradise.

The despair is not born of man – man's denial – but rather man reaches despair because the fact that society is motivated by sex and money drives him to that point.

Visconti is not an abstract artist, like Fellini, who criticizes the times without showing that the immorality of the *dolce vita* is nothing more than *a nauseating period of capitalism.*

The state of things are clear but Fellini is let down by a falsely human characteristic – his reporter is shocked by the sexual scandals – Fellini is scandalized by sex, behaving in a provincial manner, just like the Parondi's mother when Simone brings a prostitute *into* the house.

The human tragedy is within the social scenery: Ciro is a slave to Alfa Romeo, to money (he has no time for love because the factory bell calls him; he deserves Simone's repulsion as he is nothing more than a consummate worker); Vincenzo won't interfere for money (what is important to him is his petit-bourgeois family); Simone is corrupted by money; Rocco becomes a boxer and rubs shoulders with Evil because of money; their mother goes to Milan with her sons because of money (to 'make a better life for everyone after the death of her husband'); the prostitute who detests vulgarity (she won't speak of money) is already corrupted by money (Visconti makes it clear that prostitution is taken up only by poor and ignorant women because any other way, as a result of vice or moral laxity, the woman is no more than an adulterer and what she really needs is love, above all things).

Only on that point does Visconti talk of love: The prostitute is not interested in Rocco for sex. For her it's 'whatever'. With Rocco she wants to return to original purity embodied in the figure of Alain Delon. And, in the rest of the dramatic cycle, sex, which corrupts Simone and sets him against

Rocco (sex and all of the provincial preconceptions which the Parondi bring with them from Catania to Milan), envelops Rocco, not in terms of the prostitute but in relation to men – to whom the beauty of Rocco is irresistible, to the point where he becomes the lover of a boxing promoter – not due to his weakness for pleasures of the flesh but for money: money to save his brother from shame and from his crimes, to save the human being.

Rocco is amoral. Rocco helps, collaborates with Evil, he forgives Evil and he accepts Evil because he is good. Rocco does not forgive himself and it's the pure (and inconsistent) morality of Rocco that pushes him (and all the Parondi) to the precipice of tragedy.

When Rocco gives up the love of the prostitute because he prefers to help Simone, he begins to deny himself as a man.

Visconti makes it clear that purity is impossible; it is the lesson shown by the Bible itself in the resistance of Joseph to the charms of Potiphar's wife which resulted in Joseph being thrown into the dungeons. And even if he does return from thence a prince, it is also from there that the grounds for the slavery of his race are born.

Rocco in the end is the economic salvation of the Parondi family (he will earn oceans of money in boxing), but it's too late: shame and corruption have stained the name of the mother who is no longer greeted as 'Signora' in the street and therein the honour of her sons has been destroyed. And no amount of money in the entire world will undo the tragedy which has seeped into the breast of the Parondi family.

Visconti's political position is the criticism of man – on a universal level – and of Latin emotion on a cultural level, since this Marxist-homosexual-aristocrat would not for one instant deny himself to be a man of his roots.

Transgressing machismo – he doesn't hide his love for Alain Delon, nor his disdain for woman in the dramatic progress of man (the mother in the story is of no use to her sons and the prostitute is not a 'woman' in terms of the social conventions of the bourgeoisie, whether in fiction or in real life) – Visconti continues to show, in the bedroom scenes, the identification of man by man. When the two brothers howl hysterically over the death of the woman they love, within that tragedy it isn't, in fact, two brothers who both tear each other apart and comfort each other but rather two men (and their mother serves as no barrier between the two).

He doesn't fear male sensuality, gliding the camera over the bodies of the boxers, whether they're in the ring or in the shower, just like he cares little about the lack of a sister within the family to balance out the relations amongst the Parondi brothers – the archaic tragedy is indeed based on the forbidding of homosexuality as represented by Cain and Abel.

The Splendour of a God

[1]

Discussing Visconti as merely an aristocratic Marxist is no more than empty tittle-tattle. His conception of anthropomorphic cinema or his exemplary position as a purveyor of critical realism are positions created for him by the commentators who repeat the conversations of Guido Aristarco in an attempt to link literature to cinema by way of Georg Lukács. For twenty years, Visconti served to unite critics of both left and right via the myth of the aristocratic Marxist. Despite the flow of Viscontian material, cinema moved with the advent of Godard's general theory and with the rediscovery of Eisenstein. *The Stranger* (*Lo straniero*, 1967) provoked a general stampede: the master had attempted to shatter his own model, practising the alchemy of the zoom technique paired with existentialism. The loss of confidence in his work began with that zoom shot in the mirror in *Rocco and His Brothers* and reached 'unhealthy' proportions in *Sandra* aka *Sandra of a Thousand Delights* (*Vaghe stelle dell'Orsa*, 1965)... Unhealthy perhaps for the votaries of popular national cinema, which had produced a good disciple in Francesco Rosi. For Visconti, who always considered Godard 'intelligent but superficial', the zoom shot was a healthy malaise, tearing a hole through the quilt of rags woven with provincial myths which is Italian culture.

Visconti knows that Italy is a country of 'painters' and turns a blind eye to the fact that Rossellini created Godard, who has transformed cinema. Cinema was transformed, just as it was invented, in France, but the genius of Rossellini returned to the restrictions of the peninsula. Rossellini also knows (like Pasolini when talking to the press) that Italy is a country of 'painters' and it's thanks to this complex that it was Roberto himself who invented a remote-controlled zoom. If Pasolini's break with neorealism was the unleashing of the 'cinema of poetry' in *The Gospel according to St. Matthew*, emphatically employing the 'handheld camera', the real break with neorealism (two years before Pasolini did it) was *Before the Revolution* by Bertolucci, precisely because of the long zoom shots he employed, a Baroquesque introduction of vertical montage to Italian cinema. The cinema of a country of 'painters', Italian cinema could not accept the idea of using editing for anything other than rhythmical composition; the dialectic montage, advocated by Eisenstein, would be tried out in the cinema of other countries, rich in the plays of time, but visually inferior.

The person who established frontal framing in modern cinema was Rossellini, but the person who was aware of it was Godard. Expressionist cinema was only interested in set design and the camera served to capture the 'décor'. Rossellini diluted the décor within the framing and the person who gave filmic space to the décor was Antonioni. Roberto's *Journey to Italy* is, simultaneously, the mother of Michelangelo's fluid space and that of Godard's dialectically deconstructed space. While Antonioni dilated both the depth and the sides of the shot, Jean-Luc worked on the editing (at the beginning breaking it down into pieces, in the style of Joyce, then weaving in Eisenstein's lessons and, finally, 'constructing' in the manner of Dziga Vertov).

Reintroducing theatrical décor into the filmic space, Bertolucci, and above all Pasolini, were the first Italian filmmakers to become aware of the absence of editing. Pasolini theorized on this impasse in his theory 'cinema of prose, cinema of poetry' but he committed the error of approximating literary language to filmic language: for Pasolini the cinema of prose would be opposite to that of poetry (cinema of discontinuous editing). Getting behind the ball with both feet, Pier Paolo said that the handheld camera and the zoom shot were characteristic of the poetic. The ball struck the crossbar at a time when Christian Metz, Roland Barthes, Gianni Toti, Adriano Aprà and others began to evoke Roman Jakobson, thus creating a linguistic hunchback for cinema. Godard broke up the circus, saying that in the case of cinema a different, new and as yet unarticulated language was needed; the terminology applied had to be different. Barthes, now already recognising that Jean-Luc was right, and that Pasolini was offside, said:

> For written texts, unless they are very conventional, totally committed to logico-temporal order, reading time is free; for film, this is not so, since the image cannot go faster or slower without

losing its perceptual figure. The still, by instituting a reading that is at once instantaneous and vertical, scorns logical time (which is only an operational time); it teaches us how to dissociate the technical constraint from what is the specific filmic and which is the 'indescribable' meaning.[39]

The 'third sense' of which Barthes speaks is that 'obtuse' sense, the meaning of which is not immediately obvious. A sense which is historically tangible although at once impossible to describe and the pleasure resultant from it is impossible to deny. It's the same sense Eisenstein meant when he spoke of the fourth cinematic dimension, or spatial montage:

> The bringing together of binary opposites which Eisenstein thought typical of the androgynous divinities of Mexico was also found to exist in other mythological systems, by way of modern anthropological studies. This served to confirm Eisenstein's ideas, according to whom the premise served to explain the existence of numerous archetypes in culture. This bringing together of opposites (and included under this theory were the opposites of art and science) characterized, according to Eisenstein, his favourite artist, Leonardo Da Vinci. This was proven by his drawing, 'Leonardo', wherein, at the side of the painter is drawn a logarithmic spiral engraved in a circle, the symbol of the association of the *Rangées* classified as Yin and Yang.[40]

The obtuse sense spoken about by Barthes has more to do with the nucleus of the 'cinema of poetry' than the editing created by the succession of zoom coups by Pasolini: this subjective editing only decomposes a filmic space saturated with obvious sense.

Unaware of the harmonious montage which, ironically, Eisenstein had discovered when studying Leonardo Da Vinci, the Italian filmmakers present their signs on the immediate level of History.

For them, the zoom is the 'modern' paintbrush, capable of creating the 'poetic sense', a transcendence which animates the landscape and an escape from the concreteness of French cinema.

When Jean-Marie Straub says that Pasolini's cinema is more and more idealistic, we are finally provided with a comprehensible explanation for the difference between the filmic language of France and Italy, because the zoom paintbrush held by Claude Lelouch is an empty 'poetic' search and the zoom held by Visconti translates as a vertical cut into the horizontal pictorialism of Italian cinema.

Visconti's use of zoom is the only filmic detail in his literary representation. Aware that Italian cinema would never cotton on so quickly to montage using its own 'painting' technique, Visconti transformed everything into literature, even the theatrical space. And this literature, cinematographically reduced to a bad-taste melodrama, is reborn through the 'zoom to close-up' of Visconti's cinematic icons.

Before using his first zoom, in the boxing gym scene in *Rocco and His Brothers*, Visconti, at the peak of his critical prestige, had filmed nothing more than theatrical illustrations of literary works. And before that, only in the close-up of the lovers' dance at the bar in *White Nights*, which was 'the end of a zoom shot which never existed', is there any filmic concreteness (non-verbalized) in his cinema. It was in *Sandra* wherein Visconti solidified this filmic absence. And it was when faced with the zoom shots which broke down his system of set design that the critics began to badmouth him. However, it was from there that Visconti began to give his archetypes a formal filmic shape; archetypes which before had been disassembled in a theatrical play-off between Chekhov and Shakespeare.

The strength of disenchanted destiny concludes in the dance scene of *The Leopard* (*Il gattopardo*, 1963). The search outside one's own destiny takes us nowhere, given that it is the shame of being too tragic which cast a shadow over *Sandra* and eclipses *The Foreigner*. Visconti's political criticism of destiny (always an aristocratic family in literary decay) was calmly put forward in *The Damned* (*La caduta degli dei*, 1969). The zoom is not an insipid stammer (as employed by Elio Petri), it is not an enraged poetic style (Pasolini), it is not a baroque interruption (Bertolucci), it is not a natural description (Rossellini).

The zoom shot is a way of frictioning fiction like a phallus, leaving aside all other methods of intervention into reality.

The qualitative difference between a TV soap and *The Damned* is that a TV soap is fiction illustrated and constructed metrically. *The Damned* is fiction represented and constructed tonally and rhythmically: the montage formed using the rhythm of the zoom which dramatically communicates the tonal montage of the actors. In Einsteinian theory, the tonal montage is that in which: 'the movement is perceived in a wider sense. The concept of this movement embraces *all effects* of the montage piece. Here the montage is based on the characteristic *emotional sound* of the piece – of its dominant. The general *tone* of the piece.'[41]

Visconti's characters are Visconti's actors. Icons forged via the surpassing of the prosaic by the historical. The conventional unfeasibility of the placement of these characters in any other context is the very opposite in Visconti's tonal montage. The 'fallen Gods' in *The Damned*, who only differ in terms of their social position when compared with the 'demonic working classes' in *Rocco and His Brothers*, would, naturally, be restructured into non-characters in post-Brecht works by many filmmakers, including myself, who were worried about the trajectory that cinema was taking. Luchino, however, stands firm in his opinions and for him cinema is nothing more than an altar for icons. An altar born as a result of that cinema of 'painters', in the set design inherited from expressionism and which represents Italy of old (or Europe of old) which is tumbling into chaos through earthquakes and bombings but which remains in ruins and museums.

It is for this reason that Visconti, the most European of all filmmakers (being as he is Italian), had the audacity to film 'a Nazi tragedy', a work which, according to the rules of play, should have been made by Fritz Lang.

[2]

Visconti said to me that he preferred to make a film on Nazism because Italian Fascism had been a farce and he wanted to portray the greatest tragedy of the twentieth century.

I don't think it is worth discussing whether the 'historical facts' of *The Damned* are correct because it would be difficult for them to be incorrect. Nicola Badalucco and Visconti researched the period in which Nazism was founded in Germany and that which was then converted to a cinema drama is sufficient to situate Visconti's ghosts in a historical context, out of his sociologist limits, and then give them a general context which could even be reapplied line by line to other countries in the 1970s. The capitalists' 'plan', falling over themselves in a bid to seize power and making any deal necessary in the name of the bellicose National Socialism movement, was no greater a plan than that, as crass or as simplistic as it may seem. The historical repetition of an event always seems comical, as Hegel pointed out. However, within that comedy blood is spilt, as the puppet masters, be it Hitler or Trujillo, always kill. Visconti creates a whole inventory of tragic and psychoanalytical archetypes (Macbeth, Hamlet, Freud).

This is the best way of portraying it because in certain moments of History things are blatantly simplistic.

Today's tragedy is the melodrama of the past and it is for this reason that *The Damned*, a work overt in its demonstration (flourished with zoom shots) of absurd antiquities marks Visconti's return to his best filmmaking work in the style of *Senso* and *Rocco and His Brothers*, and at the same time marks an opportunity for the practice of political cinema, hovering over the polemic carcass of the debate.

As an aristocrat, the Count does not mingle but sends his message. Making melodrama out of industries and beds he transforms his autobiography on more than one occasion in order to point out to us that totalitarian fury is born out of irrationalism.

'Who will be tomorrow's victim?' is what one of the characters (Herbert in *The Damned*) is more or less asking.

Visconti belongs to the time of fiction and it was good that the zoom gave him the filmic power to show us the coarse, criminal and novelesque face of the Nazis.

Antonioni

Born in the last century, Michelangelo would have been a philosopher like Hegel and perhaps would have the same importance for the world back then as the philosopher himself did. Today, substituting written language for image and sound, Michelangelo uses cinema as a speculative tool at the same time as he founds, in the film, his moral style.

Michelangelo, understanding the communicative importance of cinema, didn't choose it like the majority of directors did, attracted as they were to a new art form.

For Michelangelo, as in the case of a few others (Godard, Rossellini, nevertheless, all from the same family), cinema is simply his language; the conscience of an artist who, counter to the general suicide of modern art, looks to unravel the facts which emerge at every stage in this reality.

Cinema, for Michelangelo, given that it is his conscience, is not a limitation: it is from this cinematic foundation that Michelangelo establishes what is known as the dialectic of alienation.

The alienation of man living in the modern world is Michelangelo's field of knowledge:

On Cinema

> Como se realizzando un film, vivendo questo periodo di tempo al servizio di una vicenda, io non mettessi in giuoco tutti i miei problemi e non li risolvessi oggettivandoli. Ma realizzando il film io sono consapevole, presente a me stesso, al mio ambiente, alla mia storia, e sono alienato nella misura in cui questo fatto mi induce a soffrire l'alienazione, a combaterla e superarla facendo il film.[42]

Through film he establishes and overcomes alienation, he widens his conscience.

In no other art form can style be the foundation of a moral code. It is simply from the relation between the filmmaker and cinema, and cinema with reality, from the synthesis of *filmmaker, cinema and reality* which is the *film as conscience* that it is possible to divide the periods of cinematographic aesthetics thus:

(a) Style as a discourse on morality (from Lumière to Visconti)
(b) Style as morality (from Rossellini to Michelangelo and from Michelangelo to the filmmakers of the future).

Or, according to Gustavo Dahl's explanation [quoting André Bazin], there exists a division between those directors who believe in the image and those who believe in reality.

Visconti, creating a historical discourse, *used image*, whereas Michelangelo surpasses his contemporary, who was representative of an era, and incorporates the reality-image, that is to say, not reality at the service of cinema, but cinema as an 'object'.

Michelangelo's cinema is disconcerting in its pace and in its frame; it is a *real cinema*, not a documentary at the periphery of reality, not a discursive connotation of reality, not an instrument through which to exercise a dialectic but rather something *historical* in itself, *dialectic* in itself.

It is from there that Michelangelo's alienation is dialectically related to the alienation of the spectator.

These relationships are the same relationships as Michelangelo's before a world where science is evolving more than morality. A world which alienates at every turn and which, either by applying *theory* or *practice*, overcomes each stage of alienation only to create a new one in its stead.

O Século do Cinema

Funeral Space

The mise-en-scène is a question of morality: mise-en-scène is not just an allegory of actors' movements.

The mise-en-scène is the new language which unites the camera with man, which breaks through the barriers of narrative photography. This new language doesn't offer what the spectator wants but rather what the spectator *needs* in order to decipher man, progress and politics.

The old rules have collapsed. The monsters have been left behind in the studios; the industry has been identified with capitalist oppression. What remains is the instrument of creation and liberty, which the artist moulds according to his politics. Today everything is becoming confused in terms of cinema: the intellectual has discovered the craftsmanship to be found within the editing when in fact this grammatical rhythm has already been destroyed by Rossellini and forgotten by the filmmakers who are now seized with the need to cast their camera lens onto real events, focusing it with another vision. The old-school critics are scandalized, acting like puritans, when faced with the anarchy of a climax which explodes in an establishing shot when it should explode in a close-up accompanied by dramatic music. The public is the victim; it is under no obligation to understand any of it since it has become sterile in the face of the industrial mode. Violating the alienation of this public is the first action of New Cinema, violating them through the mise-en-scène, because the modern mise-en-scène is always an idea in motion and what results from it is the reconstructed world, commented upon and criticized.

How best to approach an architect such as Michelangelo Antonioni: a fifty-year-old man who causes polemics within the cinematic world by bringing into it more and more disintegrated films, up to the point of *The Eclipse* which represents the end of figurative cinema, the end of the mise-en-scène, the death song for European man who has forgotten who he is, brutalized by the present?

It is necessary to have faith in humanity. All the left-wing criticism violates this artist of gesture and space who penetrated reality with the camera and blew through the emotions of the human figure to the point of eclipsing the human condition.

Antonioni is not a moralist – his is a scientific attitude mutilated through an excess of passion.

Antonioni, Visconti and Rossellini are great fighters in this Europe of defunct wild beasts – human creatures cast aside by this sanitized movement, deprived of blood and love.

They are dead, Sartre said in the terrible preface of a book about Algeria.[43]

What is *The Eclipse* if not a testament of this dead world, wherein the capitalist machine has suffocated love? What is left is a world full of objects – some solid, some rotten. And if Antonioni allows himself to be beaten, if he accepts suicide, if he simply admits like Rossellini (in a recent interview in *Cahiers du Cinéma*)[44] that cinema is a *toute petite chose* – a very small thing, you or I refuse this death because it has been thrown in our faces.

The Eclipse illuminates man – the eclipse of an idea which bubbles up to the point of violent refusal: Antonioni violates with logical argument that which Buñuel violates with passion and humour, Rossellini with poetry and mysticism, Visconti with the dialectic of a Marxist who doubts at every turn.

It is the job of the artist to violate – the artist is the eternal left-winger, logical or anarchic – the artist only begins to deny himself when he becomes part of the established order, when he stops exercising his critical powers of observation upon the world, upon the State, upon bourgeois conformity, upon the crowd pleasers. The artist is a being working in opposition – if he lives through Fascism he is anti-fascist, if he lives in Brazil, underdeveloped and starving, or in colonized North Africa, he is a revolutionary, using his head and heart to defend and liberate man from totalitarianism.

Orson Welles has acted thus ever since filming *Citizen Kane* and when he filmed *The Trial*, based on the novel by Kafka, he rained down the venom of State power on a non-descript Josef, who is a man both cornered and driven.

Liberty is oppressed by alienation and therefore any method is both valid and fair in order to break through this absurd unconsciousness, lack of strength, lack of responsibility in body and soul and lack of knowledge.

Civilization is dead and cinema cannot save it! This is what Antonioni concludes via the final sequence of his film when he removes all the characters from the scene and wanders through the empty streets, through the skeletal buildings being constructed, through objects, through sewers – when the camera comes to rest on the shot of a sun or a lamp which shines only for it to then be snuffed out.

O Século do Cinema

Two opposing forces are at work: the old culture which represents capitalism, aestheticism, contemplation, and the new culture which is revolutionary.

The capitulation of the old culture takes place via its geniuses: the artist rebels against the structure itself and grows stronger in order to destroy it, then destroys himself, annihilating the contemplative being – this man who, according to Sartre, should bow out to the new man waiting in the wings to replace him.

Antonioni, like Rossellini, Visconti, Buñuel, Orson Welles, is a son of this cinema which has destroyed itself in the fight against the old systems in place; this corpse which is resuscitated each time, only to expire once more.

The language is of hate and violence. We are, however, inheritors of a world which both amazes and humiliates us and it is within this conflict, the eternal two-way struggle, that we then discover the difficult path of reality.

I am against language used in order to deceive, to mystify, to create emotions. The masses whipped into an emotional state can just as easily follow Fascism as follow Socialism.

In Brazil, Latin America and in Africa, the mise-en-scéne is the birth.

If Brazilian *cinema novo* starts from scratch, from the point of anti-editing and anti-structure, if this revolutionary cinema ignores the past and doesn't accept the present, if our revolutionary morality is the truth and its complex, then down with demagoguery!

Herein lies the importance of Antonioni in his refusal, in his suicide, in his tragic condition.

If the mise-en-scène is the morality of the auteur, and the bourgeoisie and the alienated masses together refuse this morality, this cinema is revolutionary.

How can the people understand the revolution which is taking place if the revolution is the actual fight to liberate these closed consciences which are incapable of conceptualizing hunger?

Art marches ahead of politics; its power is greater as it is free. The artist's conflict with politics ends up taking him to the furthest extremes of crisis: when he turns on himself and on the past, the bourgeoisie applauds him because the flames have stopped lapping at his feet.

The artist consumes himself.

Buñuel doesn't: he always burns the Church and Fascism to the ground.

I don't believe that the new world is Fascist and Catholic. What will be the purpose of the artist after the cinema of spectacle, after figurative cinema, after the clean man? What will this humanity be which chooses other weapons in its fight? What grandeur is there in any gesture which argues against passion for the future, against knowing the unknown? This is what the sons of the new world are searching the answer to day after day, refusing, destroying, radicalizing.

I believe that the great importance of Antonioni and Resnais are the final images of the old world which they have bestowed upon us – abstract images, men with no souls, empty gestures, spaces which move and are then lost in a time which is eternally moving in a loop.

As strange as it may sound, the new man is responsible for the image in which his future fellow man will be created – one different from that which has died: this will be the great struggle of the artist.

Glauber Fellini

Father Arpa is a Jesuit who founded the 'Columbianum' cultural institute in the 1960s, based in Genoa, and whose objective was the promotion of cultural activities.

After a series of international festivals and cultural congresses, the Columbianum held the 'Terzo Mondo e Comunità Mondiale' [Third World and World Community] Congress.

Father Arpa was the father of emerging culture in a mega shopping centre financed by Christian-Democrat capitalists of Liberal Italy, welcoming some of the most fearful intellectuals both from Europe and the United States and from developing countries in an audiovisual saga which brought together Roland Barthes and Franz Fanon, Murilo Mendes and Georges Sadoul, Alejo Carpentier and Norman Mailer, Alberto Moravia and Nicolas Guillén, Leopold Senghor and Edgar Morin, Jean Rouch and João Guimarães Rosa, Antonio Candido de Mello e Souza and Jean-Paul Sartre, Paulo Emilio Sales Gomes and Federico Fellini, Gustavo Dahl and Visconti, Paulo Cesar Saraceni and Bernardo Bertolucci who was falling in love in the fog, Pier Paolo Pasolini, quite taken by Regina Rozemburgo, times in which Brazil shone in Italy by the light of Brazilian Ambassador Hugo Gouthier.

O Século do Cinema

The Congress grew by way of round tables, conferences, projections, interviews with global television networks, parties, tourism etc.

Father Arpa, always telephoning from his office for Fellini who had not yet arrived, tied up as he was with the filming of *Juliet of the Spirits* (*Giuletta degli spiriti*, 1965), was faced with censoring issues raised by various different reactionary embassies representing various Third World countries, who were trying to ban the screening of certain films or the circulation of various subversive books as well as requesting from the Italian police the profiles of various underdeveloped intellectuals in contact with developed intellectuals.

The CIA, KGB, G2, SNI [National Information Service of Brazil], 3/ Bureau etc. wandered the corridors of the Congress with tape recorders and handheld camcorders collecting the images and sounds of those meetings held between members of the world's intellectual vanguard.

Under the guise of the 'Alliance for Progress', multi-national cultural foundations financed projects in various colonized countries or neo-colonized countries which culminated in congresses of *Latin American only* intellectuals held in Puerto Rico, Caracas and Mexico, until the scandal of the 'Camelô Plan' blew up, revealing that the Inter-American Art Organization financed by the Rockefeller Foundation was the launch pad of the CIA Department of Culture in the universities. Political organizations and Third World underground movements corrupting the best representatives providing study grants to members of the intellectual avant-garde; colonizing them, transforming them into indirect agents or informants of the North American *Department of Culture*, converting them into advertisements for Hollywood or for the North American universities, imposing a bourgeois lifestyle, a middle-class way of life, and improving the living conditions of the proletariat and marginalized peoples with basic reforms backed by the 'Alliance for Progress'.

The Rockefeller Congress, presided over by Rockefeller's son, Rodman Rockefeller, blew up in October/November 1964 in Xyche Y Itza (State of Yucatan, Mexico) where 58,000 US dollars of whisky was drunk, served by Gabriel García Márquez in the presence of illustrious Brazilians such as Burle Marx, Aluísio Magalhães and Eros Martim Gonçalves, led by Carlos Fuentes, managing the relations between North and South America obstructed by the situation in Cuba, until the Mexican playwright Juan José Gurrolla and the Spanish writer Juan García Ponche got to their feet shouting that 'the CIA are controlling the congress; last night we climbed up the creepers to the veranda of Mr Rockefeller's room and we saw him scheming up a manifesto which was planned to be read out today, on behalf of the CIA in order to try to transform us into "faggots" controlled by imperialist corruption....'.

Father Arpa's congress, in Genoa, was in February/March of 1965 and back in Mexico I only had time to play a walk-on part in *Simon of the Desert*. I met Buñuel in the Churubuzco studios and he ordered me out to be an extra as a beatnik dancing to rock and roll at the end of the film, when Simon passes from the tower to Times Square – the God who comes to kill King Kong!

Buñuel said to me on the subject of $8\frac{1}{2}$ (*Otto e mezzo*, 1963): 'It's a fantastic film. Fellini is the best filmmaker in the world!'

I had seen $8\frac{1}{2}$ in Mexico and I sent a critical review to Zuenir Ventura, who was the editor of *Diário Carioca* [the Rio de Janeiro-based daily] at that time, revising my opinions on Fellini whom I had slated in the Bahian press as a reactionary filmmaker – and Buñuel's pronouncement on the film, which blindsided me, was equivalent to a pardon from the Pope himself.

'Fellini the Devil' was like a God to Buñuel. My critical U-turn took place before my meeting with Buñuel, but what alerted me was the fact that Buñuel, *muy de si mismo*, recognized, with such admiration and with no trace of envy, Fellini's superior talent.

I flew for the first time over frozen New York and I didn't bat an eyelid, concentrating, during the Los Angeles/New York/Milan flight on writing my thesis 'An Aesthetics of Hunger',[45] which would be my Third-World manifesto at the Genoa Congress.

I stated to the press that the Mexico Congress had been controlled by the CIA and that I represented purely national interests and therefore I did not wish to mix with any manifestation of international State interventionism, from whichever State it might come from, so that our Art might remain in all its original vitality etc....something for which I was personally praised by Guimarães Rosa who up till then had been accused of being a reactionary, like Fellini, for taking a very strong stance on personal language even if at first sight it was rendered incomprehensible by the obscuring rhetoric of orthodoxy.

The screening of *Black God, White Devil* served to confirm both in theory and practice the 'aesthetics of hunger', and at the end of the

O Século do Cinema

Congress (during which L. and I conceived a child) Father Arpa, even though he was aware of my Protestant faith, organized a meeting in Rome the following week:

'*Voglio farti conoscere Fellini...*' ['I want to introduce you to Fellini...']

Staying in the house of the diplomat and philosopher Arnaldo Carrilho, I began to write the next dialogue and scene sequences for *Entranced Earth* and to send passionate letters to Rosa Maria de Oliveira Penna in faraway Botafogo, Rio de Janeiro.

Fellini was in the air!

Gustavo Dahl, a man possessing in-depth knowledge of world cinema, said to me, 'Look, there are only two good films to come out of Italy once you take away the old communists like Visconti, De Sica, the mystics financed by the Christian Democrats like Rossellini, Antonioni and Fellini. The newest thing on the scene is Francesco Rosi's film *Salvatore Giuliano* (1961) and *The Gospel according to Saint Matthew* by Pier Paolo Pasolini, who is a fantastic and mad hellhound, a mixture of Jean-Luc Godard and Che Guevara...'.

Salvatore Giuliano preceded *Black God, White Devil*... I met Pasolini in the Karlovy Vary International Film Festival in Czechoslovakia (he was presenting *Accattone*, 1961, and I was presenting *The Turning Wind*), and when I returned from Genoa to Rome, I went to see *The Gospel according to Saint Matthew*...

As I had filmed *Black God, White Devil* almost at the same time, Pasolini's film showed me common tribal and primitive identities... But I was already thinking about *Entranced Earth*, the sea which succeeds the *sertão*, waves beyond the *nouvelle vague*.

In Rio de Janeiro back in 1958, I was at the Alcázar (in Copacabana) having a beer with Miguel Borges, Cláudio Bueno Rocha, Leon Hirszman, Carlos Peres and other *cinema novo* people when Paulo Cesar Saraceni arrived, all done up in a trousers and sweater combo in the style of Marcello Mastroianni in *La dolce vita* (1960). We paid no attention to him, he introduced himself in an offhand manner and when he suddenly left without warning someone commented:

'That guy likes Fellini...'
'What?' I asked, 'You mean that Fellini has followers here?'

Saraceni wrote an article about *I vitelloni* (1953). He defends Fellini and Rossellini .... We need to throw in Buñuel and Visconti against these reactionaries who side with Ingmar Bergman, John Ford and all the imperialists led by the critics of the Film Archive of the Museum of Modern Art [Rio de Janeiro], the Antonio Moniz Vianna group ...

One day Carrilho told me that Father Arpa had called asking for me to expect him that evening, the day on which Fellini was due to visit.

Carrilho and the filmmaker Gianni Amico, Father Arpa's 'cinematographic secretary', told a story that Fellini used the Jesuit priest for metaphysical transactions and theirs was an intimacy of such proportions that '*in that scene in which you see a harp in $8\frac{1}{2}$ ... it's a metaphor for Father Arpa ... who plays the magical, musical poetry of eternal creation ... Pagan ... Roman ... Ancient Greek.*' On a cold and windy night, we went up the hillside, myself and Father Arpa, towards the brown gateway between pale moss, an abstract room, black car, Roman roads, past misty walls and solitary squares, to a cinematographic laboratory on the 'catacombic' outskirts of the city. With us eleven Fathers (I suppose they were all Jesuits). The first copy of *Juliet of the Spirits*, Fellini's latest production and first feature-length colour film, was screened, uncut and without the final soundtrack.

In the Futurist-Fascist Italy which flourishes in the 1920s from the debris of World War I, Fellini was an outcast wise-guy who chose spectacle as a way of life.

He was born in the countryside, he had a Catholic education, he felt the violence of fascism, became an actor, magician, cartoonist, polygrapher, photographer, musician and gigolo.

Fellini is a woman! Therein lies his sublimated contradiction in the filming of *colossal, fat and lascivious women*, just like him, in his Dionysian make-up, obese, bulging eyes, fleshy lips, tremulous hands which flushed hot and cold, the frustrated desire to be Anita Ekberg or [Brazilian actress] Elvira Pagã, in the court of Ivan, The Terrible as restaged by Visconti as part of the *historical compromise* between the Catholics and Communists.

Fellini is younger than Rossellini, Visconti, De Sica, he is of the generation which contained both Pasolini and Bertolucci, equivalent in Brazil to the famous group of formalists of 1945, but this is of no consequence as Fellini doesn't link himself to any avant-garde movement. He's an abnormal case, an aesthetic eruption with no equal.

O Século do Cinema

Fellini is reflected in the mirror of $8\frac{1}{2}$.

The novelty resides in the fact that it was the first time a filmmaker made himself into the self-diagnosing psychoanalyst protagonist of his own film, extending the genre much further than the simple projection of 'myself in other characters'; a reidentification of the 'character in myself' unmasked by unfettered creativity.

Fellini learnt his cinematic art as an electrician's apprentice, a camera assistant, a co-scriptwriter, set designer, producer and distributor and ended up directing by way of his involvement with a group of young neorealist filmmakers led by Visconti, De Sica, Zavattini and Rossellini.

Fellini had a circus and theatre background and proved to be an exceptional set designer, set decorator, costume designer, make-up artist, acrobat, ballerina, choreographer and director of actors.

He was a devourer of prostitutes in the same manner as De Sica. Whereas Rossellini slept in luxury sheets and Visconti was homosexual, Fellini, due to his paganism, never refused androgyny.

Visconti came into cinema by way of Romanesque Historical Opera, De Sica by way of Psychological Theatre, Rossellini by way of journalism and Fellini through Magic, the very incarnation of Lola Montès: a fundamental character in cinema created by Martine Carol and directed by Max Ophüls.

The origins of the Fellinian circus can be found in *Lola Montès* just like the origins of Orpheus' dream in the film by Jean Cocteau; modern trends cooked up in the great cauldron of Fascist cinema produced at the Cinecittà studios in Italy, wherein History was captured on film in accordance with Mussolini's degraded project.

A cat from the green mountains of the provinces, Fellini satirized the repressed unconscious of Italy's pagan culture drowned by Nazism. Visconti filmed the symbolic representations of the tragedy. Rossellini documented the ruins. Documentary maker of dreams, Fellini would recreate his dreams magically via his set designs and actors; the dream is the projection of his *kino-eye*.

Fellini filmed his interior as reflected in the mirror of his mise-en-scène. All filmmakers film themselves in the process of making a film, but Fellini is the only one who bypasses the 'historical ruins' and projects his ecstasy straight onto the screen. He is a filmmaker guiltless of his madness and beauty; he is the pagan magician, a genius capable of getting the public to join in with the dream and of revealing, through cinema, the fantastic cine-aesthetics of the creature which is Fellini.

When he began filming *Fellini's Casanova* (*Il Casanova di Federico Fellini*) in 1975, Fellini declared to the *Corriere della Sera* (Milan) that the film would be filtered through *a hole in my unconscious*; it was in fact more like a *channel burst open by the audiovisual flow, another crater which appeared and then reconstructed Venice in the studios, a catwalk for Casanova, the Solitary and Frigid Gigolo* ...

Meta/psychoanalytically, I can corner Fellini on the edge of an abyss or in the grey ruins of a medieval church and pinpoint him as Dionysius, god of orgy and spectacle, freed from the female spirits.

After co-directing various films, Fellini premiered as an author with *The White Sheik* (*Lo sceicco bianco*, 1952), featuring Alberto Sordi in the role of the swindler who transforms himself into a superstar because he manages to trick fools with a series of scams.

Alberto Sordi is the messed-up ladies' man: ugly, middle-class, bursting with repression. A clever little swindler who despises society and his fellow man and who takes pleasure in gaining false glory, achieved by trickery. It's a complacent reflection of the fascist petit-bourgeois man who thrived on past the end of the war...

Fellini doesn't belong to Italian society, Fellini is a Persian cat.

Fellini is oriental.

These oriental origins (the sources of which are as yet unrevealed) can be found in his long lashes which conceal ruby-blue pupils, like those of the cats which Cyrus kept in Pasargadae.

The Catholic veil is the weight which suffocates Fellini.

From the circus to the Vatican and from there to cafe society, television and cinema.

Fellini recognizes the Church and ignores politics, he recognizes capitalism which finances him with success and ignores the Italian State which spends its money advertising his nationality.

Fellini doesn't need to bend to compromise: his independence is maintained by the ever-increasing wealth of Hollywood via multi-national cinematographic deals, which allows it to invest in super-cinema productions like those of his films, always lucrative due to the long and unending thirst for his work in cinema halls, on television, in universities, bookshops etc....discos...etc....

O Século do Cinema

Fellini has made an industry out of madness; he is a rich artist.

The dominance of Italian filmmakers is manifested through Fellini in his singularity of being Himself: The Filmmaker, The Star. It is Fellini that sells, not the Auteurs or the Actors. He doesn't have an agent; he simply picks up his phone and talks directly to the multi-nationals.

Ho un nuovo Fellini da fare ... [I have a new Fellini to make...]

Once his film is announced, the stampede of international distributors and producers begins towards 'the new dream...new fantasy....'.

Fellini stages the production, excites the imagination, achieves the maximum amount of money, pays himself the most inflated salary in the world and mobilizes the masses into never-ending queues.

His economic and social heyday began with *La dolce vita*, 1950s, at the end of the Cold War....

Before that point he was the juggler in *The White Sheik*, the swindler in *The Swindlers (Il bidone*, 1955), the middle-class intellectual in *I vitelloni*, Zampanò in *La strada* (1954), and the prostitute in *Nights of Cabiria (Le notti di Cabiria*, 1957).

In these first films, the stories are set in poor places peopled by the half-starved. Mad Fellinian types wander around in a picture of misery, but they are oblivious to reality; they are the dream, the beauty which Fellini creates.

La strada and *Nights of Cabiria* are films featuring Fellini's wife, Giulietta Masina.

Neorealism was responsible for launching super-women such as Silvana Mangano, Silvana Pampanini, Sophia Loren, Gina Lollobrigida, Claudia Cardinale, Monica Vitti and others who turned Italy into a hot destination for tourists.

Giulietta Masina is not pretty but she is a great actress.

Gelsomina and Cabiria are chaste characters, be it the Saint Travelling-Actor or the Cinematographic Prostitute.

Struck by passion, Fellini abandoned the 'Myself, The Swindler' character of his earlier films and made Giulietta Masina the focus of his camera's gaze. He mounted a troupe of actors. Anthony Quinn, Richard Basehart and Giulietta. He portrays a dream within a popular circus. He transforms circus and theatre into cinema, making the set design abstract, and accentuates, via the costumes and mythical performances, the historical density of drama.

His life together with Giulietta Masina served to stimulate this dream. Fellini grows in the loving arms of his new mother, who is like the wolf who fed Romulus and Remus. The mother-wife Masina, in the role of Cabiria, is a prostitute with the heart of a saint, a model which Godard would later make more sophisticated in *My Life to Live*. The mother/wife foundation as embodied by Giulietta Masina marks Fellini's independence, who moves from the role of actor (Alberto Sordi), swindler (Franco Interlenghi), magician (Anthony Quinn) to that of the filmmaker-spectator of Cabiria/Giulietta.

International success elevates Fellini into a character argued over by cinema-lovers, intellectuals and bohemian jet-setters.

The cycle of Giulietta/saint/prostitute breaks down. Fellini leaves to make *La dolce vita* in the middle of a marital breakdown. Giulietta demands more films, commercial pressures lead him to use other actors, his imagination begins to be censored by Giulietta who forbids him from having a star like Ingrid Bergman.

Fellini made a short film with the gigantic woman Anita Ekberg and *La dolce vita* with Marcello Mastroianni, the most beautiful actor in the whole of Italy, a rival of Alain Delon, who was Visconti's lover.

Tortured by Giulietta, blaming himself because he knows she is ugly, plump and short, and tells her as much, Fellini swaps her for a tall, slim and beautiful woman.

Marcello, the social affairs journalist in *La dolce vita*, who dreams one day of writing a novel, spends his time fighting with his wife and with his lovers, all part of the Roman in-crowd.

Actresses, prostitutes, rich women, intellectuals, all pass through Marcello's arms and he does not abandon his wife, always reconciling to prevent her from becoming suicidal, but he still substitutes her for superficial lovers.

His ties are with his wife, even if he has dreadful sexual relations with her.

It is the debt of Christ to the Virgin.

Marcello's wife represents the self-sacrificial mother figure who, symbolically, did not give birth to a son. From out of this divide between wife and lover, Marcello develops his perceptive abyss. Fellini/Marcello is the middle-class intellectual who discovers the world but cannot take possession of it because his wife castrates him. In the film we see the father but never the mother of Marcello. And the father is interested in women, just as the son is a man castrated by the mother/wife figure.

The repressive Mother, the unobtainable Woman, the Prostitute/Saint is Anita Ekberg who breaks into the Vatican dressed as a cardinal and takes a bath (she could have been nude but Fellini did not dare to do as much given the times...), in the Trevi Fountain, in a sequence which scandalized the censors.

Alberto Moravia compared *La dolce vita* to *Satyricon* (*Fellini-Satyricon*, 1969), the Latin classic, and the Left laid at Fellini's door the charge of *excluding the economic issues in the aesthetic description within the film*, a paradox of subjective phenomena.

However, *La dolce vita* broke the barriers of political and police censorship, conquered the public across the globe, thirsty for the pornographic sublimations of Imperial Rome.

La dolce vita was the only film after World War II which provoked a cultural revolution in morality (*above all in the Catholic public*), and opened the doors to erotica.

It is the Fall of the Roman Empire.

Fellini shows post-fascist bourgeois society, decaying under the dominance of the United States.

Lex Barker, Anita Ekberg's lover, punches Marcello. Steiner, the ex-fascist capitalist social-democrat, commits suicide. The other characters take drugs during orgies and find only a maritime monster... Marcello, faced with this horror, sees the image of a Virgin, of a Saint. The proletariat is represented by prostitutes, by Marcello's wife, bureaucracy by Marcello's father, the leftwing by the intellectuals and Marcello's journalist friends, but the Communist party, so omnipresent in Italian life, is absent, and this political absent-mindedness reveals the Pagan Egotism of Fellini.

Paganism fuelled the pre-Christian dictatorships wherein crimes were rejoiced over.

Christian Rome enjoyed the secret crime (*think of the trapdoors of the Borgia...*) and publically punished it in the interests of Cesar's rule.

The paraphernalia of Roman constitutional law (*our law is Pornography... as portrayed by Fellini in* Satyricon/La dolce vita, *a Rome with two heads, like Romulus/Satyricon/Remus La dolce vita Sons of the she-wolf Fellini...*) was not subjected to a significant overhaul by the

Vatican because the Roman Empire only adopted Christ in the new state of the Holy See, the Catechism starting to work like a metaphysical power on the temporal political power.

This Pagan Egotism, posing as Amoral, is nothing more than the hypocritical talk of a neo-Christian financed by Hollywood. Marcello, the social affairs correspondent, is the secret supporter of the Italian Communist Party (PCI). He doesn't refer to the PCI but all his existential angst can be identified by PCI intellectuals who, due to their Catholic grounding, are moralists and not...*lecherous types like Marcello, a sexual peasant of the pagan dolce vita...*

All secretly Christian, even in blasphemy!

Anita Ekberg, dressed as a cardinal climbing the stairs of St Peter's Cathedral *ad infinitum*, is the materialisation of a Fellinian desire to be both a sensual woman and a cardinal, the very vision of a *Matriarchal Pope*, the audacity which founds the *Baroque Surrealism, il vero* [the truth] ... *a fusion of paganism (Anita) and Christianity (the cardinal's robes and the cathedral) filmed via internal/external Movements; Actors and Camera moving in a transcending spiral.*

A pagan masked as a Christian or a fascist masked as a capitalist, like *un capitalista uccide proletario fascista uccide capitalista comunista...* [a capitalist killing the working-class man, a fascist killing the capitalist communist]. A basic metatextual premise in the manner that, if *La dolce vita* is properly understood, it is possible to see the Roman spiritual movement underlying the sociological representation of History.

Fellini, also touched by French surrealism...*gushes pure consciousness...* the arteries of the unconscious torn open by the Flow of Nothingness which materializes in his *creations...film...*stuff of dreams...

In *La dolce vita*, Fellini is filming *the Social Secret, the hidden side of the human being*, reality restricted by historicist methodology.

Fellini sees and hears more deeply: over and above neorealism, over and above the cultural weight of Italy and world culture. Fellini is a barbarian, he is the successor to Attila and enters Rome with the elephants of the imagination and conquers the world.

The non-identified communist violates the moral code of the Vatican, even if he is wearing a Christian mask. All manner of censors attacked Fellini and the film, repressed in its superstructure, was saved by the public. Success was the plebiscite which liberated Fellini from the Vatican and from the PCI. Success was a democratic power conferred upon him by the public and it allowed Fellini to subvert the industry.

$8\frac{1}{2}$ is the big *Olé*, the man on horseback with his sword and cape dominates the bull and proclaims himself a genius!

I am Me – that is the plot of $8\frac{1}{2}$. Marcello, the decadent newspaper correspondent, is transformed into Guido, the successful filmmaker.

The Roman society page correspondent hit the nail on the head. Fellini is now a point of reference for ordinary people, discussed by intellectuals, funded by producers, sexualized by the bourgeoisie, condescended to by the Church and the PCI.

A blaspheme. He had no aristocratic origins (Visconti), no political origins (Rossellini) nor cultural origins (De Rica) – no blood pact which defended him from the inquisition.

Taking things even further than Marcello, Guido continues the sexual party. This time, wearing the toga of a Roman Senator and a cowboy's hat, he cracks his whip like a Surrealist Tamer of women in a Sadistic Circus.

Guido is the greatest filmmaker; he's going to make the best film in the world. The world is a circus, Guido is the circus tamer, the producers are the owners of the circus and the actors are the animals, the public are the *public* and the name of the *Show is Fellini*.

> I have no idea, nor script, nor cast, nor a title...it's my eight and a half film... I hate actors and producers. I only love the mad ones....

Steiner, the capitalist who kills himself and his children in *La dolce vita*, was a slap in the face of existentialist literature of such violent proportions that it shocked Sartre and his followers.

The richness, luxury, sophistication, the nothingness, the crime, the suicide of a class with no future.

Fellini proclaimed, at the end of *La dolce vita*, the existence of a...*Paradise at Dawn*..., an obligatory metaphor in Socialist Realism...

La dolce vita has influenced public life, intellectuals, filmmakers, and Fellini has become his own theme and that of the world. $8\frac{1}{2}$ is a film of a *Man and a Half* – as it's impossible to be of just one man.

Fellini is big, fat, strong, a heavy-weight. He looks like a Roman gladiator. His erotic magnetism melts the resolve of even the most sexually repressed at a hundred yards. They tell tales of Fellini in the European brothels which would make the Marquis de Sade blush. He is the lover of his fortune teller, Madame D, a woman who shows him his *next film in her crystal ball*. But Fellini is not a fresh-faced beauty like Marcello Mastroianni, with whom he falls in love.

Guido Fellini, Marcello painted to resemble Fellini, a young Faustian Fellini with the spirit of Fellini-Mephistopheles...Dante's Beatrice or Goethe's Margarete, in the smile of the blond virgin at the end of...*La dolce vita*...

$8\frac{1}{2}$ is a Narcissistic Ecstasy.

Its *cinematographic origins* can be found in the surrealism of Jean Cocteau, Salvador Dalí and Luis Buñuel; its *literary origins* in Sigmund Freud, Carl Jung and Jorge Luis Borges.

These historical traditions feed, to some small extent, the Fellinian sap, which is self-manufactured at a pace superior to that at which cancer cells multiply.

Aesthetic production is the biggest enemy of cancer, and from there the thesis of Gozmaz as the *infra Nothingness of the Vate-Ads-Tays* (*Timothy Leary, the lysergic philosopher, said in Switzerland in 1971 that Fellini was the only man who...travels further than God*). Gozmaz, that *nothingness* surrounded by the repressive artery which, once torn open (for various reasons...what will be, will be) objectifies a vital being, son or film.

There are films with a Soul and these films are immortal. The only Art that is a Living Organism is Cinema. Cinema moves and talks. It has a colour and a smell. It has a soul. Cocteau said: 'Cinema films death at work, it's the only art form which shows death devouring actors; the characters made immortal remain stronger in our memory than the memory of living souls.'[46]

All great artists are immortal, above all in cinema: Kane is more vital than Welles because the character is the maximum force of the artist.

The artist, a mortal being, immortalizes the character in the Actor. It is the Actor who becomes immortal, not the Director, and Fellini projects his immortality onto Marcello Guido. He becomes the spirit of the Wizard.

Fellini is a neorealist, like Visconti, Antonioni or Rossellini, but his *neorealism* diverges from other dominant trends.

The contradiction between the historicism of Visconti and the mysticism of Rossellini should not exclude the *naturalism that feeds the stylistic variants of the same story*...

O Século do Cinema

Fellini breaks through the cultural blockade.

He is a Wizard; he's not a man with a Political agenda like Visconti, nor is he a Moralist like Rossellini. Visconti seeks salvation through Passion, Rossellini through Knowledge. Fellini is not worried about salvation; he wants to live the pagan savage's dream, he wants to be loved by the world, but he doesn't trust sexuality and for that reason he refuses to play the role of Guido.

Fellini is a reject, *I, Fellini, am not Anita Ekberg.*

From this frustration Guido is born, more beautiful than Anita Ekberg.

Fellini justifies Marcuse in the sense of being a better artist because he is propelled by feline sexuality.

$8\frac{1}{2}$ is a story of a filmmaker who makes a film without a script and with no title.

There are only two characters – the filmmaker and the producer.

Fellini hangs the critics and frees the Panthers which Guido whips inside the Dressing Room, preparing the troupe for the *Roman Circus Show*.

Fellini is the She-Wolf, the Mother, the Saint.

Roman Prostitute: Rome is the theme of *La dolce vita*, Roman Spirituality the theme of $8\frac{1}{2}$, *Satyricon* is the Roman Underground, *Fellini's Roma* (*Roma*, 1972) is TV journalism.

The first Fellini is provincial: Sordi the ham actor, Interlenghi the intellectual, Crawford the swindler.

The second is he himself, the Looney, Zampanò. But Zampanò kills the crazy man in *La strada*.

This crazy man is the Half (1/2) which reappears in Guido, as Calibán, Prospero's Elf in...*The Tempest*, Shakespeare's last play.

Fellini is Fellini, Mastroianni his *half*. The half is the actor, the Elf, while the God Fellini rests in Paradise.

The severed I, I and a Half, Schizophrenia. The projection of the hidden I, an orgiastic celebration of this Love towards self-criticism, humour, excretion, ritual, pleasure, orgasm, sex, art, $8\frac{1}{2}$ doesn't celebrate the *I Fellini* freed prisoner, artistic Guido Fellini, *I am My own Half* – the Half is the message...the half of the being aesthetically realized – a marvellous Vital Balance between Life and Art, the Truthful I Am My Best Theme.

$8\frac{1}{2}$ revolutionizes psychoanalysis. Guido wakes up in a clinic while Fellini enjoys it inside a car parked in the garage of Italy's social-democratic capitalism, recovered from the war. Hollywood, which in the past financed women, now finances the geniuses of cinema. Fellini is one of the greatest. For Pasolini, he is the greatest. In *La ricotta* (one of the episodes of *RoGoPaG*, 1963), Pasolini shows Orson Welles portraying Fellini:

> I won't say anything about my film but the critic will praise it because the producer is also the owner of the newspaper.

I slept during the projection of *Juliet of the Spirits*. An extremely long cinemascopic projection, loose cuts, repetitive sound, black-and-white shots, I didn't understand Italian that well, the priest would poke me, I was snoring between Fellini and the Jesuits.

I remember the first shots, the camera moving inside a house or an old man running away in an airplane... I identified the spirit of Leonardo influenced by Dalí... and *se muove* [it moves]...the immobile painting, the dynamic visuals around Gelsomina/Cabiria.

Giulietta Masina is a kind of Emília from Monteiro Lobato[47] inside a Roman Spiritist Tent, she is the Pythoness of London, Wife, Saint, Virgin Mary, the Mother of Fellini the Zarathustra.

When the projection was over, the priests surrounded Fellini, who was wearing brown trousers, a dark-blue sweater and a white scarf. I noticed that he was thinner than in pictures, he had a very thin nose and a large forehead, and was rubbing his hands:

> Brothers, do you believe that when the Pope sees this film he will believe that I believe in God? I would like the Pope to recommend this film so as to prevent censorship problems.

Father Arpa replied that Fellini was not an atheist, that the film demonstrated the existence of God but the problem was that Fellini transformed his own Spirits into Saints, and the Vatican had its own.

Fellini fled the clear winter night and Father Arpa criticized me for having slept during the projection:

> 'Fellini is a genius... You should pay more attention.'
> 'Look here, Father Arpa, Fellini was articulating the papal blessing for the film, and I am a Protestant, I think this is absurd,

it shows that there is a Catholic censorship, so I will not admit that you, Sir, in the name of the Catholic Church, speak of democracy in the Third World.'
'But we represent the new Church.... We are the apostles of John XXIII...'
'Fellini is a neo-renascentist, a neo-catholic, pagan but Christian, metaphysic. I am a materialist' – I replied, and Father Arpa smiled understandingly.

At the 1967 Venice Film Festival, Fellini was showing *Satyricon*. I watched ten minutes of it and I left the cinema slagging the film off, I booed Fellini at the press conference and I told the *Cahiers du Cinéma* people that Fellini was finished, that he did not know how to use the zoom, that only Ruy Guerra could use the zoom, that Visconti also thought that to film the novel *The Stranger* by Camus, with zoom ins in Anna Karina and Marcello Mastroianni's faces in the desert was to make modern cinema...

I went to the Palazzo for the Closing Party with Arnaldo Jabor and Danuza Leão and at the entrance I got into a fight with the doorman because I wanted to go in without a smoking jacket. I was then spotted by the producer of the TV news, Jairo Picone, who alongside Fellini came to my rescue.

I went in and Picone shouted: 'Doctor Fellini, this is Rocha...'
And I, to the astonishment of Jabor and Danuza, quickly shouted back: 'No, I don't want to meet the Devil...'

Fellini, crestfallen, with grey suit and blue tie, broken by the critical failure of *Satyricon* and the incertitude of the repercussions this would have on the public, came to me, pale and with dark circles under his eyes, and I was afraid...

I tried to see *Satyricon* again and I didn't get to the end but I felt sick; the images were rotten, sad, stinking, the overwhelming purple colouring of cancer, the cheeks of cancer, and after the cruel operation Fellini looked like Frankenstein and it was from there that this terror, faced with his worn-out public image, stemmed.

The Clowns (*I Clowns*, 1970) and *Fellini's Roma*, filmed for television, released Fellini from the crisis caused by the failure of *Juliet* and *Satyricon* and from his breakdown in a Paris hotel room, where he spent three days unconscious, with no one coming to look for him until, taken to a clinic, he declared himself resuscitated.

Fellini made a short for an episodic horror film and Terence Stamp played the Devil, whose head is sliced off in a car chase.[48]

The Cultural Revolution of 1968 questioned Fellini's Fantasy. It didn't reflect class struggles: a vision of a decadent world, its theme was not society but Fellini himself, *an Individual able to mobilize capital* in order to 'provide illusion' to the masses with his cinematographic magic.

Cowed, Fellini responded to the critics. The youth movement of 1968 was divided into two groups: guerrillas and hippies. Fellini was heralded as a guru by Timothy Leary because he had had experiences with LSD in the 1950s and his historical contract with the hippies was signed by way of *Fellini's Roma*.

At the peak of his illness, plunged deep into the Kingdom of Death, Fellini began a film in secret, a film which told the tale of his breakdown.

He retreated to the East, lived with the hippies, meditated in Buddhist monasteries, travelled around Europe, ignored the Americas and Africa and returned to Rome to film *Amarcord* which went on release in 1973–1974.

At the premiere, at a cinema on the Via Veneto, I met with Bernardo Bertolucci and Clare Peploe. Bernardo didn't like the film; Bulle Ogier and I liked it. I went to see it again with my daughter, Paloma, and I liked it even more, even though I think it a failure in human terms. Fellini is a genius. His world is a sad one. Subliminally poetic, Beautiful, *I feel*, is Fellini's desire, his art, *not his life*.

Fellini is unhappy; the beauty of his cinema doesn't heal the wound. The trauma of having the Mother's Body and the Sex of the Father, of discovering he is Male when he wanted to be Female and also that he is not Homosexual, of aesthetically sublimating the Unfillable Gap of being Fellini.

He is a Creative Anomaly, the Cinematographic Half-Fellini is born from this state of Denial.

Frustrated Sex, Fulfilled Art.

(Non)compensation, Freud writes about the childhood frustration of Leonardo Da Vinci. The same happened with Eisenstein, but with Fellini the balancing act of desire brings clarity as to how Art is still a manifestation of the illness.

Looking back to his infancy, to the child which existed before *I vitelloni*, is what eventually brings Fellini to politics, showing Fascism with such critical violence that it served to demystify the moral stance of populist aesthetics.

The boy grew up amongst colossal prostitutes and fascist criminals. Where is Catholic Italy in this plunge into the countryside? The Dionysian tradition, Eastern, conquers Catholic mass. In *Fellini's Roma*, there is a Catholic fashion parade, showing styles of cassocks and masses. Fellini criticizes, demolishes, looks for empty truths in the catacombs, a hurricane with no memory.

And through the archaeological labyrinths of Rome, Fellini returns to his infancy without discovering Christ or Marx, lost instead in a world of violence, prostitution and corruption.

Ignoring what is real, Fellini creates his own reality, films it, screens it. Fellini thrives from this reality, from the film itself, from his fight against cancer, from his volcanic pulse which identifies him with Vesuvius Reborn.

Many artists have revisited the past '...*à la recherche du temps perdu*...' [in search of lost time] – something which is always a healthy pursuit and the quality of one's memory is its specificity.

The moral censorship of the auteur is what most prevents him from admitting to be 'I', above all when manifested aesthetically.

Fellini's infancy is no more interesting than that of another person's but what is manifested from Fellini's infancy in the film *Amarcord* confirms his capacity to maintain and later to recreate his infancy.

The Child-Fellini creates. And the fundamental scene takes place in a nocturnal warehouse, the Child-Fellini and the Colossal Prostitute. The trapped femininity of Fellini, the emptiness that he tries in vain to fill with films: the Child-Fellini, the Old-Fellini, Fellini Casanova. Guido and the female circus. Fellini and the great big Woman, Casanova and the great big women. Machismo in the foreground and a multi-national brothel in the Cinecittà studios, the stage of a fantastical Venice, a *fin de siècle* oneiric orgy...

In 1975, the *ragazze* of the Piazza Navona were excited, waiting for a role in *Fellini's Casanova*.

I met Donald Sutherland at a lunch in Gillo Pontecorvo's house and the chosen Casanova was demonstrating his ignorance about the role he was about to play under Fellini's direction.

Donald was considered to be one of the most attractive actors of the time but there is nothing about him which is...*seductive*...he seems rather to be like a good-natured retired football player with his wife and child.

And the women selected for the film are nothing new.

Around the same time, Andy Warhol had swept the Roman underground scene with his two films, *Blood for Dracula* (1973) and *Flesh for Frankenstein* (1973),[49] so that Joe Dallessandro was *trash* in a *porno-western* style, and Helmut Berger was Viscontian...

Bertolucci used Donald to play a Fascist policeman in *1900* (1976), exploring his *ugliness* and latent sadism given that Donald, *possessed*, is capable of being frightening, but not sexually seductive...the frigidity of the actor impressed Fellini.

From amongst the starlets of Rome/Paris (the most talked-about are Tina Aumont, Bulle Ogier, Juliet Berto, Margareth Clementi, Haydée Politoff, Rafaella Da Vinci, Martine Zacher (or Gisela Getty) and Yuta Zacher, Milagres de las Mercedes,[50] Bettina Best...) Margareth Clementi was chosen, the ex-wife of Pierre Clementi, the actor expelled from Italy after having served a prison sentence on a drugs charge.

Bettina Best, a great big Belgian like the she-wolf, a shameless version of Anita Ekberg... *at the end of the dream*, announced that she would be one of Fellini's stars.

I stole her for my film *Claro* (1975), which I was just starting and she played the she-wolf, and hence lost her role in *Casanova*, the filming of which was interrupted because the Mafia stole the film negatives from the laboratory and then demanded money from the producers.

The prophets of doom announced in a Rome already mourning the death of Pasolini and with Visconti dying from a long and drawn-out heart attack...that *Casanova* was a disaster, that Fellini was ill and that the Yankees were branding him a madman, Donald had left the film-set, Fellini had thrown out Margareth because she didn't want to sleep with him, that Fellini had thrown out Ingmar Bergman who had come to watch the filming (Bergman, like Buñuel, considered Fellini 'the best'), that the set design had collapsed into the canal of a decadent cinema.

O Século do Cinema

Giovanni Bertolucci, Bernardo's cousin, the producer of Visconti's last film, *The Innocent* (*L'innocente*, 1976), announced that it was *The Last Film... Adesso è tutto finito... Soldi, molto soldi...sesso...politica...violenza...droga...Casanova? Bah...nessuno vuole più sapere cosa fa Fellini... Soldi?* Amarcord *ha fatto molto...*[51]

Fellini blew apart the box-office with *Amarcord* and went off the scale with *Casanova*; eight million dollars wasted due to scandals during the filming and editing, all this for the Funeral of the Great Prostitute, the Doll, the tragic Image of sexual failure in the pathetic figure of the mummified Casanova.

Life is a Theatre; *Io sono Casanova* [I am Casanova].

Casanova is a gigolo. He lived his life exploiting actresses and millionaires, seducing young girls in search of stardom, a sexual ruler like Fellini, Sultan of the historical Italian Porn Cinema, like those Superproductions commissioned by Mussolini, History falling through the holes in his body.

Fellini mummified Donald. His seductive spirit is thin. He isn't a pretty doll like Marcello, star of *La dolce vita* and $8\frac{1}{2}$. He's a man in the springtime of his life, with no faith in the possibility of complete communication between a man and a woman.

He attracts women: Fellini is rich, famous, a genius but he isn't pretty like Donald. Fellini once again hides himself behind an idealistic window display, defines his practice as the dialectic of a magician, peopling his solitude with ghosts; lecherous yet sterile.

Fellini didn't undergo complete obscenity by playing Casanova himself, parading his body in sexual acts like he sadistically forced his actors to, exposing his personal attractions and denials in order to provoke a public orgy.

Casanova is an aseptic film; it takes the moral stance of *whomsoever eats greedily is left with an empty plate...or...one thing is sex, another is love...or...he devoured so many and didn't find one brilliant soul beyond the flesh he tangled with...or...ahh if only a wonderful woman, probably big like Anita, were to fall in love with me after seeing this film.*

Casanova was a moderate success for Fellini, in a market of Cineauteurs dominated by Bergman, Antonioni, Buñuel, Resnais etc...., wherein Fellini is the most expensive, the most liberated and the least compromised by the rules of the game.

He was a very close friend of Visconti in the last twelve years and he never cut his ties with Rossellini even though the latter never revered him as much as the former.

He is not a cinematographic militant, nor is he a political demonstrator. He is an *Artist* and his medium is the cinematographic message.

Fantasies aside, Fellini is a great creator of films, gifted with an in-depth knowledge of the technology of Image and Sound. A set designer and a costume designer, both original and a perfectionist, an expressive make-up artist, a lighting director who paints pictures with reflections, a sensitive and poetic musician, a dialectic and formalist film editor.

From the filmic point of view, he integrates individual fantasy to the aesthetic aims of the cinema of Griffith, Eisenstein, John Ford, Visconti and Rossellini.

Fellini didn't invent anything in terms of framing or editing but he revolutionized the psychological structure of the script and the set design, wherein he demonstrated himself to be the best *Mobile Painter of the Century*, one of the best in the history of humanity.

Fellinian symbolism is a fertile ground for both speculation and reaction, from repulsion to delight, a stimulant that won't be bettered by the audiovisual revolution at the end of this century because it is testament to a specific time, in the manner of Kafka...

Fellini's oeuvre is the *phenomenology of decadence* and dialectically he produces jewels by the side of excrement...

No other filmmaker was as radical in their expulsion of their personal Hell, Purgatory and Paradise. Fellini (*the fact that he is called Federico, just like Garcia Lorca, always got me*) is the only one capable of filming *The Divine Comedy*, the flagship of Italian and European Metaphor.

The best horror film producer in the world, Roger Corman, announced that he would hire Fellini to film the atomic bomb dropped on Hiroshima, for which Fellini demanded an air squadron from the Pentagon, a piece of Japan, two atomic bombs and a million videos connected to the extras, Vietnamese prisoners and starving people from the region.

Fellini is still young and he could still show us God.

No other Filmmaker (and *Cinema is the greatest of all the Arts*, Lenin) travelled so far, an explorer of the unconscious, his films are ships set to travel a great course and have great depth and height. He is probably a Being from another Planet. Fellini is the greatest phenomenon of Living Imagination.

O Século do Cinema

Pasolini

Rome, 1965: the young Italian filmmakers Gianni Amico and Bernardo Bertolucci took Pier Paolo Pasolini, novelist, philologist, poet, scientist and filmmaker to a private viewing of *Black God, White Devil*. I waited outside with my friend Arnaldo Carrilho. When the screening finished, I couldn't talk long with Pasolini as he had the flu. And the hoped-for meeting didn't take place as he was leaving the next day for Morocco, where he was filming *Oedipus Rex* (*Edipo re*, 1967). The meeting was going to be about the launch of *The Gospel according to St. Matthew*, a modern version of the life of Christ, in accordance with the rulings of Pope John XXIII, to whom it is dedicated.

We met again in Venice in 1967 where Pasolini was presenting his version of *Oedipus Rex*.

Pier Paolo, as he is known by his close friends, is around forty-four. He is short and slim, he wears glasses and has black hair: he is violent, shy and ironic all at the same time. He is a legend in Italy. He began his intellectual life teaching Romance languages in a provincial school. Involved in an under-age sex scandal, Pasolini was consequently dismissed from his post and prosecuted and he began working as a poet and novelist. However, his time under the spotlight began in around 1955, ten years after the war. He was friends with Alberto Moravia, a great promoter of new literary values. Pasolini himself was heralded as an innovator in the use of the Italian language in his novels and was politically affiliated to the Communist Party, which used his image as a young rebel as promotion for its own cause.

Poems and stories and full-page articles published in newspapers, Pasolini became friends with the filmmaker Mauro Bolognini and wrote scripts for him, one of which caused a furore: *Bad Girls Don't Cry* (*La notte brava*, 1959). Further success came with *From a Roman Balcony* (*La giornata balorda*, 1960), based on a story by Moravia,[52] with a script also written for Bolognini's direction.

The fascists attacked the young, perverted communist. His personal life was the stuff of scandal in the Italian provinces. Pasolini faced his enemies, fought with his fists and was imprisoned. He was released, held up a petrol station, was prosecuted and made some shocking declarations. There was a rumour that he had broken with the Communist Party.

The whole of Europe was talking about the scandalous behaviour of the Roman. In 1962, the film *Accattone!* launched Pasolini as a director and triumphed at the Karlovy Vary International Film Festival. The main role was played by a young *ragazzo di vita*, Franco Citti. *Accattone!* is a brutal tale of society's outcasts, recounting their social, psychological and sexual conflicts. Moreover – and scandalously for the orthodox flag-bearers of social realism, it shows that ideology doesn't resolve all the human issues: the hero is a tormented soul, just like his creator.

The film wasn't successful but it was welcomed by the Italian critics who were looking for something new and alternative to Fellini and Visconti.

His second film was well publicized before its release: *Mamma Roma* (1962). Anna Magnani was the leading lady. A failure. The third film took longer to come. Few people believed in Pier Paolo. Given a chance by the producer Alfredo Bini and dragged from near obscurity, having been mocked by both left and right, Pier Paolo filmed *The Gospel according to St. Matthew.*

The film was screened in Venice in 1964: the Fascists threw eggs in the filmmaker's face when he arrived at the Festival. The jury awarded him a special prize. On general release, the life of Christ according to Pasolini was a box-office success, and, although it didn't break any records, made enough to bring Alfredo Bini returns on his investment. It was sold abroad: the French critics were divided. *Time* magazine said that the drama resembled an old art album.

Genius or mystifier: what was the Pasolini scandal all about?

The first injection of new life into the story of Christ was the context: Judea was a poor country, a Roman colony. None of the luxury seen in Cecil B. De Mille's pictures. Christ was a man of the people, dressed poorly. The Hebrew governors were at the service of Roman Imperialism. Christ emerged as a subversive figure, capable of capturing the support of the public against the hawkers of the fatherland.

A vein of moral teaching mixed with political fear runs through the film: Christ is betrayed by one of his own. On the cross, in his hour of need he shouts, 'My God, why have you forsaken me?'

Pasolini's Christ is strong, virile, and shows no tolerance towards the oppressors and crooks. Christ is violent to the extreme. When preaching he uses the incisive tone of a social agitator. The gospel of St Matthew, when used in its entirety, takes on a new dimension: this demystified and revolutionary Christ seems to have arisen from the very encyclicals of Pope John XXIII. The new Church heaps praise upon it. The orthodox leftwing accused Pasolini of making a Socialist/Christian pact. Pasolini does not dance to the Kremlin's tune even though he professes to be a die-hard Marxist.

Hawks and Sparrows (*Uccellacci e uccellini*, 1966) has an even sharper edge. A revolutionary film as well as a cinematographic and philosophical expression, it brought the ideological crisis out into the light. It's the end of ideologies (one of the pilgrims, Totò, enters into a conversation with a crow which spills out phrases and concepts, and ends up devouring him). Paul VI and Karl Marx meet at the end of the pilgrimage and we see Pasolini's fears that man is no more than a hopeless animal.

A bomb was let off at Cannes in 1966. *Hawks and Sparrows* was badly received by the majority of critics and by the public. Proclaiming the existence of an ideological crisis at a time when everyone is in desperate need of religion to keep their consciences feeling clean was, after all, 'an act of provocation and reactionarism'. And, moreover, Pasolini had already scandalized half the world's population by introducing the actor Ninetto Davoli, Totò's accomplice, as his 'fidanzata' ['fiancée'] to the hotel porter.

Venice, 1967, and everyone was waiting to behold Pasolini's vision in *Oedipus Rex*. Before this, taking part in the film project made up of short episodes alongside Rossellini, Godard and others, *RoGoPaG* (1963), Pasolini was condemned to six months imprisonment by the Italian courts for having blasphemed against the Church in his episode *La ricotta*. In it a starving actor, who plays the role of the good thief in the scene of a film about the crucifixion, eats too much between takes and dies of indigestion on the cross. When the director, played by a heavy Orson Welles, shouts *azione* [action], everyone moves, apart from the good thief, now dead on the cross.

Welles's role is a satire of Fellini in $8\frac{1}{2}$ and his character talks in a refined, presumptuous tone: 'The criticism about my film is of no importance. The film's producer owns your newspaper... I am a force from the past... Italy is the most underdeveloped country in Europe and has the most hypocritical and ignorant critics in the world.'

Religious blaspheme and an aggressive attitude towards the bourgeoisie resulted in a six-month suspended sentence and a ban from filming

The Savage Priest (*Il padre selvaggio*), a story based in Africa wherein a black man ends up eating the flesh of his white friend and becomes a poet.

On the subject of *Oedipus Rex*, Pasolini talks openly:

> With this film, I am resolving my Oedipus complex. I have freed myself from my mother. My style is crass and arbitrary. The Oedipus tragedy is a tragedy because the general public don't know it. Once the public know it, it ceases to be a tragedy. My character isn't an intellectual struggling with destiny, he's an almost primitive young man who finds himself propelled forwards into an adventure and during this adventure, he discovers that he was the lover of his own mother and killed his father. At the end of the story, when his mother, wracked with remorse, commits suicide, Oedipus gouges out his eyes but he doesn't flee from the world. He becomes a poet. He goes out into the world with his guide: sometimes he's a decadent poet, sometimes a political poet, sometimes a metaphysical one. And as a metaphysical poet, he's only obsessed with the green countryside where he played in his childhood, and with the image of his mother's breast.

The film, shot in colour, is set in the prehistoric age. The country in which it is set is not made clear to us. The costumes reflect a deliberate mixture of ancient civilizations. Shouting, bloodied, anarchic, *anti-Greek*, Pasolini's film shocks the well-intentioned unsuspecting spirits. It is an open-ended tragedy, which develops throughout the film, forcing the spectator to question the human condition. At the end, the public cannot escape the nightmare. Anti-cinema, some furious critics shout, when faced with Pasolini's disrespect of traditional technique and the grammar laid down by past glories of American cinema.

Pasolini is not interested in continuity, in acting techniques, the realism of the décor etc.

His interest is man's thoughts faced with the dilemma of incest. And only via a sublimation of violence or poetry can man be freed from his mother.

The thesis is indisputable.

The release of the film broke box-office records. But Venice doesn't award it.

I go to meet Pasolini in Rome, in a restaurant near to the slaughterhouse.

O Século do Cinema

Walter Achugar, a Uruguayan producer, is his friend and it was he who arranged the meeting for me, given the difficulties to do the same in Venice.

In person, Pasolini is a simple and shy man.

It shattered the myth that he will only speak to women from behind dark glasses: He treated Rosa Maria well and spoke quietly in fast Italian.

> 'Tomorrow I'm going to film my episode of *Vangelo 70* (aka *Amore e rabbia*). It's only one scene. One sole camera movement. We'll see Ninetto in a road talking to people passing by.' (Two days later I found out that, during filming, Pasolini's camera would spot Sartre and Simone de Beauvoir philosophizing about something on the road.)

When Pasolini speaks you get the feeling that he loves *Hawks and Sparrows* the best and that he detests being linked to the success of *The Gospel according to St. Matthew*.

I asked him if he made any money with *Oedipus Rex*:

> Not one Lira. The film was made in Morocco, in dreadful conditions. The producer's money ran out half-way through and we finished the film under great pressure. The producer, in order that we could get to the end, sold the film to other distributors... So I didn't earn anything.

Pasolini's revelation served to console me in my theory that film auteurs are all faced with the same difficulties, whether in Brazil or in Europe.

> 'Italian cinema' – Pasolini continued – 'was destroyed by the distributors who are all linked to the Americans. Nowadays everything belongs to the Americans. Carlo Ponti and Dino de Laurentis are no more than henchmen working on behalf of the Americans. That's why Italy only produces Westerns spoken in Italian and pornographic comedies or historical films. The young, talented directors don't stand a chance. A genius like Rossellini is obliged to take work in French television in order to survive. Mediocrity and coarse behaviour dominate today's Italian cinema. Visconti, for example, is a great man, who considers himself a genius and he has just stated in a magazine that he doesn't rate young directors such as Bertolucci or Bellocchio.'

Pasolini is a friend of Jean-Luc Godard. This doesn't mean they don't fight, though. Pasolini wrote theses on the existence of a cinema of prose – an equivalent to the novel – and a cinema of poetry – an equivalent to the poem. Godard disagreed and said that literary methods could not be applied to cinema criticism, that cinema is a new art form and has nothing to do with literature.

Pasolini has his own ideas; he believes that Godard speaks, thinks and films all at the same time and for that reason it's only fair that he comes out with some foolish things on occasion.

Nevertheless, Pasolini considers Godard and Bertolucci to be the best filmmakers in the world. Conversely, without wishing to say as much, he and the French-German Jean-Marie Straub, director of the film *Not Reconciled* (*Nicht versöhnt*, 1965), form another pair which completes the quartet of today's greats.

As an intellectual, Pasolini holds no reverence for Italy.

> Our language is in complete disarray; for that reason it is impossible to talk about Italian literature. In order to film *Oedipus Rex*, I decided to use the Sicilian dialect and the result is that the majority of Italians don't understand it. We are slaves to an ancient culture. The myth of the Renaissance serves only to oppress us. For that reason Italy is not a modern country. All our politics takes place behind closed doors in a game whose rules are played based on family heritage and sex. The only authentic people in Italy are the prostitutes.

For Pier Paolo, Visconti is a good representation of an individual who reaches his good conscious via an academic Marxist conception. For him, the majority of Italian critics are insensitive: they only praise traditional works of art and are not open to aesthetic invention.

> 'And they are corrupt!'

Pier Paolo wants to pay the bill.

Walter Achugar asks him about *Mamma Roma* and for the first time Pasolini raises his voice:

> The film is a failure, thanks to Anna Magnani. She is temperamental, a vulgar matron. She creates nothing; she only reflects what she

already is in life. Obviously we didn't get on. Italy is a country which habitually transforms ham actors into unscrupulous stars.

We leave the restaurant. Pasolini gets into his red Jaguar and disappears.

New Cinema in the World

[1]
Modern cinema is a break with the narrative imposed by the industry on the filmmakers and the public. This break runs parallel with the take-up of cinema by the intellectuals. The intellectuals, as a rule, produce automatically for the cinema industry. The unconscious rebellion, whose pioneers could be Griffith, Eisenstein, Buñuel or Vigo, manifested itself via neorealism. Neorealist cinema was the first postwar cinema to trigger the process of the Auteur. *Nouvelle vague* cinema, taking a critical stance of past cinema, established the politics of authorship. This politics resulted in films of varying nuances.

[2]
Auteur cinema is linked to a structure of production. Auteur cinema, independent cinema, *cinema novo*, modern cinema or free cinema is the cinema wherein cultural, artistic and political values rise above commercial interests. Throughout the world, this type of cinema is produced at low cost, that is to say: small production teams, semi-professional actors, very little film, rapid production. They use 35 mm and 16 mm film. They use direct sound and dubbing. A film of this type generally costs between five and one hundred and fifty thousand dollars, which is the average budget Godard has for his films.

As for the distribution of these films, the majority are shown in their countries of origin. There are often problems with internal distribution, either due to the censors or with the public. A rigid public, above all, which can deal only with certain forms of communication; a public which has been lulled to sleep and which is hooked on the imperialist language of industry-controlled cinema. The old-school critics, similarly drawn in by this type of culture, generally toe the line of the established cinema industry and fight against modern cinema. They collaborate with the former by ensuring the public is not disturbed from its sleep, by way of the contents of their articles in the popular press. The political and cultural consequences resulting from this imperialist conquest are very serious. Modern cinema, supported by a new wave of critics (new in the qualitative sense, not in terms of their age, as many young critics are academic or colonized), finds a way out, in its countries of origin, in the cine-clubs and art-house cinemas, a market which is developing slowly through this new production. The international outlet for these films are the film festivals. Today, thanks to the performance of some of the new critics, even some of the larger festivals permit the entrance of some examples of modern cinema. Depending on their critical success and the prizes awarded, the films then have the possibility of being shown on an international level in cine-clubs, in television culture programmes and in art-house cinemas.

[3]
The poor production style and the mechanics of distribution aside, modern cinema presents itself under the most contradictory of terms. Basically, it exists as two types of film: fictional films and documentary films filmed with direct sound. Brazilian *cinema novo*, for example, is generally characterized by the production of fictional films. Canadian *new cinema* is characterized by documentary films, which doesn't mean that fictional films aren't produced there, nor that documentary films aren't produced here in Brazil. Aesthetically, all the films are revolutionary, that is to say, they search for and experiment with a new language, different from traditional language. The widespread use of handheld cameras, discontinuous editing, narrative text, graphics, interpretive music, anti-naturalist acting (influenced by Brecht's theories), atmospheric lighting, direct sound, improvisation and free-flowing dialogue are constants of the new cinema. Obviously, there are fads and crazes which have already fallen into disuse, but these have been replaced by other experiments which are beginning to link in with the results of those experiments left over from the first period, which, on a historical timescale, could be seen as being post-*Breathless*.

The influence of Rossellini on Godard can be felt in the new generation of liberated filmmakers. A search for realism which is at the same time contradictory due to the violence of poetry. *Cinema novo* is, for that reason, much more poetic than it is documentary film. That is to say, the

O Século do Cinema

structure of the poetical editing can be felt in modern cinema, which is contrary to the case of traditional cinema, where the fictional phrase borrowed from the novel is much more evident. To illustrate this point we could compare Jean Renoir to Flaubert and Godard to Mallarmé.

In traditional cinema, the shot (the scene) serves to narrate a psychological state through a logical sequence; from this technique word follows word. In modern cinema, the shot (the scene) isn't useful for anything: it has its own *meaning*. This is the technique of *an idea per shot*, a *shot for each action taking place*. The conflict of each *full shot* (set design, light, gesture, rhythm, word, music, noise), placed next to the other *full shots* is what establishes the drama. Some theorists have begun to notice that modern cinema is taking its direction from Eisenstein's theory of the montage of conflicts, but this time developing through from the minimum shot to the *full shot*. The *full shot* is, in the final analysis, the traditional *long take* reworked using the critical spirit of the filmmaker. The *long take* (by William Wyler, for example) serves only for narrative fiction. The *full shot* at the beginning of *Barren Lives*, for example, is a revelation, a criticism and a narrative all at once. The Eisensteinian theory of the use of all visual, aural and literary elements was rendered impossible by the limitations of silent cinema. The current theory (in practice) of *everything in everything* has Eisensteinian roots. *Everything in everything* means an accumulation of contradictions in the shot. Light, image, actor, set design, voice, music, noise etc. used to create the *full shot*, but each one of these elements exerting their own expressivity. Harmony loses its sense. The cinema produced becomes polyphonic, in the definition of Alexander Kluge, theorist and filmmaker of the modern German cinema.

The trends of the *new cinema*, which unite the intuitive discovery of the real by Rossellini with the dialectic montage of Eisenstein, have in Godard its first exponent. Pasolini, Bertolucci (and other Italians), Pierre Perrault (and various Canadians), Milos Forman (and various Czechs), Jerzy Skolimowski (and various Poles) and Brazilian *cinema novo* are at the forefront of this experiment. I should, above all, cite Jean-Marie Straub, a French-German *auteur* who seems to me to be the most modern of all the filmmakers. The critical structure of this phenomenon is still in its first stages of elaboration. The linguists are trying to create a grammar (Metz, Barthes, Pasolini).

On Cinema

Figure 3.3 Glauber Rocha and Jean Renoir (Cannes, 1969).

The conquest of this new language is in its initial stages but the stage of the discovery of reality using the handheld camera has already been surpassed by the 'analysis of reality' stage, through the use of the *full shot*. It's a mysterious territory into which not even Antonioni, Bergman, Visconti nor Resnais have penetrated, even if they have manifested their interest in exploring it. The only traditional filmmakers (or modern ones) capable of carrying out this type of cinema are Buñuel, Welles and Rossellini, poets whose influence is felt more and more strongly in modern cinema, not due to their exotic characteristics but because of the permanent unfamiliar nature of their works. Before the arrival of Rossellini, Buñuel was already making modern cinema with *Un Chien Andalou*. An example of creative freedom disengaged from the industrial dictatorship.

[4]
The late arrival of cinema as a language in relation to other art forms was a consequence of the dictatorship of the industry. And, even today, when the

new cinema movement has become a universal phenomenon, and developing more and more in the spirit of solidarity, the pressures of the backers (banks, institutions, associations and parties etc. . . .) can be felt right from the beginning of the production process. And, as we have noted, the public, eventually reached once the sponsors and censors have been finally defeated, has a pre-conditioned reaction in the face of a new product. *New cinema* in the United States, quite different from that of its European and Brazilian counterparts in terms of its graphics and eroticism, is facing the same difficulties as Czech *new cinema*, and so on and so forth. The problem of communication of modern film is not a problem of content, of meaning or politics. It's the fundamental fight between the artist and the passive vice of the public, created, in capitalism, by the industrial cinema, and in socialism by propaganda cinema.

Both for the left-leaning theorist and for the capitalist publicist, the word of command is communication. But communicate what? The most revolutionary of Russian filmmakers, Eisenstein didn't manage to communicate with his public. Mayakovski had the same problem. Official State Soviet films, copying the language of American films, served only to exhaust the Russian public, given that the moral code of the positive socialist hero was just as false as that of the capitalist hero. The companies and the bureaucracy still don't understand that *dramatization* is a contradiction in terms. For them, the artist is an employee and the art itself is a potion with which to control man. The artist thinks the contrary. Art cannot be propaganda nor have commercial ends because the purpose of art is to provide man with an instrument of knowledge distinct from that of scientific knowledge.

Official cinemas preach the domination of man; they preach the ideological control of the public. American cinema, more subtle in its manner, achieved much more than Soviet cinema. This is because the language used in American film matched the colonizing moral code. In Russia, the official language became an imitation of American cinema. Destroying the outdated thesis of form and content, Russian cinema has only proven that an old, capitalist language cannot be used as the expression of a revolutionary society.

[5]
What is the purpose of modern cinema? Revolution happens in a violent way against the aesthetic, moral and political standards of the public. In the

United States, whereas politically motivated cinema had an immediate aim when the economic depression hit, today's underground cinema is apolitical because American intellectuals cannot see, within their society, even the faintest hope for change. All American political problems are played out on a world stage. American *new cinema*, however, closes its eyes to the imperialism and concentrates its efforts on an underground guerrilla movement against the country's rigid internal moral structures. It's a cinema with anarchic, dadaistic tendencies. It destroys the traditional techniques, assaults the public with obscene practices, it creates an aesthetic of sexual scandal. Although political films such as *Guns of the Trees* (1961) by Jonas Mekas do exist, the current theme seems to be of eschatological lyricism, the oldest and most enduring exponent of which is *Scorpio Rising* (1962–1964) by Kenneth Anger. A great majority of the founders of American *new cinema* have succumbed to Hollywood contracts. Another set, more focused on *cinéma vérité*, was absorbed by television, which industrialized the handheld camera and the direct sound technique. Another group, under the shadow of the success of the pioneers, combined rebellion with commercial arguments: the renowned *David and Lisa* (1962) by Frank Perry is an example of this spurious type of 'new film', the best international representation of which at the moment is *A Man and a Woman* (*Un Homme et une femme*, 1966) by Claude Lelouch. However, underground cinema (pop, dadaistic, surrealist, anarchic, automatic, abstract, neo-figurative, like the manifestations in painting) continues to be produced in great intensity in 8, 16 and 35 mm film. The driving force of the movement is still Jonas Mekas, editor-in-chief of *Film Culture*.

In England, *free cinema* was almost completely absorbed by the industry, following in the steps of the commercial route taken by Tony Richardson. Stylistically, English cinema copied the technical inventions of the *nouvelle vague* and politically it has adopted the remnants of the anti-monarchist rebellion of the *angry young men*. The sheer joy when faced with an old world fighting hard to eke out its final moments of splendour is in full, exuberant voice in Richard Lester. To modern British cinema, the nostalgic phrase, both cynical and tragic, spoken by Talleyrand and used by Bertolucci in the epigraph of his film *Before the Revolution* can be applied: 'Those who haven't lived in the last moments before the Revolution do not know the sweetness of living.'[53] John Schlesinger, Karel Reisz and

O Século do Cinema

Peter Watkins are rebels without a cause, rebels up to the limits set out by the industry.

In socialist countries, above all in Czechoslovakia and Poland, the *new cinema* has reached an impasse, faced with the socialism of Central Europe itself, where the economic problems are provoking the unleashing of existentialist problems. With his welfare guaranteed by the State, man doesn't feel secure in himself and life becomes nothing more than a monotonous flow of time towards death. The socialist filmmakers believe that the true revolution didn't take place and that there still stubbornly remain pockets of old, bourgeois mentality. However, at the same time, there is evidence of contamination by old bourgeois rules of play which emerge as development takes place and the myth of security grows. This is the central theme of the new Czech films, above all those produced by Milos Forman, Vera Chytilova, Ivan Passer and Evald Schorm. Getting past the phase of historical exaltation in order to take stock and analyse the individual, this cinema also has to disentangle itself from the academic tradition of socialist realism. The first model to draw from was the *nouvelle vague* (Godard, without barriers, is everywhere).

The same is happening in Poland, whose Skolimowski and Roman Polanski generation cannot manage, in creative terms, to match the old and politically active cinema of Jerry Kawalerowicz, Andrzej Wajda or Andrzej Munk. In Poland, the only cinema which has reacted promptly, by way of this generation, against socialist realism, the men leading the fight appear out of breath after their attempts in the driver's seat of modern cinema. Traces of theatrical dramaturgy and discursive literature are present even in the most advanced of today's works: *The Passenger* (*Pasażerka*, 1963) by Munk. Polanski and Skolimowski, losing interest in Socialism, came to Western Europe where they try to create works of low impact, always in the footsteps of Godard.

The future of socialist *new cinema* is emerging in Hungary and Yugoslavia, mainly in Hungary. Hungarian *new cinema* is dedicated to the subject of man and History. It resisted the influence of the *nouvelle vague* and it's the only cinema which returned to and reanalysed the full revolutionary line of Eisenstein. Miklós Jancsó (*The Round-Up/ Szegénylegények*, 1966), István Szabó (*Father/Apa*, 1966), Ferenc Kósa (*Ten Thousand Suns*/Tizezer nap, 1965) are the most obvious proponents of this cinema which is the descendent of the old Béla Balázs.

On Cinema

Yugoslavia brings together complacency with creative freedom. It is the most free of the socialist cinemas and yet it is the most focused on *commercial art* and aesthetics. The biggest socialist cinema industry will certainly be that of Yugoslavia, but, judging from its biggest filmmakers, Aleksandar Petrovic and Dusan Makavejev, very little of more depth can be expected from it. Petrovic (*I Even Met Happy Gypsies/Skupljači perja*, 1965–1967) is a furious director, verbose, poetic, but lacking any real critical vision. Intoxicated by the great Russian literature (he is preparing an adaptation of Dostoyevsky), Petrovic applies 'gypsyness' as an end in itself and with cultural vision. With Dusan Makavejev (*Man Is Not a Bird/Covek nije tica*, 1965; *Love Affair, or the Case of the Missing Switchboard Operator/Ljubavni slucaj ili tragedija sluzbenice P.T.T.*, 1967), it's soaring lyricism which is repeated again and again in tired *nouvelle vague* forms. Being as he is the most French of the Yugoslav filmmakers, Makavejev, like Skolimowski, is receiving a very warm welcome from the critics of Western Europe. However, his work shows within it a deep nostalgia for the bourgeois world, and its political context is obviously forced. Petrovic and Makavejev don't have the strength, awareness, expressive anguish and the love shown by Miklós Jancsó, Ferenc Kósa and István Szabó.

From Russia nothing new, unless we count *The First Teacher* (*Pervyj uticel*, 1965) by Andrei Mikhalkov-Konchalovsky. The *new cinema* virus has contaminated Finland, Denmark, Norway and Holland. Sweden has not found in the rebellious Bo Widerberg (*Elvira Madigan*, 1967) a director on a par with the classic Bergman. And Bergman himself, trying to keep up with the times, has placed himself on the edge of the abyss between language and existence (*Persona*, 1966). All movement in Sweden is directed to sex. Loyal to their traditions, even the relations between Widerberg and Lelouch fail to erase the traces of a cinema with such important traditions. Holland is poking its head out. *New cinema* in 16 or 35 mm film is reacting after the explosion of the Provo Movement. *Joseph Kautus*,[54] a mixture of Gilberto Santeiro and Rogério Sganzerla, is a guerrilla film set in the Hague and Amsterdam. And others stand out: *Paranoia* (1967), by Adriaan Ditvoorst, screened in Berlin, impressed the critics and won an award.

Germany: *nouvelle vague* is King. Here the legend of *new cinema* has won over the industry. Alexander Kluge, Edgar Reitz, Volker Schlöndorff,

O Século do Cinema

the brothers Peter, Thomas and Ulrich Schamoni and other filmmakers are in the process of being accepted by the industry. Kluge less so than the others. His theoretical arsenal is large but in *Anita G* (*Abschied von gestern*, 1966) he hasn't escaped the influences of Godard. Much is expected from this young teacher and filmmaker. The classic cinema of Friedrich W. Murnau, Lang and Ernst Lubitsch and others seems to mean nothing to the new German filmmakers. On the Eastern side nothing. On the Western side the commitment to technique and rebellion, under the common denominator of eroticism.

Italy, under attack by the Western, is living through its worst cinematic period. The domination of the greats by the Americans and the tired manifesto of the young filmmakers leave only one filmmaker acting as intermediary between the generations, Pier Paolo Pasolini, and three young filmmakers who should be kept under close watch: Bertolucci, Marco Bellocchio and Gianni Amico. Italian cinema, however, simply from the thoughts and actions of these three filmmakers, still seems to us to be one of the richest within the whole of Europe. Firstly because its rebellion against neorealism hasn't resulted in the adoption of French formulas; secondly because it's a cinema which is profoundly linked to the social problems of its times and hasn't turned its back on the critical rigor which generally marked Italian cinema of the past. *Before the Revolution*, by Bertolucci, is the most extraordinary song of poetry existent in European *new cinema*. It's a film which managed to *be new without being Godardian*, something which gained Bertolucci respect and admiration from Godard. *China is Near* (*La Cina è vicina*, 1967) by Bellocchio (for whom the success of *Fists in the Pocket/I pugni in tasca*, 1965, continues) deals with the same subject matter as *La Chinoise* (1967) by Godard: the China–Soviet conflict; the repercussions in the West of Marx/Lenin as revised by Mao.

[6]
Dispensing details and judgements on the Brazilian *cinema novo*, considered by the critics to be one of the most promising of all the *new cinemas*, we get to Jean-Marie Straub.

Straub is French, he fled the army and now lives in Germany. He worked as the assistant to some of the *nouvelle vague* directors. His film *Not Reconciled*, adapted from the novel of Heinrich Böll, one of the most famous modern German writers, was considered by some critics to be a betrayal of Böll's work, and by others the most important film in modern cinema.

The *full shot* reaches its plenitude in Straub's work. The film obeys the technique of *one shot per action* or *one idea for each shot*. It's a succession of direct frontal shots, generally immobile, which are linked through rapid fusions of black. The dialogue is dry, spoken without adjectives, like a choral recital. The actors move little. Time is free, the film is set in the present and in the past. It cuts from the past to the present and vice-versa without the artifices used by Resnais or the classic flashback techniques. *Everything takes place on the screen*. The dialogue, the text, the noise, the rare musical interventions work simultaneously. Time (the enslaving notion of time) is abolished. The film *Is*.

Politically, Straub has not reconciled himself with old cinema; neither does he give in to the lucrative deals now on offer to the rebellious, or allow his characters, living in postwar Germany, *to reconcile* themselves with the new civilian politicians, as demagogic and dangerous as the old Nazis. *Not Reconciled* alerts us to the *commitment*. It's an essay on intransigence, it is an intransigent film. It is a model essay of cinematographic politics. The viewing, reviewing and study of this film will allow the reader to evaluate the importance and strength of Jean-Marie Straub.

[7]
Embodying the typical hero of modern cinema, Straub, not reconciled himself, has lived through the greatest of personal difficulties in Munich. At present he is filming *The Chronicle of Anna Magdalena Bach*, a film about the life of Bach. Straub is a sensational figure. He likes *The Dare* by Paulo Cesar Saraceni, and *Absolute Majority* by Leon Hirszman. For eight days, in Berlin, he talked incessantly about Buñuel, Brecht, Lubitsch, Gianni Amico, Bach, pornography, Hirszman and Saraceni. His wife, Danièle Huillet, co-scriptwriter and filmmaker as well, is working by his side in the struggle to bring the image of Bach to cinema.

'A whole film in music. In the moments of silence, Bach speaks, drinks and at times loses his temper,' Straub says, and he continues: 'The actors are musicians who play baroque instruments of the era. The real work lies in getting together an orchestra which can play standing up. A shot for each movement. Direct sound. Using a Mitchell, because for immobile long takes and direct sound it's preferable to use a Mitchell. The analysis of

O Século do Cinema

an era. Bach not reconciled? The period dress, an era, is taken in part from the remains of *The Golden Coach* (*Le Carrosse d'or*, 1953) by Jean Renoir, and another part from *The Taking of Power by Louis XIV* (*La Prise du pouvoir par Louis XIV*, 1966) by Rossellini. After this film, I want to go to Brazil. Brazil's *cinema novo* is not yet as pornographic as the others.'

Pornography, for Straub, is a tidied-up art form, an art of coloured shock technique, an inoffensive art which pleases the bourgeoisie, the aesthetics of a flower, of a bird, of a beer, of cheap love. Straub, undoubtedly, would vomit all over the blue aesthetics.

The bureaucrats of German cinema were reluctant in providing Straub with financial backing as they considered him a documentary maker, a Frenchman and an academic. Incapable, therefore, of filming the life of the great Johann Sebastian Bach. Within Straub can be found all the contradictions of modern cinema. A genius without a sponsor, actively censored (*Not Reconciled* was faced with innumerous problems). His resistance and his humanism, his courage and his humour show us that success is not the easiest thing for an auteur. That the cheapest way to achieve success is by conforming. And that, faced with a choice between business and art, if it were to become impossible for art to be made and delivered directly to the public due to draconian industry decisions, the best route for the filmmaker to take would be to drop his camera and become a politician.

Just like classic art, commissioned by those in power, industry-produced cinema is no more than a mouthpiece repeating, *ad infinitum*, a moral code backed by force. *Tidied-up language* with a programme is the basis for conformism, for fascism, in all art forms.

New cinema, both throughout the world and in Brazil, is a cinema of styles. A cinema of *filmmakers without cinema* is much better than *industry-produced cinema without filmmakers*. The sterile neighbourhoods of Mexico and Spain, the frustration of Argentina, are proof that neither bureaucracy, State interventionism, sectarianism nor ingenious theories have the right to restrain a culture *that wants to be new*.

In the case of Brazilian *cinema novo*, in which are united all the hopes of Third World cinema, we must remain permanently vigilant against those who, upon seeing the opportunity to make cinema in Brazil, wish to assault and capitalize upon the talent and courage, sacrifice and indignation in the name of a *progressionist* order, suited, drunk and cowardly, sterile and sacked from its position. More than ever, Brazilian *cinema novo* will only make sense if it is brought into the forefront of the most aggressive and immediate fight. No reconciliation. Yesterday's enemies have already waved their white flags in our direction, but any deal struck at this stage by a Brazilian artist with a good conscience or with discipline would be *conciliation*. Camera in hand or on the end of a tripod, the technique evolves but that isn't important. An idea in one's head, however, always is.

[Published in *O Cruzeiro*, Rio de Janeiro, 30 March 1968]

Alphaville

[1]

For those who are completely into the Yé-Yé movement,[55] canned music, *Alphaville* will seem more like reality than fiction. At the end of the day, in a world where logic reigns, there is nothing more logical than playing just one song on a loop, with the same rhythm, always looking to the front, a pre-determined 'sensation'. Like the style of American B movies, a cartoon strip, an advert etc... The 007-style is the so-called 'mass communication'. It was born of this type of scene, planned to the nth degree. As it is reality, I am not obliged to admit it. Don't come calling me a reactionary for that. Long live the technology which now allows us to have our appendix out in a smooth, painless manner but take care when this same technology begins to measure the rhythm of the sonnet in such a manner that it eventually produces a reaction which is completely devoid of meaning: that is to say, devoid of poetry. Don't come calling me lyrical or irrational, a Godard fanatic, because, despite the humour, Godard is probably a little over-rational. Nowadays, with so many contradictions flying about attacking current values, the irrational may well be more applicable than reason itself. Nevertheless, as the empty philosophy (turned into a samba) states, there are 'reasons that reason itself cannot explain'.[56]

[2]

The introduction is meant to provoke a reaction with regards to *Alphaville*, Godard's ninth, which disappointed many, mainly the 'sons of reason'. As was noted once in an article by Luiz Carlos Maciel, our century gave birth to the 'sons of wonder'. They come to blows with the 'sons of reason' but I believe that everyone is working together for the good of humanity. The fact that man is rotten to the core is a universally known fact but it would be wrong to think that Dr Von Braun had no good intentions at heart. The electronic brain which rules *Alphaville* tolerates the *super-planning* as it believes that man is capable of good. The worst thing is that no one seems to even know what man's desires are beyond a home, food, education and good health. The brain forgets this: man needs poetry. And poetry needs the unconscious. Dictatorships exist in a state of 'super-consciousness' and their power relies on the lack of consciousness of the people they dominate. These people only react when they start to doubt: doubt is the foundation of all consciousness.

For this reason, when Lemmy Caution[57] subjects the Brain to poetry, the Brain breaks down; it short-circuits, goes mad. It is at that point that the revolution begins.

[3]
Godard is not attacking technology (nor the rule of technology), because he himself uses it in his films, in a perfect harmony of sound and image. Godard, however, like no one else in cinema, despises the technique at the service of aesthetics, and technique, as far as he is concerned, works as infrastructure and not superstructure. He himself declared in an interview that he thinks it absurd when someone comes along and says that a super-spectacle like *Ben Hur* (William Wyler, 1959) is fantastic because it is pure spectacle, it has no philosophy/message to impart. That's a ridiculous thing to say as the fact that a super-production like *Ben Hur* exists is already a basis for philosophical exercise. A film like that doesn't exist in order to entertain the masses; rather it exists to sell as many tickets to the unconscious masses as possible. The super-consciousness of the spectacle. The dictatorship of 007.

The defenders of 'popular art' think that it is enough to create an effective communication technique to solve humanity's problems. Frankly, I don't believe that humanity's issues can be solved through art, and even less so with mechanical art. The 007 style is the best example of popular art of which we are aware. Any other theory which doesn't gain audiences is said to be unpopular, therefore any theory on paper is easy but still doesn't solve anything. This doesn't mean that Brecht, for example, was wrong. The playwright was in the right and really did manage to demystify the traditional spectacle, bringing a new tradition to future generations. A tradition which Godard embodies better than anyone else in cinema, knocking Joseph Losey off his post as the filmmaker who practically embodied Brecht's thought in cinema. Godard's response, albeit of immense critical importance, continues to be unpopular. It is due to the fact that movements which are unpopular are, at base, subversive. Christians, as we all know, were fed to the lions, until Saint Peter achieved his coup d'état and founded another mass movement, more or less just as dictatorial as those which preceded it in ancient Rome.

Some artists, obviously, receive critical acclaim: Visconti, with *Rocco and His Brothers*, is an example. Visconti, however, shamelessly and uncritically opted for an operatic melodrama. He used the lead purely and simply to better his argument. And, in none of his other films, either preceding or following it, did he achieve the same result. *Rocco and His Brothers* was, above all, an inspired work, and cannot be explained away by reason. I believe, in light of this, that the roots of artistic creation are irrational. Art itself is irrational in the sense that it puts forward its own, individual reasons in explanation to reality. And the 'super-reason', which the theoreticians have tried to impose throughout the years, has created, albeit as well as clarifying a lot of situations, a lot of obstacles to artistic creation. The theoreticians, and I don't wish to attack them with impunity, always have an ideology to defend. And an ideology is typical of theoreticians, of the dominators, the drivers of society. Nothing, however, is more unbearable for an artist than an ideology which forces him down a certain path or to certain ends. The ideological end of a work of art, once achieved, goes much further than any aesthetic rules. That is the case with Visconti who, being as he is a Marxist, only achieved great things once he was gripped by irrational inspiration. Even films like *Salvatore Giuliano*, by Salvatore Rosi, or *Barren Lives*, by Nelson Pereira dos Santos, which at first appear to be products of profound ideological reason, are, once analysed in depth, of such aesthetic beauty that they leave far behind films of American production or films of Soviet persuasion. It's a widespread phenomenon, which takes place as much in Russia (see Eisenstein!) as in the United States (see Orson Welles!).

Artists obviously think they have their own points of view on things and follow ideologies. But what I mean is that the original separation between the artist and conditioning is as great (or equal to) the point of separation in the artist's infancy which caused him to take the path of liberty. There are two types of intellectual in the conflict: the irrational beings, the artists, the 'sons and daughters of wonder'; and the rationalists, the scientists, the theorists, the critics. This conflict only ceases to exist in a case of genius such as that of Sartre, wherein the ambiguity balances out. It's not necessary, however, to be a great critic to know that Sartre will continue to be known for his philosophical work and not on the premise of his artistic contribution, which works at the service of his philosophy. I'll be told that William, the Englishman, was profoundly rational, given the construction of his plays. But would the oratory tone of his characters, of great beauty, be real? Of course not. The foundation of Shakespeare is his unfettered imagination before his artisanal dominance of language, the fruit of creation. If it were a simpler thing, it would be as straightforward as joining Timon with Prospero to create a brilliant result. I have never heard of someone having had such artistic success using that method, even though I am aware that the scientists, using reason, invented the bomb.

And that's the way it goes.

[4]

Godard takes this subject forward. It's a dominant theme in our century. Rossellini, a primitive, has already pointed this out. There's no one as ignorant as Rossellini, and how rare a filmmaker of such genius. Rossellini precedes Godard, the most cultured filmmaker in existence in cinema, so cultured and rational that at times it is annoying. Godard, however, is a new breed of artist: a rational artist. I am not undoing all I've just said but I want to say that, if for the underdeveloped world the anarchic-surrealist criminality of Buñuel's style is more than fruitful, then an anarchic-critic spirit like that of Godard is more than necessary for the developed world. Even simply because, if it weren't the case, life would just not be worth living. Everything would be in its place without anyone to come along and completely mess up the order.

Jean-Luc doubts and when he poses the question which shouldn't be asked, it is shocking. It's like Van Gogh painting that which should not be painted. Jean-Luc enquires about the good or bad consciousness, the fallibility of the machine, of (in)transcendence. Transcendence is the only escape route capable of sugaring the pill of ever-suffering mankind. In the country of Dr Von Braun, whomsoever cries or loves is shot. The idea of eroticism is completely separated from that of love.

Freedom is a relative problem. If there is a State, freedom suffers from the need for things to function in a certain way and, therefore, in certain situations, the best thing to do is to put a grenade in the mouth of the poets, beings who, in years past, were taken for madmen because they walked with their lovers in the moon. It is clear, today, that the poets were right, and the fact that they were right landed many of them right in the fire. Reason is, well, like freedom, relevant to the times in which we live and it would be very pedantic to believe that here, on earth, things would be able to progress as rapidly as we might like. There is enormous cultural poverty and this poverty is demonstrated through the dominating atmosphere of intolerance. At no time in history has there been so much talk of freedom and at the same time never have so many artists and intellectuals been persecuted. The only eternal subversive in this world is the artist. Not the scientists: they may create bombs and hearts of aluminium but theirs is a moral code shared by Leaders, Military Men, Bankers and Theoreticians. Not the artist. The artist, investigating the real, can go as far as to declare the machine a failure. The machine cannot, for example, help anyone understand the subtle shades of spring. That generates death – it is illogical. Dr Von Braun condemns Lemmy Caution to death.

Lemmy Caution is a good secret agent in 007 style. He shoots Dr Von Braun. In the end, taking aim and firing is the only protection against being killed oneself. That's why so many people have taken up arms throughout the ages.

[5]
The truth of the matter is that we all have a Revolution to fight and only the revolutionaries will taste the true flavour of life or death. The revolution, however, is continuous and as it is continuous it should always ask questions, revolutionizing each time that which the reactionaries deem as ideals. A revolution, and here you'll have to forgive me one romantic image, is like a flower which opens to reveal petals which were completely unexpected. One petal may be carnal, another may be mineral.

Godard is a mineral filmmaker. *Alphaville* pits Lemmy Caution, armed with Elouard's bullets in his gun, against the dominating Brain, the fruit of the scientific genius of Dr Von Braun. At least in the fictional version Lemmy Caution escapes with the girl. Will we escape from terrorism using only verse as our weapon? Is the lesson Lemmy Caution teaches us a better way forward?

[Essay on typewriter, undated, from *Tempo Glauber* archives]

Do You Like Jean-Luc Godard? (if not, you're out)

Two films at the same time – one on even days, one on odd days – that is the rhythm in which Godard works. Jean-Luc has no scruples, he responds in a hurried manner: 'Listen, I am filming two films at the same time because of pride, because it's all a big performance. It's like a conductor conducting two orchestras at the same time....' Cynical, anarchic, irreverent, tragic, romantic, irresponsible, classic, restless, irritating and disconcerting, heads or tails: these are the many faces of this Franco-Swiss man, aged thirty-six, slim and nervous, slightly bald, considered by Aragon, a voice at the forefront of the French Communist Party, to be like a modern Cézanne, as important for cinema as the painter was for canvas. Explaining his political position in the pages of *Les Lettres Françaises*, Godard cleared up what a lot of people would like to know:

> When they need my help to organize a strike for the dockworkers of Marseille, they can ask me. I am happy to help.

Despite this, radical and reactionary critics in France dubbed his controversial film *The Little Soldier* (*Le Petit soldat*, 1963), which followed the revolutionary *Breathless* and was banned by De Gaulle's censors, a fascist film. Godard, making films, explained:

> I am a painter of letters. Just like there exist men of letters. I want to go inside Plato's cave illuminated by the light of Cézanne.

Godard is an explosion; he unbalances the so-called *cinematographic good thought*. Godard is an artist; Godard is a man of our time.

> I would like to direct the French news programmes. I want to document the Vietnam War and the teaching going on in Cuba. Cinema should be a useful tool.

But isn't Godard a fascist? If so, why would a fascist fire a bullet into an electronic dictator and kidnap a girl for a new adventure in the 'outlands'.

There are many doubts, the polemic is growing. The question is one that cannot be escaped, wherever you are in the world:

    Do you like Jean-Luc Godard?

First things first: no one with any strict principles likes Godard. It's like that story of the friend who reacts badly: 'I hate that dish!' 'But have you tried it?' 'Once and I hated it.' 'Listen, try it again.' 'Hmm, it's lovely but it's not healthy!' The critics generally want to make Godard a 'healthier meal'. 'He's great but he's not serious!' 'From an aesthetical point of view, it's OK.' 'He's politically alienated.' The kids who hang round the pavements of Paissandu[58] have got Jean-Luc on the tip of their tongues. The most well-established groups of the left speak loudly and with conviction of their dislike of him: only the most snobbish leftists speak well of him, that is to say, according to the opinion of the conformist left. Well, if a fellow who claims he is leftist likes Godard, it's because he is suffering from contamination with *bourgeois art*. If the fellow is an American Catholic and he likes Godard he is suffering, according to the right-wing radicals, from *lefty* contamination. They accuse Godard of everything apart from homosexuality, which, let's face it, is quite a feat in the circles of institutionalized backbiters.

The majority of Brazilian intellectuals haven't yet become acquainted with the phenomenon of Godard. For them, Godard is a sort of French Charlie Chaplin: a film director who is fashionable to like, a joker, like those abstract painters who painted their paintings using a donkey's tail dipped in ink. A Brazilian intellectual aged forty is quite capable of seeing *Pierrot le fou* (1965) and calmly sitting through it eating popcorn. And even if this intellectual is a poet and translator of Rimbaud he won't realize that *Pierrot* is a *new stage of hell*. He won't realize because he isn't mentally prepared for this experience. It would be like an academic art critic going to Cézanne's first exhibition.

The most incredible thing in the history of art is the reaction of formalized thought towards great revolutions in art. The impact of *Breathless* got Godard's name known but up to today he has continued to be one of the greatest sources of stupidity in the cinematographic world:

O Século do Cinema

'Everything in everything,' Godard says. That is to say, the maximum of things in the minimum of time, a simultaneous action, like Joyce, an encounter between sociology and fiction, anthropology and poetry, Shakespeare and Science Fiction, painting and philosophy. It's a pop-culture spelling book which shocks the exponents of a fossilizing formalism.

A product of a France stabilized by the De Gaulle regime, a personalized and obstinate regime, and faced with the increasing stability of the European socialist landscape, Godard finds himself in a dead end within the old continent. For a thinker who still cultivates knowledge in terms of moral ends, Godard explodes into view like a type of fanatical menace. He is like a little Lago circulating around our neighbourhood; he represents the impossible form of consciousness for those who have built their consciousness on the 'non-being', that is to say, on 'being limited' to a revolutionary *idealism*. Jean-Luc Godard is the first European artist post-Sartre: Jean-Luc Godard didn't turn his freedom into a commitment, but instead into an instrument of conquest.

As far as the reader is concerned, Godard is one of the best subjects for the so-called discussion about 'art and commitment'. This conversation, full of clichés, is the subject of choice of the so-called conservative critics. Both left-wing and right-wing conservative critics exist. The difficult task is to find a forward-thinking critic. For that reason, it is the greatest irritation for the revolutionary artist to see their work poked at on a level of shameless intimacy by hapless critics. Or by moralists set in their ways. Or by erudite fanatics. Godard, who is also a critic himself, knows these manoeuvres well. Now and then he gives an interview and throws flames onto the fire:

> Soviet cinema? Well, Soviet cinema is very bad. However, what I would ask is: will it be worthwhile to make cinema when they are constructing inter-planetary rockets?

When Carlos Drummond de Andrade wrote the poem about the stone,[59] it was a laughing stock all over Brazil. Any idiot in a tie would recite the verse about the 'stone in the middle of the road' and say 'even I could do that!' Today Drummond is seen as the great Brazilian poet and one of the best in the world. The verse about the 'stone in the middle of the road' gains its well-deserved strength, its path is now well established and its foundations

On Cinema

are now solid. The films by Jean-Luc seem like this 'stone in the middle of the road'. A little stone in a world full of pitfalls. I am going to show where the traps are set.

Cinema is like the wastebasket of Fine Art. Eisenstein, creator and thinker, developed the first cinematographic aesthetics based on painting and poetry, at a time when the constraints of Stalinism castrated him. Eisenstein, starting early with the genius of *Battleship Potemkin*, arrived late with the great orchestration of *Ivan, The Terrible* in 1944–1945, when in fact Orson Welles had already filmed *Citizen Kane* in 1941 and Rossellini finished *Rome, Open City* in 1944–1945. Looking at it this way, we see that Eisenstein arrived at the splendour of a *renaissance* cinema when Orson Welles had already thrown an extravagant leaving party for expressionism and Rossellini had similarly just planted the seeds of modern cinema. Let's explain this in more depth. Eisenstein wanted to do in cinema what Da Vinci or Michelangelo or Dante had done: he wanted to organize cinema to the image of the world, make the new Russian cinema the consecrated expression of new Russian society. It just so happened that Orson Welles, a product of a society which was revolting in another style, made a film which *disorganized* the cultural traditions of cinema in the sense that he *applied* cinema to the tragic vision of the neo-capitalist American society. In the same measure that Eisenstein *organizes*, Welles *destroys*. *Citizen Kane* is a step forward from *Ivan, The Terrible* but it is a film which Eisenstein would probably have made if he had been in the United States; I don't doubt either that the idea he had to film *An American Tragedy*, by [Theodore] Dreiser, was very different from that of *Citizen Kane*. In a Russia suspended in time thanks to Stalinism, Eisenstein grew old along with the revolution itself. Welles put the final nail in the coffin of expressionism which the German directors had brought with them to Hollywood, a school suspended in time by the cinema industry and imperialist politics.

In a Europe devastated by the war, far from the priorities of the State or from any deals with the cinema industry, Roberto Rossellini, the cameraman Roberto Rossellini, who had even worked for Mussolini in the past, picked up a camera and some pieces of film negative and filmed *Rome, Open City*. Rossellini, Open Cinema – with no literature, no studio, no dramaturgy, no actors, no make-up, no technique: just the man, the world, realism without any links to painting, visual poetry removed from the rules of composition and illumination, narrative removed from poetical pretensions, a text ignorant

O Século do Cinema

of the theatrical traditions – a new realism, *neorealism*. The loneliness of Roberto continued as *neorealism* itself was then betrayed, normalized, theorized upon, made commonplace and commercialized. Roberto, the great creator, remained on the sidelines. Luchino Visconti, restoring expressionism and Fine Art, orchestrating everything in terms of his own liberal aesthetic Marxist thought, usurped Roberto's ideas and reformulated Eisenstein, only advancing, in terms of timescale, from Leonardo Da Vinci to Dostoyevsky. From Roberto was born the sub-literary mystification of Fellini, who linked *neorealism* to mysticism, driving another paralysing stake into the form. The simplicity of Zavattini drove De Sica towards commercial projects. The 'leftist' revisions saw the rising of Francesco Rosi, attempting, in a calculated leap, to unite Roberto with Visconti in his project *Salvatore Giuliano*, that is to say, joining the cultural, literal and political organization of Visconti with the living set design and direct camera work of Roberto. And in making *Giuliano*, another cross was ceremoniously plunged into the cemetery of cinema. Roberto provided the fertile ground in which the poet Pasolini and the poet Bertolucci were to grow and Roberto was to reap the fruits of his slow-maturing crop in this future generation, twenty years later. Today, when Visconti has already begun to decompose due to the sterilizing formalism which he himself orchestrated through his aristocratic attitude towards the revolution (typical of *The Leopard*, a truly autobiographical work) – Roberto is distinguishing himself on the world stage with his modern essay on politics and poetry: *The Taking of Power by Louis XIV*, a film in colour made for French television. *Colour and Television*: modern methods of communication. Roberto, always hard at work, freed himself from industry-controlled cinema and moved to television. When Roberto made contact with the new means of communication he also touched upon a new language. Roberto is a filmmaker of our times. Roberto has nothing to do with cinema as a fantastic anachronism (wherein it is *like theatre*, to quote Welles). Roberto is the great father and master who is now, just like Louis XIV, taking power, and the direct and rightful descendant, the inheritor of new cinema, is Jean-Luc Godard.

> If you go to Rome, it is imperative that you break with all and any engagements you may have and go and enjoy a plate of spaghetti with Roberto. Roberto knows how to make spaghetti like no one else on earth... (Jean-Luc Godard, *Filmcritica*, 1964)

On Cinema

The reader, if he's still interested, will ask why I haven't spoken about Antonioni, nor Bergman, nor of Our Lord, Mr Buñuel. I will explain in reverse: Our Lord, Mr Buñuel, is a rebellious monk, a surrealist. He has nothing to do with the history of cinema. His is another path, his art is primitive. Bergman is a solitary manifestation of the existential religious anguish, he's all tied up in theatre; he's a dilutor of Eisenstein and Welles. He is a novelist in the times of visual poets, of painters of letters, of artists who penetrate into Plato's cave *bathed in the light of Cézanne* or of men who interrogate the world weighed up in Marxist terms, under the lights of the propaganda advertisements. The solitary speculator in all this is the new Michelangelo, Antonioni, who distanced himself from *neorealism* like the sacred fruit escapes from a tree in flames.

Cinema of young people, open cinema, cinema that discovers man, over and above that which has been achieved so far by Hegel and Marx and Sartre and all the vain philosophy: cinema which is an extension of that philosophy, cinema which is no longer Fine Art, dressmaking, actors and scenarios, music and painting. Instead it is that which is preached by Jean-Luc, the 'everything in everything', the new Bible, the new encyclopaedia, the new *Das Kapital*. Cinema is not an isolated art form; cinema on Television, that is, *a film shown on Television*, that is the art of the twentieth century; that is the foreshadow of the art of the future. The paths which have been trodden to reach were difficult: from Lumière to Griffith, from Griffith to Eisenstein, from Eisenstein to Welles – that is the first cycle. The second cycle goes from Roberto to Godard. In the middle of the path are Visconti, Fellini, Bergman. Circling the path with the cross on his back, Our Lord, Mr Buñuel. An artificial satellite, circling the path, is Michelangelo. Godard is the guerrilla fighter of this universe; two films a week; simultaneous creation and living. Pier Paolo Pasolini is the poet of this world. The army of this universe, I hope, will be the future filmmakers of the underdeveloped world.

INSTRUCTIONS ON HOW TO WATCH A GODARD FILM, ARMED WITH THE INFORMATION AND THE MEANDERINGS SHOWN ABOVE

1. Do not go into the cinema hall with an inferiority complex. That is to say, uttering that phrase of aversion 'I don't know anything about cinema.'

O Século do Cinema

2. Do not, under any circumstances, go in uttering that phrase of aversion to your friend but thinking to yourself 'I understand quite a bit. In fact, I have a better idea than those people over there.'
3. Do not, therefore, think that you are a 'filmmaker in the making'. Be humble. Learn to respect cinema.
4. Do not think, in a pretentious manner, that your literary background will give you the necessary tools to 'understand cinema'. Learn that the idea of 'understanding cinema' doesn't exist. What is necessary is to 'comprehend cinema'. For that it is just necessary to have a historical vision of cinema. To know, for example, what I explained before.
5. Do not think that American Westerns, crime/cop films and musicals are rubbish. It's exactly for that reason that you will be taken as 'square' when you talk to the critics. In order to defend your intellectual integrity, you fail to remember a film directed by Raoul Walsh. It's good to know Raoul Walsh and other trends of American cinema, in order to like Godard better.
6. Godard doesn't consider himself a genius. He is a modern man, free, honest. If you are right-wing, don't be so reactionary and allow Godard to attack *the* Fatherland and the Family in his own way – it's always done in an intelligent manner. If you are left-wing, don't go into the cinema calling Godard a fascist. Just wait because, deep down, he is going to talk about everything you need him to in order to keep your temper and the old Being in order. If you take no ideological position, don't look to Godard for messages.
7. Learn to *read* Godard's films. Godard's films are there to be *read* and *seen*. Godard doesn't like music very much. The music in his films is *composed of words*. It is necessary to *listen well* or *read well* all the quotations, dialogue and sounds. If you fail to read it you will miss 70 per cent of the film. Sartre has already said that, in modern cinema, the pure image is almost always neutral; the meaning comes from the words.
8. Learn, once and for all, that Godard is a realist. His characters are members of French-European capitalist society, preferably that of the twentieth century. They are outcasts, like the hero in *Breathless*, prostitutes, intellectuals etc. Godard's characters use slang, quote Corneille, Racine, Poe and other people. They are normal people, just like everyone else.

9. Learn, before and while watching Godard's films, that no one in the world lives an *organized life*. Even people who belong to *Organizations* have their hearts broken, get toothache and are frightened of dying. From that stance, Godard's cinema is as open as life itself. Learn to see and listen to life. Godard quoted another clever thing the other day. Reflect upon it. In any case, it wasn't Godard who said it, but another Frenchman, Roger Leenhardt:[60] 'To be intelligent is to comprehend before you judge.' Pay close attention: try to comprehend things and Godard's films. I would also add another phrase, by Roberto: 'It's very easy to photograph a face; it's very difficult to photograph the world.'[61]

10. Admit that Godard is modern, that he is more advanced than you are. Godard films like someone paints a picture. All the other cinema directors 'dramatize' the facts. Godard 'un-dramatizes' them. That is to say, what is important is not *telling a story* but creating a living universe, a world around and containing within it certain characters from the present and from the past. If you already understand modern literature, you will certainly understand Godard better. But do not confuse Godard with the *nouveau roman*, for the love of God! Godard is, at base, a realist. But Godard is *pop*, dig it? For example, Godard mixes scenes from American gangster movies with Humphrey Bogart in *Pierrot le fou*. That's why it's important to have seen those films. You will have a great time with the references and will comprehend a lot better how cinema is linked to life.

11. Do not think, because of what I wrote above, that Godard is pure art or anything as ridiculous as that. That sort of language has had its day. Godard, like all great avant-garde artists, is planting seeds for the future. Just like Roberto planted Godard. It was because of Roberto that *cinéma-vérité* was born, did you know that? Godard is planting for the cinema of the future: popular, industrial, in colour, international. Something which will be transmitted through space satellites by TV channels of the *Figaro-Pravda-New York Times-China Press*. That is why Godard is a pacifist. Or would you like to start a war to justify his theories? Don't confuse intelligence with pretension. Then you will be ready to understand, love (and how!) the incredible films of Jean-Luc Godard.

O Século do Cinema

Godardean

Once all preconceptions have been set aside, Godard takes on a new importance in our lives. It's a radical change. For example: you either love him or you hate him. The intelligent spectator hates any demonstration of higher intelligence than his own. This happened to me when I discovered Godard. I thought: this guy is pretentious, full of himself, a reactionary (!), inhumane. When I saw *A Woman Is a Woman* (*Une Femme est une femme*, 1961) for the first time, in Paris, I left the cinema hall hating everything which smelt of Godard. It's a typical reaction of someone who is ill adapted to the modern world. A guy who likes Visconti in the way I do needs to put Visconti in his place, that is to say, in the past, in order that he is able to like Godard. Both are to my taste but in the manner that both Bach and Noel Rosa[62] can both be to my taste, each in his own place, position and time in history. Visconti is a cinema academic. Godard is a modernist. Everything in Visconti is well-finished, organized, perfect. In Godard it is all search, imperfection, anguish, revolution. From *Ivan, The Terrible* through to *The Leopard*, cinema has been living through its first phase. What began with Roberto and resulted in Pasolini and Godard is something entirely different. Firstly, it is poetic liberty. Pasolini distinguishes the existence of 'cinema of prose' as being separate from that of the 'cinema of poetry'. All former cinema is theatrical/based on novels. It's cinema with a plot. Godard picks up cinema at the point where Joyce left the novel. *Breathless* picks up the crisis of contemporary fiction at the appropriate point in the evolution of the *verbal* novel to the *visual* novel. Joyce's best moments tend towards an impossible figurative representation: the next step forward is cinema and this step has been taken by Godard. And, in this step, cinema ceases to be prose and becomes poetry, or rather, the camera is *no longer a simple narrator* of facts but an instrument of analysis and capable of creation. Each scene takes on the value of a painting; each scene has its own value, independent of that which preceded it and that which follows. And, at the same time, this scene which *has its own value* is also profoundly linked to that which preceded it and that which follows. Godard is like a writer who gets rid of the commas; he kicks out the continuity and the formal logic imposed by the Americans. When two people have a conversation in a Godard film, they talk about life, loves, dreams, frustrations, with all the frankness of someone who is talking in real life.

For example: you, the reader, could be talking about the economic crisis while taking a shower. Or you could talk about aesthetics while eating *feijoada*.[63] Or you could laugh while you are killing somebody. Or you could do it while thinking about the atomic bomb. Godard introduced these contradictory truths in cinema. I say contradictory in terms of academic cinema. What is academic cinema? It's an artificial interpretation at the feet of a set design which matches it. For example: I speak of my romantic feelings to a backdrop of twilight. When this freedom was projected onto the screen, the public, which still hadn't grown accustomed to the disconcerting realism of Roberto Rossellini, reacted. I reacted but then I turned around and managed to work out where the error lay. The error lay with me because I was not following the eleven rules I have just presented you with.

It might seem ridiculous to say it but comprehending Godard, and here I am not joking, is one of the most important events in a person's life today. That is to say, comprehending Godard without contracting *Godarditis*, as I will now explain. *Godarditis* is an illness which occurs in the young intellectual and if it hits hard it can destroy that person for life. An adolescent could turn into a really bad character if he believes that Godard shares the ideas of Michel Poiccard, a criminal and the hero in *Breathless*. No, Godard does not embody the ideas of any of his characters, unless we count, on a wider scale, those of *Pierrot le fou*. Godard is a critic of contemporary society. Godard chronicles this society, he redacts poetical reports on this society, always maintaining the distance of someone who is observing it in the manner of a sociologist and who reacts emotionally in the manner of a poet. Godard, if my dear readers will excuse me, now sits above the Marxists and their opponents.

The filmmaker who has most influenced today's socialist cinema is Godard. Milos Forman and Jerzy Skolimowski, the greatest filmmakers in Czechoslovakia and Poland, are openly *Godardean*. This doesn't mean that Godard has no influence over the young American filmmakers. In his mantra of 'everything in everything', Godard has influenced photography, editing, dialogue style, acting, the current style of inexpensive and rapid filming. He has influenced the way of thinking, or rather, he has broken down the fictional way of thinking in terms of *the causes determining the conflicts*. For Godard, just like in real life, the causes are linked to the conflicts and that is the secret of his dramaturgy. Obviously, Godard, like everyone, makes mistakes. But they are intelligent mistakes: they are mistakes made always as a result of a doubt, of a Hamletesque certitude that the discovery of the truth means the loss of life itself. A prisoner of this terror but without articulating the conventional cries of the classic tragedy, Godard, like Pierrot, in the manner of a Greek hero, paints his face blue and blows off his own head. The Greek hero wore a mask and his cry was the excruciatingly metaphysical 'Woe is me!' Pierrot's cry, when he runs with his face all painted blue and with dynamite in his hands, is a neurotic, realistic cry, stripped of any calculated delivery. Life lives on in an eternity of colours. Man explodes and is united with the exuberance of nature. How can someone be so mineral and so romantic at the same time?

Jean-Luc Godard is the modern intellectual. Industrialist and poet, politician and sociologist, filmmaker and critic, scientist and tragic figure. A bundle of doubts; desperation born of lucidity. Making films with the vehemence and voracity of an apostle, this man has still not reached the peak of his creative experience. I believe that, in the next ten years, his creative power will assume the proportions of real genius. Like Bach, Godard is creating the structure of cinema's future. The lack of understanding which surrounds his work is entirely due to the lack of information we have at hand to solve the problems which only Godard, the artist, perceives. Time will give us the solution to all things, and once young cinema from all over the world incorportaes Godard's lessons to their own respective heritage, this generous cinematographic style will impose itself with the same force that American cinema imposed itself in the first half of the century. What is exceptional, however, is the fact that Godard is worth, just by himself, all of American cinema! He has achieved in six years that which hundreds of filmmakers achieved in sixty. He has completely reformulated cinema, learning the lessons of Roberto with all the humility of a disciple. It's from this humility that he was able, bringing together the various lines of crisis, to catalogue modern culture in a great work composed of *small-yet-great* films, the peak of which, up till now, has been *Pierrot le fou*, the modern tragedy par excellence.

His more recent films, *Made in USA*, and *Two or Three Things I Know about Her*, both filmed at the same time, are at the same advanced position. The discussion will continue. With time, all of us, in good humour and in all seriousness, will be inclined to like Jean-Luc Godard.

Notes

Preface and Acknowledgements

1. Glauber Rocha, *Cartas ao mundo*, edited by Ivana Bentes, São Paulo, Companhia das Letras, 1997.

Introduction

1. See Eric Hobsbawm, *The Invention of Tradition*, Cambridge, Cambridge University Press, 1983.
2. The expression 'tricontinental cinema' was inspired by the Tricontinental Conference in Havana, Cuba in 1967, which had a great impact on Latin American political cinema.
3. See Frantz Fanon, *The Wretched of the Earth*, New York, Grove Press, 1968, the French translation read by Rocha before writing 'An Aesthetics of Hunger' in 1965.
4. On the occasion of the release of *Antonio das Mortes* in the United States, Rocha became involved in a polemic that gave him the ideas for 'An Aesthetics of Dreams'. In response to the review by R. Callenbach, entitled 'Comparative Anatomy of Folk-Myth Film', published in *Film Quarterly*, Winter 1969–1970, Rocha exposed his anti-realist ideas and his interpretation of the link between myth and the unconscious, disavowing the form in which the reviewer used Gramsci, Lukács and Freud to criticize his film. See the article 'The Way to Make a Future' (dialogue between Rocha and Gordon Hitchens), in *Film Quarterly*, Fall 1970.
5. See Georg Lukács, *Studies on European Realism*, New York, Howard Fertig, 2002.
6. For an analysis of the impact of *Entranced Earth*, the emergence of Tropicalismo and the post-Cinema Novo era, see Ismail Xavier, *Allegories of Underdevelopment: Aesthetics and Politics in Modern Brazilian Cinema*, Minneapolis/London, University of Minnesota Press, 1997.

Notes to Pages 9-15

7. The Western was a source of inspiration when he made *Black God, White Devil* (1964). And there are some echoes of Ethan, the protagonist in *The Searchers*, in the figure of the protagonist in *Antonio das Mortes*, the enigmatic personification of violence.

Revisão Crítica do Cinema Brasileiro

1. This is the introduction to the book *Critical Review of Brazilian Cinema/ Revisão Crítica do Cinema Brasileiro*.
2. Alberto Cavalcanti (1953). *Filme e realidade*. São Paulo: Martins. [Note from Brazilian edition].
3. Alex Viany (1959). *Introdução ao cinema brasileiro*. Rio de Janeiro: Instituto Nacional do Livro-MEC. [Note from Brazilian edition].
4. Georges Sadoul (1963). *História do cinema mundial*. São Paulo: Martins. Originally published in French (1949), *Histoire du cinéma mondial des origines à nos jours*. Paris: Flammarion. [Note from Brazilian edition] [C.M.].
5. Umberto Barbaro (1965). *Elementos da estética cinematográfica*. Rio de Janeiro: Civilização Brasileira. Translation of selected chapters from Umberto Barbaro (1960). *Il film e il risarcimento marxista dell'arte*. Roma: Editori Riuniti and Umberto Barbaro (1962). *Servitù e grandezza del cinema*. Roma: Editori Riuniti. [Note from Brazilian edition] [C.M.].
6. Salvyano Cavalcanti de Paiva (1953). *Aspectos do cinema americano*. Rio de Janeiro: Páginas. [Note from Brazilian edition].
7. Carlos Ortiz (1949). *Cartilha do cinema*. São Paulo: Iris. [Note from Brazilian edition].
8. *Chanchada* films were popular musical comedies produced mainly in Rio de Janeiro and within the studio system (especially by Atlântida Studios, founded in 1941). See also note 12 of *Revisão Crítica do Cinema Brasileiro*. [C.M.]
9. In French in the original. 'There aren't good or bad films. There are only film auteurs and their politics, irreproachable by the very nature of things.' [C.M.]
10. Paulo Emilio Salles Gomes (1916-1977) was a Brazilian film critic, writer and historian, founder of the film archive of the Museum of Modern Art in São Paulo (1946, later the Brazilian Film Archive) and of the first film course in Brazil at the University of Brasília (1965). He was one of the most important thinkers of his generation within and outside the academic world, whose contribution to Brazilian cinema scholarship remains crucial to this day. Author of various books and essays on cinema including *Jean Vigo*, considered the definitive work on the French director (originally published in French in 1957, first edition in English in 1971 by University of California Press, republished by Faber & Faber in 1999). [C.M.].
11. Paulo Emilio Salles Gomes (1982). 'Artesãos e autores' in *Crítica de cinema no Suplemento Literário*, vol. 2. São Paulo: Paz e Terra. Originally published in the

Literary Supplement of the newspaper *O Estado de São Paulo*, 14 April 1961. [Note from Brazilian edition]

12. Zé Trindade, stage name of Milton da Silva Bittencourt (1915–1990), and Oscarito, stage name of Oscar Lorenzo Jacinto de la Imaculada Concepción Teresa Diaz (1906–1970), were two Brazilian actors and comedians who became well known from the late 1930s to the late 1950s through the so-called *chanchada* films. See also note 8 of *Revisão Crítica do Cinema Brasileiro*. [C.M.]

13. Macumba means 'black magic' and designates a practice amongst Afro-Brazilian syncretic religions such as Umbanda. [C.M.]

14. This note refers to the terms *cangaço* and *cangaceiro*. *Cangaço* is a historical and cultural phenomenon which took place in the north-east region of Brazil (whose dry backlands are known as the *sertão*) between 1870 and 1940, but whose origins date as far back as the eighteenth century. It can be adequately described as an instance of 'social banditry' as defined by Eric Hobsbawm in his 1959 book *Primitive Rebels* and later in his 1969 study *Bandits*, which includes an investigation of the *cangaço* and the *cangaceiro*, the social bandit of the *sertão*. The appearance and development of the *cangaço* and the *cangaceiros* are intimately linked to the agricultural and social history of the north-east during colonial (1500–1822) and imperial (1822–1889) times. In their origin, the *cangaceiros* were farm workers, known in the area as *sertanejos* (the cowboy from the *sertão*), who lived and worked in cattle farms, sugarcane and later cotton plantations in the semi-arid region of the Brazilian north-east. The *sertanejo* wore leather clothes and hats in order to protect himself from the thorny vegetation of the region, which characterize the ecosystem known as *caatinga*. From the eighteenth century onwards landowners became increasingly powerful and began to rule the political life of the region. In order to protect their properties they would arm groups of *sertanejos* who eventually formed independent groups, no longer under the control of a landowner. Towards the end of the nineteenth century these groups gradually became known as the *cangaceiros*, social bandits who would perform robberies for both economic and political reasons. Seen as common criminals by the State, the *cangaceiros* were considered by many of the local population as Robin-Hoodesque heroes, stealing from the rich to give to the poor. Different gangs of *cangaceiros* lived and hid in the secret corners of the *sertão* and were notable for their highly developed survival techniques under the harsh geographical conditions of the area, which made their capture an ever more difficult task. Eventually President Getúlio Vargas's forces won the war against the *cangaceiros* and put an end to the *cangaço* phenomenon in 1940. There are examples of Brazilian films devoted to such tales of social banditry as early as the 1920s, and a sub-genre known as *Nordestern* (*Nordeste/northeast* + Western) thrived from the 1950s to the late 1970s. See Eric J. Hobsbawm (2000). *Bandits*, revised edition. London: Weidenfeld & Nicolson. See also notes 5, 18, 21 and 25 of *Revolução do Cinema Novo*. – *Corisco, sertão, xaxado* and *Lampião*. [C.M.]

Notes to Pages 19-22

15. Alex Viany (1959). *Introdução ao cinema brasileiro*. Rio de Janeiro: Instituto Nacional do Livro-MEC. [Note from Brazilian edition]
16. There were, in fact, some film dates which were wrong. In this edition all dates and titles were amended. [Note from Brazilian edition]
17. Caio da Silva Prado Júnior was an important Brazilian historian who wrote the seminal book *Formação do Brasil contemporâneo - Colônia* (1942), translated in English as *The Colonial Background of Modern Brazil* (first published in 1967 by University of California Press). [C.M.]
18. Landeg White's translation of verse 8 of the second stanza from *Os Lusíadas* (*The Lusiads*), sixteenth-century epic poem by Luís Vaz de Camões (Oxford University Press, 1997). The original verse in Portuguese reads 'Se a tanto me ajudar o engenho e arte.' [Translator's note - S.D.]
19. Miguel Torres (1926-1962), from Bahia, was an ex-sailor, actor and screenwriter, who died in a car accident. He co-wrote with Ruy Guerra the script of *The Scoundrels* (*Os cafajestes*, Ruy Guerra, 1962) and *The Guns* (*Os fuzis*, Ruy Guerra, 1963). He never finished the documentary *The Horse of Oxumaré* (*O cavalo de Oxumaré*), and the following scripts were never produced: *ABC of Revenge* (*ABC da vingança*), *Police and Bandits* (*Volantes e cangaceiros*) and *The Road of Hunger* (*A estrada da fome*). Glauber Rocha wrote an article in his honour, 'Miguel Torres, bom cabra', in the newspaper *Diário de Notícias*, Salvador, 6 January 1963. [Note from Brazilian edition]
20. Flaherty never really worked for the GPO Film Unit (1933-1940). In 1931 he directed *Industrial Britain* for the Empire Marketing Board Film Unit (1926-1933), at the invitation of John Grierson. [C.M.]
21. José Guilherme Merquior (1965). 'Crítica, razão e lírica: ensaio para um juízo preparado sobre a nova poesia no Brasil' in *Razão do poema: ensaios de crítica e de estética*. Rio de Janeiro: Civilização Brasileira, p. 164. [Note from Brazilian edition]
22. Jorge Mateus de Lima (1893-1953) was a prominent Brazilian poet, novelist, politician and doctor. [C.M.]
23. Carlos Drummond de Andrade (1902-1987) was one of Brazil's most important and influential poets of the twentieth century. See also notes 1, 3 and 59 of *O Século do Cinema*. [C.M.]
24. João Cabral do Melo Neto (1920-1999) was a prominent Brazilian poet and diplomat of the twentieth century. He is the author of *Morte e vida severina* (1955), a narrative poem concerned with the plight of an internal migrant from the *sertão* in search of a better life in the coastal capital of the state of Pernambuco. [C.M.]
25. José Lins do Rego (1901-1957) was a Brazilian novelist and one of the chief exponents of the regionalist and critical-realist cycle in Brazilian literature in the first half of the twentieth century, alongside Graciliano Ramos (see note 27). His seminal work *Menino de engenho* (*Plantation Boy*, 1932) was adapted to the screen in 1970 by Walter Lima Jr. [C.M.]

26. Emiliano Augusto Cavalcanti de Albuquerque Melo (1897–1976), known as Di Cavalcanti, was a prominent Brazilian painter and one of the main names behind the Brazilian Modern Art Movement in the 1920s. In 1976 Glauber Rocha made a documentary short at the funeral of Di Cavalcanti. [C.M.]
27. Graciliano Ramos (1892–1953) was a prominent Brazilian writer and journalist. He is one of the chief exponents of the regionalist and critical-realist cycle in Brazilian literature in the first half of the twentieth-century, alongside José Lins do Rego (see note 25). His seminal works *São Bernardo* (1934), *Vidas secas* (*Barren Lives*, 1938) and *Memórias do cárcere* (*Prison Memories*, 1953) were adapted to the screen by Leon Hirszman in 1972 and by Nelson Pereira dos Santos in 1963 and 1984, respectively. [C.M.]
28. In this film, Humberto Mauro works as an actor and cinematographer; the director is Octávio Gabus Mendes. [Note from Brazilian edition]
29. Glauber Rocha (1961). 'Humberto Mauro e a situação histórica' in *Jornal do Brasil*, Suplemento Dominical. Rio de Janeiro, 7 October 1961. [Note from Brazilian edition]
30. Glauber Rocha (1961). 'Humberto Mauro e a situação histórica' in *Jornal do Brasil*, Suplemento Dominical. Rio de Janeiro, 7 October 1961. [Note from Brazilian edition]
31. Glauber Rocha (1961). 'Humberto Mauro e a situação histórica' in *Jornal do Brasil*, Suplemento Dominical. Rio de Janeiro, 7 October 1961. [Note from Brazilian edition]
32. Quoted in Glauber Rocha (1963). 'A linha geral de Eisenstein' in *Diário de Notícias*, Suplemento Artes e Letras. Salvador, 13 January 1963. [Note from Brazilian edition]
33. Ascenso Ferreira (1939). 'Os engenhos de minha terra' in *Cana Caiana*. Recife: author's edition. In Portuguese: '... dos engenhos da minha terra, só os nomes fazem sonhar ...'. [Note from Brazilian edition]
34. Gregório de Matos (1633–1695) was one of the most prominent poets of Colonial Brazil (1500–1822), and is considered to be one of the greatest baroque poets of the Portuguese language. His body of work includes sacred and lyrical poems as well as more popular satirical poems, which won him the nickname *Boca do Inferno* (Hell's Mouth). [C.M.]
35. Antônio Gonçalves Dias (1823–1864) is one of the first poets in the history of Brazilian literature who can be described as eminently Brazilian in subject and sensibility, unambiguously incorporating local themes and landscape in search of a nationalist sentiment. His poetry stands in opposition to the neo-classical quality of Brazilian Arcadian poetry and is one of the main manifestations of Brazilian Romanticism in the nineteenth century. While in Portugal as a law student (at the University of Coimbra) he wrote what became one of the best-known poems in Brazilian literature, 'Canção do exílio' ('The Song of Exile'), in which he sings of nostalgia for the homeland. Proud to be of mixed ethnic origin (white, native and black), he developed the 'Indianist' trend in Brazilian literature (alongside novelist José de Alencar – see note 37 of *Revisão Crítica do Cinema Brasileiro*). [C.M.]

36. Cláudio Manuel da Costa (1729–1789) was one of the most prominent poets of Colonial Brazil. His book *Obras* from 1768 marks the beginning of the Arcadian period in Brazilian poetry, which lasts until 1836 with the publication of *Suspiros poéticos e saudades* by Gonçalves de Magalhães (largely considered to have inaugurated Romanticism in Brazil). Alongside Tomás Antônio Gonzaga, Cláudio Manuel da Costa developed a neo-classical style in opposition to the excesses of baroque poetry, characterized by the idealization of nature, bucolic motifs and a praise of harmony (with a local colour). He was also involved in the most important rebellious movement in Colonial Brazil, known as the *Inconfidência Mineira* of 1789 in Ouro Preto, Minas Gerais, which attempted to overthrow the Portuguese rule and declare independence. [C.M.]
37. José Martiniano de Alencar (1829–1877) was one of Brazil's most prominent novelists in the nineteenth century and one of the main names in Brazilian Romanticism. He developed different styles such as the historical novel, the regionalist novel and the Indianist novel, creating a type of nationalist literature characterized by a use of language typical of Brazil and in opposition to the Lusitanian style. Among his most important novels are *O Guarani* (1857), *Iracema* (1865) and *Senhora* (1875). It is a widely known fact that Glauber Rocha was a great admirer of José de Alencar. [C.M.]
38. Raul d'Ávila Pompéia (1863–1895) was a Brazilian writer, largely known for his 1888 novel *O ateneu*. [C.M.]
39. Afonso Henriques de Lima Barreto (1881–1922), known simply as Lima Barreto, was a prominent Brazilian journalist and novelist (not to be confused with the filmmaker Vítor Lima Barreto, 1906–1982). Largely influenced by realist master Machado de Assis (1839–1908), his work nevertheless stands at the crossroads between realism and modernism. His most famous novel is *Triste fim de Policarpo Quaresma* (1911, first published in book form in 1915). [C.M.]
40. Joaquim Lúcio Cardoso Filho (1912–1968), known simply as Lúcio Cardoso, was a prominent Brazilian writer, playwright and journalist of the twentieth century, author of the highly praised novel *Crônica da casa assassinada* (1958). [C.M.]
41. Adonias Filho (1915–1990) was a Brazilian novelist, journalist and literary critic, whose work belongs to the third phase of Brazilian modernism (post-1945). [C.M.]

Revolução do Cinema Novo

1. The Modern Art Festival, aka Modern Art Week (*Semana de Arte Moderna*) was a festival held at the Municipal Theatre of São Paulo from 13 to 18 February 1922. It was a landmark in the history of Brazilian art and came to define the movement known as Brazilian Modernism. The festival featured exhibitions, lectures and literary-musical concerts, and was met with fierce criticism from the press and the general public. It represented a break with

the conservatism which had to a large extent dominated Brazilian artistic manifestations in the nineteenth century. Among the artists who took part in the festival were Oswald de Andrade, Menotti del Picchia, Manuel Bandeira and Mário de Andrade (literature); Anita Malfatti, Emiliano Di Cavalcanti and Vicente do Rego Monteiro (painting); Victor Brecheret, Wilhelm Haarberg and Hildegardo Velloso (sculpture); and Heitor Villa-Lobos (music). [C.M.]
2. Glauber's reference to the politician Carlos Lacerda as the 'chief critic of Guanabara' works as an irony intended to link Lacerda's political conservatism with the conservatism of the films Glauber criticizes. Carlos Frederico Werneck de Lacerda (1914–1977) was a Brazilian journalist and politician. He was a member of the National Democratic Union Party (UDN) and in 1960 became the first elected governor of the now extinct state of Guanabara (1960–1975), located in the municipality of Rio de Janeiro. In his five years as Governor, Carlos Lacerda put into practice a series of radical changes including administrative reforms, the removal of shantytowns (*favelas*) to the outskirts of the city and major public works such as the construction of tunnels, avenues and parks. His conservative and anti-communist views led to his support of the 1964 military coup which deposed President João Goulart, but as soon as 1966 he began to oppose the regime and ended up losing his political rights for ten years. Carlos Lacerda was also a prolific journalist, founder in 1949 of the influential newspaper *Tribuna da Imprensa*, and is perhaps most remembered in connection to the events which led to the suicide of President Getúlio Vargas in 1954. [C.M.]
3. Gustavo Dahl (1938–2011) was a filmmaker and film critic. After a period abroad studying cinema in Italy and France, Dahl returned to Brazil to become one of the main theorists of the *cinema novo* group in the 1960s, collaborating with various newspapers and magazines. His film *The Brave Warrior* (*O bravo guerreiro*, 1969) is one of the main titles of the second phase of the movement (post-1964 military coup). From the 1970s onwards he became involved with the public sector and occupied a series of posts within government film agencies. [C.M.]
4. Jânio da Silva Quadros (1917–1992) was Brazil's president from 31 January 1961 to 25 August 1961. He defeated Marshal Henrique Lott in the 1960 presidential elections with a campaign based on the fight against corruption and financial instability, and characterized by his exhibitionist and oftentimes dramatic style. At the time there was a separate vote for the post of vice-president, and Jânio Quadros did not manage to elect his candidate, Milton Campos, who lost to João Belchior Marques Goulart (1919–1976), aka Jango Goulart, from the Brazilian Labour Party (PTB). The new president – the first to be inaugurated in the recently built capital Brasília (1960) – represented a promise for change despite his rightist political views. In the seven months of his administration Jânio gradually lost political support from the legislative power and on 25 August 1961 he resigned from the post, an act which still remains largely unexplained in Brazilian political history. Vice-president Jango Goulart took over the presidency, not without heavy resistance from the right-

wing parties and the military. Jango was close to the Brazilian Communist Party and at the time of Jânio's resignation was visiting the People's Republic of China. He was also a close supporter of the trade unions and of agrarian reform. Jango ruled from 1961 to 1964, when he was deposed by the military coup of 31 March 1964. Glauber refers to the years between 1961 and 1964 as a period of rebellion and agitation, and his film *Black God, White Devil* is attuned with the democratic experiment and hope for political revolution experienced during the early 1960s in Brazil. [C.M.]
5. Cristino Gomes da Silva Cleto (1907–1940), nicknamed Corisco, was a legendary *cangaceiro* in the Brazilian *sertão* in the first half of the twentieth century. In 1926 he joined Lampião's gang and became known as the Blonde Devil (*diabo louro*) because of his dashing looks and long hair. It was also around this time that he kidnapped the thirteen-year-old Sérgia Ribeiro da Silva, nicknamed Dadá, who became his lifelong companion and also a member of Lampião's gang of *cangaceiros*. The couple later left Lampião's gang and started their own, but were finally killed by government forces in the state of Bahia in 1940, two years after Lampião and Maria Bonita's death. In Glauber Rocha's *Black God, White Devil*, Manuel and his wife Rosa cross paths with Dadá and Corisco (the white devil of the title, played by Othon Bastos) as they roam around the *sertão*. See also notes 14 of *Revisão Crítica do Cinema Brasileiro and 25 of Revolução do Cinema Novo*. [C.M.]
6. In English in the original. This is a reference to Howard Hawks's film *To Have and Have Not* from 1944, starring Humphrey Bogart, Lauren Bacall and Walter Brennan. The film is set in the island of Martinique, in the Eastern Caribbean. [C.M.]
7. Churubuzco Studios, founded in 1944 with 50 per cent ownership of RKO Radio Pictures. [Note from Brazilian edition]
8. In French in the original. Unidentified source. [C.M.]
9. See note 14 of *Revisão Crítica do Cinema Brasileiro*. [C.M.]
10. In French in the original: 'But almost all the films which imitate Godard are unbearable because they miss the point. They will imitate his flippancy but they will forget, and for good reason, his despair. They will imitate the puns but not the cruelty.' See Jean-Louis Comolli and Jean Narboni (1967). 'Entretien avec François Truffaut' in *Cahiers du Cinéma*, n. 190, May 1967. [Note from Brazilian edition]
11. *Amazonas, Amazonas* (documentary) and *Maranhão 66* (documentary). [Note from Brazilian edition]
12. Cordel literature could be translated as 'chapbook literature', meaning popular and cheaply printed booklets containing folk novels, songs and ballads, produced and sold mainly in the north-east region of Brazil. [C.M.]
13. The prophecy in the end of *Black God, White Devil* reads 'The backlands will turn to sea, and the sea will turn into backlands' ('O sertão vai virar mar, e o mar vai virar sertão'). For *sertão* (backlands) see note 18 of Revolução do Cinema Novo. [C.M.]

14. Glauber's intention was to invoke Che Guevara's essay 'Message to the Peoples of the World through the *Tricontinental*', published in the leftist quarterly magazine *Tricontinental* in April 1967. [Note from Brazilian edition]
15. In Portuguese in the original: 'Não conseguiu firmar o nobre pacto/Entre o cosmos sangrento e a alma pura. (...) Gladiador defunto mas intacto./(Tanta violência, mas tanta ternura).' Mário Faustino (2002).'Balada (Em memória de um poeta suicida)' in *O homem e sua hora – e outros poemas*. São Paulo: Cia das Letras. [Note from Brazilian edition]
16. In Portuguese 'A praça é do povo/Como o céu é do condor', by Antônio Frederico de Castro Alves (1847–1871), also known as the 'poet of the slaves' for his support for the abolitionist cause in the nineteenth century. [C.M.]
17. Zuenir Carlos Ventura (1931–) is a Brazilian journalist and writer. In 1964 he met Glauber Rocha at the Cannes Film Festival, where *Black God White Devil* was being nominated for the Golden Palm, and the two became friends. In December 1968, following the Institutional Act Number 5 (AI-5) – the fifth and most drastic of all decrees issued by the military dictatorship in Brazil – Zuenir Ventura was arrested under the accusation of having links with the Communist Party. Glauber's essay '*Cinema novo* and the Adventure of Creation', however, dates from before his arrest and was published on 2 February 1968 in the magazine *Visão*. [C.M.]
18. The *sertão* (backlands) is an area which spans the north-eastern states of Brazil, characterized by a semi-desert ecosystem known as *caatinga*. It also designates a culture and way of living, very much connected with the hardships of the dry land, ensuing poverty and a history of exploitation of cheap labour by local landowners. For more on *sertão*, *sertanejo* and *cangaço* See note 14 of *Revisão Crítica do Cinema Brasileiro*. [C.M.]
19. The exact verses are 'Não sei por onde vou / Não sei para onde vou / Sei que não vou por aí!' ('I don't know which way I'm going / I don't know where I'm going / I know I'm not going this way'), from 'Cântico negro' by Portuguese writer José Régio (pen name of José Maria dos Reis Pereira, 1901–1969). [C.M.]
20. See note 1 of *Revolução do Cinema Novo*. [C.M.]
21. A traditional dance which originated in the *sertão* of the state of Pernambuco, Brazil, favoured by the *cangaceiros* who would celebrate their victories by dancing the *xaxado*. For *sertão* and *cangaceiros* see notes 14 of *Revisão Crítica do Cinema Brasileiro* and 18 of *Revolução do Cinema Novo*. [C.M.]
22. In the original: '... o cineasta sabe que seu *abacaxi* espalha sementes ...' The word *pineapple* (*abacaxi*) is used in Brazilian Portuguese to mean a problem of difficult solution, and consequently 'to peel a pineapple' means to solve this difficult problem. [C.M.]
23. Nelson Rodrigues (1912–1980) was a Brazilian playwright, journalist and novelist, considered to be the inventor of modern Brazilian theatre. He remained throughout his life a controversial figure, hated by the conservative right for his domestic dramas filled with sex, incest, prostitution,

Notes to Pages 94–104

abjection and dirty hidden secrets, and by the left for his political conservatism and support for the military regime. From the 1950s onwards, Brazilian cinema 'discovered' Nelson Rodrigues as film producers gradually realized that his colourful stories, built around Rio de Janeiro's middle and lower-middle classes, had strong cinematographic potential. [C.M.]

24. Pero Vaz de Caminha (c. 1450–1500) accompanied Pedro Álvares Cabral in the expedition that set out from Lisbon in March 1500 towards India and arrived in the landmass of Brazil on 22 April 1500. Before returning to Portugal, he wrote the official report in the form of a letter, dated 1 May 1500, to King Manuel I of Portugal, describing the discovery of the new land. In this document he gives a detailed account of Cabral's expedition and registers his first impressions of what they then believed to be an island, including a description of the landscape and its native inhabitants. Pero Vaz de Caminha's letter is considered the first written document in the history of Brazil. [C.M.]

25. The most famous *cangaceiro* to roam the *sertão* was Virgulino Ferreira da Silva, known as Lampião or the King of the *Cangaço*. Lampião and his gang's deeds were notorious throughout the country in the 1920s and 1930s, and he remains to this day a legendary albeit controversial figure. In 1938 Lampião, his wife Maria Bonita and other members of his gang were caught by government forces in the state of Sergipe, killed and beheaded, their heads then preserved and exposed across the region in a symbolic display of force from the official power. For more on *cangaço*, *cangaceiro*, *sertão* and Lampião's gang (Corisco) see notes 14 of *Revisão Crítica do Cinema Brasileiro*, 5 and 18 of *Revolução do Cinema Novo*. [C.M.]

26. Glauber is referring to Cândido Portinari's 1944 painting *Retirantes*, which depicts a family of internal migrants fleeing from the drought of the Brazilian *sertão* in search of a better life. The painting as a whole and details from it are used in the credits sequence of Geraldo Sarno's documentary *Viramundo*, which focuses on the migratory movement from the north-east to the south-east of the country in the 1960s. [C.M.]

27. See note 1 of *Revolução do Cinema Novo*. [C.M.]

28. Jean-Claude Bernadet (1967). *Brasil em tempo de cinema: ensaio sobre o cinema brasileiro de 1958 a 1966*. Rio de Janeiro: Civilização Brasileira. [Note from Brazilian edition]

29. See note 1 of *Revolução do Cinema Novo*. [C.M.]

30. Glauber featured in the film *The Wind from the East* (*Vent d'est*, 1969) by Jean-Luc Godard. He plays a key role in a sequence which looks at the possible routes to be taken by cinema in the Third World, in a speech which displeased his French friend as it included, as maxims for a revolutionary cinema, the task of creating a national anti-imperialist cinema within the various Third World Countries (inspired by the proposal by Che Chevara of creating a thousand Vietnams). [Note from Brazilian edition]

31. E: Ernesto 'Che' Guevara. [Note from Brazilian edition]

32. D: Regis Debray (1967). *Révolution dans la révolution*. Paris, Maspéro. [Note from Brazilian edition]
33. Alfredo Guevara, then Director of the Instituto Cubano de las Artes e Industrias Cinematográficas [Cuban Institute of Cinematographic Arts and Industry, ICAIC] [Note from Brazilian edition]
34. Rosinha is the nickname of Rosa Maria de Oliveira Penna, Glauber's second wife from 1962 to 1971. [C.M.]
35. Bernardo Bertolucci.
36. Gianni Amico.
37. Salvyano Cavalcanti de Paiva (1923–2011) was a prolific and influential Brazilian film critic. [C.M.]
38. F: Fidel Castro. [Note from Brazilian edition]
39. Gianni Amico directed *Ah! Vem o Samba* (1968), 16mm. [Note from Brazilian edition]
40. José Flores de Jesus (1921–1999), stage name Zé Keti, was a Brazilian samba singer and composer. [C.M.]
41. *Última Hora* was a newspaper founded in Rio de Janeiro by journalist Samuel Wainer in 1951. [C.M.]
42. Brecht's maxim cited in 'Conversations with Brecht', the final chapter of Walter Benjamin's book on the German playwright, is as follows: 'Don't start from the good old things but the bad new ones.' See Walter Benjamin (1973). *Understanding Brecht*. London: NLB, p. 121. [Note from Brazilian edition]
43. See note 1 of *Revolução do Cinema Novo*. [C.M.]
44. In this case, the expression used by Glauber corresponds literally to that quoted by Walter Benjamin. See Walter Benjamin (1973). *Understanding Brecht*. London: NLB, p. 121. [Note from Brazilian edition]

O Século do Cinema

1. Carlos Drummond de Andrade (1945). 'Canto ao homem do povo Charlie Chaplin' in *A rosa do povo*. Rio de Janeiro: José Olympio. In Portuguese: '*Ó Carlito, meu e nosso amigo, teus sapatos e teus bigodes caminham numa estrada de pó e esperança.*' [C.M.]
2. Georges Sadoul (1953). *A vida de Carlitos: Charles Spencer Chaplin, seus filmes e sua época*, translated by Mário Mendes de Moura. Rio de Janeiro: Livraria Editora Casa do Estudante do Brasil, pp. 169–70. Originally published in French: Georges Sadoul (1952). *Vie de Charlot: Charles Chaplin, ses films et son temps*. Paris: Les Éditeurs Français Réunis. [Note from Brazilian edition] [C.M.]
3. Carlos Drummond de Andrade (1945). 'Canto ao homen do povo Charlie Chaplin' in *A rosa do povo*. Rio de Janeiro: José Olympio. In Portuguese: 'Sujos

de tristeza e feroz desgosto de tudo / que entraram no cinema com a aflição de ratos fugindo da vida /... e te descobriram e salvaram-se.' [C.M.]
4. Characters in the following films: *The Tragedy of Othello: The Moor of Venice* (1952), *Macbeth* (1948), *Mr Arkadin* AKA *Confidential Report* (1955) and *Chimes at Midnight* (1965). [Note from Brazilian edition]
5. In fact, when *Citizen Kane* was shot, the United States had not entered World War II yet. [C.M.]
6. Portmanteau Word: myth + irony + onanism. [C.M.]
7. The character Hank Quinlan in *Touch of Evil* (1958). [Note from Brazilian edition]
8. Cyro Siquiera (1956). 'Hollywood e o cinema da violência' in *Revista de Cinema*. Belo Horizonte, n. 21, Feb–Mar 1956. [Note from Brazilian edition]
9. Glauber is referring to the novel of the same name, *Paths of Glory* (1935) by Humphrey Cobb. [Note from Brazilian edition]
10. Sergei Eisenstein (1949). *Film Form: Essays in Film Theory*. Edited and Translated by Jay Leyda. San Diego, New York and London: Harcourt Brace & Company. [Note from Brazilian edition]
11. These are the final scenes of *The Exterminating Angel* (*El ángel exterminador*, Luis Buñuel, 1962). [LN]
12. *Viridiana* shared the Palme d'Or with *The Long Absence* (*Une Aussi longue absence*, Henri Colpi, 1961). [C.M.]
13. Oscar Dancigers was born in Russia and emigrated to Paris. After World War I he was granted French nationality. In 1940, when fleeing Nazism he went to live in Mexico where he began working as a cinema producer again. [Note from Brazilian edition]
14. Rodolfo Usigli (1905–1979), Mexican playwright, poet and essayist, whose only novel was adapted for cinema by Luis Buñuel: (1986). *Ensayo de un crimen* (*Terra nostra*). Mexico: Lecturas Mexicanas. [Note from Brazilian edition]
15. Michèle Manceaux (1960). 'Luis Buñuel: athée grâce à Dieu' in *L'Express*, 12 May 1960, p. 41. [C.M.]
16. Glauber is quoting from memory here. Rossellini actually said: 'Le cinéma est une toute petite chose [...] Et puis photographier un homme, ce n'est rien, il faudrait pouvoir photographier un monde ...', in Jean Domarchi, Jean Douchet and Fereydoun Hoveyda, 'Entretien avec Roberto Rossellini', *Cahiers du Cinéma*, n. 133, July 1962, pp. 4–14. Included in Roberto Rossellini (1984). *Rossellini: le cinéma révélé*. Textes réunis et préfacés par Alain Bergala. Paris: Flammarion/Ed. de l'Etoile, pp. 93, 106. [Note from Brazilian edition]
17. In order to make this passage clearer part of the original article was added even though it was not in the first edition of this book. [Note from Brazilian edition]
18. Glauber's article is from 1962 and the film was shot in 1964–1965, which shows the not unknown alterations he made to his own texts for the first edition of this book. [Note from Brazilian edition]

19. Glauber is talking of the novel of the same name, *Le Journal d'une femme de chambre* (1900) by Octave Mirbeau. [Note from Brazilian edition]
20. Marcel Martin, *Cinéma 64*, n. 85, Paris, April 1964, p. 121. [Note from Brazilian edition]
21. The source cited here by Glauber cannot be located. Pasolini's article 'Una visione del mondo epica-religiosa,' published in *Bianco e Nero* in June 1964, touches on the question of the sub-proletariat and the Third World. When *The Gospel according to St. Matthew* was released in France, Pasolini was faced with polemics and took part in a discussion with Jean-Paul Sartre. See 'Cristo e il Marxismo: dialogo Pasolini-Sartre,' in *L'Unità*, 22 Dec 1964. [Note from Brazilian edition]
22. Guy Gauthier (1963). *Image et Son*, n. 161–62 (Chris Marker special), Paris, Apr–May 1963. [Note from Brazilian edition]
23. The cinematographic records indicate that this film was not co-directed. Rossellini is shown as being the only director. [Note from Brazilian edition]
24. *History of Humanity*, see Adriano Aprà (ed) (2001). 'Deuxième partie: L'encyclopédie historique' in *Roberto Rossellini: la télévision comme utopie*. Paris: Cahiers du Cinéma / Auditorium du Louvre, pp. 131–90. The films mentioned are *Viva l'Italia!* (1960–1961); *The Iron Age* (*L'età del ferro*, 1964–1965, five episodes); *The Taking of Power by Louis XIV* (*La Prise du pouvoir par Louis XIV*, 1966); *Man's Struggle for Survival* (*La lotta dell'uomo per la sua sopravvivenza*, 1967–1971, 12 episodes); *Acts of the Apostles* (*Atti degli apostoli*, 1968–1969, five episodes); *Socrates* (*Socrate*, 1970); *Blaise Pascal* (1971–1972); *Augustine of Hippo* (*Agostino d'Ippona*, 1972); *The Age of Cosimo de Medici* (*L'età di Cosimo de Medici*, 1972–1973, three episodes); *Cartesius* (1973–1974); *Italy: Year One* (*Anno uno*, 1974) and *The Messiah* (*Il Messia*, 1975). [Note from Brazilian edition]
25. In 1958 Glauber was sent by Bahian daily *Diário de Notícias* to cover Roberto Rossellini's visit to Salvador. On this occasion he met painter Di Cavalcanti, who was accompanying Rossellini and who introduced the future filmmaker to the father of neorealism. Glauber later spoke of the proficuous nature of this encounter and of the conversations he had with Rossellini, which had a considerable impact on his developing views on cinema. See note 26 of *Revisão Crítica do Cinema Brasileiro* on Di Cavalcanti. [C.M.]
26. 'Dassin, Cine-Cristo às avessas', published in *Jornal do Brasil*, Rio de Janeiro, 1958. [Note from Brazilian edition]
27. Glauber is referring to *He Who Must Die* (*Celui qui doit mourir*, Jules Dassin, 1957). [Note from Brazilian edition]
28. 'Joseph and His Brothers' was one of Visconti's projects (not completed) based on Thomas Mann's four-part novel *Joseph und seine Brüder* (1926–1943). See 'Trente ans d'histoire(s)', interview with Suso Cecchi d'Amico in *Théâtres au cinéma*, n. 15, 2004, p. 47. [Note from Brazilian edition]
29. Glauber is referring to *The Brothers Karamazov* (1880) by Fyodor Dostoyevsky. [Note from Brazilian edition]

Notes to Pages 194–212

30. Glauber is referring to the novel *I Malavoglia* (1881) by Giovanni Verga. [Note from Brazilian edition]
31. Glauber is referring to the novella *Senso* (1883) by Camillo Boito. [Note from Brazilian edition]
32. Nom de guerre adopted from the anarchist movement and as a political journalist. His name at birth was Eugène-Bonaventure de Vigo. [Note from Brazilian edition]
33. Jean-Paul Sartre, *Les Chemins de la liberté* (1945–1949); *L'Âge de raison* (1945), *Le Sursis* (1945) and *La Mort dans l'âme* (1949). [Note from Brazilian edition]
34. 'Caligula', in Roger Quilliot (ed) (1962). *Théâtre, Récits et Nouvelles*. Paris: Gallimard/Pléiade. [Note from Brazilian edition]
35. Originally published as 'Ciro e i suoi fratelli' (Colloquio di Guido Aristarco con Luchino Visconti), *Cinema Nuovo*, Milan, anno IX, n. 147, Sept–Oct, 1960, p. 403. [Note from Brazilian edition]
36. *Cinema Nuovo*, Milan, anno IX, n. 147, Sept–Oct, 1960, p. 403. [Note from Brazilian edition]
37. *Cinema Nuovo*, Milan, anno IX, n. 147, Sept–Oct, 1960, p. 403. [Note from Brazilian edition]
38. Sergei Eisenstein (1949). *Film Form: Essays in Film Theory*. Edited and Translated by Jay Leyda. San Diego, New York and London: Harcourt Brace & Company. [Note from Brazilian edition]
39. Roland Barthes (1978). 'The Third Meaning: Research Notes on some Eisenstein Stills' in *Image, Music, Text – Essays Selected and Translated by Stephen Heath*. New York: Hill and Wang. [Note from Brazilian edition]
40. Viatcheslav Ivanov (1970). Eisenstein et la linguistique structurelle moderne' in *Cahiers du Cinéma*, special edition 220–221, May–June, p. 50. [Note from Brazilian edition]
41. Sergei Eisenstein (1949). *Film Form: Essays in Film Theory*. Edited and Translated by Jay Leyda. San Diego, New York and London: Harcourt Brace & Company, p. 75. [Note from Brazilian edition]
42. In Italian in the original. 'When you are making a film, living in that period of time at the service of a certain event, I do not put all my problems into the mix and I don't resolve them by objectifying them. Rather, when making the film I remain conscious, aware of myself, of my environment, of my story, and I am alienated to the point at which that event makes me suffer alienation, to then fight it and overcome it making the film.' Michelangelo Antonioni (1964). 'Preface' in *Sei film: Le amiche, Il grido, L'avventura, La notte, L'eclisse, Deserto rosso*. Torino: Einaudi, p. xii. [Note from Brazilian edition]
43. Preface of Jean-Paul Sartre to Franz Fanon (1961). *Les Damnés de la terre*. Paris, François Maspero. [Note from Brazilian edition]
44. Jean Domarchi, Jean Douchet and Fereydoun Hoveyda, 'Entretien avec Roberto Rossellini', *Cahiers du Cinéma*, n. 133, July 1962, pp. 4–14. Included in Roberto Rossellini (1984). *Rossellini: le cinéma révélé*. Textes réunis et

préfacés par Alain Bergala. Paris: Flammarion/Ed. de l'Etoile, p. 93. [Note from Brazilian edition]
45. 'Estética da fome (manifesto)' in *Revista Civilização Brasileira*, n. 3, July 1965. Reproduced in this volume ('An Aesthetics of Hunger'). [Note from Brazilian edition] [C.M.]
46. Jean Cocteau's formula 'cinema films death at work' is famous and frequently quoted by French critics. The quote cited by Glauber has not been located. For more see Jean Cocteau (1973), *Entretiens sur le cinématographe*. Édition établie par André Bernard et Claude Gauteur. Paris: Éditions Pierre Belfond. [Note from Brazilian edition]
47. Emília is the naughty and chatty rag doll in Monteiro Lobato's children's book series *Sítio do Picapau Amarelo* (1920s–1940s). [C.M.]
48. Glauber is referring to the episode *Toby Dammit* in the film *Spirits of the Dead* (aka *Histoires extraordinaires/Tre passi nel delirio*, 1968), in which the two other segments were directed by Louis Malle and Roger Vadim. [Note from Brazilian edition]
49. Films directed by Paul Morrissey. [Note from Brazilian edition]
50. The following actresses have not been located: Yuta Zacher and Milagres de la Mercedes. [Note from Brazilian edition]
51. In Italian in the original. '*It is all finished now ... money ... a lot of money ... sex ... politics ... violence ... drugs ... Casanova? ... Bah ... no one wants to know what Fellini is doing any more ... Money?* Amarcord *made a lot ...*' [C.M.]
52. The script was written by Pasolini, Marco Visconti and Alberto Moravia, based on parts of the Roman tales written by the latter including 'Il naso' (*Racconti romani*, 1954) and 'Addio alla borgata', 'Lo scimpanzè' and 'La raccomandazione' (*Nuovi racconti romani*, 1959). See Pier Paolo Pasolini ([1940] 2001). *Per il cinema*, v. II. Torino: Mondadori, p. 3200. See also Alberto Moravia (2004). *Opere. Romanzi e racconti 1950–1959*. Edited by Simone Casini. Milano: Bompiani. [Note from Brazilian edition]
53. A slight variation of the phrase 'Celui qui n'a pas vécu au dix-huitième siècle avant la Révolution ne connaît pas la douceur de vivre' ('Those who haven't lived in the eighteenth century before the Revolution do not know the sweetness of living'), attributed to French diplomat Charles Maurice de Talleyrand-Périgord (1754–1838). [C.M.]
54. Dutch film, not traced. [Note from Brazilian edition]
55. The Yé-Yé movement was a style of pop music that emerged in France in the late 1950s and early 1960s. In Brazil a similar phenomenon occurred under the banner Iê-Iê-Iê (a term equally derived from the English 'yeah-yeah-yeah'). Iê-Iê-Iê music was the quite unimaginative and sterile brand of rock and roll made in Brazil, more often than not a mere copy of British and American 1960s rock standards. [C.M.]
56. Glauber is referring to the samba 'Aos pés da cruz' ('At the Foot of the Cross'), written in 1942 by Marino Pinto and José Gonçalves, and immortalized by singer Orlando Silva. In the second stanza lyricist Marino Pinto quotes the

aphorism 'o coração tem razões que a própria razão desconhece' ('the heart has its reasons which reason does not know'), coined by Blaise Pascal (1623–1662) in his book Pensées (1669). In French: 'Le coeur a ses raisons, que la raison ne connaît point.' [C.M.]

57. Lemmy Caution is a character in Jean-Luc Godard's film *Alphaville*, inspired by British writer Peter Cheyney (1896–1951), in whose novels Lemmy Caution is an FBI agent and, in later stories, a private agent. [LN]

58. 'Estação Paissandu' (aka Cine Paissandu) was a famous film theatre in the Flamengo area of Rio de Janeiro. In the 1960s and 1970s it became a meeting point for cinephiles eager to see art-house films and discuss issues relating to cinema and the arts and politics in general. [C.M.]

59. Glauber is referring to the poem 'No meio do caminho' ('In the Middle of the Road') by Carlos Drummond de Andrade. It was first published in 1928 in *Revista de Antropofagia* and caused a great stir among the literary critics of the time, which considered it scandalous and anti-poetic for its simplicity, repetitions and informal use of grammar.

No meio do caminho

No meio do caminho tinha uma pedra
tinha uma pedra no meio do caminho
tinha uma pedra
no meio do caminho tinha uma pedra.

Nunca me esquecerei desse acontecimento
na vida de minhas retinas tão fatigadas.
Nunca me esquecerei que no meio do caminho
tinha uma pedra
tinha uma pedra no meio do caminho
no meio do caminho tinha uma pedra

In the Middle of the Road
In the middle of the road there was a stone
there was a stone in the middle of the road
there was a stone
in the middle of the road there was a stone

I shall never forget that event
in the life of my tired, tired retinas
I shall never forget that in the middle of the road
there was a stone
there was a stone in the middle of the road
in the middle of the road there was a stone.

(source: Mike Gonzalez and David Treece (eds) (1992). *The Gathering of Voices: The Twentieth-Century Poetry of Latin America*. New York and London: Verso, p. 106.) [C.M.]

60. Roger Leenhardt (1903–1985) was a French critic and essayist in the 1930s and 1940s. He was also the author and producer of short films and educational films. Leenhardt was one of the thinkers who most influenced André Bazin. He began writing for *L'Esprit 49*, a cinema-discussion club. His documentaries and works of fiction reflect his ideas on how to make an auteur cinema. [Note from Brazilian edition]
61. See note 14, in *O século do cinema*. [C.M.]
62. Noel de Medeiros Rosa (1910–1937) was one of Brazil's most important musicians in the twentieth century. A prolific composer and lyricist, his *sambas* are widely known for having established a link between the poor communities from where they originated and the middle classes, especially through their broadcasting on radio. He was also noted for his poetic use of everyday language, chronicling life in Rio de Janeiro through his songs. [C.M.]
63. Typical Brazilian dish of rice, black beans and pork meat. [Translator's note – C.S.].

Index

Page numbers in *italics* refer to figures.

007 style, 252, 253, 256

Achugar, Walter, 104, 239, 240
actor, 140
  directing actors, 61, 65–6, 114
  as image/piece of the internal editing, 158–9
  immortality of, 226
  Italian actress, 221, 232
aesthetics:
  aesthetic anthropophagy, 72
  aesthetic dictatorship, 58
  aesthetic ignorance, 107
  aesthetic realism, 6
  aesthetic technique, 143, 157
  aesthetics of the absurd, 46, 53
  'An Aesthetics of Dreams', 5–6, 121–5
  'An Aesthetics of Hunger'/'Estética da fome', xii, 5, 41–6, 74, 121, 124, 216
  aesthetics of miserabilism, 87
  aesthetics/politics relationship, 7, 8, 106–13
  aesthetics of violence, 5, 44, 121
  bourgeois aesthetic, 112
  Cinema Novo, 6, 44, 75, 82
  'Discussion of the Concept of Aesthetics and its Political Function', 106–13
  ideology and, 57
  'John Huston – Physical Technique and Aesthetic Technique', 142–4
  neo-expressionist aestheticism, 18
  periods of cinematographic aesthetics, 210
  'Revolution is an Aesthetics', 6, 46–8
  revolutionary cinematographic aesthetic, 174, 260
  social aesthetic, 152, 153
Alatriste, Gustavo, 161, 172
Alcón, Alfredo, 105
Aldrich, Robert, 142, 146
  Attack!, 148
Aleksandrov, Grigori: *The General Line/ Generalnaya Liniya*, 19
alienation, 9, 28, 81, 176, 177, 178, 196, 209–10, 211, 212
'Alliance for Progress', 215
Amado, Jorge, 22, 29, 107
'América Nuestra', 8, 104–106
American cinema, 10–11, 13, 17, 32, 76, 267
American director, 84
American narrative as recipe for success, 78–9
  Brazilian cinema and, 76–8
  cinematographic revolution and, 48–51
  colonization and, 49, 50
  gangster film, 20, 77
  hero in, 86, 88
  history of, 136
  imitation cinema and, 79, 80, 245
  language, 77, 79–80, 86, 142–3, 153, 245
  the public and, 76, 77, 78, 79, 88
  technique, 76, 77, 85, 98
  see also Hollywood; Western genre
Amico, Gianni, 105, 106, 181, 185, 218, 235, 249, 250
  Ah! Vem o Samba, 107
anarchism, 16, 104, 211, 255
Buñuel, Luis, 16, 162, 164, 167, 168, 170, 173, 176, 177, 255
Godard, Jean-Luc, 16, 166, 255

285

Andrade, Joaquim Pedro de, 29
   Garrincha: Hero of the Jungle/Garrincha, alegria do povo, 44
   Macunaíma, 74, 99
   The Priest and the Girl/O padre e a moça, 45, 93, 94
Andrade, Mário de, 86
Andrade, Oswald de, 100
Andrade, Rudá de, 106
Anger, Kenneth: *Scorpio Rising*, 246
anthropophagy, 75, 100
   aesthetic anthropophagy, 72
   Antonio das Mortes, 101
   freedom, 101
   'Tropicalism, Anthropology, Myth, Ideography', 100–104
Antonioni, Michelangelo, 9, 15, 32, 84, 104, 114, 162, 181, 185, 199, 211–12, 262
   The Adventure/L'avventura, 32
   'Antonioni', 209–10
   a bourgeois, 16, 39
   décor and space, 205
   dialectic of alienation, 9, 209–10
   The Eclipse/L'eclisse, 9, 172, 211, 212
   'Funeral Space', 211–14
   mise-en-scène, 9, 211, 213
   The Night/La notte, 32
Aprà, Adriano, 186, 205
Argentina, 6, 53–4, 55, 251
Aristarco, Guido, 104, 197–9, 204
Armendáriz, Pedro, 105
Arnheim, Rudolf, 163
Arpa, Father, 214, 215, 216, 217, 218, 228–9
   see also Instituto Columbianum
art, 99–100, 213
   'art and commitment', 259
   Brazilian Arts, 41
   cinema/film and, 30, 84, 109, 117, 137, 143, 199, 210, 226, 245, 260
   ideology and, 254
   irrationality of, 254–5
   politics and, 122
   revolution and, 6, 122
   revolutionary art, 122–3, 124–5
   Rocha: reframing art as an experimental laboratory of conflicts, 12
   as solitary activity, 119
art house cinema, 84–6, 117, 118, 242

artisan, 15, 16, 17, 31, 33, 36
artist, 211–14, 245, 254–6
   rational artist, 255–6
Asturias, Miguel Ángel, 72, 106
audience, *see* the public
auteur, 15
   amateurism, 16–17
   auteur director, 14
   'auteur method', 15, 19
   being a film auteur, 35–6, 38
   challenges, 14, 17–18, 32, 34, 36, 39, 79, 239
   creative independence, 32
   demagoguery of, 34, 36
   freedom, 14, 16, 40
   intellectual author, 31, 32, 49, 51, 241
   as a 'monster', 31, 39, 163
   revolutionary politics, 16
   truth and, 16, 26, 29
   see also auteur cinema; filmmaker/film director
auteur cinema, 7, 8, 14, 16, 52, 121, 239
   Brazil, 4–5, 38, 41
   'commercial cinema'/'auteur cinema' divide, 15, 117–18
   economic-political constraints, 4–5, 32
   independent production, 17
   Latin America, 6
   as political cinema, 18, 241
   see also auteur
Autran, Paulo, 64
avant-garde, 35, 54, 108–109, 215, 264
   Brazil, 82, 86
   France, 20, 21
   Rocha, Glauber, 58, 59
   Rough Gangue, 25
   Third World, 100

Bach, Johann Sebastian, 74, 115, 250, 265, 267
   The Chronicle of Anna Magdalena Bach/Chronik der Anna Magdalena Bach, 115, 250–1
Badalucco, Nicola, 208
Balázs, Bela, 163, 247
Barbaro, Umberto, 13, 163
Barcelloni, Gianni, 114, 116, 120, 181
Bardot, Brigitte, 31

Index

Barreto, Luiz Carlos, 85, 89, 105, 106, 107
Barthes, Roland, 205-206, 214, 243
Basehart, Richard, 221
Bastos, Othon, 63-4, 65
Bazin, André, 15, 18, 104, 131, 163, 210
Bellocchio, Marco, 181, 239, 249
  China is Near/La Cina è vicina, 249
  Fists in the Pocket/I pugni in tasca, 249
Bene, Carmelo, 181
Benedek, Laszlo, 141
  Bengal Brigade, 140
  Death of a Salesman, 140
  The Wild One, 138, 139, 140, 141, 142
Benjamin, Walter, 108, 111
Bentes, Ivana: *Cartas ao mundo*, x
Bergman, Ingmar, 15, 32, 35, 39, 54, 84, 174, 187, 192, 218, 232, 233, 244, 262
  expressionism, 40
  Jornal do Brasil, 31, 33
  Persona, 248
Bergman, Ingrid, 181-2, 185, 186, 222
Berkeley, Busby, 20
Bernadet, Jean-Claude, 99
Bertolucci, Bernardo, 8, 105, 114, 119-20, 185, 214, 230, 235, 239, 240, 243, 249, 261
  1900: 232
  Before the Revolution/Prima della rivoluzione, 114, 185, 205, 246
  The Conformist/Il conformist, 114
  décor, 205
  Partner, 114, 116
  The Spider's Stratagem/La strategia del ragno, 114
Bertolucci, Giovanni, 233
Best, Bettina, 232
Biáfora, Ruben
  Ravine/Ravina, 24
Bini, Alfredo, 236
Black God, White Devil (*Deus e o diabo na terra do sol*), 2, 43, 44, 56, 59, 60, 61-2, 75, 119, 217, 235
  'aesthetics of hunger', 216
  characters, 66, 101
  cordel/popular literature and, 61-2, 91
  directing actors, 65
  Entranced Earth and, 67, 68, 71

music, 64-5, 68
  see also Rocha's filmography
Bogart, Humphrey, 53, 86, 264
Boito, Camilio, 194
Bolívar, Simon, 107
Böll, Heinrich, 249-50
Bolognini, Mauro, 235
Borges, Jorge Luis, 8, 53, 107, 114, 122, 125, 226
Borges, Miguel, 43, 217
Borzage, Frank, 20
bourgeoisie, 16, 39, 58, 67, 78, 101, 106-107, 109
  bourgeois aesthetic, 112
  bourgeois morality, 161
  ideology and, 18, 123-4
  'the people' as the myth of the bourgeoisie, 123
box-office, 31, 78
  box-office failure, 114, 185
  box-office success, 32, 79, 233, 236, 238
Brando, Marlon, 109, 116, 127, 138, 140, 142
Brasil, Edgar, 22
Brazil:
  1964 coup, 44
  'Brazilian civilization', 80
  capitalism, 16
  Carnival, 71, 82
  dictatorship, 108, 121
  film culture, 6, 13, 23, 76
  politics, 55, 56, 66, 71, 73, 75, 83, 123
  Portuguese language, 54-5, 60, 107
  underdevelopment, 100-101
Brazilian cinema, 3, 16-17, 55, 101, 102
  American cinema and, 76-8
  auteur cinema, 4-5, 38, 41
  Brazilian filmmaker, 36, 88-9
  challenges, 36
  commercial cinema and, 14, 18
  critical realism, 23, 96
  digestive cinema, 43, 44
  economic-related issues, 4, 83
  film industry, 17, 18, 79
  history of, 4, 7, 23, 43-4
  independent production, 17
  politics and, 37-8
  see also chanchada film; Cinema Novo

287

On Cinema

Brecht, Bertolt, 1, 7, 34, 63, 65, 96, 108, 111, 112, 174, 186, 194, 195, 253–4
  The Good Person of Szechwan, 65
  The Threepenny Opera, 34, 65
Bressane, Júlio: *Face to Face/Cara a cara*, 74, 99
Breton, André, 103, 166
Brooks, Richard, 32, 141
  Blackboard Jungle, 138, 139, 141
Buñuel, Luis, 8, 9, 10, 11, 26, 38, 39, 52, 58, 72, 84, 105, 111, 120, 159, 160, 212, 241, 244, 262
  'The 12 Commandments of Our Lord Buñuel', 159–72
  anarchism, 16, 162, 164, 167, 168, 170, 173, 176, 177, 255
  Cannes Film Festival, 159, 160, 161
  cast, 63
  Catholicism/the Church, 159, 162, 165, 168, 169–70, 172, 213
  characters, 164–5, 176–7
  commercial cinema, 160–1
  editing, 163–5, 173
  France, 161, 166
  Mexico, 160, 161, 172
  mise-en-scène, 163, 165, 166
  'The Morality of a New Christ', 172–8
  political cinema, 120, 168, 173, 177
  surrealism, 159, 162, 165, 173, 176, 177, 226, 255, 262
  technique, 163
  Tropicalism and anthropophagy, 104
  violence, 164
  see also Buñuel's filmography
Buñuel's filmography:
  L'Âge d'or, 159, 161, 164, 166, 170, 177
  Belle de jour, 116
  Un Chien andalou, 159, 165, 166, 168, 244
  The Criminal Life of Archibaldo de la Cruz/Ensayo de un crimen, 160, 164, 165
  Death in the Garden/La Mort en ce jardin, 161
  Diary of a Chambermaid/Le Journal d'une femme de chambre, 173
  The Exterminating Angel/El Ángel Exterminador, 159, 161, 162, 165–8 *passim*, 171, 172
  Fever Rises in El Pao/Republic of Sin/La Fièvre monte à El Pao, 120, 161, 168, 169
  Land Without Bread/Las Hurdes, 160, 167, 176, 177
  Nazarin/Nazarín, 120, 161, 162, 164–5, 166–70, 177
  Robinson Crusoe, 160, 165
  Simon of the Desert/Simon del desierto, 172, 173, 216
  That Is the Dawn/Cela s'appelle l'aurore, 161
  This Strange Passion/Él, 160, 164, 165, 168, 177
  Viridiana, 159, 160, 161, 162–70 *passim*, 172, 176, 177
  The Young and the Damned/Los olvidados, 120, 160, 161, 164, 167, 177
  The Young One, 161, 164, 165, 169
  Wuthering Heights/Cumbres Borrascosas/Abismos de pasión, 160

Cahiers du Cinéma, 3, 13, 32, 33, 57, 96, 113, 212, 229
Cain, James M., 194
camera, 14, 25, 77, 110, 252
  camera movement, 88, 134, 148, 183, 228
  creation and, 129, 130
  handheld camera, 3, 57, 71, 204–205, 242, 244, 246
  as instrument of investigation and reflection, 181
  integration between camera, actors and set design, 95
  lie and, 26
  Mitchell camera, 250
  set design/décor and, 205
  slow camera, 21
  see also technique
Camões, Luís Vaz de, 108
Camus, Albert, 180, 197, 229
Camus, Marcel, 31
cangaceiro, 57, 61, 66, 72, 101
  The Bandit/O cangaceiro, 61, 76–7, 83, 89
cangaço, 17, 55, 76, 97
Cannes Film Festival, 2, 114, 159, 160, 161, 187, 237

Index

capitalism, 50, 122, 126, 128, 175, 176, 195, 213, 245
  Brazil, 16
  capitalist culture, 16
  cinematographic capitalism, 24
  commercial cinema and, 18
  distribution and, 49
Capovilla, Maurice: *Propaganda Girl/Bebel, a garota propaganda*, 99
Capra, Frank, 20, 21
Carné, Marcel, 20
Carpentier, Alejo, 72, 106, 107, 214
Carrilho, Arnaldo, 107, 217, 218, 235
cast, 63–4, 105, 225
Castro, Fidel, 106
Castro Alves, Antônio Frederico de, 72
Catholicism/the Church, 125, 214, 220
  Buñuel, Luis, 159, 162, 165, 168, 169–70, 172, 213
  Catholic morality, 179, 223
  Christian/Catholic mythology, 10, 168
  Fellini, Federico, 223–5, 228–9, 231
Cavalcanti, Alberto, 13, 20, 21, 24
censorship, 30, 38, 45, 52, 75, 98, 117, 118, 129, 215, 223, 224, 228, 229, 257
  moral censorship, 231
  self-censorship, 121, 231
  theatre, 59
Cervantes, Miguel de, 63, 103
Cervoni, Albert, 96
CFAC (Centre for Film Aesthetics and Cultures), xiii
Chabrol, Claude, 31, 113
chanchada film, 14, 17, 81
Chaplin, Charles, 10–11, 22, 39, 111, 118, 121, 126–9, 162, 174, 258
  The Adventurer, 126
  capitalism, 126, 128
  City Lights, 126
  A Countess from Hong Kong, 126
  The Gold Rush, 126
  The Great Dictator, 126, 127, 131
  Hollywood, 126, 128
  The Immigrant, 126
  A King in New York, 126, 127
  Limelight, 126, 127
  Modern Times, 126, 128–9
  Monsieur Verdoux, 126, 127

character, 18, 66
Andara/*Nazarin*, 166, 169
Antônio das Mortes/*Antonio das Mortes*, 62, 64, 66, 67, 68, 73, 92, 101
Black God, White Devil, 66, 101
Buñuel, Luis, 164–5, 176–7
Ciro/*Rocco and His Brothers*, 196–7, 198–9, 202
Colonel Dax/*Paths of Glory*, 148–9
Corisco/*Black God, White Devil*, 62, 63, 65, 66, 68, 71
Dadá/*Entranced Earth*, 64
Díaz/*Entranced Earth*, 65–6, 74
Dr Von Braun/*Alphaville*, 253, 256, 257
Entranced Earth, 66, 73–4
Fabiano/*Barren Lives*, 40, 44, 89–90, 92
Father Nazarin/*Nazarin*, 164–5, 166–70, 176
Fellini, Federico, 219, 222–4, 225, 227
female characters, 45, 63
Galdino/*The Bandit*, 76–7, 89
Gaúcho/*Barren Lives*, 91
Godard, Jean-Luc, 263
Guido/*8½*, 225, 227
Lemmy Caution/*Alphaville*, 253, 256–7
Luca/*Rocco and His Brothers*, 196–7, 202
Manuel/*Black God, White Devil*, 45, 64, 68, 91–2
Marcello/*La dolce vita*, 222–4
Maria/*The Big City*, 92
Paulo Martins/*Entranced Earth*, 66, 67, 68, 69, 70, 73–4
Rocco/*Rocco and His Brothers*, 193–4, 196, 197, 198, 202–203
Rosa/*Black God, White Devil*, 45, 65
Sara/*Entranced Earth*, 63, 69, 73–4
The Searchers, 153
Sebastião/*Black God, White Devil*, 62, 64, 71
Shane/*Shane*, 154
Sinhá Vitória/*Barren Lives*, 40, 45, 90
Teodoro/*The Bandit*, 76–7
Vieira/*Entranced Earth*, 59, 64, 66, 70, 71, 72, 73
Viridiana/*Viridiana*, 164, 165, 169–70
Visconti, Luchino, 208
Welles, Orson, 130, 131, 132, 226
Zulmira/*The Deceased*, 94–5

On Cinema

Chayefsky, Sidney 'Paddy', 31
Che Guevara (Ernesto Guevara), 52, 53, 54, 58, 67, 69, 87, 108, 217
　Tricontinental, 68
Chukhraj, Grigori:
　Ballad of a Soldier/Ballada o soldate, 175
　Clear Skies/Chistoe nebo, 175
　The Forty-first/Sorok pervyy, 175
Churubuzco Studios, 53, 216
CIA, 215–16
Ciment, Michel: *Positif* interview, 6, 7, 58–75
cinema, 174–5
　academic cinema, 266
　art and, 30, 84, 109, 117, 137, 143, 199, 210, 226, 245, 260
　'The Cinema Process', 4, 30–7
　communication and, 51, 56, 245
　crisis of contemporary cinema, 187
　economic aspects of, 4–5, 30–1, 32, 38, 74, 75, 83, 105, 239, 241
　future of, 120–1
　history of, 15, 38, 139, 163, 178, 262, 265
　influence of, 75–6
　as language, 35, 131, 137, 205, 206–207, 209, 244
　literature and, 136
　a method and a form of expression, 48, 51, 57
　modern cinema, 241–3, 245–6, 260, 263
　as ontology, 16
　politics and, 30
　propaganda cinema, 245
　revisionist cinema, 102
　studio-based cinema, 83
　theatrical and literary origins, 162
　theme and form, 137
　traditional cinema, 243, 244
　underground cinema, 246
　understanding a film, 88, 263
　as vehicle of ideas, 35–6, 37
　see also film
Cinema Novo, 1, 14, 17, 55, 74, 82–3, 213, 243, 249, 251–2
　V Festival of Latin American Cinema, Genoa, 41
　1930s and, 21

　1960s 17, 43, 74–5, 99
　aesthetics, 6, 44, 75, 82
　anti-industrial film principle, 24
　as challenge to mechanical cinema, 29
　'Cinema Novo and the Adventure of Creation', 7, 75–100
　communication, 81–2
　creation and, 81–2
　crisis, 60, 75
　definition, 45–6
　female characters in, 45
　fictional film, 242
　freedom, 46, 74, 75, 82, 121–2
　hunger and, 43–4, 46
　imitation cinema and original cinema, 79–80
　an international cultural phenomenon, 109
　international festivals, 44
　miserabilism, 43
　music, 64
　non-acceptance within Brazil, 98, 119
　origins, 17, 19, 37–8, 163
　polemic and controversy, 56
　politics and, 6, 38, 46, 60, 75, 99
　Rocha, Glauber, 2, 4, 5, 6, 11–12
　socio-political content of, 5, 82
　themes and traditions, 55
　truth and, 25, 43, 45
　see also Brazilian cinema; language; the public
Cinema Nuovo, 13
cinema of poetry, 62, 204, 205, 206, 240, 265
cinéma-vérité, 26, 96, 163, 185, 246, 264
cinemascope, 143–4
Cinemateca Brasileira, São Paulo, xiii
Clair, René, 20, 32
　À nous la liberté, 129
Claude Antoine, 2, 104
Clementi, Margareth, 232
Clementi, Pierre, 8, 114, 116, 118–19, 120, 232
Cobb, Humphrey, 149
Cocteau, Jean, 219, 226
　Beauty and the Beast/La Belle et la bête, 110
　Orpheus/Orphée, 110

290

Index

colonialism, 75, 101, 121, 123
American cinema and colonization, 49, 50
colonial culture, 46-7, 81, 101
cultural colonization, 96
Latin America, 42
colour, 15, 57, 59, 88, 238, 261
see also technique
Columbia Pictures, 83, 84
comedy, 133, 158
commercial cinema, 17, 113, 117, 118
Brazilian cinema and, 14, 18
Buñuel, Luis, 160-1
capitalism and, 18
'commercial cinema'/'auteur cinema' divide, 15, 117-18
director/filmmaker and, 15
discursive editing, 28
false notion of culture, 18
themes, 18
Truffaut, François, 113
truth, 18
communication, 81, 98, 261
cinema and, 51, 56, 245
cinema as method and form of expression, 48, 51, 57
Cinema Novo, 81-2
mass communication, 252
communism, 15, 16, 73, 128, 175, 192, 194, 197, 223
communist morality, 179
French Communist Party, 257
Italian Communist Party, 179, 217, 224-5, 235
Latin America, 66, 67
Corneille, Pierre, 115, 263
Cortázar, Julio, 53, 107
CosacNaify, x, xii, xiii
counter-cinema, 7, 52, 187, 188, 190
Coutard, Raoul, 15, 22
crime genre, 77, 136, 145, 263
O Cruzeiro, 252
Cuba, 2, 6, 37, 54, 108, 109
culture, 52
Brazilian film culture, 6, 13, 23, 76
capitalist culture, 16
cinematographic culture, 76, 79
colonial culture, 46-7, 81, 101

cultural colonization, 96
cultural poverty, 256
cultural revolution, 85, 86, 100
cultural underdevelopment, 98
revolutionary culture, 46, 47-8, 213
Cunha, Euclides da, 86, 97
Czechoslovakia, 175, 217, 245, 247, 266

Da Vinci, Leonardo, 110, 181, 206, 230, 260, 261
Dahl, Gustavo, 43, 98, 106, 210, 214, 217
The Brave Warrior/O bravo guerreiro, 56, 74, 99
Dalí, Salvador, 103, 159, 165-6, 226, 228
Dancigers, Oscar, 160, 172
Das Gupta, Sonali, 186
Dassin, Jules, 188, 190
Rififi/Du rififi chez les hommes, 147
Daves, Delmer: *3:10 to Yuma*, 156
De Gaulle, Charles, 55, 257, 259
De Sica, Vittorio, 181, 190, 217, 218, 219, 261
Bicycle Thieves/Ladri di Biciclette, 191
Umberto D, 191
Dean, James, 11, 132-3, 138, 142, 158
Deheinzelin, Jacques, 19
D'El Rey, Geraldo, 64, 105
Delon, Alain, 202, 203, 222
Democratic Republic of the Congo, 2
Demy, Jacques: *The Umbrellas of Cherbourg/Les Parapluies de Cherbourg*, 113
developed world, 5, 46, 56, 98, 100, 174
see also underdevelopment/undeveloped country
Di Cavalcanti, 22
Díaz, Jesús, 54
Dickens, Charles, 133, 200
dictatorship, 108, 111, 121, 244, 253
aesthetic dictatorship, 58
artistic dictatorship, 76
Diegues, Carlos, 93, 106
The Big City/A grande cidade, 56, 92
Ganga Zumba, 43, 45, 56, 93
The Heirs/Os herdeiros, 74, 99
Dietrich, Marlene, 20
DIFILM, 85-6
documentary, 97, 160, 180, 242
Amico, Gianni, 107

291

British documentary, 20, 21
didactic documentary, 35
Dutch documentary, 20
Mauro, Humberto, 23, 28–9
Rocha, Glauber, 2, 59
social documentary, 163
Dostoyevsky, Fyodor, 114, 193, 194, 197, 200, 248, 261
Douglas, Kirk, 149, 158
Dovzhenko, Alexander: *Earth/Zemlya*, 20
dramaturgy, 1, 200, 247, 266
Visconti, Luchino, 9, 187–92, 193, 194
Dreiser, Theodore, 195
An American Tragedy, 195, 260
Dreyer, Carl, 15
The Passion of Joan of Arc/La Passion de Jeanne d'Arc, 95, 137, 158, 159
Drummond de Andrade, Carlos, 22, 94, 107, 127, 129, 259
Duvivier, Julien, 20
Dziga Vertov Group, *xii*, xiv

editing, 15, 40, 129, 189, 211
actor as image/piece of the internal editing, 158–9
aesthetic technique, 143, 157
Buñuel, Luis, 163–5, 173
Citizen Kane, 132
creation and, 129, 130
discursive editing, 28
Godard, Jean-Luc, 28, 205
internal editing, 146, 187
Kubrick, Stanley, 145, 146, 147, 150
Mauro, Humberto, 25, 27–8
narrative editing, 28, 35, 110, 131, 193
poetical editing, 243
Resnais, Alain, 28
rhythm, 25, 65, 137, 145
Rocha, Glauber, 61, 65, 72
Visconti, Luchino, 187
Eisenstein, Sergei M., 8, 15, 22, 38, 105, 162, 163, 175, 194, 195, 204, 230, 241, 254, 262
Alexander Nevsky/Aleksandr Nevskiy, 61, 130
Battleship Potemkin/Bronenosets Potyomkin, 15, 19, 26, 108, 118, 121, 137, 195, 260

Film Form, 157, 158, 199
The General Line/Generalnaya Liniya, 19, 26–7, 195
graphics, ideograms, 6, 9
Ivan, The Terrible I, 130, 178, 195, 260, 265
Ivan, The Terrible II, 11, 61, 130
montage, 26, 27, 60–1, 157, 187, 205, 206, 207, 243
October/Oktyabre, 19, 26, 27, 195
Que Viva Mexico!, 52, 53, 61, 110, 195
revolutionary cinematographic aesthetic, 174, 260
Rocha's admired filmmaker, 9–10, 61, 108, 130
Stalinism and, 39, 195, 260
Strike/Stachka, 19, 195
Ekberg, Anita, 218, 222, 223, 224, 227, 232
England, 20, 21, 180, 246
GPO/General Post Office Film Unit, 20
Entranced Earth (Terra em transe), 2, 7, 56, 59, 63, 64, 70–1, 75, 104, 217
'An Aesthetics of Hunger', 121
Black God, White Devil and, 67, 68, 71
characters, 66, 73–4
a dialectic film, 111
final shot, 71
Maldoror, 69
monologue, 69
music, 68, 71, 72, 74
sound/image relationship, 10, 71
theme, 67
violence, 73
see also Rocha's filmography
epic, 108, 135–6
the epic and the didactic, 47, 48
epic/didactic cinema, 6, 7, 51, 52, 58
Epstein, Jean, 158
Escorel, Eduardo, 106
Europe, 5, 62–3, 96, 178
expressionism, 110, 162, 205, 208
Bergman, Ingmar, 40
German expressionism, 19, 27, 132, 178, 260
Latino expressionism, 201
neo-expressionist aestheticism, 18
Visconti, Luchino, 261
Welles, Orson, 110, 260

Index

Falconetti, Maria, 158, 159
Fanon, Frantz, 5, 214
Farias, Marcos, 43
Farias, Roberto, 79
   Assault on the Pay Train/Assalto ao trem pagador, 77-8
   Every Maiden Has a Father Who Is Angry/Toda donzela tem um pai que é uma fera, 78
   Roberto Carlos in the Rhythm of Adventure/Roberto Carlos em ritmo de aventura, 78-9
   Tragic Jungle/Selva trágica, 78, 79
Fascism, 55, 100, 109, 117, 131, 162, 171, 172, 179, 208, 212, 213, 218, 231, 251
   neo-fascism, 111
Faulkner, William, 10, 60, 72, 199, 200
   The Wild Palms, 72
Faustino, Mário, 69-70
favela, 17, 81
   Five Times Favela/Cinco vezes favela, 43
   Shantytown of My Loves/Favela dos meus amores, 23
Fellini, Federico, 32, 35, 61, 84, 104, 162, 174, 181, 202, 214, 216, 218-19, 228, 231, 261, 262
   8½ /Otto e mezzo, 216, 218, 219, 225-6, 227, 233, 237
   Amarcord, 230, 231, 233
   Catholicism, 223-5, 228-9, 231
   characters, 219, 222-4, 225, 227
   The Clowns/I Clowns, 229
   La dolce vita, 217, 221, 222-4, 225-6, 227, 233
   Fellini's Casanova/Il Casanova di Federico Fellini, 220, 231-3
   'Glauber Fellini', 214-34
   Juliet of the Spirits/Giulietta degli spiriti, 215, 218, 228, 229
   magician/magic, 218, 219, 222, 227, 230, 233
   mise-en-scène, 219
   neorealism, 226
   Nights of Cabiria/Le notti di Cabiria, 221
   Roma/Fellini's Roma, 227, 229, 231
   Satyricon, 223, 227, 229
   La strada, 221
   surrealism, 224, 226
   The Swindlers/Il bidone, 221
   I vitelloni, 218, 221, 231
   The White Sheik/Lo sceicco bianco, 220, 221
Feyder, Jacques, 20
fictional film, 195, 242
fictional-reportage cinema, 163
Figueroa, Gabriel, 22, 163
Filho, Jardel, 64
film:
   film as conscience, 210
   understanding a film, 88, 263
   'What is a film?', 35
   see also cinema
film archive, 13, 21, 60
film club, 13, 55, 58, 60
film critic, 13-14, 31-2, 33, 88, 96, 104, 241-2
   cinematographic revolution and, 49
   didactic criticism, 136
film distribution, 48, 49, 74, 83-4, 85, 96, 100, 117, 239
   auteur cinema, 241
   future of, 121
film exhibitor, 49, 83, 84, 89
film industry, 79, 116-19, 241, 244-5
   Brazil, 17, 18, 79
   marketing, 4
   regulating powers, 4
film production, 83, 105
   filmmaker and, 33, 48, 102, 241
   independent production, 50
   industry-produced cinema, 251
   producer-creator instead of *capitalist producer*, 49
filming technique, *see* technique
filmmaker/film director, 14, 15, 50-1, 84, 189
   American director, 84
   auteur director, 14
   Brazilian filmmaker, 36, 88-9
   commercial cinema, 15
   directing actors, 61, 65-6, 114
   film production and 33, 48, 102, 241
   independent filmmaker, 48-50, 120
   as man of action, 51
   as poet, 37
   story as one of the elements of direction, 88

tricontinental filmmaker, 2, 4, 57–8
  see also auteur
Filmology, 137, 143
Films and Filming, 13
Flaherty, Robert, 15, 20, 21, 26, 38, 53, 174, 180, 181
Flaubert, Gustave, 39, 62, 243
Fonda, Henry, 87
Ford, John, 11, 20, 21, 72, 87, 142, 218, 234
  Fort Apache, 154
  'The Searchers', 152–4
  Stagecoach, 77, 154, 155
  Western genre, 27, 57, 138, 152, 153, 154, 155
  Young Mr Lincoln, 87
formalism, 9, 129–30, 133, 218, 259, 261
  'anti-formalism' of Italian cinema, 141
  French formalism, 116
Forman, Milos, 243, 247, 266
framing, 143, 144, 155, 181, 187, 188, 189, 234
  frontal framing, 205
France, xiv, 2, 121, 204
  Communist Party, 257
  formalism, 116
  French cinema, 20, 34, 104, 206–207
  surrealism, 103, 224
  see also nouvelle vague
Francis, Paulo, 106–107
Franco, Francisco, General, 159, 162, 168, 172
Franju, Georges, 31
Freitas, Jânio de, 107
Freud, Sigmund, 27–8, 132, 226, 230
Fuller, Samuel, 32

Gabus Mendes, Octávio, 25
gangster film, 9, 17, 20, 77, 264
García Márquez, Gabriel, 107
Gatti, Armand, 16
Gauthier, Guy, 176
GEICINE (Executive Group of the Film Industry), 19
Germany, 179, 195, 248–9
  German expressionism, 19, 27, 132, 178, 260
  see also Nazism

Ginsberg, Allen: *Guns of the Trees*, 162
Godard, Jean-Luc, 8, 9, 15, 31, 55, 102, 104, 105, 110, 119, 162, 174, 185, 187, 199, 204, 240
  Alphaville, 252–7
  anarchism, 16, 166, 255
  Breathless/À bout de souffle, 15, 16, 111, 242, 257, 258, 265, 266
  British Sounds, 111
  budget for films, 241
  characters, 263
  La Chinoise, 111, 249
  as dialectical filmmaker, 110, 111
  (dis)montage, 41
  'Do You Like Jean-Luc Godard? ...', 257–64
  editing, 28, 205
  'everything in everything', 243, 259, 262, 266
  'Godard syndrome', 57
  'Godardean', 265–7
  Godarditis, 266
  instructions on how to watch a Godard film, 262–4
  The Little Soldier/Le Petit soldat, 257
  Made in USA, 111, 267
  My Life to Live, 111, 222
  Pierrot le fou, 9, 258, 264, 266, 267
  political cinema, 58, 102
  a rational artist, 255–6
  Rocha's admired filmmaker, 9, 108
  Rossellini's influence on, 242
  space, 205
  technology and, 253
  as tricontinental filmmaker, 57–8
  Two or Three Things I Know about Her, 111, 267
  Wind from the East, xii, xiv
  A Woman Is a Woman/Une Femme est une femme, 265
Gomes, Carlos, 74
Gonzaga, Adhemar, 23, 24
Goulart, João, 44, 55
Gouthier, Hugo, 214
Gramsci, Antonio, 179
Grierson, John, 20
Griffith, David Wark, 21, 22, 105, 126, 127, 162, 174, 179, 234, 241, 262

Index

Guerra, Ruy, 64, 91, 229
  The Guns/Os fuzis, 56, 57, 75, 90–1, 119
  The Scoundrels/Os cafajestes, 56, 99
  guerrilla, 55, 69, 246
  guerrilla cinema, 7, 52, 57–8, 248
Guevara, Alfredo, 104
Guillén, Nicolás, 72, 214
Guimarães Rosa, João, 8, 93, 94, 107, 214, 216
Gullar, Ferreira, 99–100

Has, Wojciech, 175
Hathaway, Henry, 20
Hawks, Howard, 57, 72
hero, 26, 64, 66, 67, 86, 94, 97, 167, 168, 175, 176–7, 250
  American cinema, 86, 88
  anti-hero, 90
  Brazilian hero, 89
  filming technique and, 92
  from rural heroes to urban heroes, 92
  hero couple, 86–7
  heroine, 88, 95
  'Western – Introduction to the Genre and to the Hero', 150–1
  Western genre, 150–1, 152, 153, 154, 159
Hirszman, Leon, 43, 60–1, 106, 217
  The Deceased/A falecida, 56, 57, 93, 94–6
  The Deceased: Absolute Majority/Maioria absoluta, 96, 250
  Girl from Ipanema/Garota de Ipanema, 64, 74
  São Diogo Quarry/Pedreira de São Diogo, 61
Hitchcock, Alfred, 32, 35, 119
Hobsbawm, Eric, 12
Hollywood, 11, 18, 20, 76, 119, 120, 126, 128, 136, 246
  Brazilian market and, 4
  challenges, 34
  ideology of, 78
  language, 132, 140, 142
  pornography, 116
  see also American cinema
Hossein, Robert, 31
Huillet, Danièle, 115, 250

Humildes, Sônia dos, 64
Hungary, 247
Huston, John, 39, 142–4, 146
  The Asphalt Jungle, 148
  Heaven Knows, Mr Allison, 143, 144
  The Treasure of Sierra Madre, 148

ideographic cinema, 8, 103, 104
ideology, 237, 254
  aesthetics and, 57
  art and, 254
  bourgeoisie and, 18, 123–4
  Hollywood, 78
image, 210, 263
  sound/image relationship, 10, 71
  as word, 35
imitation, 57, 77, 78, 81, 98, 116
imitation cinema, 79, 80, 85, 245
imperialism, 51, 58, 87, 102, 130, 131–2, 236, 241, 242, 246
INCE (National Institute for Educational Cinema), 23
independent cinema, 50, 120–1, 241
independent film, 51, 60
independent filmmaker, 48–50, 120
independent production, 50
  Pereira dos Santos, Nelson, 60
industrial cinema, 21, 245, 251
lies and exploitation, 46
inferiority complex, 4, 77, 107, 109, 262
Instituto Columbianum (Genoa), 5, 41, 214
  Terzo Mondo e Comunità Mondiale/Third World and World Community Congress, 214–15, 216
  see also Arpa, Father
intellect/intellectual, 18, 22, 62
  film/cinema and, 35, 40, 109, 110
  Godard, Jean-Luc, 267
  intellectual author, 31, 32, 49, 51, 241
  intellectual poverty, 14
  Paulo Martins, 66, 67
Italy/Italian cinema, 2, 119–20, 179, 204, 205, 206–207, 217, 239, 240–1, 249
  'anti-formalism' of Italian cinema, 141
  Communist Party, 179, 217, 224–5, 235
  Fascist cinema, 219

295

On Cinema

Italian actress, 221, 232
Italian neorealism, 1, 9, 41, 137, 140-1, 181, 219, 221, 261, 262
opera, 10, 219
Itamaraty (Brazil's Ministry of External Relations), 95
Ivanov, Viatcheslav, 206
Ivens, Joris, 20

Jabor, Arnaldo, 229
   Public Opinion/Opinião pública, 96, 97
   Racial Integration/Integração racial, 96
James Bond, 118, 121
Jancsó, Miklós, 8, 114-15, 117, 118, 247, 248
   The Confrontation aka *Sparkling Winds/Fényes Szelek*, 114
   The Red and the White/Csillagosok, Katonák, 114
   The Round-Up/Szegénylegények, 114, 247
   Silence and Cry/Csend és Kiáltás, 114
   Winter Wind/Téli Sirokkó, 114
John XXIII, Pope, 235, 237
Johnson, Nunnally: *The Man in the Gray Flannel Suit*, 141
Jornal do Brasil, 24-5, 31, 33
Joyce, James, 63, 111, 112, 133, 174, 200, 205, 259, 265
   Ulysses, 39, 195, 199
Jung, Carl, 226

Kafka, Franz, 6, 131, 175, 212, 234
Karlovy Vary International Film Festival, Czechoslovakia, 217, 236
Kawalerowicz, Jerzy, 175, 247
Kazan, Elia, 31, 106, 140
   A Streetcar Named Desire, 140
Keaton, Buster, 118
Kluge, Alexander, 243, 248
   Anita G/Abschied von gestern, 249
Kósa, Ferenc, 248
   Ten Thousand Suns/Tizezer nap, 247
Kramer, Stanley, 139
Kubrick, Stanley, 142, 144-50, 174
   editing, 145, 146, 147, 150
   Killer's Kiss, 144
   The Killing, 144, 145-8
   Paths of Glory, 148-50, 183-4
   Spartacus, 32

Lacerda, Carlos, 43
Lang, Fritz, 20, 110, *112*, 174, 179, 208, 249
   Die Nibelungen: Siegfried/Die Nibelungen: Siegfrieds Tod, 110
   M, 110
   Metropolis, 179
Langlois, Henri, 110, 118
language, 17, 82-3, 118, 213
   American cinema, 77, 79-80, 86, 142-3, 153, 245
   artistic language, 86
   awareness/consciousness and, 80, 99, 103
   cinema as, 35, 131, 137, 205, 206-207, 209, 244
   Hollywood, 132, 140, 142
   language of domination, 83
   Portuguese language, 54-5, 60, 107
   the public and, 77, 79-80
   revolution in cinematic language, 144-5
Latin America, 7, 8, 41-2
   auteur cinema, 6
   colonialism and, 42
   communism, 66, 67
   concrete surrealism, 71-2
   hunger, 43
   indigenous and black roots of, 124
   Latin America/Europe alterity, 5
   surrealism, 103-104
   see also Third World
Lautréamont, Comte de, 103
   The Songs of Maldoror, 69
Lean, David, 133-6
   Brief Encounter, 133
   Great Expectations, 133
   Hobson's Choice, 133-4
   music, 134
   Oliver Twist, 133
   The Sound Barrier, 133, 134-6
   Summertime, 133, 134
Leenhardt, Roger, 264
Lelouch, Claude, 206-207, 248
   A Man and a Woman/Un Homme et une femme, 246
Lewgoy, José, 64
lighting, 29, 64, 143, 146-7, 163, 234, 242
   natural light, 95
   see also technique

Index

Lima, Cavalheiro, 19
Lima, Jorge de, 22, 29
Lima, Waldemar, 65
Lima Jr, Walter, 24, 65, 106
Brazil Year 2000/Brasil ano 2000,
  74, 75, 99
Plantation Boy/Menino de engenho,
  56, 93
Lima Barreto, Afonso Henriques de, 28
The Bandit/O cangaceiro, 61, 76-7, 83, 89
The First Mass/A primeira missa, 24, 25
Lins do Rego, José, 22, 29, 93, 107
literary cinema, 35
literature, 29, 37, 62
  baroque tradition, 63
  cantadores, 61-2
  cinema and, 136
  concretist poetry movement, 37
  cordel literature, 61-2
  European tradition, 62-3
  popular literature, 61-2, 63, 91
Loren, Sophia, 127, 221
Losey, Joseph, 112, 174, 254
Lubitsch, Ernst, 20, 249, 250
Lukács, Georg, 6, 96, 177, 204
Lumière Brothers, 15, 82, 105, 178, 210, 262
lyricism, 22, 26, 27, 36, 52, 133, 134, 136,
  137, 202, 246, 248

Maciel, Luiz Carlos, 252
Magnani, Anna, 186, 236, 240-1
Makavejev, Dusan, 248
  Love Affair, 248
  Man Is Not a Bird/Covek nije tica, 248
Mallarmé, Stéphane, 60, 111, 243
Malle, Louis, 26, 31
  The Fire Within/Le Feu follet, 113
  Viva Maria!, 113
Mamoulian, Rouben, 20
Mann, Daniel: *Come Back, Little Sheba*, 140
Mann, Anthony: *Men in War*, 148
Marcorelles, Louis, 106
Marker, Chris, 163, 176
  The Jetty/La Jetée, 113
Martelli, Otello, 22
Martín Fierro, 72
Martin, Marcel, 173
Martinez Corrêa, José Celso, 100, 120

Marx, Karl, 27-8, 56, 186, 187, 195, 237, 262
Marxism, 11, 111, 195
Visconti, Luchino, 197, 204, 212, 240,
  254, 261
Masina, Giulietta, 221-2, 228
Mastroianni, Marcello, 217, 222, 226, 227,
  229, 233
Mauro, Humberto, 4, 19-29, 37, 39
  Cataguazes, 4, 21, 23, 24
  Cinema Novo, 20-1, 29
  *The Discovery of Brazil/O descobrimento
    do Brasil*, 22, 23
  documentary, 23, 28-9
  editing, 25, 27-8
  filmography, 23
  lyricism, 22
  *Mills and Power Plants/Engenhos e
    usinas*, 28-9
  mise-en-scène, 25, 27
  Rough Gangue/Ganga bruta, 21-2, 23,
    24, 25, 27-8
  *Shantytown of My Loves/Favela dos meus
    amores*, 23
  silent film, 4
  sound cinema, 23
  Valadião, The Rogue/Valadião, o cratera,
    21, 23
Medeiros, José, 95
Medeiros, Marcos, 2
Mekas, Jonas:
  Film Culture, 246
  Guns of the Trees, 162, 246
Méliès, George, 15, 105, 178
Melo Neto, João Cabral de, 22, 29, 107
melodrama, 10, 18, 27, 45, 95, 190, 194,
  207, 209, 254
Mendes, Murilo, 214
Merquior, José Guilherme, 22
Metro-Goldwyn-Mayer, 88, 109
Metz, Christian, 205, 243
Mexico, 6, 120, 251
  Buñuel, Luis, 160, 161, 172
  Mexican cinema, 22, 52, 53, 54-5
  nationalism, 52, 53
Migliaccio, Flávio: *The Beggars/Os mendigos*,
  44
Mikhalkov-Konchalovsky, Andrei: *The First
  Teacher/Pervyj uticel*, 248

On Cinema

Milestone, Lewis: *All Quiet on the Western Front*, 148
Miller, Arthur: *Death of a Salesman*, 140
Mirbeau, Octave, 173
mise-en-scène, 11, 41, 131, 142, 144, 163
   Antonioni, Michelangelo, 9, 211, 213
   Buñuel, Luis, 163, 165, 166
   Mauro, Humberto, 25, 27
   morality and, 211, 213
   Rough Gangue/Ganga bruta, 25
   Visconti, Luchino, 188, 189–90, 193, 194, 198, 201
Mix, Tom, 152, 154
Modern Art Week/*Semana de Arte Moderna*, São Paulo (1922), 37, 86, 109
Molinaro, Edouard, 31
monologue, 9, 69, 99, 199
montage, 35, 60, 108, 131
   dialectical montage, 26, 27, 61, 108, 110–11, 187, 205, 243
   Eisenstein, Sergei M., 26, 27, 60–1, 157, 187, 205, 206, 207, 243
   epic montage, 108
   Godard's (dis)montage, 41
   Hollywood, 116
   shock montage, 155–6, 157, 193
   spatial montage, 206
   vertical montage, 205, 207
   Visconti, Luchino, 207, 208
   see also technique
morality, 46, 50, 119, 176, 210
   bourgeois morality, 161
   Catholic morality, 179, 223
   communist morality, 179
   mise-en-scène and, 211, 213
   'The Morality of a New Christ', 172–8
Moravia, Alberto, 114, 214, 223, 235
Munk, Andrzej, 174, 247
   Passenger, 175, 247
Murnau, Friedrich W., 22, 53, 162, 174, 249
   Sunrise, 118
music, 74
   Black God, White Devil, 64–5, 68
   The Chronicle of Anna Magdalena Bach/Chronik der Anna Magdalena Bach, 250
   Cinema Novo, 64
   Entranced Earth, 68, 71, 72, 74

Gunfight at the O.K. Corral, 158
   importance of, 64
   Lean, David, 134
   samba, 56, 71, 81, 107, 252
   Straub, Jean-Marie, 115
   Sturges, John, 158
   The Turning Wind, 68
musical genre, 20, 64, 136, 263
Mussolini, Benito, 179, 219, 233, 260
mysticism, 36, 92, 95, 97, 106, 123–4, 162, 212, 261
   colonizing mysticism of Catholicism, 125
   hunger/mysticism relationship, 103
   political mysticism, 123
   poverty and, 124
   Rossellini, Roberto, 16, 184, 226
   social mysticism, 184
   The Turning Wind, 58
myth, 11, 68, 94, 97
   Eldorado, 70
   as the first ideograph, 103
   Hollywood, 18
   'the people' as the myth of the bourgeoisie, 123
   'Tropicalism, Anthropology, Myth, Ideography', 7–8, 100–104
mythology, 6, 10, 103, 168

narrative, 145
narrative cinema, 67, 111–12, 130
narrative editing, 28, 35, 110, 131, 193
National Institute of Cinema, 83
nationalism, 47, 54, 75, 100, 179
   anti-nationalism, 36, 43
   Mexican nationalism, 52, 53
   romantic nationalism, 46, 53, 80
Nazism, 20, 115, 131, 178, 179, 208–209, 219, 250
   The Damned, 208–209
   Modern Times, 129
neorealism, 22, 31, 60, 103, 113, 114, 204–205, 241
   British realist documentary, 20
   Fellini, Federico, 226
   Italian neorealism, 1, 9, 41, 137, 140–1, 181, 219, 221, 261, 262
   'The Neorealism of Rossellini', 178–87
   social neorealism, 185

Index

Visconti, Luchino, 190, 201
  see also realism
Neruda, Pablo, 8, 71, 103, 106
Neto, Triguerinho, 106
  Bahia of All Saints/Bahia de todos os santos, 107
Neves, David, 106
  Memories of Helen/Memória de Helena, 99
new cinema ('New Cinema in the World'), 9, 241–52
  Canada, 242
  Czechoslovakia, 245, 247
  England, 246
  Germany, 248–9
  Italy, 249
  Poland, 247
  Russia, 248
  socialist new cinema, 247–8
  United States, 245, 246
  see also Cinema Novo
newspaper, 13, 31, 90, 235
Nichols, Mike: The Graduate, 120
Noronha, Linduarte, 29
  Aruanda, 43, 96
nouvelle vague, 1, 18, 22, 38, 50, 84, 113, 166, 174, 217, 246, 248, 249
  bourgeois aesthetic, 112
  politics of authorship, 241
  production coup, 31

Ogier, Bulle, 230, 232
Oliveira Penna, Rosa Maria de (Rosinha), 105, 217, 239
Ophüls, Max, 38, 219
  Lola Montès, 113, 219
Ortiz, Carlos, 13

Pagnol, Marcel, 20
Paiva, Salvyano Cavalcanti de, 13, 106
Pallero, Edgardo, 104
Pasolini, Pier Paolo, 10, 120, 181, 185, 204, 206, 214, 235, 243, 249, 261, 262, 265
  Accattone, 217, 235–6
  décor, 205
  The Gospel According to Saint Matthew/Il vangelo secondo Matteo, 175–6, 204–205, 217, 235, 236–7, 239
  Hawks and Sparrows/Uccellacci e uccellini, 237, 239
  Mamma Roma, 236, 240–1
  Oedipus Rex/Edipo re, 235, 237, 238, 239, 240
  'Pasolini', 235–41
  La ricotta/RoGoPaG, 228, 237
  The Savage Priest/Il padre selvaggio, 238
  script, 235
  Vangelo 70/Amore e rabbia, 239
Paxton, John, 139
Peixoto, Mário, 23, 24, 37
  Limit/Limite, 21, 22, 23
Pereira dos Santos, Nelson, 5, 17, 29, 37, 38, 60, 82, 106, 113
  Comme il était bon mon petit français/ HowTasty was my Little Frenchman, 75
  independent cinema, 60
  Rio 40 Degrees/Rio, 40 graus, 60
  Rio, Northern Zone/Rio, zona norte, 60
  The Turning Wind, 58, 60
  Vidas secas/Barren Lives, 23, 37–41, 43, 44, 45, 56, 57, 62, 74, 75, 89–90, 91–2, 95, 96, 119, 243, 254
Perrault, Pierre, 243
Perry, Frank: David and Lisa, 246
Person, Luís Sérgio: São Paulo S.A., 45
Pesaro, Festival of, 115
Pessoa, Fernando, 108
Petrarch, 111
Petrovic, Aleksandar: I Even Met Happy Gypsies/Skupljači perja, 248
Pinal, Sílvia, 105, 173
Pitanga, Antônio, 106
Poland, 175, 247, 266
Polanski, Roman, 247
political cinema, 7, 11, 18, 52, 56, 163, 209, 241
  Buñuel, Luis, 120, 168, 173, 177
  Godard, Jean-Luc, 58, 102
  Rocha, Glauber, 1–2, 3, 72
politics, 16, 122
  aesthetics/politics relationship, 7, 8, 106–13
  Brazil, 55, 66, 71, 73, 75, 83, 123
  Brazilian cinema and, 37–8
  cinema and, 30
  Cinema Novo, 6, 38, 46, 60, 75, 99

political mysticism, 123
Rocha, Glauber, 8-9, 10
Visconti, Luchino, 194, 195-7, 207
popular art, 42, 80, 81, 253
popular cinema, 11, 105
popular culture, 6, 102, 124, 152
populism, 80, 81, 82
pornography, 14, 45, 117, 120, 223
   Hollywood, 116
   Straub on, 116, 117, 119, 250, 251
   see also sex/sexuality
Portabella, Pere, 120
Portinari, Candido, 22, 97
Portugal, 3, 180
Positif, 6, 7, 58-75
poverty, 17, 28, 77, 81, 91, 92, 121-2, 123, 160, 177, 179, 195
   'An Aesthetics of Hunger', xii, 5, 41-6, 74, 121, 124, 216
   cultural poverty, 256
   intellectual poverty, 14
   mental poverty, 43
   moral poverty, 43
   mysticism of, 124
   starvation, 96
Prado Júnior, Caio da Silva, 19
primitive, 15, 21, 25-6, 66, 67, 162, 217, 255, 262
   Antônio das Mortes, 66, 67
   primitive culture, 46
   primitive man, 28, 29
   violence and, 44
Proust, Marcel, 107, 193, 194, 199, 200
the public, 17, 80-1, 85, 102, 211, 241-2
   American cinema and, 76, 77, 78, 79, 88
   imitation cinema/original cinema, 79-80
   public/film conflict, 96-9, 245
   Public Opinion, 97
   respect for, 118
   shock and rejection by, 92, 93, 94, 95
   understanding a film, 88
Pudovkin, Vsevolod, 142, 175, 187
   Mother/Mat, 19
   Storm over Asia/Potomok Chingis-Khana, 19-20

Quadros, Jânio, 44
Quine, Richard 32
Quinn, Anthony, 221, 222

Rabal, Francisco, 105, 169
Ramos, Graciliano, 22, 29, 37, 40, 62, 63, 89
rationality/reasoning, 6, 108, 123-4, 162, 173, 183, 252, 255
   dominant reasoning, 123
Rattigan, Terence, 134, 135
Ray, Man, 159
Ray, Nicholas, 32, 141
   Rebel Without a Cause, 138, 139, 141-2
Ray, Satyajit, 26, 32, 33, 34, 162
   Pather Panchali, 34
realism, 6, 10, 22, 62, 63, 87, 89, 110
   aesthetic realism, 6
   'choreographic realism', 138, 139, 141, 157
   critical realism, 23, 96, 174, 204
   fatalistic realism, 95
   psychological realism, 10, 156
   social realism, 194, 236
   socialist realism, 40, 54, 68, 225, 247
   see also neorealism
Reichenbach, François, 163
Reisz, Karel, 246-7
Renoir, Jean, 20, 21, 105, 181, 243, *244*
   The Golden Coach, 251
   Grand Illusion, 148
   Madame Bovary, 110
Resnais, Alain, 15, 31, 32-3, 104, 112-13, 162, 166, 174, 175, 199, 214
   a bourgeois, 39, 112
   editing, 28
   Far from Vietnam/Loin du Vietnam, 113
   Hiroshima mon amour, 32, 35, 112, 199, 200
   interior monologue, 9
   Last Year in Marienbad/L'Année dernière à Marienbad, 113
   Marienbad, 113
   Night and Fog/Nuit et brouillard, 113
   Toute la mémoire du monde, 113
   The War Is Over/La Guerre est finie, 112, 113
resources, 5, 136
   lack of, 3, 4, 17, 24, 35, 101, 136

Index

Revisão crítica do cinema brasileiro (*A Critical Review of Brazilian Cinema*), 2, 3-4
  Introduction, 3, 13-14
  Method, 15-19
  see also Mauro, Humberto; Rocha, Glauber
Revolução do Cinema Novo (*The Cinema Novo Revolution*), 3, 4-8
  see also Rocha, Glauber
revolution, 213, 245-6, 256
  art and, 6, 122
  'The Cinematographic Revolution', 7, 48-51
  cultural revolution, 85, 86, 100
  'Revolution is an Aesthetics', 6, 46-8
  'revolution by the word', 55
  revolutionary art, 122-3, 124-5
  revolutionary cinematographic aesthetic, 174, 260
  revolutionary culture, 46, 47-8, 213
  revolutionary politics, 16
  socialist revolution, 108
  'This Is How the Revolution in Cinema Is Made', 8, 114-21
  Tricontinental, 51-2
rhythm, 55, 77, 82, 114, 115, 134, 136, 137-9
  editing, 25, 65, 137, 145
  external/internal rhythm, 25, 28, 110, 137, 146, 155
  juvenile delinquency, 138-9
  rhythmical composition, 205
  Visconti, Luchino, 188-9
  Western genre, 138, 154, 155, 157, 158
Richardson, Tony, 246
Rio Film Festival, 96
Ritt, Martin, 32
Rivette, Jacques, 104
Robbe-Grillet, Alain, 33, 113
Rocha, Anecy, 92
Rocha, Glauber, *112, 160, 180*, 217, *244*
  admired filmmakers, 8, 9-10
  avant-garde, 58, 59
  biography, 1-3
  Cinema Novo, 2, 4, 5, 6, 11-12
  development as filmmaker, 1, 2-3
  directing actors, 61, 65-6
  editing, 61, 65, 72

epic/didactic cinema, 6, 7, 51
exile, xiv, 2, 5, 11
in Godard's *Wind from the East*, *xii*, xiv, 102
influences on, 60-1, 105-106
politics, 8-9, 10
as 'tricontinental filmmaker', 2, 4
violence, 73
see also Rocha's filmography; Rocha's writings
Rocha's filmography, 9
  América Nuestra, 105, 106, 107, 108, 110
  Antonio das Mortes/O dragão da maldade contra o Santo Guerreiro, 2, 5, 101, 103, 104, 111
  Barravento/The Turning Wind, 1, 44, 56, 58-61, 63, 64, 65, 68, 99, 217
  Cabezas Cortadas/Cutting Heads, 2, 5
  Câncer/Cancer, 2
  Claro, 2, 232
  Cruz na Praça/The Cross in the Square, 58-9, 60
  Di Cavalcanti, 2, 187
  documentary, 2, 59
  essay in colour, 59
  female characters, 63
  História do Brazil, 2
  A idade da terra/The Age of the Earth, 2, 3
  Jorjamado no cinema, 2
  Der leone have sept cabeças/The Seven-Headed Lion, 2, 5, 105, 106, 108
  A morte de Dom Quixote/The Death of Don Quixote, 105
  Pátio, 1, 59-60
  political cinema, 1-2, 3, 72
  Rampa/Ramp, 59
  short film, 1, 58-9
  see also Black God, White Devil; *Entranced Earth*
Rocha's writings, x, 12
  film critique, x, 1, 3
  language and writing style, xii-xiii, 3, 8, 11
  screenplay, 2
  see also O século do cinema; *Revisão crítica do cinema brasileiro*; *Revolução do Cinema Novo*
Rockefeller, Rodman, 215-16

Rockefeller Congress, 215–16
Rockefeller Foundation, 215
Rodrigues, Nelson, 94–6
RoGoPaG, 228, 237
romanticism, 22, 28, 47, 97, 105, 174
Rosi, Francesco, 40, 174, 181, 185, 204
　Salvatore Giuliano, 217, 254, 261
Rossellini, Roberto, 8, 9, 15, 26, 32, 38, 39,
　61, 104, 105, 120, 162, 163, *180*, 204,
　212, 219, 244, 255, 260–1, 262, 264,
　265, 266, 267
　cine-journalism, 185
　Europa '51, 181–2
　*The Flowers of St Francis/Francesco
　　giullare di Dio*, 183
　Il generale Della Rovere, 26, 181, 182, 183,
　　184
　*Germany, Year Zero/Germania, anno
　　zero*, 182
　History of Humanity, 186
　*India as Seen by Rossellini/L'India vista
　　da Rossellini*, 186
　Journey to Italy/Viaggio in Italia, 110,
　　185, 205
　The Man of the Cross/L'uomo dalla croce,
　　181
　The Messiah/Il Messia, 186
　mysticism, 16, 184, 226
　'The Neorealism of Rossellini', 178–87
　Paisan/Paisà, 61, 182
　Rome, Open City/Roma, città aperta, 39,
　　61, 181, 182, 185, 260
　Stromboli/Stromboli, terra di Dio, 182
　*The Taking of Power by Louis XIV/La
　　Prise du pouvoir par Louis XIV*, 251,
　　261
　technique, 179, 181, 183, 204
　television, 186, 239, 261
　The White Ship/La nave bianca, 181
　Year One/Anno Uno, 186
Rouch, Jean, 15, 163, 185, 214
Russia, *see* USSR/Soviet Union

Sadoul, Georges, 13, 128, 214
Salles Gomes, Paulo Emilio, 15, 26–7, 34,
　106, 214
Sanders, George, 182
Santos, Carmen, 23, 24

Santos, Luiz Paulino dos:
　Rampa/Ramp, 59
　The Turning Wind, 58, 59
Santos, Roberto: *The Hour and Turn of
　Augusto Matraga/A hora e vez de
　Augusto Matraga*, 93–4
Saraceni, Paulo Cesar, 24, 25, 29, 61, 106,
　214, 217–18
　Capitu, 74, 99
　The Dare/O desafio, 45, 56, 92, 250
　Porto das Caixas/The Port of Caixas, 23,
　　43, 44, 99
Sarno, Geraldo: *Viramundo*, 97
Sartre, Jean-Paul, 180, 196, 197, 212, 213,
　214, 225, 239, 255, 262, 263
　Les Chemins de la liberté, 197
Schlesinger, John, 246–7
　Midnight Cowboy, 116, 120
script, 69, 71, 95, 104, 107, 163, 189, 234, 235
O século do cinema (*The Century of
　Cinema*), xi, 3, 8–11
　O Sekulo do Kynema, xii;
　see also Rocha, Glauber
sertão, 76, 81, 90, 91, 97, 217
set design, 88, 110, 181, 205, 221, 232,
　261, 266
　importance of, 95
　integration between camera, actors and
　　set design, 95
sex/sexuality, 9, 10, 27, 169–71, 201,
　202–203, 227
　homosexuality, 164, 204, 219, 258
　see also pornography
Shakespeare, William, 11, 255
short film, 1, 57, 58–9, 61, 99, 144, 222
shot, 163, 184, 211
　aerial shot, 147
　deep focus shot, 131
　full shot, 243, 244, 250
　importance of, 29
　long take, 243
　modern cinema, 243
　panning shot, 157, 188
　panoramic shot, 138, 142, 147, 188, 193
　tracking shot, 61, 110, 113, 134, 138,
　　173, 184
　traditional cinema, 243
Sight and Sound, 13

Index

silent film/cinema, 4, 15, 25, 128, 243
Silveira, Walter da, 106
Siquiera, Cyro, 138
Skolimowski, Jerzy, 243, 247, 248, 266
Soares, Paulo Gil, 59
   Memories of the Cangaço/Memória do cangaço, 62, 97
   Satan's Feats in the Town of Back and Forth/Proezas de Satanás na vila do Leva-e-Traz, 74, 99
socialism, 50, 57, 108, 122, 213, 245
   'dogmatic socialism', 7
socialist cinema, 50, 58, 266
socialist *new cinema*, 247–8
socialist realism, 40, 54, 68, 225, 247
Solanas, Fernando: *The Hour of the Furnaces/La hora de los hornos*, 122
Sordi, Alberto, 220, 222, 227
sound, 20, 246
   direct sound, 59, 241, 242, 246, 250
   dubbing, 64, 241
   sound cinema period, 15, 20
   sound/image relationship, 10, 71
Spain, 2, 120, 180, 251
spectator, *see* the public
Stalinism, 39, 175, 195, 260
Steinbeck, John: *The Grapes of Wrath*, 87–8
Stendhal, 62, 194, 197, 200
Sternberg, Josef von, 20
Stevens, George, 142
   Giant, 158
   Shane, 138, 154, 155, 156
Straub, Jean-Marie, 8, 106, 110, 114, 115, 116–20 *passim*, 206, 240, 243, 249, 250
   The Chronicle of Anna Magdalena Bach/Chronik der Anna Magdalena Bach, 115, 250–1
   as dialectical filmmaker, 110–11
   music and, 115
   Not Reconciled/Nicht versöhnt, 115, 240, 249–50, 251
   Othon, 115
   on pornography, 116, 117, 119, 250, 251
Stroheim, Erich von, 20, 21, 174
   Greed, 95
Sturges, John:
   Bad Day at Black Rock, 156–7
   Escape from Fort Bravo, 157
   Gunfight at the O.K. Corral, 154–5, 156, 157–9
   music, 158
surrealism, 6
   Buñuel, Luis, 159, 162, 165, 173, 176, 177, 226, 255, 262
   concrete surrealism, 71–2, 103
   Fellini, Federico, 224, 226
   French surrealism, 103, 224
   Latin America, 71–2, 103–104
   tropical surrealism, 44
   Tropicalismo, 103–104
Sutherland, Donald, 232, 233
Szabó, István, 248
Father/Apa, 247

technique, 56–7, 97–8, 252
   aesthetic technique, 143, 157
   American cinema, 76, 77, 85, 98
   Buñuel, Luis, 163
   cinemascope, 143–4
   close-up, 26, 27, 34, 60, 88, 92, 143, 148, 150, 151, 159, 183, 184, 207, 211
   deep focus shot, 131
   direct cinema, 57, 74, 89
   fusion, 21
   graphism, 21
   hero and, 92
   'John Huston, Physical Technique and Aesthetic Technique', 142–4
   jump cut, 3
   physical technique, 143, 157
   remote-controlled zoom, 204
   Rossellini, Roberto, 179, 181, 183, 204
   superimposition, 21
   technical body of the film, 143
   tracking shot, 61, 110, 113, 134, 138, 173, 184
   zoom, 9, 57, 204–207, 209, 229
   see also camera; colour; editing; framing; lighting; montage; shot; sound
technology, 30, 54, 75, 123, 128, 234, 252
   Godard, Jean-Luc and, 253
   technology of production, 51
television, 33, 51, 84, 98, 117, 246, 261, 264
   film shown on, 262
   Rossellini, Roberto, 186, 239, 261

On Cinema

Tempo Glauber archives, 257
theatre, 33–4, 37, 63–4, 84, 94, 106, 109
   Brazilian theatre, 109
   censorship, 59
   'cinematographic' theatre, 140
   expressionist theatre, 110
   Rocha, Glauber: staging poems, 58, 59
Third World, 5, 41, 71, 121, 178
   avant-garde, 100
   Tricontinental, 51–2
   see also colonialism; Latin America; underdevelopment/undeveloped country
Tiempo de Cine, 197–9
time, 156
   cinematographic time, 150, 188, 199, 205–206, 250
   psychological time, 150
   Visconti, Luchino, 188, 191–2, 200
Tissé, Eduard, 15, 22, 26
Toland, Gregg, 22
Torre Nilsson, Leopoldo, 54, 72
Torres, Miguel, 19
Toti, Gianni, 205
tragedy, 10, 11, 55, 66, 78, 94, 115, 133, 183, 238
   imperialist tragedy, 9, 130
   Visconti, Luchino, 197, 198, 200, 202, 203, 208–209, 219
tricontinental:
   'Tricontinental', 7, 51–8
   tricontinental cinema, 57
   tricontinental cinema as guerrilla cinema, 7, 52
   tricontinental filmmaker, 2, 4, 57–8
Tricontinental, 68
Tropicalismo, 7
   ideography, 8, 103, 104
   surrealism, 103–104
   'Tropicalism, Anthropology, Myth, Ideography', 7–8, 100–104
   underdevelopment and, 101
   see also anthropophagy
Truffaut, François, 15, 31, 57, 104, 112, 162, 166, 174
   The 400 Blows/Les Quatre-cents coups, 113
   commercial cinema, 113

Jules and Jim/Jules et Jim, 113, 175
The Soft Skin/La Peau douce, 113
truth, 21, 266
   auteur and, 16, 26, 29
   Cinema Novo and, 25, 43, 45
   commercial cinema and, 18

Última Hora, 107
underdevelopment/undeveloped country, 34, 46, 79, 81, 92, 120, 255, 262
   artistic creation in, 41
   cultural underdevelopment, 98
   see also developed world; Latin America; Third World
United States, 5, 20, 87, 245, 246, 254
   see also American cinema; Hollywood; Western genre
University of Reading, School of Art and Communication Design, xiii
USSR/Soviet Union, 119, 131, 175, 178, 179, 254
   classical period, 19–20, 27
   new cinema, 248
   Soviet cinema, 10, 117, 137, 165, 180, 245, 254, 259, 260

Vadim, Roger, 31, 33
Valle, Maurício do, 64
Varda, Agnès: *Happiness/Le Bonheur*, 113
Veloso, Caetano, xiv
Venice Film Festival, 2, 3, 229, 236, 237, 238
Ventura, Zuenir Carlos, 75, 216
Vera Cruz (production company), 83–4
Verdi, Giuseppe, 74
Verga, Giovanni, 194
Vertov, Dziga, xiv, 10, 22, 180, 181, 205
Viana, Zelito, 104, 105, 106, 107, 113
Viana Filho, Oduvaldo, 92
Viany, Alex, 13, 19, 23, 24, 106
   Sun on The Mud/Sol sobre a lama, 43–4
Vidor, King, 20, 21
Vigo, Jean, 15, 16, 20, 21, 22, 26, 38, 162, 194–5, 241
   L'Atalante, 39
   Zero for Conduct, 195
Villa-Lobos, Heitor, 22, 23, 64–5, 74
violence, 12, 44–5, 73, 156–7, 164
   aesthetics of violence, 5, 44, 121

Index

century of the cinema as the century of violence, 11
hunger and, 44
poetics of violence, 27, 242
Western genre, 156–7
youth and, 138, 139, 141, 142
Visconti, Luchino, 8, 15, 32, 38, 61, 104, 105, 108, 162, 174, 210, 212, 214, 219, 226, 239, 261, 262, 265
characters, 208
'Cinema's Form and Sense', 192–3
communism, 16
editing, 187
expressionism, 261
'Filmic Dramaturgy: Visconti', 187–92
Italian opera, 10, 219
Marxism, 197, 204, 212, 240, 254, 261
mise-en-scène, 188, 189–90, 193, 194, 198, 201
montage, 207, 208
neorealism, 190, 201
politics 194, 195–7, 207
rhythm, 188–9
'The Splendour of a God', 9, 204–209
time, 188, 191–2, 200
tragedy, 197, 198, 200, 202, 203, 208–209, 219
'Visconti and the Nerves of Rocco', 193–9
'Viscontian Baroque', 9, 199–204
zoom, 207
see also Visconti's filmography
Visconti's filmography:
América Nuestra, 105
The Damned/La caduta degli dei, 207–209
The Earth Trembles/La terra trema, 194
The Foreigner, 207
The Innocent/L'innocente, 233
The Leopard/Il gattopardo, 207, 261, 265
Obsession/Ossessione, 10, 192, 194, 201
Rocco and His Brothers/Rocco e i suoi fratelli, 193, 196, 199, 200–204, 207, 208, 209, 254
Sandra of a Thousand Delights/Vaghe stelle dell'Orsa, 204, 207
Senso, 10, 187–8, 190, 191, 200, 209
The Stranger/Lo straniero, 204, 229

White Nights/Le notti bianche, 192, 193, 200, 207

Wajda, Andrzej 174, 175, 247
Walsh, Raoul, 263
war film, 148–9
Warhol, Andy:
 Blood for Dracula, 232
 Flesh for Frankenstein, 232
Watkins, Peter, 247
Welles, Orson, 9, 22, 38, 39, 72, 105, 129–32, 146, 237, 244, 254, 262
 characters, 130, 131, 132, 226
 Citizen Kane, 11, 32, 118, 121, 130–2, 178, 212, 226, 260
 class struggle, 131
 expressionism, 110, 260
 Hollywood, 130
 imperialism, 130, 131–2
 The Magnificent Ambersons, 131
 RKO and, 39
 Rocha's admired filmmaker, 9, 130
 Touch of Evil, 130
 The Trial, 131, 212
Western genre, 9, 17, 18, 72, 76–7, 102, 136, 263
 cowboy, 138, 150–1, 152, 154
 epic Western, 154
 Ford, John, 27, 57, 138, 152, 153
 hat, 138, 150, 225
 hero, 150–1, 152, 153, 154, 159
 historical Western, 154
 'The New Western', 154–9
 psychology/psychological Western, 31, 155, 156, 159
 rhythm, 138, 154, 155, 157, 158
 'The Searchers', 152–4
 social aesthetic, 152, 153
 tragedy, 158
 violence, 156–7
 'Western – Introduction to the Genre and to the Hero', 150–1
 see also Ford, John
Widerberg, Bo: *Elvira Madigan*, 248
Wiene, Robert: *The Cabinet of Dr Caligari/Das Kabinet Des Doktor Caligari*, 110
Wilder, Billy, 142
Wise, Robert: *The Set-Up*, 144

305

World War II, 19, 174, 178, 179, 223
Wright, Basil, 20
Wyler, William, 20, 21, 22, 142, 243
   Ben Hur, 253
   Detective Story, 140, 143

Yé-Yé movement, 252
youth:
   cultural background of, 60, 63

'Juvenile Delinquency', 136-42
   leather jacket, 138, 139, 141
   rebellious youth, 136, 138, 140, 142
   violence, 138, 139, 141, 142
Yugoslavia, 247, 248

Zavattini, Cesare, 163, 181, 219, 261
Zinnemann, Fred: *High Noon*, 143, 154, 155, 156, 157

www.ingramcontent.com/pod-product-compliance
Lightning Source LLC
Chambersburg PA
CBHW072123290426
44111CB00012B/1751